Race, Equity, and Education

Pedro A. Noguera · Jill C. Pierce · Roey Ahram
Editors

Race, Equity, and Education

Sixty Years from *Brown*

 Springer

Editors
Pedro A. Noguera
University of California, Los Angeles
Los Angeles, CA
USA

Roey Ahram
New York University
New York, NY
USA

Jill C. Pierce
New York University
New York, NY
USA

ISBN 978-3-319-23771-8   ISBN 978-3-319-23772-5   (eBook)
DOI 10.1007/978-3-319-23772-5

Library of Congress Control Number: 2015950880

Springer Cham Heidelberg New York Dordrecht London

Printed on acid-free paper

Springer International Publishing AG Switzerland is part of Springer Science+Business Media (www.springer.com)

Contents

Contributors

Roey Ahram New York University, New York, NY, USA

Antwi A. Akom San Francisco State University, San Francisco, CA, USA

Cynthia M. Alcantar UCLA Institute for Immigration, Globalization, and Education, Los Angeles, CA, USA

Jennifer B. Ayscue UCLA, Los Angeles, CA, USA

Sonya Douglass Horsford Graduate School of Education, College of Education and Human Development, George Mason University, Fairfax, VA, USA

Evelyn Hu-DeHart American Studies and Ethnic Studies, Brown University, Providence, RI, USA

Jorge López Claremont Graduate University, Claremont, CA, USA

Ernest Morrell Teachers College, Columbia University, New York, NY, USA

Aaron Nakai I-SEEED, Oakland, CA, USA

Bach Mai Dolly Nguyen UCLA Institute for Immigration, Globalization, and Education, Los Angeles, CA, USA

Pedro A. Noguera UCLA, Los Angeles, CA, USA

Gary Orfield UCLA, Los Angeles, CA, USA

Jill C. Pierce New York University, New York, NY, USA

Richard Rothstein Economic Policy Institute, Washington, DC, USA

Cati V. de los Ríos Teachers College, Columbia University, New York, NY, USA

Casandra D. Salgado Department of Sociology, UCLA, Los Angeles, CA, USA

Aekta Shah Stanford University, Stanford, CA, USA

Lisa M. Stulberg Steinhardt School of Culture, Education, and Human Development, New York University, New York, NY, USA

Robert T. Teranishi UCLA Institute for Immigration, Globalization, and Education, Los Angeles, CA, USA

Lawrence T. Winn University of Wisconsin, Madison, WI, USA

Maisha T. Winn University of Wisconsin, Madison, WI, USA

About the Authors

Roey Ahram   is the Director of Research and Evaluation at New York University's Metropolitan Center for Research on Equity and the Transformation of Schools. His work focuses on understanding the causes for educational inequities and examining how schools can reduce those inequities through changes in policies and practices.

Antwi A. Akom   is part of a new generation of college professors, innovators, and entrepreneurs building technology to inspire, equip, and mobilize people to solve some of the world's greatest challenges. In 2012 he co-founded the Institute for Sustainable Economic, Educational, and Environmental Design (I-SEEED), an award-winning nonprofit organization dedicated to building sustainable cities and schools. In 2013 Dr. Akom co-founded Streetwyze (A Benefit Corporation)—a best-in-class mobile, mapping, and SMS platform for residents to find goods and services, take action on important issues, and visualize neighborhood health and well-being. Dr. Akom has held academic appointments at UC Berkeley, the Lawrence Berkeley National Laboratory, the University of California, San Francisco (UCSF), and San Francisco State University. He holds a Ph.D. from the University of Pennsylvania in Environmental Sociology, an M.A. in Education from Stanford University, and a B.A. in Political Science/Economics from the University of California, Berkeley.

Cynthia M. Alcantar   is a doctoral student in Social Science and Comparative Education and research associate for the Institute for Immigration, Globalization, and Education at the University of California, Los Angeles and the National Commission on Asian American and Pacific Islander Research in Education (CARE). Cynthia earned her Master's degree in Education from Claremont Graduate University (CGU). Prior to her current roles, Cynthia worked as an administrator for the Upward Bound Program at Norco Community College and as an adjunct faculty and advisor for the McNair Scholars program at CGU. Her research centers on college access, persistence, and completion of underserved and underrepresented students, especially as they relate to higher education policy and practice.

Jennifer B. Ayscue is a research associate at The Civil Rights Project/*Proyecto Derechos Civiles* and a doctoral candidate in the Graduate School of Education and Information Studies at University of California, Los Angeles. Her research interests focus on desegregation in K-12 schools and the role of policy in furthering the goal of diversity. Before attending UCLA, Ayscue earned an M.A. in Social Sciences in Education from Stanford University and a B.A. in Elementary Education from the University of North Carolina at Chapel Hill.

Cati V. de los Ríos is a former ESL, Spanish, and Ethnic Studies high school teacher. She is currently a Ph.D. candidate in the Department of Arts and Humanities at Teachers College, Columbia University and a research fellow at the Institute for Urban and Minority Education (IUME) in Harlem. Cati received her B.A. from Loyola Marymount University, an M.T.S and secondary teaching credential from Harvard University, and an Ed.M. in Curriculum and Teaching from Teachers College, Columbia University.

Sonya Douglass Horsford is an Associate Professor of Education in the Graduate School of Education and College of Education and Human Development at George Mason University. Her research interests include the political and policy contexts of education leadership with a focus on school desegregation, racial inequality, and education reform in the post-Civil Rights Era. She is the editor of three books and author of *Learning in a Burning House: Educational Inequality, Ideology, and (Dis)Integration* (Teachers College Press, 2011).

Evelyn Hu-DeHart is Professor of History, American Studies and Ethnic Studies, and past director of the Center for the Study of Race and Ethnicity in America, Brown University. She has been researching and publishing on the history of Chinese and other Asian migration to the Americas, especially Latin America and the Caribbean and the U.S.-Mexico borderlands.

Jorge López is a National Board certified social studies teacher and an activist at Roosevelt High School in the community of Boyle Heights in Los Angeles. He has been teaching since 2002, after graduating from UCLA's Teacher Education Program. In 2009 he earned a second Master's degree from UCLA's Principal Leadership Institute. He has taught courses in ethnic and cultural studies that address youth of color, community history, social movements, counter-narratives, critical media literacy, decolonization, and social justice. He recently co-authored the book *Critical Media Pedagogy: Teaching for Achievement in City Schools.* Jorge is pursuing a Ph.D. in Teaching, Learning, and Culture at Claremont Graduate University.

Ernest Morrell is the Macy Professor of Education and Director of the Institute for Urban and Minority Education (IUME) at Teachers College, Columbia University. He is also a Fellow of the American Educational Research Association and past-president of the National Council of Teachers of English (NCTE). A former high school teacher, Ernest focuses his research on innovative socially, culturally, and technologically relevant pedagogical practices that promote academic achievement and civic engagement. He is the author of 60 articles and chapters and six books. He received his Ph.D. in Language, Literacy, and Culture from UC Berkeley.

Aaron Nakai is a critical educator who has served as a trainer, mentor, and youth development specialist in a variety of community and education spaces for the past 13 years. His graduate studies include a Master's of Education focused on Equity and Social Justice from San Francisco State University. He is currently the Program Director of Health Equity and Community Engagement at the Institute for Sustainable Economic, Educational and Environmental Design (I-SEEED) in Oakland, CA. His work includes designing health and environmental equity curriculum, implementing community-based action research projects, and co-teaching early college/model high school classes in urban ecology, Ethnic Studies and environmental justice. He is an expert facilitator who trains youth and youth-serving adults to develop a range of projects for low-income youth of color, their families, and their communities.

Bach Mai Dolly Nguyen is a doctoral student in Social Science and Comparative Education and a research associate in the Institute for Immigration, Globalization, and Education at the University of California, Los Angeles. Her research aims to improve the educational outcomes of underrepresented students of color through examining the impact of educational practice and policy, with particular attention to Asian American and Pacific Islander students. She is currently the team lead on the iCount data disaggregation initiative for the National Commission on Asian American and Pacific Islander Research in Education (CARE).

Pedro A. Noguera is Distinguished Professor of Education at the Graduate School of Education and Information Sciences at UCLA. He is author of several books and serves at numerous national and local boards related to education and social justice.

Gary Orfield is Distinguished Research Professor of education, law, political science, and urban planning at University of California, Los Angeles. His research interests are civil rights, education policy, urban policy, and minority opportunity. He co-founded and directed the Civil Rights Project at Harvard and now serves as co-director of the Civil Rights Project/*Proyecto Derechos Civiles* at UCLA. Orfield's central interest has been the development and the implementation of social policy, with a focus on the impact of policy on equal opportunity for success in American society.

Jill C. Pierce is a former high school English teacher, college counselor, education coordinator, and research assistant. She is a Ph.D. candidate in urban education and has a Master's degree in Secondary English Education and an undergraduate degree in Comparative Literature.

Richard Rothstein is a research associate of the Economic Policy Institute and a senior fellow of the Chief Justice Earl Warren Institute on Law and Social Policy, University of California (Berkeley) School of Law. He has authored *Grading*

Education: Getting Accountability Right (Teachers College Press and EPI, 2008); *Class and Schools: Using Social, Economic and Educational Reform to Close the Black-White Achievement Gap* (Teachers College Press and EPI 2004); and *The Way We Were? Myths and Realities of America's Student Achievement* (Century Foundation, 1998). His work on residential segregation and schools includes the "The Making of Ferguson" (2014), on the Economic Policy Institute website.

Casandra D. Salgado is a Ph.D. candidate in Sociology at the University of California, Los Angeles. Her research interests focus on educational and wealth inequality, and immigrant-native relations. Casandra is currently writing her dissertation, which examines the racial and immigration attitudes and wealth resources of latter-generation Hispanics and Anglos in Albuquerque, New Mexico. She earned her B.A. in Peace and Conflict Studies from the University of California, Berkeley and M.A. in Sociology from the University of California, Los Angeles.

Aekta Shah is currently a Ph.D. candidate at Stanford University in Technology Design and Program Director of Technology and Youth Engagement at the Institute for Sustainable Economic, Educational and Environmental Design (I-SEEED). At Stanford Aekta is engaged in research and development on issues including technology, GIS mapping, education, and sustainable community development. Committed to providing college and career opportunities to traditionally underserved youth, Aekta has been recognized by organizations such as the Aspen Institute, Green for All, and Bioneers and has presented for the UN on issues of sustainable development and education. Aekta holds an Ed.M. in Education Policy and Management from Harvard and a B.A. in Developmental Psychology and Education from Dartmouth College.

Lisa M. Stulberg is Associate Professor of Educational Sociology at New York University's Steinhardt School of Culture, Education, and Human Development. She is the author of *Race, Schools, and Hope: African Americans and School Choice After Brown* (Teachers College Press, 2008). She co-edited (with Eric Rofes) *The Emancipatory Promise of Charter Schools: Toward a Progressive Politics of School Choice* (SUNY Press, 2004). She co-edited (with Sharon Lawner Weinberg) *Diversity in American Higher Education: Toward a More Comprehensive Approach* (Routledge, 2011). She currently is co-writing a book with Anthony S. Chen on the origins of race-conscious affirmative action in college admissions.

Robert T. Teranishi is Professor of Social Science and Comparative Education, the Morgan and Helen Chu Endowed Chair in Asian American Studies, and co-director for the Institute for Immigration, Globalization, and Education at the University of California, Los Angeles. He is also a senior fellow with the Steinhardt Institute for Higher Education Policy at New York University and principal investigator for the National Commission on Asian American and Pacific Islander Research in Education. His research examines the causes and consequences of the stratification of college opportunities, with a particular interest on the impact of higher education practice and policy on the mobility of marginalized and vulnerable communities.

Lawrence T. Winn is a doctoral student in the School of Human Ecology in the Civil Society and Community Research program at the University of Wisconsin, Madison. Winn is a consultant for strategic partnerships for Race to Equity in Madison, Wisconsin. He also served as Director of the Martin Luther King, Sr. Community Resources Collaborative, Director of Development and Strategic Partnerships for St. HOPE Academy, and the Executive Director of Uth Turn. Winn earned a B.A. in English from the University of California, Berkeley, a Juris Doctorate from Vanderbilt University Law School, and a Master of Divinity degree from Princeton Theological Seminary.

Maisha T. Winn is the Susan J. Cellmer Chair in English Education and Professor of Language and Literacy in the Department of Curriculum and Instruction at the University of Wisconsin, Madison. Winn is the author of many books including *Girl Time: Literacy, justice, and the school-to-prison pipeline*, *Humanizing Research: Decolonizing research with youth and communities* (with Django Paris), and *Education and Incarceration* (with Erica Meiners) as well as articles published in *Harvard Educational Review*; *Review of Research in Education*, *Race, Ethnicity, and Education*; *Anthropology and Education Quarterly*; *Research in the Teaching of English*, *Journal of African American History*, *Written Communication*, and *English Education*.

Part I
Introduction

Race, Education, and the Pursuit of Equity in the Twenty-First Century

Pedro A. Noguera

When W.E.B. Du Bois, the renowned African-American historian and sociologist, predicted that the question of the "color line" would be the primary problem for American society in the twentieth century (Du Bois, 1903), he had no way of knowing that the problem he alluded to would extend well into the twenty-first century. Similarly, when Swedish sociologist Gunnar Myrdal characterized America's race problem as a moral dilemma in the 1940s, one that threatened the veracity of the nation's proclaimed commitment to equality and democracy (Myrdal, 1944), like Du Bois, he had no way of knowing that the moral threat posed by America's inability to make progress in eliminating barriers related to race would persist to the present day.

The barriers observed by Du Bois and Myrdal have changed but in many ways they are still firmly intact today, and they are apparent most clearly and profoundly in the field of education.

It was not supposed to be this way. When the U.S. Supreme Court rendered its historic decision in *Brown versus Board of Education* in 1954, it was supposed to commence the beginning of the end of racial separation, in American schools and throughout American society (Bell, 2004). However, more than 60 years after the decision, it appears that the prediction of Du Bois has indeed extended into the twenty-first century, and the observation of Myrdal continues to be painfully accurate in the present day. Racial problems remain as intractable as ever, and progress in the pursuit of racial equality remains exceedingly slow. This is particularly the

This chapter expands significantly on text from the following article: Noguera, P. A., Pierce, J. C., & Ahram, R. (2015). Race, education, and the pursuit of equality in the twenty-first century. *Race and Social Problems, 7*(1), 1–4.

P.A. Noguera (✉)
UCLA GSEIS, 1041 Moore Hall, 405 Hilgard Avenue, Los Angeles, CA 90095–1521, USA
e-mail: pednoguera@gmail.com

© Springer International Publishing Switzerland 2016
P.A. Noguera et al. (eds.), *Race, Equity, and Education*,
DOI 10.1007/978-3-319-23772-5_1

case in the field of education, where the lack of progress on matters pertaining to racial equality has contributed to considerable controversy, conflict, and polarization throughout American society.

Lack of racial progress is evident on numerous fronts, from depictions of people of color in U.S. history and social studies textbooks (Loewen, 1995) to the *de facto* segregation of non-English speaking children and the absence of effective bilingual education in most schools and school districts (García, 2005). Racial controversies show up most prominently in the heated battles over standardized testing and in simmering conflicts over disparities in school discipline practices. In fact, although it is rarely stated, the increasingly acrimonious debate over the direction of education policy, particularly as it plays itself out in America's cities, is largely about who will determine the best way to educate poor children of color who constitute the overwhelming majority of students in these districts (Brill, 2011; Lipman, 2011). As the number of children from racial "minority" backgrounds continues to grow and children of color[1] become the majority of students in more American public schools,[2] how these children will be educated will undoubtedly continue to be a matter of considerable debate because of the social, economic, and political importance associated with this challenge.

Defining the Race Problem in American Education

To a large degree, the reason that race continues to be a persistent source of controversy in American education is because even as the number of children of color in American schools continues to grow, disparities in academic outcomes and opportunities continue to be pervasive and persistent in American education. On every measure of achievement and attainment, race continues to be a salient factor in defining and dividing the American student population. Policymakers are increasingly aware of these patterns, and since 2001 they have typically framed the problem as an "achievement gap" (Miller, 1995). Others have framed the problem as an "education debt" (Ladson-Billings, 2006) and an "opportunity gap" (Carter & Welner, 2013; Schott Foundation for Public Education, 2015): a critical part of the legacy of racism and racial discrimination in the U.S., a legacy that has produced and perpetuated unequal educational opportunities in the present, particularly for low-income children of color.

---

[1]Some authors in this volume use the term "racial minorities," while others refer to students, children, or people "of color." Both terms typically denote Black and Latino groups, though sometimes they encompass groups representing other racial-ethnic backgrounds, including Asian Americans/Pacific Islanders and Native Americans.

[2]According to a report by *Education Week*, minority children were projected to become the majority of children in U.S. public schools in 2014. The increase is "driven largely by dramatic growth in the Latino population and a decline in the white population, and, to a lesser degree, by a steady rise in the number of Asian-Americans" (Maxwell, 2014).

In many schools throughout the country, the conditions under which racial minority children are educated are often woefully inadequate and profoundly unequal. This is particularly the case in communities where poverty is concentrated (Kozol, 1991). A recent study commissioned by the U.S. Department of Education (2013) documented pervasive disparities in resources, educational opportunities, and the treatment afforded to children of color. The study concluded that

> …any honest assessment must acknowledge that our efforts to date to confront the vast gaps in educational outcomes separating different groups of young Americans have yet to include a serious and sustained commitment to ending the appalling inequities—in school funding, in early education, in teacher quality, in resources for teachers and students and in governance—that contribute so mightily to these gaps…(U.S. Department of Education, 2013, p. 14)

Of course, these problems are not new. Rather, they are the direct result of racial discrimination and unequal treatment that have been present throughout U.S. history and have been pervasive in other aspects of American society. Invariably, schools reflect broader patterns of privilege and inequality in American society, but while there is considerable pressure placed upon schools to equalize academic outcomes, there is little evidence of similar efforts being waged in other institutions and parts of society. In a widely read article for *The Atlantic*,[3] journalist Ta-Nehisi Coates (2014) persuasively made the case for reparations to African-Americans, documenting the numerous ways in which the legacy of slavery and racial segregation has contributed to disadvantages in economic opportunities and housing experienced by African-Americans. Like others (Conley, 2009; Massey & Denton, 1998; Rothstein, 2014), Coates argues that the legacy of racial discrimination has contributed to the prevalence of racial inequality in wealth and income today: disparities that have substantially increased in the last 20 years.[4] Law professor Michelle Alexander has made similar arguments in her work *The New Jim Crow* (2010), which documents the continuities between slavery and the emergence of mass incarceration as a system of social control.

One should not be surprised that similar continuities between racial injustice in the past and racial inequities in the present are common in education today. For example, Central High School in Little Rock, Arkansas, which in 1957 was the epicenter of a bitter battle over racial integration, a battle so intense that President Dwight D. Eisenhower found it necessary to deploy U.S. troops to enforce his integration order, nonetheless remains racially imbalanced today. Whereas in 1957 the school had a student body that was nearly all white, in 2012–2013 it had a minority population of 67 % (U.S. News and World Report, 2015). The largely minority (Black) student population is noteworthy because the city itself is

---

[3]This was one of the most widely read essays ever published by *The Atlantic*.

[4]In an analysis of current trends, the Federal Reserve Survey of Consumer Finances found that the average white household had 13 times the median wealth of the average Black household. According to a report by the Pew Research Center, the Black-white wealth gap is the highest it has been since 1989. For a detailed analysis see Kochhar and Fry (2014).

relatively integrated (48 % white, 42 % Black). Unlike the past, when segregationist laws and the threat of violence by white mobs kept racial barriers intact, in the current period, *de facto* segregation is maintained through "choice" and enrollment patterns that are viewed as voluntary.

Even more extreme patterns of racial concentration can be found in cities and towns, especially in the north and west (Orfield, Kucsera, & Siegel-Hawley, 2012). Ironically, today school integration is more likely in the south than in other parts of the country. In most large cities, a dual system of education has emerged: a private, well-resourced system that serves a largely white, affluent student population, and an under-resourced public system that primarily serves poor children of color. The latter schools are often chaotic, occasionally unsafe, and from an academic standpoint, generally inferior in quality. U.S. Secretary of Education Arne Duncan has described many urban high schools as "dropout factories" because they manage to graduate so few of the students who enroll there.[5]

Yet, while there is substantial continuity in the way that issues pertaining to race (and often class) intersect with educational opportunities, it would be a mistake to conclude that there are not important differences in education in the pre- and post-*Brown* period. In the current period the issues are not only different; in many ways they are also more complex than they were in 1954 when the *Brown* decision was rendered. As a result of immigration, many schools are more diverse linguistically and ethnically, having incorporated Latinos, a wide variety of Asians (now outnumbering African-Americans in several states), and immigrants from dozens of nations across the globe (Orfield & Lee, 2006). For many immigrant students, language barriers are as significant as racial barriers in denying students access to critical resources (e.g., college prep classes and advanced placement courses), and in some cases, high quality schools (Olsen, 1997). Moreover, as a result of changes in state and federal policies, the supports that were once made available to economically disadvantaged children under the Elementary and Secondary Education Act (ESEA) have shifted to a more narrow focus on standards and accountability. This has occurred even as poverty rates have risen and schools serving the greatest concentration of poor children have been more likely to fail (Barton & Coley, 2010; Boykin & Noguera, 2011). The evidence shows that in schools and districts where poverty is concentrated and academic performance tends to be substantially lower, there has still been relatively little willingness to address poverty and devise new strategies to alleviate the issues that frequently accompany it (U.S. Department of Education, 2013).

A number of researchers have described the current issues as "second generation" forms of discrimination to distinguish them from the issues that were prevalent prior to *Brown* (Meier, Stewart, & England, 1989). Unlike the first-generation issues which largely pertained to legally sanctioned racial discrimination, and

---

[5]Duncan claims that there are approximately 2,000 high schools with dropout rates that exceed 50 %. He has labeled these "dropout factories" and called for dramatic action to turn them around (see Gewertz, 2009).

that could therefore be addressed through legal challenges, the second-generation issues have been largely impervious to legal intervention.

The chapters in this volume document and describe a variety of second-generation issues related to the ways in which children of color, especially those from poor families, have been denied access to high quality educational opportunities and other barriers related to race. We have described the elimination of these barriers as the pursuit of the as yet unfulfilled promise of *Brown*. The very fact that over 60 years after the rendering of this historically important milestone many schools throughout the U.S. continue to be characterized by racial hyper-segregation (Orfield & Frankenberg, 2014) is just one of many indications that insufficient progress has been made in the journey toward racial equality in education.

However, this does not mean that *Brown* is no longer important or that it has become irrelevant. Many of the authors in this volume will show that *Brown*, despite its unfinished legacy, continues to be important because it serves as a legal precedent for challenging new racial barriers. While the law may be less effective today in challenging second-generation forms of discrimination, *Brown* continues to provide a moral basis for asserting the civil and educational rights of children who are poorly served. The mere fact that *Brown* brought about a formal end to *legally sanctioned* racial discrimination, what might be thought of as America's own version of Apartheid (Hacker, 1992; Omi & Winant, 2015), should serve as a reminder of the importance embedded within the Supreme Court's ruling.

However, with every year that passes since its rendering, it becomes clear that as written, and even more importantly, as enforced by the courts and the government, *Brown* is a limited tool and a weak lever for change. In fact, it could be argued that not only has the promise of *Brown*—racial integration in the nation's schools—been largely ignored, but the will to realize its promise has largely faded away. After significant progress in the 1960s and 1970s, and considerable backlash and resistance (Titus, 2011), today there is substantial evidence that public schools, especially in the largest cities in the north and west, have become more segregated on the basis of race and class (Orfield & Eaton, 1996; Orfield & Frankenberg, 2014). The U.S. Congress has not supported any measure for school desegregation since 1972. No Supreme Court decisions expanding desegregation have been rendered since 1973, and since 1981 there has been no funding allocated by the federal government for research and training on school desegregation (Orfield & Frankenberg, 2014). Nationwide, 74 % of African-Americans and 80 % of Latinos attend schools where the majority of students are from the same racial background (Orfield et al., 2012). Furthermore, more often than not, America's poorest children of color are concentrated together, typically in under-resourced schools that struggle in meeting their academic and social needs (Orfield & Lee, 2006). It is becoming increasingly clear that we have not only failed to live up to the promise of *Brown*, but we have not even achieved the more limited separate but equal goal of *Plessy*: the Supreme Court decision rendered in 1896 that was used to rationalize racial segregation.

Despite assertions from policymakers and pundits that education is the civil rights issue of the twenty-first century,[6] there is ample evidence of vast and persistent racial disparities in educational opportunities throughout American education. Consider the following patterns and trends included in a report from the U.S. Department of Education, Office for Civil Rights (2015: Data reflects FY 2013–2014):

- Black children represent 18 % of the preschool enrollment but 42 % of preschool children suspended once.
- Black students are suspended and expelled at three times the rate of white students.
- Black girls are suspended at higher rates (12 %) than any other girls.
- A quarter of the high schools with the highest percentage of Black and Latino students do not offer Algebra II, and a third do not offer chemistry.
- English learners represent 5 % of students but only 2 % of students enrolled in Advanced Placement courses.

The report also documents significant disparities in teacher salaries, in the likelihood that a student will be taught by a certified or experienced teacher, and in access to a guidance counselor. Moreover, throughout the United States, schools in poor communities generally spend less per pupil—and often many thousands of dollars less per pupil—than schools in nearby affluent communities, meaning poor schools cannot compete for the best teaching and principal talent in a local labor market and cannot implement the high-end technology and rigorous academic and enrichment programs needed to enhance student performance.

Finally, the international comparisons are equally troubling and revealing. The poverty rate for school-age children—currently more than 22 %—is twice the Organisation for Economic Co-operation and Development (OECD) average and nearly four times that of leading countries such as Finland. Twenty-two percent of American schoolchildren live in conditions of poverty, and among the 35 wealthiest nations, the U.S. ranks 34th in the relative child poverty rate (PISA, 2009).

This is by no means an exhaustive list. As I have pointed out already, racial disparities show up in most facets of life in America—in health (Auerbach, Krimgold, & Lefkowitz, 2000), in housing (Massey & Denton, 1998; Rothstein, 2014), nutrition, wealth (Conley, 2009), income (DeNavas-Walt & Proctor, 2014), and most blatantly, the criminal justice system (Alexander, 2010). The presence of these disparities reinforces an even more disturbing reality: the journey toward racial justice is far from over, and in some areas, has barely evinced signs of

---

[6]U.S. Secretary of Education Arne Duncan has described education as "the civil rights issue of the twenty-first century" on numerous occasions. Though he and others who use the phrase never follow it with an explanation of how education should be used to advance civil rights, the slogan continues to have considerable currency among both Democrats and Republicans. Some of the other public officials who have borrowed this phrase include former New York Mayor Michael Bloomberg (and his Chancellor Joel Klein), former President Bill Clinton, and New Jersey Governor Chris Christie. (For a critique of facile associations between education and civil rights, see Barry, 2011; Jones, 2014; Ravitch, 2012, 2013).

progress. In fact, given how consistent and pervasive these disparities are throughout American society, it is truly remarkable that policymakers would attempt to address racial disparities in education alone.

The presence of these disparities reminds us that not only does race still matter in American society; it matters a great deal. It matters not only with respect to the so-called "achievement gap"—the unequal academic outcomes that consistently correspond to the race and socioeconomic status of students that national leaders have claimed to be fixated on closing since 2001—but also with respect to gaps in educational opportunity. However, as the authors of the following chapters show, we have done relatively little to address gaps in opportunity—access to good schools, to highly qualified teachers, to rigorous courses, to a culturally relevant curriculum, to quality preschool, etc.—even though our policymakers decry with great frequency the gaps in achievement.

For this reason, the question of why race continues to matter in American education more than 60 years after *Brown* is the central focus of this book. The editors of this volume accept the notion that race is largely a political and social construct: a social category less related to biology than to power, created for the purpose of rationalizing domination and subordination—slavery, colonization, conquest, and even genocide (Omi & Winant, 2015; Roediger, 1991). Yet, in describing race as a social construct we by no means intend to suggest that it is insignificant and not a defining feature of life in American society today. The evidence shows that race matters in a wide variety of ways in American education. The question is why, especially given that racial discrimination has been outlawed and *Brown* continues to be the law of the land.

An Impoverished View of Reform

Close examination of the persistent and widespread disparities in academic outcomes that correspond to the race and class backgrounds of students reveals that they are actually part of a multidimensional phenomenon related first and foremost to larger patterns of inequality in society. Family income and to a lesser degree parental education continue to be strong predictors of academic performance (Barton & Coley, 2010). This means that more often than not, rather than expanding opportunity, education serves as a means through which inequality is reproduced (Carnoy, 1994). Additionally, gaps in academic performance are closely tied to unequal access to quality early childhood education (the preparation gap), inequities in school funding (the allocation gap), and differences in the amount of support that well-educated, affluent parents can provide to their children as compared to poorer, less-educated parents (the parent gap).

Research also suggests that gaps in academic outcomes are sometimes related to strained relations between students and their teachers and may be influenced by lower expectations and bias, particularly toward poor and minority students (the teacher–student gap). In many schools throughout the country, there is a significant imbalance between the racial composition of the teaching force and the student population (Darling-Hammond, 2010). Recent research suggests that this imbalance can result in lowered expectations (Boykin, Tyler, & Miller, 2005) and strained relations between teachers and students that become manifest in frequent discipline referrals (Gregory, Skiba, & Noguera, 2010). This is not only the case in urban and rural schools that serve large concentrations of poor children of color; it is also often the case in affluent school districts with ample resources and relatively small numbers of minority students (Noguera, 2001). In such communities, ability grouping or tracking often re-segregates students within schools and has the effect of denying students of color access to college preparatory courses and the most highly qualified teachers (Noguera & Wing, 2006; Oakes, 1989; Sealey-Ruiz, Handville, & Noguera, 2008). Similar patterns can be observed in special education placements (Ahram, Fergus, & Noguera, 2011) and discipline patterns (Gregory et al., 2010). Disproportionally, students of color (African-Americans, Latinos, and Native Americans particularly) are overrepresented in categories associated with risk and failure, and underrepresented in categories associated with academic success (Meier et al., 1989; Skiba et al., 2008).

Finally, as many parents know, there are often gaps between how well students do in school (as measured by grades or test scores) versus how well they might have actually done if they were motivated to work to their ability (the performance gap). Many students of all kinds report feeling bored and alienated in school, and researchers who have studied these phenomena find that students who feel disconnected from school and the educators who teach them do less well academically (Goodenow & Grady, 1993; Stipek & Gralinski, 1996). There is growing awareness that these problems are particularly acute among students of color and may be exacerbated by a curriculum that emphasizes the acquisition of basic skills and preparation for standardized tests but ignores the need for students to be challenged by rigorous and stimulating material (Noguera, Darling-Hammond, & Friedlaender, 2015). Several studies have shown that low-income children of color are more likely than other students to be subjected to a curriculum that lacks access to science, art, and higher-order thinking (Boykin & Noguera, 2011).

All of these dimensions are important to understanding the relationship between race and student performance, but none of these are considered or addressed in most of the efforts to address the so-called achievement gap. Most often, the achievement gap is conceived of as either a problem caused by low student motivation or teacher ineffectiveness. Based on these assumptions, policymakers have typically relied on strategies aimed at pressuring students and teachers to perform at higher levels such as using high-stakes testing (Darling-Hammond, 2010). These strategies include threatening both parties (and frequently principals as well) with sanctions (e.g., withholding a diploma) or job loss for inadequate performance.

In addition to tough accountability, policymakers have assumed that it might be possible to improve student performance by elevating academic standards. Although it is now fairly controversial, the new Common Core standards were heralded as a way to increase college readiness on a mass scale (Noguera et al., 2015).

Though some have championed these measures as a means to advance racial equity in education, they have typically paid scant attention to learning conditions within schools or to the challenges faced by teachers who must devise strategies to meet the learning needs of a diverse array of students (Darling-Hammond, 2010).

Additionally, in much of the literature on school failure, there has been relatively little attention paid to the ways in which the challenges rooted in low-income urban neighborhoods impact the performance of students and schools (Bowen, Bowen, & Ware, 2002; Noguera, 2003). This is also the case with respect to the public policies that in recent years have been used to guide and shape the direction of school reform. Consistently, education policies have been adopted and reforms have been carried out without sufficient attention to how they interact with and are affected by social and economic conditions present within economically depressed urban, suburban, or rural communities. Since the adoption of No Child Left Behind (NCLB), school reform has become the primary national strategy used to combat poverty, as other antipoverty policies have become less politically viable (Noguera, 2003; Rothstein, 2004). However, there is no evidence to support the notion that schools alone can counter the effects of poverty on children. There is, however, ample evidence that when the basic social needs of children are unaddressed, the academic challenges they face tend to become more severe (Rothstein, 2004). Nonetheless, the de-contextualized approach to school reform that began with the adoption of NCLB in 2001 (Rothstein, 2004 has called this "the schools alone approach") has persisted despite evidence that it has failed as a strategy for improving the most disadvantaged schools (Payne, 2008).

For large numbers of students of color, the persistent failure of school reform has also contributed to the social crises confronting Black and Latino males in society. Numerous studies have demonstrated a strong link between school failure and higher rates of unemployment and incarceration (Schott Foundation for Public Education, 2015). Recent research shows that Black males are particularly likely to end up "disconnected" from employment and other opportunities, and to become ensnared by the criminal justice system. Rather than schools serving as essential elements of a community's support system for children, they are too frequently the settings where the problems facing disadvantaged students of color emerge and worsen over time.

A study conducted by Anthony Bryk and his colleagues at the Consortium for School Improvement at the University of Chicago examined 10 years of intensive reform that included: closure of dozens of "failing" schools, massive investments in technology and professional development for educators, and the creation of new "innovative" school models (Bryk, Sebring, Allensworth, Luppescu, & Easton, 2010). The researchers found that these measures did little to improve academic outcomes or the quality of schools, particularly in Chicago's poorest neighborhoods (p. 37). Bryk and his colleagues found that problems related to poverty—crime, substance abuse, child neglect, unmet health needs, housing shortages, interpersonal violence, etc.—were largely ignored by the reform policies pursued in Chicago, and consequently the reforms yielded little in the way of sustained improvement (Bryk et al., 2010).

The Chicago case mirrors patterns observed in cities throughout the United States. This is because education policy has focused on raising academic standards and increasing accountability but largely ignored the social and economic conditions that impact school environments and learning opportunities for students. The emphases on standards and accountability (especially high-stakes testing) have left many of the schools that serve low-income children of color mired in persistent failure.

History Matters: From Cultural to Structural Explanations of Racial Disparities in Education

Throughout American history, racial inequality and the corresponding disparities or "gaps" in achievement, attainment, and measures of intellectual ability were attributed to innate genetic differences between population groups (Omi & Winant, 2015). Until relatively recently, much of education policy and practice that addressed matters related to race was premised on the notion that racial differences were immutable, and the inherent superiority of whites over non-whites was regarded as an indisputable "natural" phenomenon (Fredrickson, 1981). Intelligence was regarded as an innate human property rooted in the particular genetic endowments of individuals and groups (Duster, 2003; Gould, 1981), and as such, altering patterns of academic achievement was not considered feasible, much less desirable.

White supremacist views about the relationship between race and intelligence have had considerable influence on public policy and social science research throughout much of America's history (Duster, 2003; Lemann, 1996). Though overtly racist views have largely faded from public discourse (even if not entirely repudiated), it is important to understand how they helped to maintain larger patterns of racial subjugation in American society throughout much of U.S. history. For example, beliefs about the inherent inferiority of Africans rationalized 300 years of slavery and racial discrimination, in schools and other institutions (Feagin, 2000; Twombly, 1971). Similarly, racist views toward Native Americans provided justification for war and genocide and the forcible removal of many Indian children from reservations into boarding schools (Spring, 1994). Finally, imperial aggression and colonial domination in places like the Philippines, Hawaii, Puerto Rico, and Cuba were sold to the American public as "Manifest Destiny" and premised on the notion that subjugated people were uncivilized and would be better off under American rule (Fredrickson, 1981; Takaki, 1989; Zinn, 1980).

Early in the twentieth century advocates of Eugenics—the "science of genetic engineering"—propagated the notion that groups and individuals with superior intellect and physical ability should be encouraged to procreate to strengthen the national gene pool, while inferior groups should be actively discouraged and even prevented from reproducing their progeny (Duster, 2003). Some Eugenicists became leaders in the effort to devise tests for measuring intelligence (Lemann, 1996) in order to provide an "objective" scientific measure of intellectual acumen and ability. They also pushed for the results from these standardized tests to be used to determine who should be recruited for top occupations and for enrollment at elite universities (Fischer et al., 1996).

Beliefs about the relationship between race and intelligence in the United States that were used to rationalize slavery and racial segregation may seem like part of America's ugly past, but there is considerable evidence that the past is not irrelevant to current efforts aimed at closing the achievement gap. Although it is increasingly regarded as politically incorrect to attribute differences in achievement to genetic differences between racial groups, *The Bell Curve* (Hernstein & Murray, 1994) made precisely this point, and the book received a mix of condemnation and acclaim at the time of its release (Fischer et al., 1996). Although such views have not been supported by research on genetics, this did not prevent the authors of *The Bell Curve* from making arguments about the genetic basis of intellectual ability or the inferiority of racial minorities. The authors of *The Bell Curve*, Richard Hernstein (a psychologist) and Charles Murray (a political scientist), were not geneticists. However, lack of knowledge about the field in which they engaged in scholarly research did not prevent them or others from making similar claims. For example, not long ago, former Harvard University President Lawrence Summers suggested that one of the reasons why women were not well represented in mathematics- and science-related fields was due to innate differences in intellectual ability (Bombardieri, 2005). If the President of Harvard University, an economist by training, felt comfortable making remarks about the genetic basis of intelligence, it would not be a stretch of logic to conclude that similar views about the relationship between race, gender, and innate ability continue to be widely held throughout American society.

In place of arguments that attribute differences in achievement to innate differences in intelligence, a number of scholars in recent years have argued that disparities in academic performance can be explained by cultural differences (McWhorter, 2000; Ogbu, 1987), parental influences (Epstein, 1994; Farkas, 2004), and even the act of listening to gangsta rap music (Ferguson, 2007). Though such arguments differ significantly from previous arguments related to the inherent inferiority of certain minority groups, in practice they serve a similar purpose. Unlike biology, culture is often seen as less politically distasteful when offered as an explanation of academic differences among racial groups because it is assumed that culture, unlike biology, is not immutable and can be changed over time. Among those advocating this perspective are scholars such as anthropologist John Ogbu (1987; Ogbu & Davis, 2003), who argued that nonvoluntary minorities— groups that were incorporated into the U.S. through conquest, slavery, or force (i.e. Native Americans, African-Americans, Puerto Ricans, and Mexican Americans)— consistently do less well in school because they adopt an "oppositional culture" in relation to schooling (Ogbu, 1987). According to Ogbu, nonvoluntary minorities tend to regard schooling as a form of forced assimilation, and as such Ogbu argued they were less likely to embrace the behaviors that contribute to school success (e.g., obeying school rules, studying for examinations, speaking standard English, etc.). Ogbu's views have been embraced by many scholars as an effective way to explain why many "voluntary" immigrant minorities (especially Asian-Americans) do well in school while many domestic minorities do not. Although such arguments cannot explain exceptions to the patterns (e.g., members of domestic minority groups that succeed) or why large numbers of white students are not successful, cultural arguments continue to have enormous currency.

For example, similar arguments have been made most recently by Chua and Rubenfeld (2014), two Yale law professors who have argued that certain immigrant and religious groups (their favorites are Jews, Mormons, Chinese, Indians, Iranians, Nigerians, and some West Indians) outperform others because they possess a combination of cultural attributes they refer to as the triple package— a belief in their inherent superiority, deep-seated insecurity, and impulse control (Chua & Rubenfeld, 2014). The authors write:

> The good news is that it's not some magic gene generating these groups' disproportionate success. Nor is it some 5000-year-old "education culture" that only they have access to. Instead their success is significantly propelled by three simple qualities open to anyone. The way to develop this package of qualities—not that it's easy, or that everyone would want to—is through grit. It requires turning the ability to work hard, to persevere and to overcome adversity into a source of personal superiority. This kind of superiority complex isn't ethnically or religiously exclusive. It's the pride a person takes in his own strength of will.

Neither Chua nor Rubenfeld is an anthropologist, but like the nonexperts who made claims about genetics before them, lack of training in the study of culture has not prevented either from making broad generalizations about the relationship between culture and achievement. Though his arguments are more nuanced, sociologist Orlando Patterson, whose most recent book is *The Cultural Matrix* (Patterson & Fosse, 2015), makes similar generalizations in his attempt to explain the culture of disconnected Black youth. Like Chua and Rubenfeld, and Ogbu (who was an anthropologist), Patterson and many of the contributors to his edited volume make broad generalizations about Black youth and discount the influence of structural factors like class, neighborhood, and economic opportunities. Patterson asserts that disconnected Black youth "...create a virtual state of siege for all others who live in the ghetto" (2015, p. 78). His concern is that this group of individuals has an enormous influence over life in the inner city, particularly because of its association with the Hip Hop industry. He writes:

> ...being bad and nonconforming are simultaneously identified with real, 'authentic' blackness... an exaggerated performance of everything that distinguishes them from the mainstream: black talk; black dress; loud black music; disruptive classroom performance; fighting; heterosexual power and misogynistic attitudes toward women; identification with the pimp, drug pusher, gangster, the incarcerated, and the ex-con (p. 86).

While there is evidence that such behaviors exist, Patterson has trouble explaining why some youth who grow up in similar neighborhoods and circumstances do not exhibit them. He also cannot explain why these behaviors appear among some middle-class Black children and a large number of youth from different ethnic and socioeconomic backgrounds. Patterson regards the influence this group has over American culture generally as one of his central concerns:

> Here we come upon one of the central paradoxes of American civilization: the near complete socioeconomic isolation of disadvantaged black youth from middle class American mainstream culture and from its most critical procedural knowledge base, in conjunction with the complete integration and constitutive role of black youth in its popular culture, to the degree that the very identity of this culture, in America and in the world, is in good part recognized as black. (p. 92)

Cultural explanations of the relationship between race and academic achievement cannot explain variations within groups (e.g., not all Chinese are good at math and not all Puerto Ricans underachieve in school), nor can they explain why it is that when structural circumstances change—students enroll in better schools, families move out of neighborhoods where poverty is concentrated—behaviors can change too (Fergus, Noguera, & Martin, 2014). Sociologist William Julius Wilson, who has also studied Black, urban youth culture, points out that culture is malleable (2009), and observable behavior patterns often transform as opportunity structures change (Wilson, 1996).

Working in a similar vein as Patterson, Columbia University linguist John McWhorter has attributed the lower achievement of many African-American students to what he describes as a "culture of anti-intellectualism" (McWhorter, 2000). Similarly, former English professor Shelby Steele has attributed lower achievement among Black students to what he calls "victimology": the tendency on the part of Blacks to blame "the White man" for their problems (Steele, 1996). Embracing the concept, McWhorter (2000) contends that "victimology stems from a lethal combination of this inherited inferiority complex with the privilege of dressing down the former oppressor," and he adds that it "condones weakness and failure" (p. 28). Others, such as economist Ron Ferguson and journalist Juan Williams (Ferguson, 2007; Williams, 2006), have cited the culture of "gangsta rap," with its emphasis on "bling" (flashy jewelry), violence, and disdain for hard work, as producing a culture of failure.

Undoubtedly, certain aspects of human behavior may in fact be attributed to what might be described as culture. However, in order to be helpful in finding ways to ameliorate or at least reduce disparities in achievement, the specific aspects of culture that seem to be most influential to academic success must be identified. For example, certain child-rearing practices such as parents reading to children during infancy or posing questions rather than issuing demands when speaking to children are associated with the development of intellectual traits that contribute to school success (Epstein, 1994; Rothstein, 2004). Similarly, parental expectations about grades, homework, and the use of recreational time have been shown to influence adolescent behavior and academic performance (Ferguson, 2007). In his research at the University of California, Uri Treisman found that many Asian-American students studied in groups and helped one another to excel, reinforcing norms that contribute to the importance of academic success. In contrast, the African-American students he studied were more likely to socialize together but study alone (Treisman, 1993). Whether or not such behaviors can be attributed to culture can be debated, but clearly identifying specific behaviors that seem to positively influence academic achievement is more helpful than making broad generalizations about "oppositional" and "anti-intellectual" cultures.

Even when behaviors that appear rooted in culture are identified, educators must be careful about relying on cultural explanations to guide their thinking about academic achievement. Such thinking often has the effect of reinforcing negative stereotypes (Boykin & Noguera, 2011) and fostering practices that aim at uprooting or eliminating the culture of the children being educated. In fact, many of the so-called "No Excuses" charter schools have adopted practices and rituals with this specific purpose in mind (Whitman, 2008). Such practices typically ignore the cultural assets that research shows could actually assist children in learning (Perry, Steele, & Hilliard III, 2003).

Differences related to socioeconomic status and income, the educational background of parents, the characteristics and resources available in particular neighborhoods, and most importantly the quality of school a student attends significantly affect student achievement (Barnett, 2010; Miller, 1995; Noguera, 2003). Such factors influence the academic performance of all students, but because of the tendency to overemphasize the influence of culture on the performance of racial minority groups, they are often ignored. Again, there are a number of white students who do poorly in school and who do not attend college (Jencks, & Phillips, 1998), but there is substantially less attention paid to this problem than to the issues facing racial minority students. Academic failure among white students and the existence of poverty among white people in the U.S. are phenomena that are rendered invisible due to the high degree of emphasis placed on race in many aspects of American social policy. Moreover, it is rare to hear "experts" cite culture as an explanation for why some white students do poorly in school.

Finally, from a policy standpoint it is hard to imagine how we might go about changing the culture of individuals who seem to embrace attitudes and norms that undermine possibilities for academic success. It is far more sensible for public policy to focus on factors that can be more easily influenced, such as reducing poverty and racial segregation, equalizing funding between middle-class and poor schools, lowering class size, and ensuring that teachers who are qualified and competent are assigned to schools in high poverty neighborhoods. These are factors that several of the authors in this volume show can have a positive effect on student achievement, and none of these factors involve trying to figure out how to change a person or group's culture.

Moving Toward Racial Equality in Education in the Twenty-First Century

Given America's history with race, the fact that federal educational policy has made the goal of closing the achievement gap a national priority is a truly remarkable shift in assumptions related to race. Although policymakers have not called attention to the fact that the effort to eliminate racial disparities in student achievement represents a repudiation of America's past views on race, educators at the center of this effort are often forced to confront views on the relationship between race and intellectual ability that remain rooted in the not-so-distant past.

As a result of the pressure applied on schools by NCLB and the strict accountability that has led some school districts to fire superintendents and principals when test scores do not improve, educators across the country have been scrambling, and in some cases even cheating, to find ways to raise student test scores and show that gaps in performance can be closed. Despite their efforts, it is becoming increasingly clear that neither pressure nor a narrowed focus on test preparation will work as an effective means of eliminating the achievement gap or of substantially raising achievement levels for all students.

Scores on the National Assessment of Educational Progress (NAEP), also referred to as the nation's report card, were flat and in some cases declined in recent years (Perie, Moran, & Lutkus, 2005); graduation rates have improved but controversy remains about whether or not the progress is real; and on most international measures of academic performance, American children have fallen farther behind children in other wealthy nations (Darling-Hammond, 2010). A close look at PISA—the Programme for International Student Assessment, which is used to compare the performance of students in various nations on a variety of academic measures—reveals that when the performance of U.S. students is disaggregated by income, school districts with poverty rates lower than 25 % score as high as the top performing nations in the world (National Center for Education Statistics, 2009). In effect, the international comparisons reveal that inequality, particularly related to race and class, is America's greatest educational challenge.

The evidence also shows that the pursuit of integration has largely halted and become increasingly difficult to advance. In a series of rulings, the courts have removed or eliminated many of the legal tools that were once used to promote, encourage, or even mandate integration in schools (Milliken v. Bradley, 1974; Parents Involved in Community Schools v. Seattle School District, 2007; see Garland, 2013; Orfield & Eaton, 1996). Aside from their pronouncements about education being the civil rights issue of the twenty-first century, policymakers have ignored the empirical evidence that shows that racial isolation in schools is growing. Even as the nation marked the 60th anniversary of the *Brown* decision, politicians have largely been silent about the retreat from racial integration.

Throughout much of his career Du Bois was an advocate of racial integration. However, in his later years he became more cynical and disheartened about prospects for achieving meaningful racial integration in schools as he became more aware of how deeply entrenched racist beliefs were in American society. Du Bois was clear that it was not sufficient to merely enroll children from different backgrounds in the same schools. His primary concern was with ensuring that the academic and social needs of children, particularly African-American children, would be met. In the following passage he spells out what this education should entail:

...there must be sympathetic touch between teacher and pupil; knowledge on the part of the teacher, not simply of the individual taught, but of his surroundings and background, and the history of his class and group; such contact between pupils, and between teacher and pupil, on the basis of perfect social equality, as will increase this sympathy and knowledge;...and the promotion of such extra-curricular activities as will tend to induct the child into life (Du Bois, 1935, p. 328)

The conditions Du Bois describes as essential are not present in many ostensibly integrated schools, and for that reason, integration must be seen as only one of several important issues to be addressed on the subject of race and education. As I have pointed out, race and class issues figure prominently in a variety of educational issues. Many, though not all, of these issues are addressed by the authors of the chapters in this volume, who also make significant efforts to demonstrate how these issues are influenced by persistent and pervasive inequality both in school (particularly with respect to funding) and beyond (Carnoy, 1994; Carter & Welner, 2013). These pervasive disparities provide the contexts that shape and give meaning to other educational issues we examine in this book. Unlike policymakers and often the media, who generally prefer to discuss the state of public education without any reference to how it may be influenced by America's history of racial inequity, this book makes those connections explicit.

As noted above, children of color were projected to comprise the majority of children in U.S. public schools in 2014—the 60th anniversary of the *Brown* decision. Beyond schools, demographers project that by 2044, those who have historically been in the minority nationwide (at least as determined by membership in specified racial and ethnic groups) will be in the majority (Colby & Ortman, 2015; see also Clark, 1998), and those who previously were in the majority (those historically categorized as "whites"), will constitute the largest of several minority groups that make up the U.S. population. Additionally, regardless of efforts to close the border to stop illegal immigration, it is projected that by 2050, more than one-third of U.S. children will be of Latino origin (Murphy, Guzman, & Torres, 2014). We have yet to fully understand what these changes will mean for America's future, but we know for sure that major changes are inevitable. As the one institution charged with providing access to all children regardless of their backgrounds, education will undoubtedly play an important role in shaping patterns of mobility in the years ahead. In that critical role, it will either serve as a pathway to opportunity that helps in integrating the nation and its people, or it will continue to serve as the means through which existing inequalities are reinforced and reproduced over time. Whatever role it plays, there is little doubt that education will profoundly influence the kind of nation we become.

References

Ahram, R., Fergus, E., & Noguera, P. (2011). Addressing racial/ethnic disproportionality in special education: Case studies of suburban school districts. *Teachers College Record, 113*(10), 2233–2266.

Alexander, M. (2010). *The new Jim Crow: Mass incarceration in the age of colorblindness*. New York, NY: The New Press.

Auerbach, J. A., Krimgold, B. K., & Lefkowitz, B. (2000). *Improving health: It doesn't take a revolution*. Washington, DC: National Policy Association.

Barnett, W. S. (2010). Universal and targeted approaches to preschool education in the United States. *International Journal of Child Care and Education Policy, 4*(1), 1–12.

Barry, E. (2011, August 31). *Who says education reform is the 'civil rights issue of our time'?*. Retrieved from http://editbarry.wordpress.com/2011/08/31/who-says-education-reform-is-the-'civil-rights-issue-of-our-time'.

Barton, P. E., & Coley, R. J. (2010). *The black-white achievement gap: When progress stopped*. NJ: Princeton. Educational Testing Service.

Bell, D. (2004). *Silent covenants: Brown versus Board of Education and the unfulfilled hopes for racial reform*. New York, NY: Oxford University Press.

Bombardieri, M. (2005, January 17). Summers' remarks on women draw fire. *Boston Globe*. Retrieved from http://www.boston.com/news/education/higher/articles/2005/01/17/summers_remarks_on_women_draw_fire/?page=full.

Bowen, N. K., Bowen, G. L., & Ware, W. (2002). Neighborhood social disorganization, families, and the educational behavior of adolescents. *Journal of Adolescent Research, 17*, 468–489.

Boykin, A. W., & Noguera, P. (2011). *Creating the opportunity to learn: Moving from research to practice to close the achievement gap*. Washington, DC: ASCD.

Boykin, A. W., Tyler, K. M., & Miller, O. A. (2005). In search of cultural themes and their expressions in the dynamics of classroom life. *Urban Education, 40*(5), 521–549.

Brill, S. (2011). *Class warfare: Inside the fight to fix America's schools*. New York, NY: Simon and Schuster.

Brown versus Board of Education of Topeka, 347 U.S. 483 (1954).

Bryk, A. S., Sebring, P. B., Allensworth, E., Luppescu, S., & Easton, J. Q. (2010). *Organizing schools for improvement: Lessons from Chicago*. Chicago, IL: University of Chicago Press.

Carnoy, M. (1994). *Faded dreams: The politics and economics of race in America*. New York, NY: Cambridge University Press.

Carter, P., & Welner, K. G. (2013). *Closing the opportunity gap: What America must to do give every child an even chance*. New York, NY: Oxford University Press.

Chua, A., & Rubenfeld, J. (2014, January 26). *The triple package: How three unlikely traits explain the rise and fall of cultural groups in America*. New York Times. Retrieved from http://www.nytimes.com/2014/01/26/opinion/sunday/what-drives-success.html?_r=0.

Clark, W. A. V. (1998). *The California cauldron*. New York, NY: The Guilford Press.

Coates, T. (2014, June). *The case for reparations*. The Atlantic. Retrieved from http://www.theatlantic.com/features/archive/2014/05/the-case-for-reparations/361631/.

Colby, S. L., & Ortman, J. M. (2015). *Projections of the size and composition of the U.S. population: 2014 to 2060: Population Estimates and Projections: Current Population Reports*, P25-1143. U.S. Census Bureau. Washington, D.C. Retrieved from https://www.census.gov/population/projections/data/national/2014/publications.html.

Conley, D. (2009). *Being black, living in the red*. Berkeley, CA: University of California Press.

Darling-Hammond, L. (2010). *The flat world and education*. New York, NY: Teachers College Press.

DeNavas-Walt, C., & Proctor, B. D. (2014). *Income and poverty in the United States: 2013*. U. S. Department of Commerce: Economics and Statistics Administration: U. S. Census Bureau. Retrieved from http://www.census.gov/content/dam/Census/library/publications/2014/demo/p60-249.pdf.

Du Bois, W. E. B. (1903). *The souls of black folk*. Chicago, IL: A.C. McClurg and Co.

Du Bois, W. E. B. (1935). Does the Negro need separate schools? *Journal of Negro Education, 4*(3), 328–335.

Duster, T. (2003). *Backdoor to Eugenics*. New York, NY: Routledge.

Epstein, J. L. (1994). Theory to practice: School and family partnerships lead to school improvement and school success. In C. L. Fagnano & B. Z. Werber (Eds.), *School, Family, and Community Interactions: A View from the Firing Lines* (pp. 39–52). Boulder, CO: Westview Press.

Farkas, G. (2004). The black-white test score gap. *Contexts, 3*, 12–19.

Feagin, J. (2000). *Racist America: Roots, current realities, and future reparations*. New York: Routledge.

Fergus, E., Noguera, P. A., & Martin, M. (2014). *Schooling for resilience: Improving the life trajectory of Black and Latino boys*. Cambridge, MA: Harvard Education Press.

Ferguson, R. (2007). *Toward excellence with equity*. Cambridge, MA: Harvard University Press.

Fischer, C., Hout, M., Sánchez Jankowski, M., Lucas, S. R., Swidler, A., & Voss, K. (1996). *Inequality by design: Cracking the bell curve myth*. Princeton, NJ: Princeton University Press.

Frederickson, G. (1981). *White supremacy*. Oxford, UK: Oxford University Press.

García, E. (2005). *Teaching and learning in two languages: Bilingualism and schooling in the United States*. New York, NY: Teachers College Press.

Garland, S. (2013). *Divided we fail: The story of an African American community that ended the era of school desegregation*. Boston, MA: Beacon Press.

Gewertz, C. (2009, October 2). What to do about 'dropout factories.' *Education Week*. Retrieved from http://blogs.edweek.org/edweek/high-school-connections/2009/10/httpwwwall4edorgfi lesprioritiz.html?qs=gewertz+dropout

Gregory, A., Skiba, R., & Noguera, P. A. (2010). The achievement gap and the discipline gap. *Educational Researcher, 39*(1), 59–68.

Goodenow, C., & Grady, K. (1993). The relationship of school belonging and friends' values to academic motivation among urban adolescent students. *The Journal of Experimental Education, 62*, 60–71.

Gould, A. (1981). *The mismeasure of man*. New York, NY: W. W. Norton.

Hacker, A. (1992). *Two nations: Black and White, separate, hostile, unequal*. New York, NY: Scribner.

Hernstein, R. J., & Murray, C. (1994). *The bell curve: Intelligence and class structure in American life*. New York, NY: Free Press.

Jencks, C., & Phillips, M. (Eds.). (1998). *The Black-White test score gap*. Washington, DC: Brookings.

Jones, D. (2014, February). *Beware of education reformers who co-opt the language of the civil rights movement*. emPower. Retrieved from http://www.empowermagazine.com/beware-education-reformers-co-opt-language-civil-rights-movement/.

Kochhar, R., & Fry, R. (2014, December 12). *Wealth inequality has widened along racial, ethnic lines since end of Great Recession*. Pew Research Center. Retrieved from http://www.pewresearch.org/fact-tank/2014/12/12/racial-wealth-gaps-great-recession/.

Kozol, J. (1991). *Savage inequalities*. New York, NY: Crown Publishers.

Ladson-Billings, G. (2006). From the achievement gap to the education debt: Understanding achievement in US schools. *Education Researcher, 35*(7), 3–12.

Lemann, N. (1996). *The big test: The secret history of the American meritocracy*. New York, NY: Farrar, Straus, and Giroux.

Lipman, P. (2011). *The new political economy of urban education: Neo-liberalism, race and the right to the city*. New York, NY: Routledge.

Loewen, J. W. (1995). *Lies my teacher told me: Everything your American history textbook got wrong*. New York, NY: New Press.

McWhorter, J. (2000). *Losing the race: Self-sabotage in Black America*. New York, NY: The Free Press.

Massey, D. S., & Denton, N. A. (1998). *American Apartheid: Segregation and the making of the underclass*. Cambridge, MA: Harvard University Press.

Maxwell, L. A., (2014, August 19). *U.S. school enrollment hits majority minority milestone*. Education Week. Retrieved from http://www.edweek.org/ew/articles/2014/08/20/01demogr aphics.h34.html.

Meier, K., Stewart, J., & England, R. (1989). *Race, class, and education: The politics of second-generation discrimination*. Madison, WI: University of Wisconsin Press.

Milliken v. Bradley, 418 U.S. 717. (1974).

Miller, L. (1995). *An American Imperative: Accelerating minority educational advancement.* New Haven, CT: Yale University Press.

Murphy, D., Guzman, L., & Torres, A. (2014). *America's Hispanic children: Gaining ground, looking forward* (Publication #2014-38). Child Trends Hispanic Institute. Retrieved from http://www.childtrends.org/wp-content/uploads/2014/09/2014-38AmericaHispanicChildren.pdf.

Myrdal, G. (1944). *An American dilemma: The negro problem and modern democracy.* New York, NY: Harper and Brothers.

National Center for Education Statistics. (2009). *Report on PISA.* Washington, DC: US Department of Education.

No Child Left Behind Act of 2001. (2002). Pub. L. No. 107–110, 115 Stat. 1425.

Noguera, P. (2001). The elusive quest for equity and excellence. *Education and Urban Society, 34,* 18–41.

Noguera, P. (2003). *City schools and the American dream: Reclaiming the promise of public education.* New York, NY: Teachers College Press.

Noguera, P. A., Darling-Hammond, L., & Friedlaender, (2015). *Equal opportunity for deeper learning.* Boston, MA: Jobs for the Future.

Noguera, P. A., & Wing, J. Y. (2006). *Unfinished business: Closing the racial achievement gap in our nation's schools.* San Francisco, CA: Jossey Bass.

Oakes, J. (1989). *Keeping track: How schools structure inequality.* New Haven, CT: Yale University Press.

Ogbu, J. (1987). Opportunity structure, cultural boundaries, and literacy. In J. Langer (Ed.), *Language, literacy, and culture: Issues of society and schooling* (pp. 265–283). Norwood, NJ: Ablex.

Ogbu, J., & Davis, A. (2003). *Black American students in an affluent suburb: A study of academic disengagement.* New York, NY: Lawrence Erlbaum.

Olsen, L. (1997). *Made in America: Immigrant students in our public schools.* New York, NY: The New Press.

Omi, M., & Winant, H. (2015). *Racial formation in the United States* (3rd ed.). New York, NY: Routledge.

Orfield, G., & Eaton, S. E. (1996). *Dismantling desegregation.* New York, NY: New Press.

Orfield, G., & Lee, C. (2006). *Racial transformation and the changing nature of segregation.* Cambridge, MA: The Civil Rights Project at Harvard University.

Orfield, G., Kucsera, J., & Siegel-Hawley, G. (2012). *E Pluribus...Separation: Deepening Double Segregation for More Students.* Los Angeles, CA: The Civil Rights Project/Proyecto Derechos Civiles. Retrieved from http://civilrightsproject.ucla.edu/research/k-12-education/integration-and-diversity/mlk-national/e-pluribus...separation-deepening-double-segregation-for-more-students/orfield_epluribus_revised_omplete_2012.pdf.

Orfield, G., & Frankenberg, E. (with Ee, J. & Kuscera, J.). (2014). *Brown at 60: Great progress, a long retreat and an uncertain future.* Los Angeles, CA: The Civil Rights Project/Proyecto Derechos Civiles. Retrieved from http://civilrightsproject.ucla.edu/research/k-12-education/integration-and-diversity/brown-at-60-great-progress-a-long-retreat-and-an-uncertain-future/Brown-at-60-051814.pdf.

PISA (2009). *Equally prepared for life? How 15-year-old boys and girls perform in school.* OECD. Retrieved from http://www.oecd-ilibrary.org/education/equally-prepared-for-life_9789264064072-en

Parents Involved in Community Schools v. Seattle School District No. 1, 551 U.S. 701 (2007).

Patterson, O., & Fosse, E. (2015). *The cultural matrix: Understanding black youth.* Cambridge, MA: Harvard University Press.

Payne, C. (2008). *So much reform, so little change.* Cambridge, MA: Harvard Education Press.

Perie, M., Moran, R., & Lutkus, A.D. (2005). *NAEP 2004: Trends in academic progress: Three decades of student performance in reading and mathematics* (NCES 2005–464). U.S. Department of Education, Institute of Education Sciences, National Center for Education Statistics. Washington, DC: Government Printing Office.

Perry, T., Steele, C., & Hilliard, A, I. I. I. (2003). *Young, gifted and black: Promoting high achievement among African-American students.* New York, NY: Beacon Press.

Ravitch, D. (2012, August 30). Is education the civil rights issue of our day?. Retrieved from http://dianeravitch.net/2012/08/30/is-education-the-civil-rights-issue-of-our-day/.

Ravitch, D. (2013). *Reign of error: The hoax of the privatization movement and the danger to America's public schools.* New York, NY: Knopf.

Roediger, D. R. (1991). *The wages of whiteness: Race and the making of the American working class.* New York, NY: Verso Press.

Rothstein, R. (2004). *Class and schools: Using social, economic, and educational reform to close the black-white achievement gap.* Washington, D.C. and New York, N.Y.: Economic Policy Institute and Teachers College Press.

Rothstein, R. (2014). *The making of Ferguson: Public policies at the root of its troubles.* Washington, DC: Economic Policy Institute.

Schott Foundation for Public Education. (2015). *Black lives matter: The Schott fifty state report on public education and black males.* Schott Foundation for Public Education. Retrieved from http://www.blackboysreport.org/2015-black-boys-report.pdf.

Sealey-Ruiz, Y, Handville, N., & Noguera, P. (2008). In pursuit of the possible: Lessons learned from district efforts to reduce racial disparities in student achievement. *The Sophists Bane, 6*(2).

Stipek, D., & Gralinski, J. H. (1996). Children's beliefs about intelligence and school performance. *Journal of Educational Psychology, 88*(3), 397–407.

Skiba, R. J., Simmons, A. B., Ritter, S., Gibb, A. C., Rausch, M. K., Cuadrado, J., & Chung, C. (2008) Achieving equity in special education: History, status, and current challenges. *Exceptional Children, 74*(3), 264–288.

Spring, J. (1994). *American education.* New York, NY: McGraw Hill.

Steele, S. (1996). *The content of our character.* New York: St. Martin's Press.

Takaki, R. (1989). *Strangers from a different shore: A history of Asian Americans.* New York, NY: Penguin.

Titus, J. O. (2011). *Brown's battleground: Students, segregationists, and the struggle for justice in Prince Edward County, Virginia.* Chapel Hill, NC: University of North Carolina Press.

Treisman, U. (1993). *Lessons learned from a FIPSE project.* Berkeley, CA: University of California Professional Development Program.

Twombly, R. C. (Ed.). (1971). *Blacks in White America.* New York, NY: David McKay Company.

U.S. Department of Education (2013). *For each and every child: A strategy for education equity and excellence.* Washington, D.C. Retrieved from https://www2.ed.gov/about/bdscomm/list/eec/equity-excellence-commission-report.pdf.

U.S. Department of Education, Office for Civil Rights. (2015). *Protecting civil rights, advancing equity: Report to the President and Secretary of Education, under Section 203(b)(1) of the Department of Education Organization Act, FY 13–14.* Washington, D.C.

U.S. News and World Report. (2015). *Little rock school district: Central high school: Overview.* Retrieved from http://www.usnews.com/education/best-high-schools/arkansas/districts/little-rock-school-district/central-high-school-1373.

Whitman, D. (2008). *Sweating the small stuff: Inner-city schools and the new paternalism.* Washington, D.C.: Thomas B. Fordham Institute.

Williams, J. (2006). *Enough: Phony leaders, dead-end movements and the culture of failure that are undermining black America—and what we can do about it.* New York, NY: Random House.

Wilson, W. J. (1996). *When work disappears: The world of the new urban poor.* New York: Vintage Books.
Wilson, W. J. (2009). *More than just race: Being Black and poor in the inner city.* New York: W.W. Norton.
Zinn, H. (1980). *A people's history of the United States.* New York, NY: Harper.

Part II
Roots and Forms of Segregation

School Policy Is Housing Policy: Deconcentrating Disadvantage to Address the Achievement Gap

Richard Rothstein

We cannot substantially improve the performance of the poorest African-American students—the "truly disadvantaged," in William Julius Wilson's phrase—by school reform alone. It must be addressed primarily by improving the social and economic conditions that bring too many children to school unprepared to take advantage of what even the best schools have to offer.

There are two aspects to this conclusion:

- First, social and economic disadvantage—not poverty itself, but a host of associated conditions—depresses student performance, and
- Second, concentrating students with these disadvantages in racially and economically homogeneous schools depresses it further.

The individual predictors of low achievement are well documented:

- With less access to routine and preventive health care, disadvantaged children have greater absenteeism (Aysola, Orav, & Ayanian, 2011; Starfield, 1997), and they cannot benefit from good schools if they are not present.

This chapter was originally published as an article with the following citation: Rothstein, R. (2015). The racial achievement gap, segregated schools, and segregated neighborhoods: A constitutional insult. *Race and Social Problems, 7*(1), 21–30. Springer New York.

R. Rothstein (✉)
Economic Policy Institute, 1333 H Street NW Suite 300 East Tower,
Washington, DC 20005, USA
e-mail: rrothstein@epi.org

- With less literate parents, they are read to less frequently when young, and are exposed to less complex language at home (Ayoub et al., 2009; Brooks-Gunn & Markman, 2005).
- With less adequate housing, they rarely have quiet places to study and may move more frequently, changing schools and teachers (Mehana & Reynolds, 2004; Raudenbush, Jean, & Art, 2011).
- With fewer opportunities for enriching after-school and summer activities, their background knowledge and organizational skills are less developed (Entwisle, Alexander, & Olson, 2000; Neuman & Celano, 2001).
- With fewer family resources, their college ambitions are constrained (Johnson, In Progress).

As these and many other disadvantages accumulate, lower social class children inevitably have lower average achievement than middle-class children, even with the highest quality instruction.

When a school's proportion of students at risk of failure grows, the consequences of disadvantage are exacerbated.

In schools with high proportions of disadvantaged children:

- Remediation becomes the norm, and teachers have little time to challenge those exceptional students who can overcome personal, family, and community hardships that typically interfere with learning.
- In schools with high rates of student mobility, teachers spend more time repeating lessons for newcomers, and have fewer opportunities to adapt instruction to students' individual strengths and weaknesses.
- When classrooms fill with students who come to school less ready to learn, teachers must focus more on discipline and less on learning.
- Children in impoverished neighborhoods are surrounded by more crime and violence and suffer from greater stress that interferes with learning (Buka, Stichick, Birdthistle, & Earls, 2001; Burdick-Will et al., 2010; Farah et al., 2006).
- Children with less exposure to mainstream society are less familiar with the standard English that is necessary for their future success (Sampson, Sharkey, & Raudenbush, 2008).
- When few parents have strong educations themselves, schools cannot benefit from parental pressure for higher quality curriculum, children have few college-educated role models to emulate and have few classroom peers whose own families set higher academic standards.

Nationwide, low-income black children's isolation has increased. It is a problem not only of poverty but of race.

- The share of black students attending schools that are more than 90 % minority has grown from 34–39 % from 1991 to 2011 (Orfield & Frankenberg, 2014, Table 8; Orfield & Lee, 2006, Table 3). In 1991, black students typically attended schools where 35 % of their fellow students were white; by 2011, it had fallen to 28 % (Orfield & Frankenberg, 2014, Table 4; Orfield, Kucsera, & Siegel-Hawley, 2012, Table 5).
- In 1988, black students typically attended schools in which 43 % of their fellow students were low-income; by 2006 it had risen to 59 % (Orfield, 2009).
- In cities with the most struggling students, the isolation is even more extreme. The most recent data show, for example, that in Detroit, the typical black student attends a school where 3 % of students are white, and 84 % are low income (Detroit Public Schools, 2009, Enrollment Demographics as of 11/19/2009).

It is inconceivable that significant gains can be made in the achievement of black children who are so severely isolated.

This school segregation mostly reflects neighborhood segregation. In urban areas, low-income white students are more likely to be integrated into middle-class neighborhoods and less likely to attend school predominantly with other disadvantaged students. Although immigrant low-income Hispanic students are also concentrated in schools, by the third generation their families are more likely to settle in more middle-class neighborhoods. Illustrative is that Latino immigrants who had resided in California for at least 30 years had a 65 % homeownership rate prior to the burst of the housing bubble (Myers, 2008).[1] It is undoubtedly lower after the bubble burst, but still extraordinary.

The racial segregation of schools has been intensifying because the segregation of neighborhoods has been intensifying. Analyzing census data, Rutgers University Prof. Paul Jargowsky has found that in 2011, 7 % of poor whites lived in high poverty neighborhoods, where more than 40 % of the residents are poor, up from 4 % in 2000; 15 % of poor Hispanics lived in such high poverty neighborhoods in 2011, up from 14 % in 2000; and a breathtaking 23 % of poor blacks lived in high poverty neighborhoods in 2011, up from 19 % in 2000 (Jargowsky, 2013).

In his 2013 book *Stuck in Place*, the New York University sociologist Patrick Sharkey defines a poor neighborhood as one where 20 % of the residents are poor, not 40 % as in Paul Jargowsky's work. A 20-percent-poor neighborhood is still severely disadvantaged. In such a neighborhood, many, if not most other residents are likely to have very low incomes, although not so low as to be below the official poverty line.

Sharkey finds that young African-Americans (from 13 to 28-years old) are now ten times as likely to live in poor neighborhoods, defined in this way, as young whites—66 % of African Americans, compared to 6 % of whites (Sharkey, 2013,

---

[1]Compare to overall national rates in 2007 (in percents): all, 68; whites, 75; blacks, 47; Hispanics (all generations), 50 (U.S. Census Bureau, 2014).

p. 27, Fig. 2.1). What is more, for black families, mobility out of such neighborhoods is much more limited than for whites. Sharkey shows that 67 % of African-American families hailing from the poorest quarter of neighborhoods a generation ago continue to live in such neighborhoods today. But only 40 % of white families who lived in the poorest quarter of neighborhoods a generation ago still do so (Sharkey, 2013, p. 38, Fig. 2.6).

Considering all black families, 48 % have lived in poor neighborhoods over at least two generations, compared to 7 % of white families (Sharkey, 2013, p. 39). If a child grows up in a poor neighborhood, moving up and out to a middle-class area is typical for whites but an aberration for blacks. Black neighborhood poverty is thus more multigenerational while white neighborhood poverty is more episodic; black children in low-income neighborhoods are more likely than others to have parents who also grew up in such neighborhoods.

The implications for children's chances of success are dramatic: For academic performance, Sharkey uses a scale like the familiar IQ measure, where 100 is the mean and roughly 70 % of children score about average, between 85 and 115. Using a survey that traces individuals and their offspring since 1968, Sharkey shows that children who come from middle-class (non-poor) neighborhoods and whose mothers also grew up in middle-class neighborhoods score an average of 104 on problem-solving tests. Children from poor neighborhoods whose mothers also grew up in poor neighborhoods score lower, an average of 96.

Sharkey's truly startling finding, however, is this: Children in poor neighborhoods whose mothers grew up in middle-class neighborhoods score an average of 102, slightly above the mean and only slightly below the average scores of children whose families lived in middle-class neighborhoods for two generations. But children who live in middle-class neighborhoods—yet whose mothers grew up in poor neighborhoods—score an average of only 98 (Sharkey, 2013, p. 130, Fig. 5.5).

Sharkey concludes that "the parent's environment during [her own] childhood may be more important than the child's own environment." He calculates that "living in poor neighborhoods over two consecutive generations reduces children's cognitive skills by roughly eight or nine points … roughly equivalent to missing 2–4 years of schooling" (Sharkey, 2013, pp. 129–131).

Integrating disadvantaged black students into schools where more privileged students predominate can narrow the black–white achievement gap. Evidence is especially impressive for long term outcomes for adolescents and young adults who have attended integrated schools (e.g., Guryan, 2001; Johnson, 2011). But the conventional wisdom of contemporary education policy notwithstanding, there is no evidence that segregated schools with poorly performing students can be "turned around" while remaining racially isolated. Claims that some schools, charter schools in particular, "beat the odds" founder upon close examination. Such schools are structurally selective on non-observables, at least, and frequently have high attrition rates (Rothstein, 2004, pp. 61–84). In some small districts, or in areas of larger districts where ghetto and middle-class neighborhoods adjoin, school integration can be accomplished by devices such as magnet schools, controlled choice, and attendance zone manipulations. But for African-American students living in the ghettos of large cities, far distant from middle-class suburbs, the racial isolation of their schools cannot be remedied without undoing the racial isolation of the neighborhoods in which they are located.

The Myth of *De Facto* Segregation

In 2007, the Supreme Court made integration even more difficult than it already was, when the Court prohibited the Louisville and Seattle school districts from making racial balance a factor in assigning students to schools, in situations where applicant numbers exceeded available seats (Parents Involved in Community Schools v. Seattle School District No. 1, 2007).

The plurality opinion by Chief Justice John Roberts decreed that student categorization by race (for purposes of administering a choice program) is unconstitutional unless it is designed to reverse effects of explicit rules that segregated students by race. Desegregation efforts, he stated, are impermissible if students are racially isolated, not as the result of government policy but because of societal discrimination, economic characteristics, or what Justice Clarence Thomas, in his concurring opinion, termed "any number of innocent private decisions, including voluntary housing choices."

In Roberts' terminology, commonly accepted by policymakers from across the political spectrum, constitutionally forbidden segregation established by federal, state, or local government action is *de jure*, while racial isolation independent of state action, as, in Roberts' view, in Louisville and Seattle, is *de facto*.

It is generally accepted today, even by sophisticated policymakers, that black students' racial isolation is now *de facto*, with no constitutional remedy—not only in Louisville and Seattle, but in all metropolitan areas, North and South.

Even the liberal dissenters in the Louisville-Seattle case, led by Justice Stephen Breyer, agreed with this characterization. Breyer argued that school districts should be permitted voluntarily to address *de facto* racial homogeneity, even if not constitutionally required to do so. But he accepted that for the most part, Louisville and Seattle schools were not segregated by state action and thus not constitutionally required to desegregate.

This is a dubious proposition. Certainly, Northern schools have not been segregated by policies assigning blacks to some schools and whites to others—at least not since the 1940s; they are segregated because their neighborhoods are racially homogeneous.

But neighborhoods did not get that way from "innocent private decisions" or, as the late Justice Potter Stewart once put it, from "unknown and perhaps unknowable factors such as in-migration, birth rates, economic changes, or cumulative acts of private racial fears" (Milliken v. Bradley, 1974).

In truth, residential segregation's causes are both knowable and known—twentieth-century federal, state, and local policies explicitly designed to separate the races and whose effects endure today. In any meaningful sense, neighborhoods and in consequence, schools, have been segregated *de jure*. The notion of *de facto* segregation is a myth, although widely accepted in a national consensus that wants to avoid confronting our racial history.

De Jure Residential Segregation by Federal, State, and Local Government

The federal government led in the establishment and maintenance of residential segregation in metropolitan areas.

From its New Deal inception and especially during and after World War II, federally funded public housing was explicitly racially segregated, both by federal and local governments. Not only in the South, but in the Northeast, Midwest, and West, projects were officially and publicly designated either for whites or for blacks. Some projects were "integrated" with separate buildings designated for whites or for blacks. Later, as white families left the projects for the suburbs, public housing became overwhelmingly black and in most cities was placed only in black neighborhoods, explicitly so. This policy continued one originating in the New Deal, when Harold Ickes, President Roosevelt's first public housing director, established the "neighborhood composition rule" that public housing should not disturb the preexisting racial composition of neighborhoods where it was placed (Hirsch, 1998/1983, p. 14; Hirsch, 2000, p. 209; e.g., Hills v. Gautreaux, 1976; Rothstein, 2012). This was *de jure* segregation.

Once the housing shortage eased and material was freed for post-World War II civilian purposes, the federal government subsidized relocation of whites to suburbs and prohibited similar relocation of blacks. Again, this was not implicit, not mere "disparate impact," but racially explicit policy. The Federal Housing and Veterans Administrations recruited a nationwide cadre of mass-production builders who constructed developments on the East Coast like the Levittowns in Long Island, Pennsylvania, New Jersey, and Delaware; on the West Coast like Lakewood and Panorama City in the Los Angeles area, Westlake (Daly City) in the San Francisco Bay Area, and several Seattle suburbs developed by William and Bertha Boeing; and in numerous other metropolises in between. These builders received federal loan guarantees *on explicit condition* that no sales be made to blacks and that each individual deed include a prohibition on resales to blacks, or to what the FHA described as an "incompatible racial element" (FHA, 1938; Jackson, 1985, pp. 207–209, 238; e.g., Silva, 2009). This was *de jure* segregation.

In addition to guaranteeing construction loans taken out by mass production suburban developers, the FHA, as a matter of explicit policy, also refused to insure individual mortgages for African-Americans in white neighborhoods, or even to whites in neighborhoods that the FHA considered subject to possible integration in the future (Hirsch, 2000, pp. 208, 211–212). This was *de jure* segregation.

Although a 1948 Supreme Court ruling barred courts from enforcing racial deed restrictions, the restrictions themselves were deemed lawful for another 30 years and the FHA knowingly continued, until the Fair Housing Act was passed in 1968, to finance developers who constructed suburban developments that were closed to African-Americans (Hirsch, 2000, pp. 211–212). This was *de jure* segregation.

Bank regulators from the Federal Reserve, Comptroller of the Currency, Office of Thrift Supervision, and other agencies knowingly approved "redlining" policies by which banks and savings institutions refused loans to black families in white suburbs and even, in most cases, to black families in black neighborhoods— leading to the deterioration and ghettoization of those neighborhoods (see, e.g., USCCR, 1961, pp. 36–37, 42–51). This was *de jure* segregation.

Although specific zoning rules assigning blacks to some neighborhoods and whites to others were banned by the Supreme Court in 1917, explicit racial zoning in some cities was enforced until the 1960s. The Court's 1917 decision was not based on equal protection but on the property rights of white owners to sell to whomever they pleased. Several large cities interpreted the ruling as inapplicable to their racial zoning laws because they prohibited only residence of blacks in white neighborhoods, not ownership. Some cities, Miami the most conspicuous example, continued to include racial zones in their master plans and issued development permits accordingly, even though neighborhoods themselves were not explicitly zoned for racial groups (Mohl, 1987, 2001). This was *de jure* segregation.

In other cities, following the 1917 Supreme Court decision, mayors and other public officials took the lead in organizing homeowners' associations for the purpose of enacting racial deed restrictions. Baltimore is one example where the mayor organized a municipal Committee on Segregation to maintain racial zones without an explicit ordinance that would violate the 1917 decision (Power, 1986, 2004). This was *de jure* segregation.

In the 1980s, the Internal Revenue Service revoked the tax-exemption of Bob Jones University because it prohibited interracial dating. The IRS believed it was constitutionally required to refuse a tax subsidy to a university with racist practices. Yet the IRS never challenged the pervasive use of tax-favoritism by universities, churches, and other nonprofit organizations and institutions to enforce racial segregation. The IRS extended tax exemptions not only to churches where such associations were frequently based and whose clergy were their officers, but to the associations themselves, although their racial purposes were explicit and well known. This was *de jure* segregation.

Churches were not alone in benefitting from unconstitutional tax exemptions. Robert Hutchins, known to educators for reforms elevating the liberal arts in higher education, was president and chancellor of the tax-exempt University of Chicago from 1929 to 1951. He directed the University to sponsor neighborhood associations to enforce racially restrictive deeds in its nearby Hyde Park and Kenwood neighborhoods, and employed the University's legal department to evict black families who moved nearby in defiance of his policy, all while the university was subsidized by the federal government by means of its tax-deductible and tax-exempt status (Hirsch, 1998/1983, pp. 144–145; Plotkin, 1999, pp. 122–125). This was *de jure* segregation.

Urban renewal programs of the mid-twentieth century often had similarly undisguised purposes: to force low-income black residents away from universities, hospital complexes, or business districts and into new ghettos. Relocation to stable and integrated neighborhoods was not provided; in most cases, housing quality for those whose homes were razed was diminished by making public housing high-rises or overcrowded ghettos the only relocation option (Hirsch, 2000, pp. 217–222; Weaver, 1948, p. 324; USCCR, 1961, p. 96). This was *de jure* segregation.

Where integrated or mostly-black neighborhoods were too close to white communities or central business districts, interstate highways were routed by federal and local officials to raze those neighborhoods for the explicit purpose of relocating black populations to more distant ghettos or of creating barriers between white and black neighborhoods. Euphemisms were thought less necessary then than today: according to the director of the American Association of State Highway Officials whose lobbying heavily influenced the interstate program, "some city officials expressed the view in the mid-1950s that the urban Interstates would give them a good opportunity to get rid of the local 'niggertown'" (Schwartz, 1976, p. 485 n. 481). This was *de jure* segregation.

For a sense of how federal policy was infused with segregationist impulses, consider the 1949 Congressional debate over President Harry S. Truman's proposal for a massive public housing program. Conservative Republicans, opposed to federal involvement in the private housing market, devised a "poison pill" guaranteed to defeat the plan. They introduced amendments in the House and Senate requiring that public housing be operated in a non-segregated manner, knowing that if such amendments were adopted, public housing would lose its Southern Democratic support and the entire program would go down to defeat.

The Senate floor leader of the housing program was the body's most liberal member, Paul Douglas, a former economist at the University of Chicago. Supported by other leading liberal legislators (Senator Hubert Humphrey from Minnesota, for example), Senator Douglas appealed on the floor of the Senate to his fellow Democrats and civil rights leaders, beseeching them to defeat the pro-integration amendment: "I should like to point out to my Negro friends what a large amount of housing they will get under this act… I am ready to appeal to history and to time that it is in the best interests of the Negro race that we carry through the housing program as planned, rather than put in the bill an amendment which will inevitably defeat it…"

The Senate and House each then considered and defeated proposed amendments that would have prohibited segregation and racial discrimination in federally funded public housing programs, and the 1949 Housing Act, with its provisions for federal finance of public housing, was adopted (Davies, 1966, p. 108; Julian & Daniel, 1989, pp. 668–669). It permitted local authorities in the North as well as the South to design separate public housing projects for blacks and whites, or to segregate blacks and whites within projects. And they did so.

Although there was an enormous national housing shortage at the time, one that denied millions of African-Americans a decent place to live, it remains an open question whether it really was in their best interests to be herded into segregated projects, where their poverty was concentrated and isolated from the American mainstream.

It was not, however, federal policy alone that segregated the metropolitan landscape. State policy contributed as well.

Real estate is a highly regulated industry. State governments require brokers to take courses in ethics and exams to keep their licenses. State commissions suspend or even lift licenses for professional and personal infractions—from mishandling escrow accounts to failing to pay personal child support. But although real estate agents openly enforced segregation, state authorities did not punish brokers for racial discrimination, and rarely do so even today when racial steering and discriminatory practices remain (Galster & Godfrey, 2005). This misuse of regulatory authority was, and is, *de jure* segregation.

Local officials also played roles in violation of their constitutional obligations. Public police and prosecutorial power was used nationwide to enforce racial boundaries. Illustrations are legion. In the Chicago area, police forcibly evicted blacks who moved into an apartment in a white neighborhood; in Louisville, the locus of *Parents Involved*, the state prosecuted and convicted (later reversed) a white seller for sedition after he sold his white-neighborhood home to a black family (Braden, 1958). Everywhere, North, South, East, and West, police stood by while thousands (not an exaggeration) of mobs set fire to and stoned homes purchased by blacks in white neighborhoods, and prosecutors almost never charged well-known and easily identifiable mob leaders (Rubinowitz & Perry, 2002). This officially sanctioned abuse of police power also constituted *de jure* segregation.

An example from Culver City, a suburb of Los Angeles, illustrates how purposeful state action to promote racial segregation could be. During World War II, its state's attorney instructed the municipality's air raid wardens, when they went door-to-door advising residents to turn off lights to avoid providing guidance to Japanese bombers, also to solicit homeowners to sign restrictive covenants barring blacks from residence in the community ("Communiques from the housing front," 1943). This was *de jure* segregation.

Other forms abound of racially explicit state action to segregate the urban landscape, in violation of the Fifth, Thirteenth, and Fourteenth Amendments. Yet the term "*de facto* segregation," describing a never-existent reality, persists among otherwise well-informed advocates and scholars. The term, and its implied theory of private causation, hobbles our motivation to address *de jure* segregation as explicitly as Jim Crow was addressed in the South or apartheid was addressed in South Africa.

Private prejudice certainly played a very large role. But even here, unconstitutional government action not only reflected but helped to create and sustain private prejudice. In part, white homeowners' resistance to black neighbors was fed by deteriorating ghetto conditions, sparked by state action. Seeing slum conditions invariably associated with African-Americans, white homeowners had a reasonable fear that if African-Americans moved into their neighborhoods, these refugees from urban slums would bring the slum conditions with them.

Yet these slum conditions were supported by state action, by overcrowding caused almost entirely by the refusal of the federal government to permit African-Americans to expand their housing supply by moving to the suburbs, and by municipalities' discriminatory denial of adequate public services (Colfax, 2009; Kerner Commission, 1968, pp. 14, 145, 273; Satter, 2009). In the ghetto,

- garbage was collected less frequently,
- predominantly African-American neighborhoods were re-zoned for mixed (i.e., industrial, or even toxic) use,
- streets remained unpaved,
- even water, power, and sewer services were less often provided.

This was *de jure* segregation, but white homeowners came to see these conditions as characteristics of black residents themselves, not as the results of racially motivated municipal policy.

The Continuing Effects of State Sponsored Residential Segregation

Even those who understand this dramatic history of *de jure* segregation may think that because these policies are those of the past, there is no longer a public policy bar that prevents African-Americans from moving to white neighborhoods. Thus, they say, although these policies were unfortunate, we no longer have *de jure* segregation. Rather, they believe, the reason we do not have integration today is not because of government policy but because most African-Americans cannot afford to live in middle-class neighborhoods.

This unaffordability was also created by federal, state, and local policy that prevented African-Americans in the mid-twentieth century from accumulating the capital needed to invest in home ownership in middle-class neighborhoods, and then from benefiting from the equity appreciation that followed in the ensuing decades.

Federal labor market and income policies were racially discriminatory until only a few decades ago. In consequence, most black families, who in the mid-twentieth century could have joined their white peers in the suburbs, can no longer afford to do so.

The federal civil service was first segregated in the twentieth century, by the administration of President Woodrow Wilson. Under rules then adopted, no black civil servant could be in a position of authority over white civil servants, and in consequence, African-Americans were restricted and demoted to the most poorly paid jobs (King, 1995).

The federal government recognized separate black and white government employee unions well into the second half of the twentieth century. For example, black letter carriers were not admitted to membership in the white postal service union. Black letter carriers had their own union but the Postal Service would only hear grievances from the white organization ("Same work, different unions," 2011).

At the behest of Southern segregationist Senators and Congressmen, New Deal labor standards laws, like the National Labor Relations Act and the minimum wage law, excluded from coverage, for undisguised racial purposes, occupations in which black workers predominated (Katznelson, 2013).

The National Labor Relations Board certified segregated private sector unions, and unions that entirely excluded African-Americans from their trades, into the 1970s (Foner, 1976; Hill, 1977; Independent Metal Workers, 1964).

State and local governments maintained separate, and lower, salary schedules for black public employees through the 1960s (e.g., Rothstein & Miles, 1995).

In these and other ways, government played an important and direct role in depressing the income levels of African-American workers below the income levels of comparable white workers. This, too, contributed to the inability of black workers to accumulate the wealth needed to move to equity-appreciating white suburbs.

Today (2010), median black family income is 61 % of the white median, but black median family wealth (net worth, or assets minus debts) is an astonishingly low 5 % of the white median (Mishel, Bivens, Gould, & Shierholz, 2012, Tables 2.5 and 6.5). The wealth gap does not only reflect the desperate financial situation of the poorest disadvantaged families. Thomas Shapiro, co-author of *Black Wealth/White Wealth* (1995), has estimated the relative wealth by race for *middle-class* families. Calculating relative wealth for black and white families with annual incomes of $60,000—slightly above the national median—from his most recent data in 2007, he found that black middle-class wealth was only 22 % of whites' (T. Shapiro, personal communication, May 3, 2014). This gap has undoubtedly widened since 2007 because the housing collapse harmed blacks—who were targeted disproportionately for exploitative subprime loans and exposed to foreclosure—more than whites.

In short, middle-class African-Americans and whites are in different financial straits. Total family wealth (including the ability to borrow from home equity) has more impact than income on high-school graduates' ability to afford college. Wealth also influences children's early expectations that they will attend and complete college. White middle-class children are more likely to prepare for, apply to, and graduate from college than black children with similar family incomes. This widely acknowledged difference in educational outcomes is, in considerable part, the enduring effect of *de jure* segregated housing policies of the twentieth century, policies that prevented African-Americans from accumulating, and bequeathing, wealth that they might otherwise have gained from appreciating real estate.

Levittown, described above as a Long Island suburban development built with federal financing and restricted to whites, illustrates these enduring effects. William Levitt sold his houses to whites in 1947 for $7,000, about two and a half times the national median family income (Jackson, 1985, pp. 231–245; Williamson, 2005). White veterans could get VA or FHA loans with no down payments. Today, these homes typically sell for $400,000, about six times the median income, and FHA loans require 20 % down. Although African-Americans are now permitted to purchase in Levittown, it has become unaffordable. By 2010 Levittown, in a metropolitan region with a large black population, was still less than 1 % black. White Levittowners can today easily save for college. Blacks denied access to the community are much less likely to be able to do so.

Segregation in many other suburbs is now locked in place by exclusionary zoning laws—requiring large setbacks, prohibiting multi-family construction, or specifying minimum square footage—in suburbs where black families once could have afforded to move in the absence of official segregation, but can afford to do so no longer with property values appreciated.

Mid-twentieth century policies of *de jure* racial segregation continue to have impact in other ways, as well. A history of state-sponsored violence to keep African-Americans in their ghettos cannot help but influence the present-day reluctance of many black families to integrate.

Today, when facially race-neutral housing or redevelopment policies have a disparate impact on African-Americans, that impact is inextricably intertwined with the state-sponsored system of residential segregation that we established.

Miseducating Our Youth

Reacquainting ourselves with that history is a step toward confronting it. When knowledge of that history becomes commonplace, we will conclude that *Parents Involved* was wrongly decided by the Supreme Court in 2007: Louisville, Seattle and other racially segregated metropolitan areas not only have permission, but a constitutional obligation to integrate.

But this obligation cannot be fulfilled by school districts alone. As noted above, in some small cities, and in some racial border areas, some racial school integration can be accomplished by adjusting attendance zones, establishing magnet schools, or offering more parent–student choice. This is especially true—but only temporarily—where neighborhoods are in transition, either from gradual urban gentrification, or in first-ring suburbs to which urban ghetto populations are being displaced. These school integration policies are worth pursuing, but generally, our most distressed ghettos are too far distant from truly middle-class communities for school integration to occur without racially explicit policies of residential desegregation. Many ghettos are now so geographically isolated from white suburbs that voluntary choice, magnet schools, or fiddling with school attendance zones can no longer enable many low-income black children to attend predominantly middle class schools (Rothstein & Santow, 2012).

Instead, narrowing the achievement gap will also require housing desegregation, which history also shows is not a voluntary matter but a constitutional necessity—involving policies like voiding exclusionary zoning, placing scattered low and moderate income housing in predominantly white suburbs, prohibiting landlord discrimination against housing voucher holders, and ending federal subsidies for communities that fail to reverse policies that led to racial exclusion.

We will never develop the support needed to enact such policies if policymakers and the public are unaware of the history of state-sponsored residential segregation. And we are not doing the job of telling young people this story, so that they will support more integration-friendly policies in the future. Elementary and secondary school curricula typically ignore, or worse, misstate this story. For example:

- In over 1,200 pages of McDougal Littell's widely used high-school textbook, *The Americans* (Danzer, de Alva, Krieger, Wilson, & Woloch, 2007, p. 494), a single paragraph is devoted to twentieth-century "Discrimination in the North." It devotes one passive-voice sentence to residential segregation, stating that "African Americans found themselves forced into segregated neighborhoods," with no further explanation of how public policy was responsible.
- Another widely used textbook, Prentice Hall's *United States History* (Lapanksy-Werner, Levy, Roberts, & Taylor, 2010, pp. 916–917), also attributes segregation to mysterious forces: "In the North, too, African Americans faced segregation and discrimination. Even where there were no explicit laws, *de facto* segregation, or segregation by unwritten custom or tradition, was a fact of life. African Americans in the North were denied housing in many neighborhoods."
- *History Alive*! (Alavosus, 2008, p. 423), a popular textbook published by the Teachers' Curriculum Institute, teaches that segregation was only a Southern problem: "Even New Deal agencies practiced racial segregation, especially in the South," failing to make any reference to what Ira Katznelson, in his 2013 *Fear Itself*, describes as FDR's embrace of residential segregation nationwide in return for Southern support of his economic policies.

Avoidance of our racial history is pervasive and we are ensuring the persistence of that avoidance for subsequent generations. For the public and policymakers, relearning our racial history is a necessary step because remembering this history is the foundation for an understanding that aggressive policies to desegregate metropolitan areas are not only desirable, but a constitutional obligation. Without fulfilling this obligation, substantially narrowing the achievement gap, or opening equal educational opportunity to African-Americans, will remain a distant and unreachable goal.

References

Alavosus, L. (Ed.). (2008). *History alive!: Pursuing American ideals*. Palo Alto, CA: Teachers' Curriculum Institute.

Ayoub, C., O'Connor, E., Rappolt-Schlictmann, G., Vallotton, C., Raikes, H., & Chazan-Cohen, R. (2009). Cognitive skill performance among young children living in poverty: Risk, change, and the promotive effects of Early Head Start. *Early Childhood Research Quarterly, 24*(3), 289–305. doi:10.1016/j.ecresq.2009.04.001.

Aysola, J., Orav, E. J., & Ayanian, J. Z. (2011). Neighborhood characteristics associated with access to patient-centered medical homes for children. *Health Affairs, 30*(11), 2080–2089. doi:10.1377/hlthaff.2011.0656.

Braden, A. (1958). *The wall between*. New York, NY: Monthly Review Press.

Brooks-Gunn, J., & Markman, L. B. (2005). The contribution of parenting to ethnic and racial gaps in school readiness. *The future of children, 15*(1), 139–168.

Buka, S. L., Stichick, T. L., Birdthistle, I., & Earls, F. J. (2001). Youth exposure to violence. Prevalence, risks, and consequences. *American Journal of Orthopsychiatry, 71*(3), 298–310. doi:10.1037/0002-9432.71.3.298.

Burdick-Will, J., Ludwig, J., Raudenbush, S. W., Sampson, R. J., Sonbonmatsu, L., & Sharkey, P. (2010). Converging evidence for neighborhood effects on children's test scores: An experimental, quasi-experimental, and observational comparison. Paper prepared for the Brookings Institution *Project on Social Inequality and Educational Disadvantage: New Evidence on How Families, Neighborhoods and Labor Markets Affect Educational Opportunities for American Children*. Retrieved from http://cas.uchicago.edu/workshops/education/files/2010/03/Burdick-Will-Ed-Workshop-20100301.pdf.

Colfax, R. N. (2009, Fall). *Kennedy v. City of Zanesville*: Making the case for water. *Human Rights, 36*(4). American Bar Association. Retrieved from http://www.americanbar.org/publications/human_rights_magazine_home/human_rights_vol36_2009/fall2009/kennedy_v_city_of_zanesville_making_a_case_for_water.html.

Communiques from the housing front: Venice race-hate meet reported on. (1943, November 18). *California Eagle, 64*(32), pp. 1–2. Retrieved from http://www.archive.org/details/la_caleagle_reel26.

Danzer, G. A., de Alva, J. J. K., Krieger, L. S., Wilson, L. E., & Woloch, N. (2007). *The Americans*. Evanston, IL: McDougal Littell.

Davies, R. O. (1966). *Housing reform during the Truman administration*. Columbia, MO: University of Missouri Press.

Detroit Public Schools (2009). *Detroit city school district*. Retrieved from http://detroitk12.org/schools/reports/profiles/district_profile.pdf.

Entwisle, D. R., Alexander, K. L., & Olson, L. S. (2000). Summer learning and home environment. In R. D. Kahlenberg (Ed.), *A notion at risk: Preserving public education as an engine for social mobility* (pp. 9–30). New York, NY: Century Foundation Press.

Farah, M. J., Shera, D. M., Savage, J. H., Betancourt, L., Giannetta, J. M., Brodsky, N. L., … & Hurt, H. (2006). Childhood poverty: Specific associations with neurocognitive development. *Brain Research, 1110*(1), 166–174. doi: 10.1016/j.brainres.2006.06.072.

FHA (Federal Housing Administration) (1938). *Underwriting manual: Underwriting and valuation procedure under Title II of the National Housing Act*. Excerpts in J. M. Thomas & M. Ritzdorf (Eds.). (1997). *Urban planning and the African American community: In the shadows* (pp. 282–284). Thousand Oaks, CA: Sage Publications.

Foner, P. S. (1976). *Organized labor and the black worker, 1619–1973*. New York, NY: International Publishers.

Galster, G., & Godfrey, E. (2005). By words and deeds: Racial steering by real estate agents in the U.S. in 2000. *Journal of the American Planning Association, 71*(3), 251–268.

Guryan, J. (2001). *Desegregation and black dropout rates*. Working Paper 8345, Cambridge, MA: National Bureau of Economic Research.

Hill, H. (1977). *Black labor and the American legal system*. Washington, DC: Bureau of National Affairs.

Hills v. Gautreaux. 425 U. S. 284 (1976).

Hirsch, A. R. (1998). *Making the second ghetto: Race and housing in Chicago, 1940–1960*. (Original work published 1983). Chicago, IL: University of Chicago Press.

Hirsch, A. R. (2000). Choosing segregation: Federal housing policy between Shelley and Brown. In J. F. Bauman, R. Biles, & K. M. Szylvian (Eds.). *From tenements to the Taylor Homes: In search of an urban housing policy in twentieth century America* (pp. 206–225). University Park, Pennsylvania: The Pennsylvania State University Press.

Independent Metal Workers, Local 1. 147 N.L.R.B. 1573 (1964).

Jackson, K. T. (1985). *Crabgrass frontier*. New York, NY: Oxford University Press.

Jargowsky, P. A. (2013). *Concentration of poverty in the new millennium: Changes in the prevalence, composition, and location of high-poverty neighborhoods*. The Century Foundation and Rutgers Center for Urban Research and Education. Retrieved from http://www.tcf.org/assets/downloads/Concentration_of_Poverty_in_the_New_Millennium.pdf.

Johnson, R. C. (2011). *Long-run impacts of school desegregation & school quality on adult attainments*. Cambridge, Massachusetts: Working Paper 16664. Cambridge, MA; National Bureau of Economic Research.

Johnson, R. C. (In Progress). *The impact of parental wealth on college enrollment & degree attainment: Evidence from the housing boom & bust*. Working Paper, 2012. University of California Berkeley: Goldman School of Public Policy. Retrieved from http://socrates.berkeley.edu/~ruckerj/RJabstract_ParentalWealth_KidCollege_12-11.pdf.

Julian, E. K., & Daniel, M. M. (1989). Separate and unequal: The root and branch of public housing segregation. *Clearinghouse Review, 23*, 666–676.

Katznelson, I. (2013). *Fear itself: The New Deal and the origins of our time*. New York, NY: Liveright Publishing Corporation.

Kerner Commission (National Advisory Commission on Civil Disorders). (1968). *Report of the national Advisory Commission on Civil Disorders*. New York, NY: Bantam Books.

King, D. (1995). *Separate and unequal: Black Americans and the U.S. federal government*. Oxford, England: Clarendon Press.

Lapanksy-Werner, E. L., Levy, P. B., Roberts, R., & Taylor, A. (2010). *United States history*. Upper Saddle River, NJ: Pearson.

Mehana, M., & Reynolds, A. J. (2004). School mobility and achievement: A meta-analysis. *Children and Youth Services Review, 26*(1), 93–119. doi:10.1016/j.childyouth.2003.11.004.

Milliken v. Bradley, 418 U.S. 717 (1974).

Mishel, L., Bivens, J., Gould, E., & Shierholz, H. (2012). *The state of working America* (12th Edition). Washington, DC: The Economic Policy Institute. Retrieved from http://www.stateofworkingamerica.org/subjects/overview/?reader.

Mohl, R. A. (1987, Spring). Trouble in paradise: Race and housing in Miami during the New Deal era. *Prologue: The Journal of the National Archives, 19*(1), 7–21.

Mohl, R. A. (2001). Whitening Miami: Race, housing, and government policy in twentieth-century Dade County. *The Florida Historical Quarterly, 79*(3), 319–345.

Myers, D. (2008). Immigrants' contributions in an aging America. *Communities and Banking, 19*(3), 3–5. Retrieved from http://www.bostonfed.org/commdev/c&b/2008/summer/myers_immigrants_and_boomers.pdf.

Neuman, S. B., & Celano, D. (2001). Access to print in low-income and middle income communities: An ecological study of four neighborhoods. *Reading Research Quarterly, 36*(1), 8–26. doi:10.1598/RRQ.36.1.1.

Orfield, G. (2009). *Reviving the goal of an integrated society: A 21st century challenge*. Los Angeles, CA: The Civil Rights Project/Proyecto Derechos Civiles. Retrieved from http://civilrightsproject.ucla.edu/research/k-12-education/integration-and-diversity/reviving-the-goal-of-an-integrated-society-a-21st-century-challenge/orfield-reviving-the-goal-mlk-2009.pdf.

Orfield, G., & Frankenberg, E. (with Ee, J. & Kuscera, J.). (2014). *Brown at 60: Great progress, a long retreat and an uncertain future*. Los Angeles, CA: The Civil Rights Project/Proyecto Derechos Civiles. Retrieved from http://civilrightsproject.ucla.edu/research/k-12-education/integration-and-diversity/brown-at-60-great-progress-a-long-retreat-and-an-uncertain-future/Brown-at-60-051814.pdf.

Orfield, G., Kucsera, J., & Siegel-Hawley, G. (2012). *E pluribus...separation: Deepening double segregation for more students*. Los Angeles, CA: The Civil Rights Project/Proyecto Derechos Civiles. Retrieved from http://civilrightsproject.ucla.edu/research/k-12-education/integration-and-diversity/mlk-national/e-pluribus...separation-deepening-double-segregation-for-more-students/orfield_epluribus_revised_omplete_2012.pdf.

Orfield, G., & Lee, C. (2006). *Racial transformation and the changing nature of segregation.* Cambridge, MA: The Civil Rights Project at Harvard University. Retrieved from http://civilrights project.ucla.edu/research/k-12-education/integration-and-diversity/racial-transformation-and-the-changing-nature-of-segregation/orfield-racial-transformation-2006.pdf.

Parents Involved in Community Schools v. Seattle School Dist. No. 1, 551 U. S. 701 (2007).

Plotkin, W. (1999). *Deeds of mistrust: Race, housing, and restrictive covenants in Chicago, 1900–1953.* Doctoral Dissertation. Retrieved from Proquest. (9941500).

Power, G. (1986, March). *The development of residential Baltimore, 1900–1930.* Paper presented at the Chancellor's Colloquium, University of Maryland at Baltimore.

Power, G. (2004). Meade v. Dennistone: The NAACP's test case to "…sue Jim Crow out of Maryland with the Fourteenth Amendment." *Maryland Law Review, 63*(4), 773-810. Retrieved from http://digitalcommons.law.umaryland.edu/cgi/viewcontent.cgi?article=3230 &context=mlr.

Raudenbush, S. W., Jean, M., & Art, E. (2011). Year-by-year and cumulative impacts of attending a high-mobility elementary school on children's mathematics achievement in Chicago, 1995 to 2005. In G. J. Duncan & R. J. Murnane (Eds.), *Whither opportunity: Rising inequality, schools, and children's life chances* (pp. 359–376). New York, NY: Russell Sage Foundation.

Rothstein, R. (2004). *Class and schools: Using social, economic, and educational reform to close the Black-White Achievement Gap.* Washington, D.C. and New York, N.Y.: Economic Policy Institute and Teachers College Press.

Rothstein, R. (2012). Race and public housing: Revisiting the federal role. *Poverty and Race, 21*(6), 1–2; 13-17. Retrieved from http://prrac.org/newsletters/novdec2012.pdf.

Rothstein, R.; & Miles, K. H. (1995). *Where's the money gone? Changes in the level and composition of education spending.* Washington, D.C.: The Economic Policy Institute. Retrieved from http://www.epi.org/page/-/old/books/moneygone.pdf.

Rothstein, R., & Santow, M. (2012). *A different kind of choice.* Working Paper. Washington, D.C.: The Economic Policy Institute. Retrieved from http://www.epi.org/files/2012/Different_Kind_Of_Choice.pdf.

Rubinowitz, L. S., & Perry, I. (2002). Crimes without punishment: White neighbors' resistance to black entry. *Journal of Criminal Law and Criminology, 92*(2), 335–428.

Same work, different unions: Carriers content with legacy of segregation. (2011, June). *Postal Record,* 8–13. National Association of Letter Carriers. Retrieved from http://www.nalc.org/news/precord/ArticlesPDF/june2011/06-2011_segregation.pdf.

Sampson, R. J., Sharkey, P., & Raudenbush, S. W. (2008). Durable effects of concentrated disadvantage on verbal ability among African-American children. *Proceedings of the National Academy of Sciences, 105*(3), 845–852. doi:10.1073/pnas.0710189104.

Satter, B. (2009). *Family properties: Race, real estate, and the exploitation of black urban America.* New York, NY: Metropolitan Books.

Schwartz, G. T. (1976). Urban freeways and the interstate system. *Southern California Law Review, 49*(3), 406–513.

Sharkey, P. (2013). *Stuck in place: Urban neighborhoods and the end of progress toward racial equality.* Chicago, IL: University of Chicago Press.

Silva, C. (2009). *Racial restrictive covenants: Enforcing neighborhood segregation in Seattle.* Seattle Civil Rights and Labor History Project, University of Washington. Retrieved from http://depts.washington.edu/civilr/covenants_report.htm.

Starfield, B. (1997). Health indicators for preadolescent school-age children. In R. M. Hauser, B. V. Brown, & W. R. Prosser (Eds.), *Indicators of children's well-being* (pp. 95–111). New York, NY: Russell Sage Foundation.

U.S. Census Bureau. (2014). *People and households, housing vacancies and homeownership (CPS/HVS), Historical tables. Table 16: Homeownership rates by race and ethnicity of householder:1994 to present.* Retrieved June 2, 2014 from http://www.census.gov/housing/hvs/data/histtabs.html.

USCCR (United States Commission on Civil Rights). (1961). *Book 4: Housing: 1961 Commission on Civil Rights report.* Washington, D.C.: Government Printing Office. Retrieved from http://www.law.umaryland.edu/marshall/usccr/documents/cr11961bk4.pdf.
Weaver, R. C. (1948). *The negro ghetto.* New York, NY: Russell & Russell.
Williamson, J. (2005). Retrofitting 'Levittown'. *Places Journal, 17*(2), 46–51. Retrieved from http://escholarship.org/uc/item/0r57v5j3.

Perpetuating Separate and Unequal Worlds of Educational Opportunity Through District Lines: School Segregation by Race and Poverty

Jennifer B. Ayscue and Gary Orfield

In U.S. society, space within metropolitan areas, divided by invisible school district boundary lines and attendance boundary lines within many districts, defines and perpetuates separate and unequal worlds of opportunity. Decisions made long ago have created lines of profound and lasting difference, lines now built into public images of communities and school systems and their related housing markets. Simply reading the real estate ads in any Sunday newspaper is sufficient to convey that school districts and school attendance areas within school districts are used for advertising because districts and schools are viewed as important assets that people will pay to obtain if they have the money to do so. Sometimes districts or schools are clearly capitalized into the value of the home (Kane, Staiger, & Samms, 2003). In other words, geography matters and boundary lines matter a lot (Carter & Welner, 2013; Clotfelter, 2004). Curiously, the concern of middle-class families to live within certain district or school boundary lines is omitted, almost entirely, from discussions of opportunity for poor and non-white children. Recognizing the link between geography and opportunity was a central goal during the desegregation era but has been systematically neglected in the past

This chapter is adapted from Ayscue, J. B., & Orfield, G. (2015). School district lines stratify educational opportunity by race and poverty. *Race and Social Problems, 7*(1), 5–20. Springer New York.

J.B. Ayscue (✉) · G. Orfield
University of California, Los Angeles, 8370 Math Sciences, 951521,
Los Angeles, CA 90095–1521, USA
e-mail: jayscue@ucla.edu

G. Orfield
e-mail: orfield@gmail.com

© Springer International Publishing Switzerland 2016

P.A. Noguera et al. (eds.), *Race, Equity, and Education*,
DOI 10.1007/978-3-319-23772-5_3

three decades (Mickelson, Smith, & Nelson, 2015). This analysis seeks to reintroduce the issue of boundary lines to the policy discourse by exploring the relationship between fragmentation—the degree to which metropolitan areas are split into many separate school districts—and segregation. Our central analysis revolves around the question: *How are different school district structures related to patterns of school segregation?* This chapter urges consideration of spatial segregation and school districting systems as fundamental barriers to equity.

Beginning with President Reagan in the 1980s, Americans have focused on individual-level education policies affecting students and teachers (Sunderman, 2009). The challenges have been to find ways to make students study harder and learn more, as measured by test scores, and to hold their schools and teachers accountable if they do not (Logan, Minca, & Adar, 2012). If that fails—and it failed spectacularly in No Child Left Behind—then the back-up policy is to provide individual leaders with public school funds to create semiprivate schools, which are intended to be better than traditional public schools because individuals created them outside of educational systems and individual families are afforded a choice about where to go to school (Roda & Wells, 2013). However, ensuring an opportunity for students in inferior, segregated schools to choose to enroll in other districts is ignored by most choice advocates (Orfield & Frankenberg, 2013b).

This dominant ideology, which has now been embraced for more than three decades by both Republican and Democratic administrations, has downplayed the importance of structural forces related to educational inequality, forces that affect entire groups of people and are systematically linked to unequal opportunity and outcomes (Rothstein, 2004). Race and class are dimensions of inequality which were central to the educational reforms of the mid-twentieth century, and which almost always are significant in empirical analyses of American schools. Another dimension, which has received less attention, is geographic space.

This chapter provides an overview of the history of metropolitan development and two theoretical perspectives on the consequences of metropolitan organization. We then highlight legal developments affecting district structures in metropolitan areas, the relationship between-district boundaries and segregation, and the significance of segregation in limiting educational opportunities and outcomes. After explaining our data and methods, we analyze enrollment and segregation trends in the public schools of North Carolina, Virginia, New York, and New Jersey and the main metropolitan areas of each state. We conclude with a discussion of key findings, suggestions for future research, and policy recommendations.

Literature Review

The organization of metropolitan areas has consequences for the everyday experiences of residents as well as the future success of communities. In addition to the structure of metropolitan areas, several key legal decisions have influenced the ways in which school districts create boundary lines and pursue desegregation.

The structure of school districts can either facilitate desegregation efforts or add further challenges to achieving desegregation, as can be seen in North Carolina, Virginia, New York, and New Jersey. The differences in school district structure are important because of the educational consequences that are associated with segregated schooling.

Development of Metropolitan Areas and Educational Institutions

American municipal and educational institutions were formed generations ago in a predominantly rural society with many small communities separated by distances too long to walk. In our oldest states, many communities formed before the United States became a nation and their boundaries have been set for generations. As the country became a nation of metropolitan areas, often encompassing dozens of these small communities, the metropolitan areas found ways to cooperate in many sectors, including transportation, water, and sewer systems, as well as in environmental controls, business promotion, and agencies running parks, museums, sports facilities, and many other institutions. However, in most metropolitan areas, school district lines remain untouched and school systems operate as independent villages disconnected from the rest of the metro. This is also true for housing, zoning, and land use policies that are fundamental to the social stratification of metropolitan areas and their school districts. In the absence of school desegregation plans or voluntary cooperation among independent school districts, housing patterns determine educational opportunity. Recent studies of two intensely segregated states have confirmed that housing remains highly stratified by race and class.[1] Housing patterns and lines on maps define two separate worlds of great educational privilege and greatly diminished opportunity.

After World War II, there was a reform movement in American education, the "school consolidation movement," which sought to eliminate thousands of school districts that were too small to offer adequate curricula and professional staffs. Between 1939 and 2006, 88 % of the nation's school districts disappeared, declining in number from 117,108 to 13,862 districts and making the basic units sufficiently large, for example, to support a comprehensive high school (Duncombe & Yinger, 2010). No such movement, however, affected urban and suburban communities in most of the nation's states.[2] As the differentiation of the metropolitan

---

[1]Recent reports analyzing the states with the most severe segregation of blacks (New York) and Latinos (California) found clear relationships with residential segregation (Kucsera & Orfield, 2014; Orfield & Ee, 2014).

[2]North Carolina was a notable exception where there was a long-lasting state policy strongly supporting consolidation of districts within a given county. There have been consolidations in some Tennessee metros and in court decisions in metro Louisville, Kentucky, and Wilmington, Delaware.

areas intensified, so too did the differences among their small, almost neighbor-hood-based school districts. Those with costly housing and restrictive housing and zoning policies had the best prepared students and teachers and the most educated and affluent parents, usually from overwhelmingly white families. The preserva-tion of this fragmented system of school districts in metropolitan areas has become a basic mechanism for perpetuating educational and social inequality in the United States.

In American law, it is illegal to treat students differently on the basis of their race but legal and normal to treat heavily white and affluent schools and districts differently from those serving areas of concentrated non-white residence and more poverty.[3] Since this differentiation is legal and well known, especially by white and Asian families, it creates an intense demand for what many parents see as ways to transfer intergenerational advantages to their children. That drives up the cost of housing in privileged areas and makes those areas even more exclusive and inaccessible while other areas experience downward mobility (Kane, Riegg, & Staiger, 2006; Liebowitz & Page, 2015). All of these are facilitated by the use of test scores, which are directly related to family social class and often taken as objective measures of educational quality, furthering the cycle of deepening ine-quality (Ladd & Fiske, 2011).

Theoretical Perspectives on the Consequences of Metropolitan Organization

School districts' success with desegregation and other issues is often supported or constrained by the metropolitan context in which the districts operate. Therefore, an understanding of the political and social organization of the metropolitan areas in which school districts exist is essential.

After World War II, as suburbanization was underway and cities became less dense, metropolitan development moved outward. Rusk (1999) contends that the current social, economic, and fiscal health of a metropolitan area is largely related to the city's elasticity during this time. Some "elastic" cities were able to cap-ture new growth through annexation or city-county consolidation. Most elastic cities are located in the South (e.g., Charlotte and Nashville) and the West (e.g., Albuquerque). On the other hand, "inelastic" cities, most of which are located in the Northeast (e.g., New York and Harrisburg) and Midwest (e.g., Cleveland and Detroit), were unable to capture new growth, leading instead to suburban sprawl and fragmented metropolitan areas. If a city's growth was cut off long ago by fixed boundaries, it has no elasticity. Postwar elastic areas with expanding cities had higher rates of job creation and income growth, and the difference in income

---

[3]*San Antonio Independent School District v. Rodriguez,* 411 U.S. 1 (1973) was the Supreme Court decision holding that there is no right to equal school resources in the U.S. Constitution.

between residents of the city and suburbs was less substantial. Conversely, inelastic cities lost middle-class households, businesses, retail shops, and factories to the suburbs, leaving many inelastic cities in financial crisis. Racial and economic segregation was more pronounced in inelastic metropolitan areas. A city's elasticity determines its level of fragmentation and has social and economic consequences for the metropolitan area, with inelasticity perpetuating segregation and inequality of opportunity between the city and suburban areas.

Moreover, Weiher (1991) argues that the thousands of invisible political lines that are used to delineate separate spaces in the United States become social boundaries, segregating people by race and class. The creation and maintenance of social boundaries occurs through two complementary processes: exclusion and recruitment. Exclusion occurs through zoning ordinances, discriminatory real estate practices, violence, hostility, and other mechanisms, all of which sort populations within metropolitan areas by prohibiting some populations, often racial groups, from residing in certain areas. However, exclusion alone does not account for enduring segregation by race and class. Weiher contends that political boundary lines support the recruitment of selected populations into certain spaces because the boundary lines themselves are associated with information that makes it possible to identify particular places with specific populations and the characteristics (e.g., race, occupation, education, income, and socioeconomic status) and lifestyles of those populations. People use this information to match their preferences with the attributes of a place. Through the processes of exclusion and recruitment, political boundary lines become social boundary lines that separate people by race and socioeconomic status and ultimately result in very different social contexts for people living on different sides of boundary lines. Through the creation of political boundaries, distinct spaces into which people can be segregated have also been created.

Together, Rusk and Weiher highlight the consequences that metropolitan organization has for residents living across boundary lines. Highly fragmented metropolitan areas have numerous political boundary lines that generate social boundaries and promote segregation. These boundaries become barriers that define separate and unequal opportunities, including inequitable access to high-quality integrated education.

Legal Influence on Metropolitan Desegregation

Along with the structure of metropolitan areas, key legal decisions over the last 60 years have influenced the ways in which school districts within a metropolitan area can pursue desegregation. In the 1954 *Brown v. Board of Education* decision, the Supreme Court declared segregated schools to be unconstitutional and inherently unequal. This decision ushered in the era of school desegregation across the nation, beginning with token integration followed by more full compliance.

In the 1971 *Swann v. Charlotte-Mecklenburg Board of Education* decision, the Supreme Court required that districts desegregate their schools to the greatest extent possible and approved busing as a tool for doing so. This case was influential across the country because it struck down race-neutral student assignment plans that produced segregation by relying on existing residential patterns of segregation. In making this decision, the Supreme Court recognized the relationship between geography and opportunity and concluded that the former should not dictate the latter.

However, in 1974, after the appointment of more conservative justices by President Nixon, the pivotal 5-4 Supreme Court decision in *Milliken v. Bradley* ruled against a metropolitan desegregation remedy for Detroit. The Court affirmed that local control of the suburbs around Detroit was more important than including the suburban school districts in the highly segregated metropolitan Detroit area in the remedy. This decision made metropolitan-wide desegregation more difficult to achieve unless it was voluntary because it required plaintiffs to show that individual suburbs were guilty of intentional discrimination, thus limiting the ability of predominantly non-white central city school districts to achieve desegregation by using interdistrict remedies that would cross district lines to include the suburbs.

Two years later, in *Pasadena Board of Education v. Spangler* (1976), the Supreme Court ruled that courts did not have to update desegregation plans as the communities' demographics changed. Together, *Milliken* and *Spangler* created strong barriers to urban school desegregation, making it difficult for communities to desegregate across metropolitan areas and allowing desegregation plans to become outdated when populations changed, as has occurred across the nation over the last several decades.

More recently, the Supreme Court of Connecticut ruled that district boundary lines separating city and suburban school districts in Hartford led to racially segregated schools and therefore violated the state constitution's guarantee of an equal education (Sheff v. O'Neill, 1996). In doing so, the court identified the metropolitan area's districting system as the fundamental problem in creating racial and socioeconomic isolation in Hartford. In response, the state legislature created a voluntary desegregation program that includes a regional magnet school system and an interdistrict transfer program.

District Structures and Segregation

Given the consequences of boundary lines for metropolitan organization and the legal constraints on metropolitan-wide approaches to desegregation, it is not altogether surprising that urban and suburban schools continue to enroll student bodies that are racially distinct, particularly when metropolitan areas are fragmented (Table 1). Urban schools continue to educate a student body in which white students are underrepresented and black and Hispanic students are overrepresented when compared to the nation's enrollment. On the other hand, suburban schools

Table 1 Student enrollment by race and locale, 2010–2011

	White (%)	Black (%)	Hispanic (%)	Asian (%)
All U.S. Schools	52	16	23	5
Urban Schools	30	25	34	7
Suburban Schools	54	14	23	6

Source National Center for Education Statistics (2013). *The condition of education 2013*. Washington, DC: U.S. Department of Education

are more closely mirroring the nation's enrollment, with more than half of their student bodies comprised of white students.

Although both urban and suburban schools are becoming more multiracial, there are still distinct differences between the experiences of students attending schools in each part of the metropolitan area unless they live in a metro that has one consolidated city-suburban school district.

Metropolitan-Wide Districts Facilitate Successful Desegregation. The major exceptions to these trends are the states where the basic unit of school organization is the county rather than the municipality. The county-wide structure tends to exist in states that were more rural states where urbanization occurred later and county government was historically more central. This can mean, for example, that city and suburban schools in an entire metropolitan area are largely or totally within one school district. When this is the case, the small communities are not separate worlds of educational policy but part of a single school district with metropolitan-wide reach and systems of governance that reflect a much broader range of residents by race and class. In this circumstance, it becomes a central interest of all the major institutions to make the school system work (Mickelson et al., 2015; Orfield, 1996).

Some metropolitan areas, most of which are located in the South, implemented comprehensive city-suburban desegregation plans. In some cases, including North Carolina, state policies incentivized the consolidation of city and suburban districts into school systems that would serve large parts of a metropolitan area as these metropolitan-wide school districts were believed to be more efficient and effective in providing strong educational programs (Orfield, 2001). Although the original intent of district consolidation was not to promote desegregation, the county-wide structure allowed for more extensive and comprehensive desegregation by ensuring that, in many cases, county-wide districts were more diverse than they would have been if there had been separate city and county districts. It also meant that when desegregation efforts were underway, it was more difficult for white families to flee the desegregating schools to attend other nearby schools because all public schools in the metropolitan area were part of the same district and all were participating in the same desegregation efforts (Orfield, 2001; U.S. Commission on Civil Rights, 1977). Thus, when school districts cover entire metropolitan areas, they are often associated with more stably integrated schools (Orfield, 2001).

Fragmented Metropolitan Areas Associated with Segregation. However, because of the limitations on city-suburban desegregation that were created by *Milliken*, in most large metropolitan areas, metropolitan-wide districts have not been created. In these cases, the basic situation of municipalities and school districts within metropolitan areas is an unregulated competitive system with no incentives for cooperation on the part of the more powerful communities that possess abundant resources and commanding market positions. The more powerful communities can use their zoning and land use powers as well as other development tools to continually build on their advantages and to exclude certain segments, such as low-income families with children and less attractive residential, commercial, and industrial development. Advantages create more advantages. In contrast, disadvantaged, non-white, and low-income communities have very little leverage (Danielson, 1976; Sager, 1969; Wachter, 1990). They often face a continuing loss of residential and commercial development and a decline in demand for housing and other facilities. Thus, there is less incentive to maintain property or protect their housing market from increasing concentrations of poor families who have limited taxable resources and many children needing schooling and other services. At their worst, these communities can face a vicious cycle of continuing decay, disinvestment, and isolation in the lower income non-white sector of the housing market. These trends have notable impacts on the schools. There are no institutions with the responsibility to seek the common good of the larger community.

When districts are fragmented and boundary lines are drawn between city and suburban areas, school segregation patterns in urban and suburban districts often differ, with more students of color attending intensely segregated schools in urban districts than in suburban districts (Orfield & Frankenberg, 2008). A recent case study of Birmingham, Alabama, found that the growing number of separate school districts in the metropolitan area had the same stratifying effect as earlier laws that had mandated racial segregation (Frankenberg, 2009). For the last several decades, the majority of segregation has occurred and continues to occur between school districts rather than between schools within the same district (Bischoff, 2008; Clotfelter, 2004), demonstrating the significant impact of district boundary lines and fragmentation in segregating students.

County-Wide Districts in North Carolina and Virginia; Fragmentation in New York and New Jersey. Unless there is a violation of the federal constitution and laws, school districting is a power of state governments. In general, metropolitan areas in the Northeast and Midwest have higher levels of school district fragmentation than those in the West and South, where school districts are less fragmented (Bischoff, 2008). These differences are similar to differences in municipal fragmentation, with Northeastern states having more separate, independent municipalities.

North Carolina is a particularly interesting case in this regard since it has had a strong policy incentivizing consolidation into county-wide school districts that began before the desegregation era and has continued to the present. In 1960, the Charlotte City and Mecklenburg County districts merged and during the 1975–76 academic year, both city and county school boards in Wake County voted in favor of unifying the systems (Douglas, 1995; Grant, 2011). In 1992, city and county schools in Durham merged, and the next year, Guilford County Schools also merged its city and county systems. At present, of North Carolina's 100 counties, only 15 city districts have not yet merged with the 11 counties in which they are located to form a consolidated county-wide district. Virginia has a different history in which cities are not part of, but separate from, counties, but the state schools are largely organized at the county level. A noteworthy exception occurs in metropolitan Richmond where urban and suburban districts remain separate (Ryan, 2010). In 1972, a federal district court ordered Richmond City to merge with the city's two neighboring suburban districts—Henrico and Chesterfield—but the decision was overturned by the Fourth Circuit Court of Appeals and this ruling was later upheld by the Supreme Court (Bradley v. Richmond School Board, 1974).

Outside of the South, county-wide school districts are far less common. In New Jersey, the 1971 *Jenkins v. Morris Township* ruling authorized the state commissioner of education to mandate the crossing of school district boundary lines if needed to achieve racial balance. Consequently, in 1973, the urban school district in Morristown was forced to merge with the suburban white school district in Morris Township. However, soon after this merger occurred, the commissioner of education lost his job and subsequent commissioners did not support regional efforts; therefore, other urban districts across New Jersey failed to merge with surrounding suburban districts. Similarly, past efforts at district consolidation in New York have been unsuccessful. For example, in 1969, the state education commissioner's proposals for merging and consolidating several districts in Long Island were rejected, and in 2002, there was strong opposition to the Rochester mayor's suggestion of a county-wide school district. Aside from a small voluntary transfer plan in Rochester, there are no regional policies in New York, which now has the nation's highest level of segregation for black students (Kucsera & Orfield, 2014).

Inequality of Educational Opportunities and Outcomes Related to Segregation

Because of the ways in which school district structures are related to segregation, these structures have important educational consequences for students. Decades of social science research demonstrate that racially desegregated schools have a variety of benefits for students, including improved academic outcomes, improved near-term intergroup relations, and advantageous long-term effects (Linn & Welner, 2007; Mickelson & Nkomo, 2012). Conversely, segregated schools are systematically linked to unequal educational opportunities and outcomes.

Benefits of Desegregation. The academic effects of racially integrated learning environments are positive for students of all races. Students of color achieve at higher levels in racially diverse schools than in segregated schools (Borman et al., 2004; Hallinan, 1998). For white students attending racially diverse schools, there is no corresponding detrimental impact on academic achievement (Crain & Mahard, 1983).

Based on intergroup contact theory, Pettigrew and Tropp's (2006) meta-analysis of more than 500 studies confirms that increased contact between members of different groups can have positive impacts on all groups by reducing prejudice, negative attitudes, and stereotypes while at the same time increasing friendships among members of different groups. In examining school settings in particular, Tropp and Prenovost (2008) found that intergroup contact theory operates similarly in schools as it does in other environments. These positive impacts are enhanced when four optimal conditions exist: equal status within the contact situation, cooperation toward mutually valued goals, opportunity for people to get to know each other as individuals, and the support of relevant authorities (Allport, 1954).

Further, desegregated schooling has positive long-term effects. Research based on perpetuation theory shows that segregation repeats itself across various stages of life. When individuals have early and sustained experiences in desegregated schools, they are more likely to live and work in desegregated environments later in life (Braddock & McPartland, 1989; Wells & Crain, 1994). Racially diverse schools are beneficial not only to individuals but also to communities and society. In the long term, students who attended integrated schools have high levels of civic engagement (Kurlaender & Yun, 2005). These benefits of diverse schools provide the foundation for social cohesion in multiethnic, democratic societies, such as the United States (Mickelson & Nkomo, 2012).

Harms of Segregation. On the other hand, segregated, predominantly non-white schools tend to be schools of concentrated poverty that are systematically linked to unequal educational opportunities and outcomes (Orfield & Ee, 2014; Orfield & Lee, 2005). Opportunities for students at non-white segregated schools are often limited by a variety of insufficient resources. Segregated schools tend to have fewer experienced and less qualified teachers (Clotfelter, Ladd, & Vigdor, 2005; Jackson, 2009) as well as high levels of teacher turnover (Clotfelter, Ladd, & Vigdor, 2010). In addition, the student enrollment at segregated schools is less stable (Rumberger, 2003). Segregated schools tend to have inadequate facilities and learning materials as well as fewer curricular options, such as advanced placement courses (Yun & Moreno, 2006). Consequently, it is not surprising that the outcomes for students who attend non-white segregated schools are worse than for students who attend desegregated schools, including lower academic performance (Mickelson, Bottia, & Lambert, 2013; Mickelson & Heath, 1999) and higher dropout rates (Balfanz & Legters, 2004; Swanson, 2004).

This study explores the relationship between fragmentation—the degree to which a metropolitan area is divided into many separate school districts—and segregation by race and poverty. We hypothesize that higher levels of fragmentation will be associated with higher levels of segregation.

Methods[4]

Data Source

Our data comes from the National Center for Education Statistics, Common Core of Data (NCES CCD), Public Elementary/Secondary School Universe Survey, and Local Education Agency Universe Survey. NCES is a reliable data source that uses an annual survey to collect the federal government's enrollment figures for all public elementary and secondary schools and school districts. Our analysis uses race/ethnicity data and free and reduced-price lunch (FRL) data as measures of poverty from the 1989–1990, 1999–2000, and 2010–2011 school years.

Sample

We explore enrollment and segregation trends between 1989 and 2010 in the public schools of four states—New York, New Jersey, North Carolina, and Virginia—and the main metropolitan areas in each state. This chapter is part of a larger, in-depth study by The Civil Rights Project analyzing school segregation in states along the East Coast from Maine to North Carolina. From this larger project, we selected these four states for further analysis because state policies regarding metropolitan consolidation and desegregation and the subsequent levels of fragmentation in the two Southern states are quite different from that of the two Northern states. North Carolina and Virginia have substantially larger, more consolidated public school districts than New York and New Jersey, which have highly fragmented district structures. In 2010–2011, New York's districts had an average student enrollment of 3,856 students and New Jersey's districts enrolled an average of 2,282 students. On the other end of the spectrum, Virginia and North Carolina's districts enrolled an average of two to five times more students. Virginia's districts had an average enrollment of 9,234 students and North Carolina's districts enrolled an average of 12,592 students. In addition, the racial composition of public school enrollment was similar in all four states, thus allowing for an informative comparison of the relationship between fragmentation and segregation. In 2010–2011, the non-white portion of public school enrollment was 48 % in New Jersey, 50 % in New York, 47 % in North Carolina, and 46 % in Virginia. There was more variation in the share of students eligible for FRL: 33 % in New Jersey, 48 % in New York, 50 % in North Carolina, and 37 % in Virginia.

We used the 1999 metropolitan statistical area (MSA) definitions for the metropolitan area base. The MSA is used as the unit of analysis rather than the district because the MSA reflects the overall demographic changes and housing conditions more accurately than the district. Within each of the four states, the main MSAs—those enrolling

---

[4]The authors gratefully acknowledge the assistance of John Kucsera in data collection and analysis.

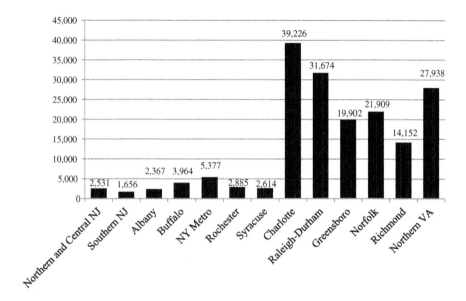

Fig. 1 Average student enrollment per district, 2010–2011. *Note* Total number of districts for each metropolitan area: Northern and Central New Jersey = 403; Southern New Jersey = 171; Albany = 53; Buffalo = 39; New York = 325; Rochester = 58; Syracuse = 44; Charlotte = 7; Raleigh–Durham = 8; Greensboro = 11; Norfolk = 11; Richmond = 13; Northern Virginia = 16

more than 100,000 students in 1989—are included in our analysis. To make these areas geographically comparable over time, we matched and aggregated enrollment counts for MSAs with the current definitions of Core-Based Statistical Areas (CBSAs). We then applied 2010 boundary codes to all years. Although some metropolitan boundaries span two or more states, we restricted the analysis for each metropolitan area to schools within the specified state. For example, our analysis of the Charlotte–Gastonia–Rock Hill MSA is restricted to the portions of the metro that are located in North Carolina and does not include any schools located in South Carolina. North Carolina and Virginia's metros have larger (2.5–25 times larger), more comprehensive school districts, ranging in size from 14,000 to 40,000 students in 2010–2011 (Fig. 1). New York and New Jersey's main metropolitan areas are more fragmented with smaller districts that enroll an average of 1,600–5,400 students. The non-white portion of student enrollment ranges from 21 to 65 %.

Measures

We measure fragmentation by calculating the average number of students per district at the state and metropolitan levels. The segregation analyses consist of three measures of school segregation over time: exposure/isolation, concentration, and evenness. In order to identify trends in segregation over the last 20 years, we analyze these measures at three time points: 1989–1990, 1999–2000, and 2010–2011.

Exposure and isolation are inversely related indices that describe the racial and socioeconomic composition of schools that the typical member of a given racial group attends. Exposure and isolation are calculated by computing the percent of a specified group of students (e.g., white students) who attend the same school as a particular student (e.g., Latino student) in a larger geographical area and finding the average of these results. *Exposure* refers to the degree of potential contact between the typical student of one racial group and other members of a *different* group, while *isolation* refers to the degree of potential contact between the typical student of one racial group and other members of the *same* group (Massey & Denton, 1988). In our analysis, we explore exposure by race and poverty (as measured by FRL) and isolation by race. Both measures range from 0 to 1. Higher exposure values and lower isolation values indicate greater integration, while lower exposure values and higher isolation values indicate greater segregation.

Concentration measures the proportion of non-white students in a school. We identify three categories of non-white segregated schools: (1) majority non-white schools, which enroll 50–100 % non-white students; (2) intensely segregated schools, which enroll 90–100 % non-white students; and (3) apartheid schools, which enroll 99–100 % non-white students. Non-white students include black, Latino, Asian, and American Indian students. We also measure the proportion of low-income students in each type of non-white segregated school.

Evenness refers to the extent to which members of a group are evenly distributed across schools in a larger geographic area. This measure identifies the proportion of students of a particular race that would need to move to a different school in order to achieve an even distribution of students by race (Massey & Denton, 1988). We use Theil's entropy index of multigroup segregation, *H*, to measure the evenness of multiple racial groups (Reardon & Firebaugh, 2002). *H* ranges from 0 to 1. A score of 0.40–1.00 indicates extreme segregation, 0.25–0.40 indicates high segregation, 0.10–0.25 indicates moderate segregation, and 0.00–0.10 indicates low segregation (Reardon & Yun, 2002–2003). For example, a score of 0.25 would indicate that the average school is 25 % less diverse than the metropolitan area as a whole.

Together, measures of exposure, concentration, and evenness provide a nuanced description of the nature of school segregation at the state and metropolitan levels (Orfield, Siegel-Hawley, & Kucsera, 2014).

Results

Our results are divided into two sections. We begin with an analysis of state-level data and then turn to metropolitan-level data. In each section, we explore enrollment and segregation.

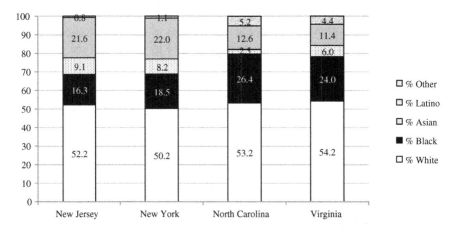

Fig. 2 Public School Enrollment by Race 2010–2011. *Note* Other includes American Indian and two or more races

Similar Racial Compositions in North Carolina, Virginia, New Jersey, and New York

Public school enrollment is becoming more multiracial, but in 2010, white students still accounted for just over half of the enrollment in all four states (Fig. 2). In New Jersey and New York, Latino students accounted for the second largest share of enrollment (22 %), and in North Carolina and Virginia, black students comprised the second largest share (24–26 %). While these differences are important, the overall level of non-white students in each of the four states is similar, allowing for an informative comparison of segregation patterns of non-white students from white students in these four states.

Black and Latino Students Exposed to Smaller Shares of White Students and White Students More Isolated in Fragmented States

The typical black and Latino students in Virginia and North Carolina are exposed to larger shares of white students than in New York and New Jersey (Fig. 3). In each state, the typical black student is exposed to the smallest share of white students, although the typical black student's exposure to white students is more limited in New York (17 %) and New Jersey (24 %) than in Virginia (36 %) and North Carolina (35 %). A similar pattern of more limited exposure to white students exists for Latino students in New York and New Jersey while Latino students in the less fragmented states of Virginia and North Carolina, while still underexposed to white students, are exposed to larger shares of white students.

In addition to higher levels of segregation for black and Latino students in the two more fragmented Northern states, the typical white student in New York and New

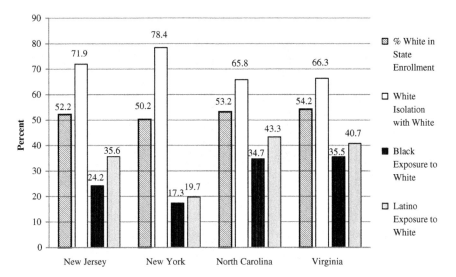

Fig. 3 Exposure to white students by race and isolation of white students 2010–2011

Jersey is more isolated with other white students (72–78 %) than the typical white student in Virginia and North Carolina who attends a school with 66 % white peers.

Gaps in exposure to white students compared to the overall share of white enrollment are larger in New Jersey and New York than in North Carolina and Virginia. In New York, there is a 61 percentage point gap between white isolation with white classmates and black exposure to white classmates and in New Jersey, the gap is 48 % points. On the other hand, at 31 % points, the gap is much smaller in both Virginia and North Carolina. A similar trend, though to a lesser extent, exists for Latino students in all the four states. These gaps indicate a disparate exposure to white students, with both the isolation of white students with other white peers and an underexposure of black and Latino students to white classmates. While there are gaps in all the four states, they are substantially larger in the two highly fragmented states of New York and New Jersey.

Larger Racial Disparity in Exposure to Low-Income Students in More Fragmented States

Unlike the share of white students, which is relatively similar in all the four states, the share of low-income students in each of these four states has greater variation, ranging from 33 % in New Jersey to 50 % in North Carolina (Fig. 4). It is informative to explore disparities in exposure to low-income students by examining gaps between the exposure to low-income students of students of different races across the four states.

The gaps in exposure to low-income students are larger in New York and New Jersey than in North Carolina and Virginia. In New York, black and Latino

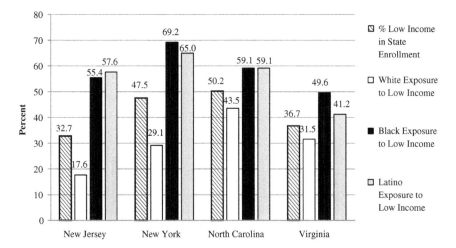

Fig. 4 Exposure to low-income students by race 2010–2011

students are exposed to more than double the share of low-income students than white students are, and in New Jersey they are exposed to more than three times as many low-income students. Although disparities exist in North Carolina and Virginia, they are much smaller. These gaps reveal a double segregation of students by race and poverty, which is more extreme in the highly fragmented states than in those with less fragmentation.

Larger Shares of Non-white Segregated Schools in More Fragmented States

There are substantially larger shares of intensely segregated and apartheid schools in New York and New Jersey, the states with highly fragmented districts, than in North Carolina and Virginia (Fig. 5). In North Carolina and Virginia, 6–10 % of schools are intensely segregated—enrolling 90–100 % non-white students—while 19–30 % of schools are intensely segregated in New York and New Jersey. At a more extreme level, only 1 % of North Carolina and Virginia's schools enroll 99–100 % non-white students while closer to 10 % of New Jersey and New York's schools are apartheid schools.

The share of intensely segregated schools is increasing in all the four states and the share of apartheid schools is increasing in all the states except North Carolina. However, in 2010, the share of both types of schools in North Carolina and Virginia was lower than the share of both types of schools in New York and New Jersey was even two decades ago.

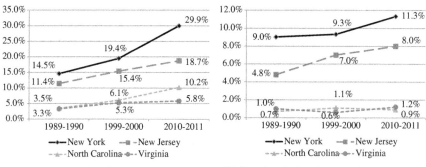

This figure shows the share of intensely segregated schools—those with an enrollment of 90-100% non-white students.

This figure shows the share of apartheid schools—those with an enrollment of 99-100% non-white students.

Fig. 5 Share of non-white segregated schools

Higher Statewide Levels of Multiracial Unevenness in More Fragmented States, Due to Unevenness Between Districts

The overall level of multiracial unevenness in New Jersey (0.35) and New York (0.42) is higher than in North Carolina (0.22) and Virginia (0.25), indicating that students in New Jersey and New York are more unevenly distributed across school districts by race than are students in North Carolina and Virginia (Fig. 6). New Jersey's unevenness is considered high and New York's is extreme. North Carolina and Virginia's levels of unevenness are considered moderate.

When comparing the within- and between-district components of this overall measure of multiracial unevenness, segregation between districts accounts for the majority of the segregation in all the four states. However, the level of segregation between districts accounts for a greater proportion of unevenness in New Jersey and New York than it does in North Carolina and Virginia. The segregation between districts accounts for almost all (91 %) of the segregation in New Jersey. Accounting for 69 % of the segregation in New York, unevenness between districts is close to the level in Virginia (68 %) and higher than the level of between-district unevenness in North Carolina (55 %). This measure reveals that district boundary lines contribute to the majority of segregation in all the four states but to a greater extent in the more fragmented states, particularly New Jersey.

Greater Variation in Racial Compositions of Metros in More Fragmented States

Each of the main metropolitan areas in North Carolina and Virginia enrolls a student body with a racial composition that is relatively similar to the other main metros and to the overall composition of the state's enrollment (Fig. 7). In the state

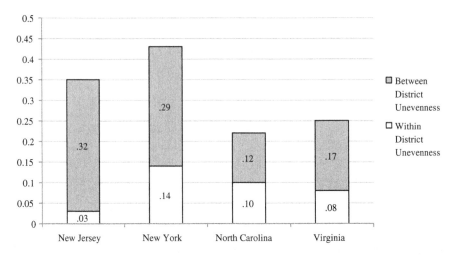

Fig. 6 Entropy index of multiracial unevenness, within and between school districts, by state, 2010–2011. *Note* the total unevenness for each state: New Jersey = 0.35; New York = 0.42; North Carolina = 0.22; Virginia = 0.25

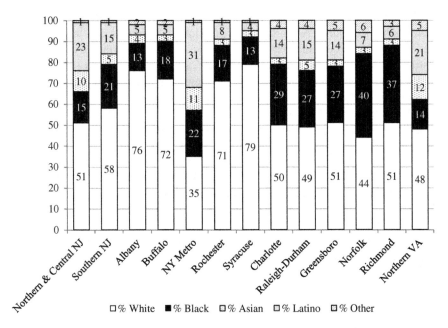

Fig. 7 Metropolitan public school enrollment by race 2010–2011. *Note* Other includes American Indian and two or more races

of New York, there are substantial differences between the racial composition of the enrollment in different metropolitan areas, with the New York metro enrolling a smaller share of white students (35 %) and larger shares of black (22 %) and

Latino (31 %) students than the other four main metros in the state, where white students account for more than 70 % of the total enrollment. Southern New Jersey also enrolls a student body in which white students account for a larger share of the enrollment (58 %) than Northern and Central New Jersey (51 %) and the state as a whole (52 %).

Larger Racial Disparities in Exposure to White Students in More Fragmented Metros

In all metropolitan areas, the typical black and Latino students are underexposed to white students and the typical white student is isolated with a disproportionately large share of other white peers (Table 2). However, the disparities in exposure to white students differ substantially between more fragmented metropolitan areas, which have larger disparities, and less fragmented areas with smaller disparities.

In 2010, in New Jersey and New York's metros, the gap in exposure to white students between the typical white student and the typical Latino student ranges from 34 to 51 % points, indicating a large disparity between the racial composition of the typical Latino student's school and that of the typical white student. While there is also a disparity in the metro areas of North Carolina and Virginia, it is smaller, ranging from 13 to 32 % points.

The pattern was similar for black students' exposure to white students in 2010. The gap in exposure to white students between the typical white student and the typical black student was larger in almost all of New Jersey and New York's metros, ranging from a gap of 49–56 % points, than in the metros of North Carolina and Virginia, which had a gap of 17–38 % points. The one exception is Southern New Jersey where, at 35 % points, the gap between the typical black student's exposure to white peers and the typical white student's isolation with white peers was more similar to that of metros in North Carolina and Virginia. Overall, the different levels of disparity in exposure to white students indicate that the typical black and Latino students are more segregated in fragmented metropolitan areas than they are in less fragmented metros.

Larger Racial Disparities in Exposure to Low-Income Students in More Fragmented Metros

Similar to the state-level data, there is considerable variation in the share of low-income students across the metro areas, ranging from 27.4 % in Northern Virginia to 52.0 % in New York Metro (Table 3). In all metro areas, white students are exposed to the smallest share of low-income students, while black and Latino students are exposed to larger shares of low-income students.

Table 2 Isolation with and exposure to White students by race

	White share of enrollment (%)	White isolation with white (%)	Black exposure to white (%)	Latino exposure to white (%)	Gap between white and black (%)	Gap between white and Latino (%)
Northern and Central NJ						
1989–1990	65.1	84.0	20.4	27.6	63.6	56.4
1999–2000	59.5	79.3	20.4	27.7	58.9	51.6
2010–2011	50.7	72.0	19.5	25.6	52.5	46.4
Southern NJ						
1989–1990	70.5	82.5	40.6	35.6	41.9	46.9
1999–2000	66.3	79.5	38.6	34.8	40.9	44.7
2010–2011	57.7	71.7	36.4	33.8	35.3	37.9
Albany–Schenectady–Troy						
1989–1990	91.0	93.5	58.1		35.4	
1999–2000	86.0	90.7	49.2		41.5	
2010–2011	76.4	85.7	37.0	51.8	48.7	33.9
Buffalo–Niagara Falls						
1989–1990	80.4	88.4	45.4		43	
1999–2000	77.2	88.5	35.3		53.2	
2010–2011	71.8	85.4	29.6		55.8	
New York Metro						
1989–1990	45.8	76.9	15.0	19.3	61.9	57.6
1999–2000	39.2	73.1	13.2	16.6	59.9	56.5
2010–2011	35.1	67.9	11.5	17.0	56.4	50.9
Rochester						
1989–1990	80.0	89.4	38.1		51.3	
1999–2000	77.1	89.1	30.9		58.2	
2010–2011	70.5	84.3	28.8	39.5	55.5	44.8
Syracuse						
1989–1990	89.1	92.3	59.6		32.7	
1999–2000	86.5	91.5	49.1		42.4	
2010–2011	78.5	87.6	35.8		51.8	
Charlotte–Gastonia–Rock Hill						
1989–1990	68.2	73.3	57.2		16.1	
1999–2000	62.8	72.0	46.7		25.3	
2010–2011	50.4	67.1	29.4	35.6	37.7	31.5
Raleigh–Durham–Chapel Hill						
1989–1990	63.5	69.2	52.3		16.9	
1999–2000	59.9	65.9	49.4		16.5	
2010–2011	49.1	57.8	37.2	41.9	20.6	15.9
Greensboro–Winston Salem–High Point						
1989–1990	72.7	78.3	57.5		20.8	
1999–2000	64.8	76.3	41.6		34.7	

(continued)

Table 2 (continued)

	White share of enrollment (%)	White isolation with white (%)	Black exposure to white (%)	Latino exposure to white (%)	Gap between white and black (%)	Gap between white and Latino (%)
2010–2011	51.4	65.8	32.4	38.7	33.4	27.1
Norfolk–Virginia Beach–Newport News						
1989–1990	57.2	66.1	43.5		22.6	
1999–2000	52.5	63.1	38.8		24.3	
2010–2011	43.8	56.0	30.0	43.5	26	12.5
Richmond–Petersburg						
1989–1990	59.9	77.7	30.7		47	
1999–2000	57.5	76.1	29.5		46.6	
2010–2011	50.6	66.4	29.1	41.7	37.3	24.7
Northern VA						
1989–1990	69.5	74.6	57.6	52.3	17	22.3
1999–2000	65.3	71.3	55.1	47.4	16.2	23.9
2010–2011	47.4	56.1	38.8	35.5	17.3	20.6

Note Blank cells indicate that Latino students accounted for less than 5 % of the total enrollment, thus analyses were not calculated for those years

The gaps in exposure to low-income students between black and white students are larger in the more fragmented New Jersey and New York metros than in the less fragmented metros of North Carolina and Virginia. Richmond is the only exception to this pattern, but Richmond is also the most fragmented of the North Carolina and Virginia metros, having failed to merge the city and neighboring suburban districts. In all but one metro (Charlotte), the gaps in exposure to low-income students between Latino and white students are larger in the more fragmented metros of New York and New Jersey than in North Carolina and Virginia's less fragmented metros. The racial disparities in exposure to low-income students reveal that students in all metro areas experience a double segregation by both race and poverty, and these disparities are larger in the more fragmented metro areas.

Largest Shares of Non-white Segregated Schools in Fragmented Metropolitan Areas

The New York metro has a much larger share of intensely segregated schools (46 %) and apartheid schools (19 %) than the other metropolitan areas in these four states. However, New York metro also enrolls a much larger share of non-white students (65 %) so the concentration of non-white students within the metro's schools must be interpreted within this context. The two New Jersey metros also have large shares of apartheid schools. In 2010, 8.5 % of Northern and Central New Jersey's schools and 6.5 % of Southern New Jersey's schools were apartheid schools.

Table 3 Exposure to low-income students by race, 2010–2011

	Low-income share of enrollment (%)	White exposure to low-income students (%)	Black exposure to low-income students (%)	Latino exposure to low-income students (%)	Gap between white and black (%)	Gap between white and Latino (%)
Northern and Central NJ	31.8	15.0	57.1	57.6	42.1	42.6
Southern NJ	35.9	25.8	50.8	57.6	25.0	31.8
Albany–Schenectady–Troy	30.6	24.3	58.6	48.4	34.3	24.1
Buffalo–Niagara Falls	40.4	29.8	73.0		43.2	
New York Metro	52.0	24.0	70.2	69.7	46.2	45.7
Rochester	38.5	28.1	70.0	63.3	41.9	35.2
Syracuse	38.8	32.4	68.7		36.3	
Charlotte–Gastonia– Rock Hill	47.3	36.2	60.1	62.1	23.9	25.9
Raleigh–Durham–Chapel Hill	37.8	31.6	46.4	46.6	14.8	15.0
Greensboro–Winston Salem–High Point	51.8	42.3	62.1	65.5	19.8	23.2
Norfolk–Virginia Beach–Newport News	40.2	30.7	51.5	40.2	20.8	9.5
Richmond–Petersburg	35.4	23.5	52.1	42.3	28.6	18.8
Northern VA	27.4	20.8	35.5	39.4	14.7	18.6

Note Blank cells indicate that Latino students accounted for less than 5 % of the total enrollment

Raleigh–Durham, Northern Virginia, Syracuse, and Albany have the smallest shares of intensely segregated schools, accounting for less than 10 % of the schools in these four metros. In Raleigh–Durham and Northern Virginia, the small share of intensely segregated schools is likely related to county-wide districts. However, in Syracuse and Albany, it is likely related to the disproportionately large share of white students (79 % in Syracuse and 76 % in Albany) and correspondingly small shares of non-white students in the metros. These two New York metros have the largest shares of white students and smallest shares of non-white students in our sample of metros; therefore, it is not unexpected that they would have small shares of intensely segregated schools.

Higher Levels of Multiracial Unevenness in More Fragmented Metros, Due to Unevenness Between Districts

Total unevenness levels are higher in almost all of New Jersey and New York's metros than in North Carolina and Virginia's metros, indicating that the diversity of the schools in New Jersey and New York's metros is less similar to the diversity of the overall metro areas than in North Carolina and Virginia's metros (Fig. 8). An exception occurs in Richmond, which is likely related to the failure of Richmond City Schools to consolidate with its two neighboring suburban districts; therefore, metro Richmond is more fragmented than the other metros represented

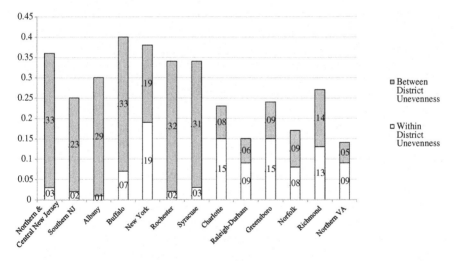

Fig. 8 Entropy index of multiracial unevenness, within and between school districts, by metropolitan area 2010–2011. *Note* The total unevenness for each metropolitan area: Northern and Central New Jersey = 0.36; Southern New Jersey = 0.25; Albany = 0.30; Buffalo = 0.40; New York Metro = 0.38; Rochester = 0.34; Syracuse = 0.34; Charlotte = 0.23; Raleigh–Durham = 0.15; Greensboro = 0.24; Norfolk = 0.17; Richmond = 0.26; Northern Virginia = 0.15

in North Carolina and Virginia. The levels of unevenness in all the more fragmented metros of New Jersey and New York are considered high. The level of
unevenness in the majority of the less fragmented metros in North Carolina and
Virginia is considered moderate. Again, Richmond, a more fragmented metro
within Virginia, is an exception, bordering on moderate-to-high unevenness.

The vast majority of the segregation in six of the seven New Jersey and New
York metros is due to segregation between school districts: Northern and Central
New Jersey (92 %), Southern New Jersey (92 %), Albany (97 %), Buffalo (83 %),
Rochester (94 %), and Syracuse (91 %). In metro New York, unevenness between
and within districts is more evenly split. Conversely, in most of North Carolina
and Virginia's metros, the majority of unevenness occurs within districts. In these
less fragmented metros, unevenness between districts is less influential in contributing to overall levels of unevenness: Charlotte (35 %), Raleigh–Durham (40 %),
Greensboro (38 %), and Northern Virginia (33 %). In Norfolk and Richmond,
unevenness between and within districts is more evenly split. This data demonstrates that in the more fragmented metro areas, districts' overall level of diversity
is less similar to that of the larger metro area and school district lines are largely
responsible for this unevenness. On the other hand, in less fragmented metros,
there are lower levels of overall unevenness, which is largely due to within-district
segregation.

Discussion

Our analysis reveals greater fragmentation in New York and New Jersey's metropolitan areas as well as racial compositions that are less similar to one another and
to the racial composition of the state's overall enrollment. The racial disparities
in exposure to white students and the share of non-white segregated schools are
larger in the more fragmented metropolitan areas. There are also larger disparities
in exposure to low-income students by race in the more fragmented metropolitan
areas. More fragmented metropolitan areas have higher levels of unevenness, most
of which is due to an uneven distribution of students between school districts. In
summary, in comparison to the less fragmented states, in the more highly fragmented states of New York and New Jersey, the typical black and Latino students
are exposed to smaller shares of white students, the typical white student is more
isolated with other white peers, there are greater disparities in exposure to low-
income students by race, the shares of intensely segregated and apartheid schools
are substantially larger, and levels of multiracial unevenness are higher, with the
majority due to unevenness between school districts. Although the measures cannot determine cause, these results indicate that states and metropolitan areas with
more fragmented district structures are associated with higher levels of segregation, thus confirming our hypothesis.

The data shows that segregation is becoming more extreme in fragmented areas
but it is also present and increasing in all areas, including those with county-wide

districts. Our findings are consistent with patterns of intensifying segregation across the nation (Orfield & Frankenberg, 2014). Therefore, the responsibility for addressing segregation is not confined only to fragmented metropolitan areas. States and districts across the nation must adopt policies that seek to achieve racial diversity; without such explicit efforts, intensifying segregation is likely to continue. In fact, a recent study of four Southern metropolitan areas found that although consolidated city-suburban district structures provide more potential for integration to occur, in order to achieve desegregation, districts must also implement comprehensive and cohesive desegregation plans (Siegel-Hawley, 2014).

Policy Implications

One approach for addressing segregation is developing and implementing multi-factor, race-conscious student assignment policies. Berkeley, California, has successfully maintained racially and socioeconomically desegregated schools through a controlled choice system that considers various characteristics such as income, educational attainment, and share of students of color in the neighborhood where the student resides (Frankenberg, 2013). Louisville adopted a similar approach after the Supreme Court struck down its race-conscious student assignment plan in 2007. Berkeley and other school districts using multifactor, race-conscious student assignment policies have been able to devise policies that are successful in creating diverse schools while abiding by current legal constraints.

In the vast majority of situations, attempts to improve educational opportunities for students in urban districts while keeping students isolated from opportunities available in suburban districts have been unsuccessful. Rusk (1999) emphasizes that in order to improve the opportunities in central cities, metropolitan areas must not rely solely on efforts to address urban decline but such efforts must be complemented with strong regional strategies. Several regional strategies to address metropolitan fragmentation include interdistrict transfer programs, regional magnet schools, and consolidation. These approaches require cooperation across boundary lines and therefore might require considerable time to implement; however, they are essential for making boundaries and fragmentation less powerful by providing access to opportunities across district lines.

Interdistrict transfer programs encourage students to cross district boundaries voluntarily and therefore create more diverse learning environments in spite of fragmented metropolitan areas. There are currently eight unique interdistrict transfer programs in the country that allow students from central city schools to transfer to suburban schools. Multiple positive outcomes are associated with these programs, including increased student achievement, improved racial attitudes and growing acceptance, and better long-term outcomes (Wells, Warner, & Grzesikowski, 2013). The Metropolitan Council for Educational Opportunity (METCO), which was established in 1966 and is the longest running interdistrict transfer program, allows students from Boston to attend more than 30 suburban districts. It has proven educational and long-term benefits (Eaton, 2001). However, funding for METCO has been historically unstable and demand for the program has exceeded its capacity (Eaton & Chirichigno, 2011). The consistent success of and persistent interest in METCO and other interdistrict transfer programs suggest that interdistrict transfer programs could be successful models for creating diverse schools in other fragmented metropolitan areas as well.

Connecticut serves as an example of another regional approach that incorporates both an interdistrict transfer program and regional magnet schools. Following the declaration of Hartford's districting system as unconstitutional in *Sheff*, the state developed a system of regional magnet schools designed to desegregate students across district lines (Cobb, Bifulco, & Bell, 2011). Additionally, the state expanded what had been an interdistrict transfer program in Hartford to also include the cities of New Haven and Bridgeport, subsidizing transportation and providing funding for receiving districts.

Finally, districts in fragmented metropolitan areas could consider consolidating multiple districts to form larger, metropolitan-wide districts. There are numerous successful examples of district consolidation, including Louisville and Jefferson County, Kentucky, which merged in 1976, Raleigh and Wake County, North Carolina, which merged in 1976, and Chattanooga and Hamilton County, Tennessee, which merged more recently in 1997. Jefferson County Public Schools is a particularly interesting example because its voluntary student assignment policy was declared unconstitutional in *Parents Involved in Community Schools* (2007). Rather than giving up on the goal of diversity following the ruling, this county-wide district modified its policy and continues to implement a voluntary, multifactor student assignment plan to promote racial diversity across the metro (Orfield & Frankenberg, 2013a; Phillips, Rodosky, Munoz, & Larsen, 2009).

Limitations and Future Research Directions

New Jersey, New York, North Carolina, and Virginia are illustrative examples that allow us to explore the problems associated with fragmentation and segregation. A detailed national analysis of fragmentation and segregation is beyond the scope of this exploratory project; therefore, we cannot be certain that these four states are representative of the other 46 states and results should not be overgeneralized. Further analysis of fragmentation and segregation at the national level or using different states and metropolitan areas for comparison would serve as a complement to this study. We also encourage future research to conceptualize and explore alternative ways of measuring fragmentation.

Fragmentation is one mechanism related to segregation. Additional factors are also likely related to segregation patterns in these four states, such as residential segregation and racial steering in real estate markets, student assignment policies, desegregation orders, legal constraints, and migration patterns. This analysis demonstrates the relationship between fragmentation and segregation, but does not assert that fragmentation causes segregation as the measures employed cannot be used to identify causation.

Future research might also underscore the significance of the problem of fragmentation and segregation by examining the relationships between segregation and academic achievement, short-term outcomes, and long-term outcomes within the context of fragmentation.

Conclusion

The time is long past for trying to provide equal education to children in our fragmented metropolitan areas within a structure that builds in, perpetuates, and multiplies inequalities. We need to move toward cooperation, federation, and even unified metropolitan institutions of school governance. It is clear that less fragmented metropolitan school districts have been the most successful not only in achieving lasting diversity but also in avoiding the precipitous decline and virtual destruction that has been inflicted on a number of highly impoverished, virtually all non-white central city systems.

References

Allport, G. W. (1954). *The nature of prejudice*. Reading, MA: Addison Wesley.

Balfanz, R., & Legters, N. E. (2004). Locating the dropout crisis: Which high schools produce the nation's dropouts? In G. Orfield (Ed.), *Dropouts in America: Confronting the graduation crisis* (pp. 57–84). Cambridge, MA: Harvard Education Press.

Bischoff, K. (2008). School district fragmentation and racial residential segregation: How do boundaries matter? *Urban Affairs Review, 44*(2), 182–217.

Borman, K. M., Eitle, T. M., Michael, D., Eitle, D. J., Lee, R., Johnson, L., & Shircliffe, B. (2004). Accountability in a postdesegregation era: The continuing significance of racial segregation in Florida's schools. *American Educational Research Journal, 41*(3), 605–631.

Braddock, J. H., & McPartland, J. M. (1989). Social-psychological processes that perpetuate racial segregation: The relationship between school and employment desegregation. *Journal of Black Studies, 19*(3), 267–289.

Bradley v. Richmond School Board, 416 U.S. 696 (1974).

Brown v. Board of Education of Topeka, 347 U.S. 483 (1954).

Carter, P. L., & Welner, K. G. (Eds.). (2013). *Closing the opportunity gap: What America must do to give every child an even chance*. New York, NY: Oxford University Press.

Clotfelter, C. T. (2004). *After Brown: The rise and retreat of school desegregation*. Princeton, NJ: Princeton University Press.

Clotfelter, C. T., Ladd, H. F., & Vigdor, J. L. (2005). Who teaches whom? Race and the distribution of novice teachers. *Economics of Education Review, 24*(4), 377–392.

Clotfelter, C. T., Ladd, H. F., & Vigdor, J. L. (2010). Teacher mobility, school segregation, and pay-based policies to level the playing field. *Education, Finance, and Policy, 6*(3), 399–438.

Cobb, C. D., Bifulco, R., & Bell, C. (2011). Legally viable desegregation strategies: The case of Connecticut. In E. Frankenberg & E. DeBray (Eds.), *Integrating schools in a changing society: New policies and legal options for a multiracial generation* (pp. 131–150). Chapel Hill, NC: University of North Carolina Press.

Crain, R. L., & Mahard, R. (1983). The effect of research methodology on desegregation achievement studies: A meta-analysis. *American Journal of Sociology, 88*, 839–854.

Danielson, M. N. (1976). *The politics of exclusion*. New York, NY: Columbia University Press.

Douglas, D. M. (1995). *Reading, writing, and race: The desegregation of the Charlotte schools*. Chapel Hill, NC: The University of North Carolina Press.

Duncombe, W. D., & Yinger, J. M. (2010). School district consolidation: The benefits and costs. *The School Administrator, 67*(5), 10–17.

Eaton, S. (2001). *The other Boston busing story: What's won and lost across the boundary line*. New Haven, CT: Yale University Press.

Eaton, S., & Chirichigno, G. (2011). *METCO merits more: The history and status of METCO*. Boston, MA: Pioneer Institute.

Frankenberg, E. (2009). Splintering school districts: Understanding the link between segregation and fragmentation. *Law and Social Inquiry, 34*, 869–909.

Frankenberg, E. (2013). The promise of choice: Berkeley's innovative integration plan. In G. Orfield & E. Frankenberg (Eds.), *Educational delusions? Why choice can deepen inequality and how to make schools fair* (pp. 69–88). Berkeley, CA: University of California Press.

Grant, G. (2011). *Hope and despair in the American city: Why there are no bad schools in Raleigh*. Cambridge, MA: Harvard University Press.

Hallinan, M. (1998). Diversity effects on student outcomes: social science evidence. *Ohio State Law Journal, 59*, 733–754.

Jackson, K. (2009). Student demographics, teacher sorting, and teacher quality: Evidence from the end of school desegregation. *Journal of Labor Economics, 27*(2), 213–256.

Jenkins v. Morris Township School District, 58 N.J. 483, 279 A. 2d. 619 (1971).

Kane, T., Riegg, S., & Staiger, D. (2006). School quality, neighborhoods, and housing prices. *American Law and Economics Review, 8*(2), 183–212.

Kane, T., Staiger, D., & Samms, G. (2003). School accountability ratings and housing values. *Brookings-Wharton Papers on Urban Affairs, 2003*, 83–137.

Kucsera, J., & Orfield, G. (2014). *New York state's extreme school segregation: Inequality, inaction and a damaged future*. Los Angeles, CA: The Civil Rights Project/Proyecto Derechos Civiles.

Kurlaender, M., & Yun, J. (2005). Fifty years after *Brown*: New evidence of the impact of school racial composition on student outcomes. *International Journal of Educational Policy, Research and Practice, 6*(1), 51–78.

Ladd, H. F., & Fiske, E. B. (2011, December 11). Class matters: Why we won't admit it, *The New York Times*.

Liebowitz, D., & Page, L. (2015). Residential choice as school choice. In R. Mickelson, S. Smith, & A. Nelson (Eds.), *Yesterday, today, and tomorrow: School desegregation and resegregation in Charlotte*. Cambridge, MA: Harvard Education Press.

Linn, R., & Welner, K. (2007). *Race-conscious policies for assigning students to schools: Social science research and the Supreme Court cases*. Washington, D.C.: National Academy of Education.

Logan, J. R., Minca, E., & Adar, S. (2012). The geography of inequality: Why separate means unequal in American public schools. *Sociology of Education, 85*(3), 287–301.

Massey, D. S., & Denton, N. A. (1988). The dimensions of residential segregation. *Social Forces, 67*(2), 281–315.

Mickelson, R. A., Bottia, M. C., & Lambert, R. (2013). Effects of school racial composition on K-12 mathematics outcomes: A metaregression analysis. *Review of Educational Research, 83*(1), 121–158.

Mickelson, R. A., & Heath, D. (1999). The effects of segregation on African American high school seniors' academic achievement. *The Journal of Negro Education, 68*(4), 566–586.

Mickelson, R. A., & Nkomo, M. (2012). Integrated schooling, life course outcomes, and social cohesion in multiethnic democratic societies. *Review of Research in Education, 36*, 197–238.

Mickelson, R. A., Smith, S. S., & Nelson, A. H. (Eds.). (2015). *Yesterday, today, and tomorrow: School desegregation and resegregation in Charlotte*. Cambridge, MA: Harvard Education Press.

Milliken v. Bradley, 418 U.S. 717 (1974).

National Center for Education Statistics. (2013). *The condition of education 2013*. Washington, DC: U.S. Department of Education.

Orfield, G. (1996). Metropolitan school desegregation: Impacts on metropolitan society. *Minnesota Law Review, 80*, 825.

Orfield, G. (2001). Metropolitan school desegregation: Impacts on metropolitan society. In J. A. Powell, G. Kearney, & V. Kay (Eds.), *In pursuit of a dream deferred: Linking housing and education policy* (pp. 121–157). New York: Peter Lang.

Orfield, G., & Ee, J. (2014). *Segregating California's future: Inequality and its alternative 60 years after Brown v. Board of Education*. Los Angeles, CA: The Civil Rights Project/Proyecto Derechos Civiles.

Orfield, G., & Frankenberg, E. (2008). *The last have become first: Rural and small town America lead the way on desegregation*. Los Angeles, CA: The Civil Rights Project/Proyecto Derechos Civiles.

Orfield, G., & Frankenberg, E. (2013a). Experiencing integration in Louisville: Attitudes on choice and diversity in a changing legal environment. In G. Orfield & E. Frankenberg (Eds.), *Educational delusions? Why choice can deepen inequality and how to make schools fair* (pp. 238–254). Berkeley, CA: University of California Press.

Orfield, G., & Frankenberg, E. (Eds.). (2013b). *Educational delusions? How choice can deepen inequality and how to make schools fair*. Berkeley, CA: University of California Press.

Orfield, G., & Frankenberg, E. (2014). *Brown at 60: Great progress, a long retreat, and an uncertain future*. Los Angeles, CA: The Civil Rights Project/Proyecto Derechos Civiles.

Orfield, G., & Lee, C. (2005). *Why segregation matters: Poverty and educational inequality*. Cambridge, MA: The Civil Rights Project.

Orfield, G., Siegel-Hawley, G., & Kucsera, J. (2014). *Sorting out deepening confusion on segregation trends*. Los Angeles, CA: The Civil Rights Project/Proyecto Derechos Civiles.

Parents Involved in Community Schools v. Seattle School District No. 1, 551 U.S. 701 (2007).

Pasadena City Bd. of Educ. v. Spangler, 427 U.S. 424 (1976).

Pettigrew, T., & Tropp, L. (2006). A meta-analytic test of intergroup contact theory. *Journal of Personality and Social Psychology, 90*(5), 751–783.

Phillips, K. J. R., Rodosky, R. J., Munoz, M. A., & Larsen, E. S. (2009). Integrated schools, integrated futures? A case study of school desegregation in Jefferson County, Kentucky. In C. E. Smrekar & E. B. Goldring (Eds.), *From the courtroom to the classroom: The shifting landscape of school desegregation* (pp. 239–269). Cambridge, MA: Harvard Education Press.

Reardon, S. F., & Firebaugh, G. (2002). Measures of multigroup segregation. *Sociological Methodology, 32*(1), 33–67.

Reardon, S. F., & Yun, J. (2002–2003). Integrating neighborhoods, segregating schools: The retreat from school desegregation in the South, 1990–2000. *North Carolina Law Review, 81*, 1563–1596.

Roda, A., & Wells, A. S. (2013). School choice policies and racial segregation: Where white parents' good intentions, anxiety, and privilege collide. *American Journal of Education, 119*(2), 261–293.

Rothstein, R. (2004). *Class and schools: Using social, economic, and educational reform to close the black-white achievement gap*. New York, NY: Teachers College Press.

Rumberger, R. (2003). The causes and consequences of student mobility. *The Journal of Negro Education, 72*(1), 6–21.

Rusk, D. (1999). *Inside game, outside game: Winning strategies for saving urban America*. Washington, D.C.: Brookings Institution Press.

Ryan, J. (2010). *Five miles away, a world apart: One city, two schools and the story of modern educational inequality*. New York: Oxford University Press.

Sager, L. G. (1969). Tight little islands: Exclusionary zoning, equal protection, and the indigent. *Stanford Law Review, 21*(4), 767–800.

San Antonio Independent School District v. Rodriguez, 411 U.S. 1 (1973).

Sheff v. O'Neill, 238 Conn. 1 (1996).

Siegel-Hawley, G. (2014). Mitigating Milliken? School district boundary lines and desegregation policy in four Southern metropolitan areas, 1990–2010. *American Journal of Education, 120*(3), 391–433.

Sunderman, G. L. (2009). The federal role in education: From the Reagan to the Obama administration. *Voices in Urban Education, 24*, 6–14.

Swann v. Charlotte-Mecklenburg Board of Education, 402 U.S. 1 (1971).

Swanson, C. B. (2004). Sketching a portrait of public high school graduation: Who graduates? Who doesn't? In G. Orfield (Ed.), *Dropouts in America: Confronting the graduation rate crisis* (pp. 13–40). Cambridge, MA: Harvard Education Press.

Tropp, L. R., & Prenovost, M. A. (2008). The role of intergroup contact in predicting children's interethnic attitudes: Evidence from meta-analytic and field studies. In S. R. Levy & M. Killen (Eds.), *Intergroup attitudes and relations in childhood through adulthood* (pp. 236–248). New York, NY: Oxford University Press.

U.S. Commission on Civil Rights. (1977). *Statement on metropolitan desegregation*. Washington, D.C.: U. S. Commission on Civil Rights.

Wachter, S. M. (1990). The effects of land-use constraints on housing prices. *Land Economics, 66*, 315–324.

Weiher, G. R. (1991). *The fractured metropolis: Political fragmentation and metropolitan segregation*. Albany, NY: State University of New York Press.

Wells, A. S., & Crain, R. L. (1994). Perpetuation theory and the long-term effects of school desegregation. *Review of Educational Research, 64*(4), 531–555.

Wells, A. S., Warner, M., & Grzesikowski, C. (2013). The story of meaningful school choice: Lessons from interdistrict transfer plans. In G. Orfield & E. Frankenberg (Eds.), *Educational delusions? Why choice can deepen inequality and how to make schools fair* (pp. 187–218). Berkeley, CA: University of California Press.

Yun, J. T., & Moreno, J. F. (2006). College access, K-12 concentrated disadvantage, and the next 25 years of education research. *Educational Researcher, 35*(1), 12–19.

Kids, Kale, and Concrete: Using Participatory Technology to Transform an Urban American Food Desert

Antwi A. Akom, Aekta Shah and Aaron Nakai

Introduction

Although Americans have been quick to condemn the apartheid system of South Africa, they have been slow to recognize the consequences of institutionalized racial segregation in their own backyards. South Africa's racial caste system draws parallels to Jim Crow segregation faced by African-Americans in the deep south—in both instances Blacks and Whites had separate schools, buses, education, housing, and health care—and economic opportunities available to Black and Brown communities were vastly different than those available to Whites. Moreover, even though South African apartheid was dismantled in the 1990s, and Jim Crow was legally abolished by the Civil Rights Act (1964) and the Voting Rights Act (1965), many view segregation as a remnant of a racist past, one that is fading progressively over time. Few, however, recognize that America is still a segregated society, and even fewer appreciate the continued perseverance of Black/Brown "separateness" or the degree to which it is maintained by modern institutional arrangements and individual actions.

A.A. Akom
San Francisco State University, 1600 Holloway Avenue, Burk Hall 521,
San Francisco, CA 94132, USA
e-mail: akom@sfsu.edu

A. Shah (✉)
Stanford University, 485 Lasuen Mall, Stanford, CA 94305–3096, USA
e-mail: Aekta_Shah@mail.harvard.edu

A. Nakai
I-SEEED, 1625 Clay Street, Suite 600, Oakland, CA 94612, USA
e-mail: anakai@iseeed.org

© Springer International Publishing Switzerland 2016
P.A. Noguera et al. (eds.), *Race, Equity, and Education*,
DOI 10.1007/978-3-319-23772-5_4

The topic of racial segregation, or "American Apartheid"—as coined by Massey and Denton (1993)—has all but disappeared from the public dialogue; it is gone from the list of issues on political platforms; and is dismissed by most researchers who continue to hurl endless deficit theories like the "culture of poverty" at low income and communities of color. Segregation has woven itself seamlessly into all aspects of our daily lives and in doing so has become the forgotten footnote of American race relations. The twenty-first century racial reality is that until political leaders, decision-makers, researchers, and everyday people recognize and make visible the crucial role of America's own apartheid-like system in perpetuating urban poverty and racial injustice, the United States will remain racially divided between the rich and the poor, the eco haves and have nots, and the healthy and the sick.

Fifty years of social-science research has documented the relationships between racially and economically isolated neighborhoods and employment, health, crime, and violence, educational outcomes, and a range of other factors. Researchers are now moving beyond descriptive relationships among race, space, place, and waste, and toward an understanding of the underlying causes and how they interact to have a cumulative impact. Conceptual frameworks including "eco-apartheid" (Akom, 2011a) examine the social, emotional, economic, and environmental manifestations of structural racialization that limit Black and Brown communities from accessing key institutional resources and privileges that promote health and academic achievement. This holistic approach brings into view ways in which health and educational outcomes are systematically racialized—accumulating across institutional domains and concentrating poverty over time.

After persisting for more than five decades, apartheid in Black and Brown communities will not be addressed by passing a few amendments or by implementing a medley of "red-tape" laden reforms. Apartheid is deeply entrenched in modern American society; manufactured by whites earlier in the century to isolate and control growing urban Black and Brown populations, it is maintained today by a set of institutions, attitudes, and practices that are deeply embedded in the structure of American life. As the recent grand-jury decisions in the Ferguson and Eric Garner police brutality cases highlight, in many ways conditions have worsened for Black and Brown communities and Apartheid has assumed ever greater importance as an institutional tool for propagating the consequences of racial oppression: crime, drugs, violence, illiteracy, poverty, despair, and their growing health, educational, environmental and economic costs not only for Black and Brown communities, but for the country as a whole.

Resistance, Agency, and Political Contestation: Using Civic Technology to Combat "American Apartheid"

This chapter aims to highlight the ways that low income and communities of color are combating "American Apartheid" by using technology—particularly the ways in which American Apartheid impacts access to healthy food and educational achievement. In section one, we place the need for food justice—access to nutritious, affordable, cultur-ally appropriate food—in the context of structural racialization, racial formation, and racialized geographies. In section two, we describe some of the innovative ways that low income and communities of color are fighting back by using technology and Youth Participatory Action Research (YPAR) to engage youth in community planning and health promotion. In section three, we introduce an innovative mobile technology tool called Streetwyze—which utilizes data visualization, mapping, and crowd-sourcing to increase community engagement and shed light on how the food ecosystem has been shaped by institutionalized racism. We conclude by demonstrating how food apartheid serves as a theoretical and political bridge between scholarship and activism on school-ing, sustainability, educational achievement, and environmental justice.

Long before the *Brown* decision, race was, and remains, a powerful organiz-ing feature of American social life. All across the United States, racial ideologies operate politically, legally, and socially to limit Black people/people of color's access to economic, educational, and environmental resources (Bonilla-Silva, 2001; Bullard, 1990; Corburn, 2005; Freudenburg, 2005; Pulido, 2000). We sug-gest that efforts to eliminate well-established racial disparities must consider the historical relationships between food apartheid—which we define as the structural, political, and experiential limits on the availability of nutritious, healthy, afford-able, and culturally appropriate foods, and/or limited or uncertain access to food—and health and educational outcomes. We present evidence that outlines how food apartheid is an important cause of racial disparities in health and education, one that (1) influences access to institutional resources and privileges that promote health, and (2) influences educational outcomes (Link & Phelan, 1995; Williams & Collins, 2001). Our conceptual framework draws from environmental sociology, public health, urban education, and decolonized research methodologies to exam-ine the relationship between school desegregation, environmental inequality, struc-tural racialization, and health and educational outcomes.

Drawing from previously published literature, food apartheid places the need for food justice—access to nutritious, affordable, culturally appropriate food—in the context of structural racialization, racial formation, and racialized geographies (Alkon & Nogaard, 2009; Omi & Winant, 2004). This concept of food apartheid brings the environmental justice emphasis on racial stratification to bear on the schooling and sustainability movement's desire to demonstrate an association between nutrition, students' academic performance, and food deserts—socially marginalized areas where residents have little or no access to healthy afford-able food—and as a result, higher incidences of obesity, diabetes, morbidity, and mortality.

This chapter is focused on the city of Oakland, California; however, we also build on a larger body of work, situated in other racially segregated urban con-texts. We argue that the concept of food justice can help the schooling and sus-tainability movement move beyond several limitations of the place-based approach and meaningfully incorporate issues of race-based residential segregation, commu-nity defense, social equity, and social justice into the lived experiences of ghetto formation, toxic waste, and academic achievement. Additionally, food justice may help activists, teachers, community leaders, and policymakers working on food security inside and outside of schools to better understand the institutionalized nature of denied access to healthy foods and the important role that community-based organizations can play in transforming food deserts into food oases— community defense tactics that community-based organizations like the Black Panther Party understood from the very beginning. The racial segregation that produces food apartheid and the community defense tactics used to resist are the subject of this chapter.

For over 50 years as the birthplace of the Black Panther Party and the Slow Food movement, California has come to embody the critical ways in which race and class shape sustainable food systems, community defense, and environmental change at the neighborhood level (Self, 2005). Youth Uprising, a community-based organization in East Oakland, follows in this historic tradition. In 1997, as a result of the racial tensions that erupted in violence in East Oakland, the county of Alameda and the city of Oakland made an unprecedented investment in East Oakland by providing support for the planning of a one-stop health and human service center designed by-and for-youth. Youth, residents, public officials, and other key stakeholders researched national best practices, designed the space, planned the initial programming, and raised capital support from public and private sources. Youth Uprising broke ground in 2003 and the doors opened to a 25,000 square foot state-of-the-art facility in 2005 that attracted more than 1,600 visitors in its first year.

As the rates of childhood obesity have surged in East Oakland, where 48 % of teens are overweight (UCLA Center for Health Policy Research, 2011), Youth Uprising has begun to reframe the local community's food insecurity and high rates of diet-related diseases not as the result of poor individual food choices, but rather due to institutionalized racism, and to document the disproportionate burden of disparities—in terms of access to healthful foods—on people of color and the poor (Alkon & Norgaard, 2009). Although University partnerships have helped to inform this crucial work, some of the resulting research is highly inaccessible to everyday people at the street level. Also, because some researchers may not collaborate with youth partners in ways that promote policy change or help youth feel empowered by their racio-ethnicity or other axis of social identity, there is sometimes tension between academics, youth activists, and educators about whose research it is, who owns it, and whose interest it really serves (Akom, Cammorota, & Ginwright, 2008; Akom, 2011b; Duncan-Andrade & Morrell, 2008; Ginwright, Noguera, & Cammarota, 2006; Morello-Frosch, Zuk, Jerrett, Shamasunder, & Kyle, 2011; Morrell, 2008).

In recent years, Youth Uprising has begun to collaborate with University researchers and public health specialists to move past documenting disparities and instead develop transparent and scientifically valid technology tools to put the power back in the hands of everyday people (Akom, Shah, & Nakai, 2014; Parikh, 2006; Van Wart, Tsai, & Parikh 2010). More specifically, in 2011 Youth Uprising in collaboration with a research team from San Francisco State University, UC Berkeley, The Institute for Sustainable Economic Educational and Environmental Design (I-SEEED), Oakland Unified School District's Office of Research, Assessment, and Development (RAD) and Castlemont High School, formed the Mapping to Mobilize collaborative (M2M) utilizing Local Ground—a participatory mapping platform—and later "Streetwyze," a new mobile, mapping, and SMS platform that allows young people to find goods and services, take action on important issues, and visualize health and well-being in their neighborhoods.

Traditional models of urban redevelopment rarely provide urban youth with the design assistance they need to maximize their own benefit from development dollars (or under-development dollars) being spent in their communities and often fail to address the role that technology can play in bridging civic infrastructure with the built environment (Marable, 2000). Technology has the power to transform our democracy, making it more transparent, efficient, and inclusive of community input (Patel, Sotsky, Gourley, & Houghton, 2013). Community engaged technology provides an important scale to test and replicate data visualization platforms that enable community members to verify the accuracy of public data sets in real-time, in order to make our neighborhoods and ultimately our cities more sustainable, vibrant, and strong.

We begin with a discussion of food apartheid and the contemporary racialized geographies through which structural racialization shapes the physical landscape where Black and Brown youth live, learn, work, and play. Structural racism defines how lack of geographic and economic access often confines choices in Black and Brown neighborhoods to processed, fast, and commodity foods (Alkon & Norgaard, 2009; Kwate, 2008). We then highlight the challenges of doing YPAR—or what Corburn refers to as "street science"—and the "data distrust" that can emerge between researchers and youth of color (Corburn, 2002; Sadd et al., 2013). In the third section, we provide a description of the Mapping 2 Mobilize collaborative (M2M) including its use of the Local Ground mapping platform and Streetwyze community engagement platform, and how this led to ground-truthing. We conclude by summarizing our findings and results, and discuss the ways in which local knowledge completes and complements "professional" knowledge in improving educational and environmental research and outcomes.

Bringing Social Justice Back into Schooling and Sustainability

In the past two decades, environmental justice scholars have successfully documented the unequal distribution of environmental toxins through which low-income people and people of color bear the burdens of Eco-Apartheid and environmental degradation (Akom, 2011a; Pastor, Sadd, & Morello-Frosch, 2002). Schools and communities have organized numerous campaigns against the companies that are responsible (Bullard, 1990; Kaplan & Morris, 2000; Sze, 2008). However, despite the central importance of food to educational achievement and overall public health, surprisingly little educational literature devotes attention to food access. While Gottlieb and Fisher (1996) first highlighted an environmental justice approach to food security more than a decade ago, few educational scholars have incorporated food or nutrition into their analyzes.

Examining the health impact of fast food and liquor stores in Black and Brown neighborhoods is critical. Specifically, according to NHANES data, in 2011–2012, obesity for Blacks was 47.8 and 42.5 % for Hispanics (Kwate, 2008; Ogden, Carroll, Kit, & Flegal, 2013). And women are disproportionately affected (between 1997–2008, Black women were 44 % more likely to be obese than White women), Black males are 2 % more likely to be obese than White men (Kwate, 2008; Jackson et al., 2013), and Mexican-American women are 31 % more likely to be obese compared with White women (National Center for Health Statistics, 2013). While all groups in the U.S. exhibit rising rates of obesity, diabetes, and other diet-related diseases, the rates are highest among low-income communities and communities of color (Drewnowski & Spector, 2004; Kwate, 2008)

Studies on high caloric food further depict how access plays a major role in the connection between economic-status and health (Drewnowski & Spector, 2004; Kwate, 2008). Fast food is high in sugar, carbohydrates, fats, and cholesterol and low in several important nutrients (French, Harnack, & Jeffery, 2000), as well as in price. Prior research has shown that fast food consumption is related to obesity (Jeffery, Baxter, McGuire, & Linde, 2006; Kwate, 2008). On a regional level, heart disease and fatalities are higher in places with high concentrations of fast food chains (Alter & Eny, 2005; Kwate, 2008). Cumulatively, the data support the concept of food apartheid as a conceptual bridge between education and environmental justice that situates low–income communities' lack of food access within the historical processes of structural racialization, racial identity formation, and racialized geographies (Akom, 2008).

Food Apartheid's Impacts on Health and Education

It is a tragedy when it is easier to get "fried chicken," waffles, and churros rather than chayotes, carrots, or cherries (Brownell & Horgen, 2004; Kwate, 2008). And yet, evidence shows that for many Black and Brown folks it is more challenging, and often more expensive, to get chayotes or cherries—and this is because of systematic and cumulative racial and spatial discrimination (Kwate, 2008; Morland, Wing, Diez Roux, & Poole 2002; Zenk et al., 2005). With the disproportionately higher exposure to fast food and liquor stores in Black and Brown communities, it becomes convenient and affordable to purchase high calorie, fast, and fried food instead (Block, Scribner, & DeSalvo 2004; Kwate, 2008; Lewis et al., 2005).

Today, food apartheid has connections to the end of *de jure* segregation and the prevailing patterns of re-segregation and other forms of continuing apartheid in the US—and more specifically—impacts education and well-being in Black and Brown communities (Kwate, 2008). Research shows that the food that is available to communities impacts their health (Kwate, 2008; Morland et al., 2002; Morland, Diez Roux, & Wing, 2006). And, on a positive note, programs and policies that improve access to healthy food have been shown to lead to the higher consumption of these foods (Kwate, 2008; Wrigley, Warm, & Margetts, 2003).

In educational spaces, school cafeterias are often the largest "restaurants" in town—and collectively schools, large institutions, and grass roots organizations can help create enough demand to support sustainable regional agriculture transformation across entire communities (Stone, Brown, Weiden, & Barlow, 2014). A 2011 report calculated that each dollar spent locally for school food adds $1.86 to the local economy, and every job created by a district's purchasing power results in an overall increase of 2.43 jobs (Ecotrust, 2011). School meals are especially critical for low-income students and students of color. In 2012, 49 million Americans, including 15.9 million children, lived in food insecure households. One out of five households with children reported food insecurity (Coleman-Jensen et al., 2013).

Historically, programs like the Black Panther Party's Free Breakfast for School Children program have spearheaded the Black community's presence in the school food legislation movement. Shortly after the passage of the Civil Rights Act of 1964, civil rights organizations lobbied to appropriate federal funds to expand the free school meal program. Unlike other civil rights groups who used legislative reform tactics, the Black Panther Party fought directly to end hunger in the Black community through direct service and the implementation of community-based "survival programs," which addressed the universal depravity of poverty in the Black community (Powell, 2014).

One of the most successful "survival and anti-poverty programs" in the history of the Black community was the free breakfast initiative, which was headquartered in Oakland, California in St. Augustine's church. Prior to the program's implementation in 1969, Black Panther Party members consulted with nutritionists to determine what foods constituted a healthy breakfast and made sure the kitchen was in compliance with all safety code regulations. The program proved to be a tremendous success and expanded to 45 sites across the country. Educators reported that students who received free breakfast no longer complained of hunger pangs and were more attentive during classroom instruction (Heynen, 2009). According to Professor Nik Heynen, the free breakfast program would serve as "both the model for, and impetus behind, all federally funded school breakfast programs currently in existence within the United States" (Heynen, 2009, p. 411).

Fifty years ago, the Black Panther Free Breakfast Program demonstrated an association between nutrition, students' academic performance, and food justice. The program was visionary because today there is increasing evidence that supports the Panthers' fundamental belief that there is an association between nutrition and students' academic performance. Recent findings from a variety of studies support this hypothesis including the following: improving school meals can make almost immediate difference in students' academic achievement (Belot & James, 2011); increased fruit and vegetable consumption and reduced dietary fat intake have been significantly linked to improved academic performance (Florence, Asbridge, & Veugelers, 2008); increases in participation of school breakfast programs are associated with an increase in math and reading test scores, daily attendance, class participation, and reductions in tardiness and absenteeism (Basch, 2010); and nutrient deficiencies, refined sugars and carbohydrates, pesticide residues, preservatives, and artificial colorings in food have all been associated with altered thinking and behavior and with neuro-developmental disorders such as Attention Deficit/Hyperactivity Disorder (Greene, online publication).

Thus, the racialization of space is a fundamental cause of food apartheid and shapes access to resources (e.g., income, wealth, health, knowledge, food access, prestige) that impact educational achievement (Basch, 2010; Link & Phelan, 1995). Racial residential segregation has created "two Americas" (Hacker, 1992; Kwate, 2008; LaVeist, 2003)—delineated between the "haves" and "have nots" in terms of access to health care (William & Collins, 2001), parks and open space, economic capital, jobs, exposure to environmental toxins (Bullard, Johnson, & Torres, 2004; Sadd et al., 2013; Sze & London, 2008), high quality education (Akom, 2011a), social and public services, and overall safety, peace, and well-being.

This concept of food apartheid sheds light on how the food ecosystem has been shaped by institutionalized racism (Akom, 2011a; Alkon & Norgaard, 2009) and brings an environmental justice emphasis on racial stratification to bear on the schooling and sustainability movements' desire to demonstrate an association between nutrition, students' academic performance, and food deserts. As a result, food apartheid serves as a theoretical and political bridge between scholarship and activism on schooling, sustainability, educational achievement, and environmental justice.

Research Approach: Youth Participatory Action Research

Data for this research project was collected through YPAR. Although statistical research on health and educational disparities tends to dominate academic debates, YPAR has also emerged as an important part of the work (Akom, 2008, 2009a; Cammarotta & Fine, 2010; Smith, 1999; Wallerstein & Duran, 2006). YPAR is defined as a collaborative approach to research that engages community partners and academic partners as equals in both knowledge generation and intervention strategies that benefit the communities involved (Akom, 2009b; Akom, Scott, & Shah, 2013; Tuck & Yang, 2013; Van Wart et al., 2010; Wallerstein & Duran, 2006).

The knowledge that the youth have about their experiences of living with multiple environmental health hazards and chronic disease is one of the fundamental assets they can contribute to schools and community-based organizations and is often a key resource that the community organizes to avoid being exploited and exposed to health risks and social toxins (Corburn, 2002, 2006). When youth engage in environmental health research, their primary goal is often to help themselves and their communities by generating usable or actionable knowledge—information that goes beyond description and analysis and suggests proactive or precautionary intervention strategies. By taking action to transform the social and material conditions in their communities, youth build self-respect, self-confidence, and self-determination while fostering positive relationships with caring adults (Camino, 2005; Fergus, Noguera, & Martin, 2014; Nasir, Rosebery, Warren, & Lee, 2006). Although high levels of social and cultural capital are needed to carry out YPAR, this approach itself can build community capacity and increase civic engagement throughout the research process (Ruglis & Freudenberg, 2010; Wallerstein & Duran, 2006).

YPAR Collaboration

In 2011, the Mapping 2 Mobilize (M2M) collaboration was formed to research and address environmental justice issues in East Oakland and beyond as identified and defined by the community. The stages of our YPAR collaboration began with identification of a problem and progressed toward deciding on research questions, conducting a study, and developing and implementing action plans (Vasquez et al., 2007).

The collaboration was first anchored by Youth Uprising, a youth development organization with strong roots in East Oakland, and I-SEEED, a community-based organization with national expertise in education, technology, economic development, and environmental justice. Over time, the collaborative grew in size and scope to include major universities, K-12 institutions, and additional community-based partners. The goals of M2M are threefold: (1) improve health and educational outcomes in low-income communities of color like East Oakland; (2) conduct research on food security, community assets, and environmental health hazards; and (3) develop the expertise and capacity of local youth-serving organizations by linking research to policy advocacy and community organizing locally, regionally, and statewide.

Youth Uprising was influential in helping to develop the initial focus of the M2M collaboration and in defining the food apartheid problem. An important focus of Youth Uprising is to educate youth and communities about the impact of food apartheid on people and communities locally. The definition of food apartheid in practice here is: the structural, political, and experiential limits on the availability of nutritious, healthy, affordable, and culturally appropriate foods, and/or limited or uncertain access to food. Measured at the community level, food apartheid investigates the underlying social, economic, and institutional factors—or in other words structural racialization impacts—within a community that affect the quantity and quality of available food and its affordability relative to the financial resources available to acquire it (Cohen, 2002). Thus, the relationship between environmental health and the structural racialization of the food apartheid system became an integral part of the M2M problem definition and later policy intervention.

M2M's research plan was adapted from that developed by Sadd et al. (2013) to ensure scientific rigor and objectivity through the process of peer review by community, youth researchers (i.e., youth as public intellectuals, see Akom, 2008) and scientific colleagues (through youth and adult-led professional conference presentations and publishing in environmental health and social-science literature) as well as youth and adult-led presentations to regulatory scientists at the county and state level, leadership at regulatory agencies, schools, and policy think tanks. This method of validation was developed and documented by Community-Based Participatory Research (CBPR) researchers in Los Angeles (Sadd et al., 2013). The research plan began by using secondary data collected by regulatory authorities such as the Alameda County Public Health Department to document the impacts of food apartheid in East Oakland. M2M adopted this strategy in the belief that analyzing the government's own data to assess racial and other health disparities would be a powerful way to draw regulatory attention to the intersection between educational and environmental justice issues impacting East Oakland (Sadd et al., 2013).

Method: Ground-Truthing Using Community-Driven Technology

Ground-truthing as a methodology emerged from the field of cartography—where images taken from airplanes or satellites documenting features such as "open space," "vegetation," or "tree cover" are validated, using observations conducted by researchers on the ground (Sadd et al., 2013; Sharkey & Horel, 2008). For this project, ground-truthing was adapted from the methodology developed by Sadd et al. (2013), and involved validating regulatory databases (i.e., county grocery store data) with community-driven data. The technological innovation that the M2M collaborative integrated into the research design was the Local Ground participatory mapping platform developed at UC Berkeley with community engagement support from I-SEEED. Local Ground combines the best of the paper and the digital world by using paper maps to capture rich qualitative data and using a QR-code to create digital versions of hand-drawn annotations and to import them onto an online map. Using paper maps makes the Geographic Information Systems (GIS) data collection process more accessible, cheap, portable, and, most importantly, easy to learn. Digitizing the data then allows planners and community members to collate and analyze the data with the Local Ground user interface, and the Local Ground digital visualization tools then enable community members to share findings with key decision-makers (Van Wart et al., 2010).

Based on this work, I-SEEED recognized the need to develop culturally and community responsive technology platforms that combine both analog research tools (i.e., paper maps, surveys, etc.) and digital tools (i.e., mobile apps, GPS devices, smartphones, FlipCams) to accelerate ground-truthing processes—verifying in real time whether information indicated in regulatory databases really exist and whether there are additional hazards or assets identified by local residents on the ground that are not captured by these databases. In the summer of 2012, I-SEEED conceptualized Streetwyze, a more comprehensive mapping application, and piloted the platform over a five-city M2M project across the State of California (Oakland, San Francisco, San Diego, Merced, and Planada).

Streetwyze is a mobile, mapping, and SMS platform that enables users to find, rank, and share information about local goods and services or environmental issues impacting their communities. Streetwyze makes it easy for community members to (1) Find the services they need to thrive; (2) Rate the quality of services; (3) Increase community engagement through community asset mapping; (4) Share best practices through digital storytelling; and (5) Visualize community resiliency through GIS mapping technology. By providing the most underserved populations with tools to find and communicate directly with regulatory, health, educational, or social service sectors, Streetwyze puts the power back in the hands of everyday people to transform our democracy, making it more transparent, efficient, and inclusive of community input.

Mapping the Neighborhood

Our ground-truthing process followed the well-documented methodology developed by scholars Sadd et al. (2013) in LA. We adapted the methodology to fit the particular population, context of East Oakland, as well as our study-goals of analyzing "food desert" conditions.

As the first step of the ground-truthing process, we conducted workshops where youth were trained on theories of structural racialization, youth empowerment, resistance, problem-posing education, the science of environmental health, cumulative impacts, social vulnerability, as well as state and federal databases that keep locational and other records of food security (Sadd et al., 2013). Technical assistance and training included: introduction to mapping platform and user interface, uploading data, research design, YPAR methodology, planning and conducting data analysis, crowd-sourcing data collection, community-driven indicators and metrics, collecting multimedia and GIS data, dissemination, social media, and publication training.

To ground-truth what regulatory databases were recognizing as food oases but youth were experiencing as food deserts, the youth researchers also conducted store-mapping research in over 30 retail food outlets in East Oakland to determine how many were in fact grocery stores, versus liquor stores or corner stores. To ground-truth food retail outlets in East Oakland, youth were equipped with clipboards, paper maps embedded with digital QR-codes, handheld digital devices (iPhones, Smartphones, Mobile Phones, Flip Cameras), and step-by-step instructions on data collection. Group leaders organized participants into teams of three—with each team trained and responsible for conducting street-by-street assessments of their portion of the study area and locating and categorizing grocery stores, liquor stores, and/or any other type of food/retail outlets. One block overlaps at the boundaries were included to ensure that the mapping was complete (Sadd et al., 2013).

Teams were tasked with the following (adapted from Sadd et al., 2013):

- Verify the location and correct information of all retail outlets/"grocery stores" documented in regulatory agency (Alameda County Public Health Department) databases—Collect written data on paper maps as well as pictures and audio field-notes of observations.
- Verify the type of retail outlet as defined by the local community (liquor store, corner store, grocery store, ethnic food store, smoke shop, gas station, etc.)—Collect written data on paper maps, written field-notes, as well as pictures, and audio field-notes.
- Locate and map any additional food retail outlets and healthy food locations not included in the regulatory agency databases—Collect written data on paper maps, written field-notes, as well as pictures, and audio field-notes.

Youth recorded locations, either using portable GPS receivers or smartphones and/or by writing the retail outlet name on paper maps encoded with specialized QR-codes. Youth also recorded the name, type of business or activity, and other notes about the retail outlet on a field-notes sheet (i.e., types of food/beverage prominently displayed, existence of any fresh/whole foods, price of kitchen staples such as milk, bread, fruits/vegetables, prominence of alcohol/cigarettes/other controlled substances). Teams also recorded observations about types of accessibility issues not necessarily tied to types of food/beverage/items sold, that is, perceived safety of surrounding area, visible public transportation stops in the vicinity, general upkeep/signage/visibility of retail location, etc. The data collected by youth participants was transferred to the mapping database through embedded QR-code using geo-coded addresses (adapted from Sadd et al., 2013).

During the food retail outlet ground-truthing project, teams mapped 5 neighborhoods in East Oakland: MacArthur Blvd, International Blvd, Eastmont District, High Street, and Fruitvale District. Oakland Uptown, Oakland Chinatown, and Piedmont were also mapped as comparative communities, but used a different protocol—this data are not the subject of this study and thus are not reported here. Following the techniques developed by Sadd et al. (2013), variations in categorization of retail outlet by each youth researcher were characterized by sampling sites that they felt represented both the worst and best food options, as well as locations where large numbers of residents shopped for groceries. Youth researchers developed a plan to visit these sites in groups of at least three (to internally check for variation in outlet categorization), between 11 a.m. and 6 p.m. Youth researchers used portable GPS-enabled mobile devices and paper maps encoded with specialized QR-codes. Monitoring was done during the summer, fall, and spring months (adapted from Sadd et al., 2013).

To understand the extent of food apartheid in East Oakland, the M2M collaborative undertook several types of research including: direct participant observation, semi-structured interviews, surveys, and secondary data from regulatory databases. The problem identification phase of the project lasted 1 year (one summer and two school-year semesters with Castlemont High School)—and provided a wealth of relevant information about the diverse dimensions of the problem of food apartheid across East Oakland neighborhoods.

Results

The ground-truthing process revealed that categorization of retail food outlets in regulatory agency databases is often incorrect. Most often, retail food outlets were categorized by regulatory agencies as "grocery stores," while the community identified them as either "liquor stores" or "corner stores". The basis for community categorization is provided in Fig. 4.

Youth researchers further found that the top three nontobacco or alcohol-related products available at these stores were chips, soda, and candy/confection-items (i.e., Snickers, Skittles, Honeybuns), many of which had high sugar, fat, and salt content. Figure 1 shows an itemized list of most sold items (as reported by store owners) at seven retail outlets on MacArthur Boulevard. Asterisked items depict items containing some nutritional value as identified by the US FDA's nutritional guide. Sales tended to peak between 12–8 pm, according to store owners, corresponding with school lunch-time, after-school, and dinner periods during which most youth consume the majority of their daily calories. This is not unique to the MacArthur community: each of the five communities mapped had a similar distribution of types of food/beverage items sold as well as peak hours of consumption. In Fig. 1, we show results for the MacArthur Boulevard community (though the same data were collected for all five neighborhoods).

Most Sold Items	Frequency (# of store owners reporting)
Alcohol	7
Cigarettes	7
Chips (i.e. Doritos, Cheetos, Takis)	7
Soda (i.e. Coke, Pepsi, Mtn. Dew)	6
Candy (i.e. Snickers, Starburst, Skittles)*	5
Other confections (i.e. Honeybuns, Mrs. Fields Cookies, etc.)	5
*some candy-bars contain levels of protein high enough to be recognized on FDA nutritional standards, however most calories from candy-bars come from sugar	

Fig. 1 Itemized list of most sold items at seven food retail outlets on MacArthur Boulevard

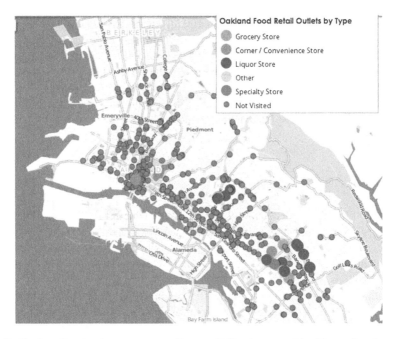

Fig. 2 Food retail outlets by type—across five east Oakland communities (*Source* Local ground;
http://www.localground.org)

Youth data on locations of grocery stores versus liquor stores and corner stores
was also generated across the five communities. Figure 2 shows the retail outlets
across all types for all five ground-truthed areas.

Figure 3 shows ground-truthing results for MacArthur and International
Boulevards with red markers indicating the youth-identified liquor stores, pink
markers identifying corner stores (categorized as stores selling primarily snack
foods but without alcohol/cigarettes), blue markers identifying specialty stores
(categorized as outlets selling primarily tobacco and tobacco related paraphernalia), and green markers identifying grocery stores (categorized as outlets selling
food staples such as milk, bread, cereal, and eggs, as well as at least 1−2 shelves-
or 10−15 different types- of fresh produce).

Figure 4 further describes the categorization of retail outlets based on indicators developed by youth researchers. On MacArthur Boulevard, youth researchers identified almost seven sites that they considered to be liquor stores or corner/
convenience stores that were typed as "grocery stores" in regulatory databases.
These facilities tended to sell primarily alcohol and cigarettes, along with chips,
sweets, soda, and sometimes milk and bread (most often whole milk and white
bread). The results for MacArthur Boulevard are not anomalous: in each ground-
truthed neighborhood, residents identified more liquor stores, corner/convenience
stores, and specialty stores than grocery stores—as enumerated in county regulatory databases.

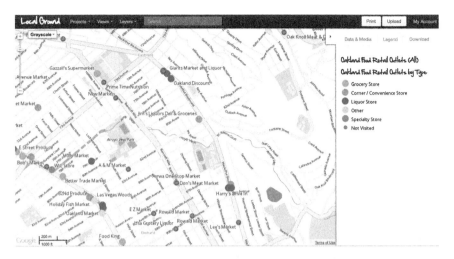

Fig. 3 Food retail outlets by type – MacArthur and international Boulevards (*Source* Local Ground; http://www.localground.org)

The collaboration felt strongly about building relationships with store owners, so during this initial problem identification phase of the project, interviews were conducted with local storeowners at 15 of the retail food outlets stores. Storeowners were at times reluctant to speak with youth who, carrying clipboards and cameras, were perceived to be "Health Auditors" or "Inspectors." In keeping with true participatory research practice, youth researchers convened, and they discussed and adapted the original research methodology, leaving their clipboards and cameras outside with an adult group leader when they intended to interview a storeowner. This strategy proved successful—and the storeowners who agreed to participate stressed the hardships of owning businesses and keeping late hours in locations that are prone to violent behavior, along with the struggles they experience to keep their businesses afloat. Merchants also pointed out that alcohol, cigarettes, and processed foods were the most profitable products they sell due to the cheap bulk price that distributors offer for these items.

To gain additional information for better defining the problem of food apartheid in East Oakland, youth researchers used the mapping platform to produce maps highlighting locations of corner stores, supermarkets/grocery stores, school locations, and relevant demographic characteristics of the community. Findings from the GIS mapping component showed that access to healthy food was indeed racialized and spatialized since the census tracts where the majority of the East Oakland youth attend school are primarily in the flatlands and predominantly African-American and Latino/a, whereas the local grocery stores are in the hillside areas more than one to two miles away where the demographics are predominantly White. Additionally, when transportation routes were overlaid on the maps, they revealed that existing public transportation often requires about 1 hour and an average of two bus transfers from the East Oakland flats to reach many of these

Store Type	Indicators	Marker
Grocery Store	More than 1 shelf of fresh produce; More than 10 types of fresh produce; Organic produce; WIC; Percentage of produce to other food/retail items greater than 30%	Green
Corner/Convenience Store	Majority of items for sale are processed foods or other retail; No Alcohol; Cigarettes may or may not be sold; Less than 1 shelf of fresh produce; Less than 10 types of fresh produce	Pink
Liquor Store	Majority of items for sale are processed foods or other retail; Alcohol sold; Cigarettes may or may not be sold; Less than 1 shelf of fresh produce; Less than 10 types of fresh produce	Red
Specialty Shop	Sells specialty items such as: tobacco products, rolling papers, and other tobacco-related paraphernalia	Dark Blue
Other	Other type of retail (i.e. automotive, clothing, etc.)	Light Blue

Fig. 4 Food retail outlets categorization—based on indicators developed by youth researchers

supermarkets—further illuminating the role that racialized geographies play in exacerbating the transportation gap and urban grocery gap.

Following the example of the ground-truthing collaborative in LA, led by researchers Sadd et al. (2013), M2M's collaborative model is based on the collective sharing, interpretation, and dissemination of research results. Following, once results were collected and verified, researchers reported back to participants in workshops. At these workshops, youth researchers were asked to compare the maps they had created with those from the county regulatory agency data. Youth researchers were then led through a question asking, analysis, and discussion activity in order to develop findings and recommendations to report back to the county regulatory agency.

Policy-Related Outcomes

The M2M collaborative has realized policy outcomes at the local, municipal, and state levels. According to those interviewed and the multiple documents reviewed, the collaborative's research and policy actions have contributed to these outcomes. The collaborative's impact on the involved youth has been detailed elsewhere (Akom et al., 2014).

The types of health-promoting changes recommended by youth researchers to help spark a food revolution in liquor/corner stores were

- Stock more fresh produce (encouraging organic and locally grown);
- Stock more healthy staple foods (for example, whole wheat bread or skim milk);
- Stock healthy products at more affordable prices through participation in food stamp, WIC and other related programs;
- Adhere to environmental standards and codes that address loitering, cleanliness, and safety;
- Limit tobacco and alcohol advertising, promotion, and sales;

To further mitigate food apartheid conditions in East Oakland, youth researchers recommended

- Locate farmers' markets in central youth-serving locations throughout East Oakland—such as at school-sites or at organizations like Youth Uprising (NOTE: this recommendation was implemented with a farmers' market at Castlemont High School launched during the 2011–12 school year).
- Examine alternate uses for empty lots prevalent throughout East Oakland— recommendations included: Pop-up farmers' market sites, urban farm sites, or future grocery store locations.

Corner store and other health-promoting recommendations were disseminated through a presentation that the M2M collaboration helped develop under the direction of lead organization I-SEEED.

The pilot store-mapping project was seen as a local success generating broad interest in replication and expansion. Community and school-based partners shared that the combination of research and media both raised awareness of the issues and influenced decision-makers to address food apartheid in preliminary ways. More specifically, in 2011 with training and ongoing technical assistance from additional school-based and community-based partners, I-SEEED led an expanded M2M pilot project statewide funded by the Robert Wood Johnson Foundation that utilized ground-truthing, the Local Ground participatory mapping platform, and Streetwyze community engagement platform, as well as targeted surveys from 168 youth across five communities in California. The surveys covered needs and desires relating to local markets, health behaviors, daily nutrition, physical activity habits, and what incentives or changes it would take to get young people to eat healthier food. Additionally, in Fall 2011, Castlemont High School launched a weekly farmers' market—featuring produce grown on the school's student-run urban farm. And in 2012, Oakland Unified School District announced a central Food Commissary in West Oakland (a community that experiences food apartheid conditions in similar ways to East Oakland) featuring a forty-four thousand square foot specialized kitchen space, four thousand square foot healthy food education center, and a 4-acre urban farm accessible to OUSD students.

Most recently, in 2014, I-SEEED secured additional funding through the Surdna Foundation, Kresge Foundation, and The California Endowment to expand use of the Streetwyze mapping tool to eight cities across the country– including Los Angeles, CA, Denver, CO, Washington, DC, and Newark, NJ—as well as to evaluate target populations like Black and Latino boys and men (Sons and Brothers) in statewide and national efforts. I-SEEED is the lead partner on these expansion plans and has local partners in each city to support scaling of the effort.

Decision-makers at the state level have credited the M2M collaborative for producing credible research evidence of food insecurity regionally and for playing a key role in persuading school district, city, and state officials of the importance of the problem and finding appropriate policy solutions. One important local policy outcome from this work was the adaptation of *The ACE Study* led by the Center for Youth Wellness in San Francisco—specifically, findings from the collaborative's work were used to re-conceptualize how social determinants of health are measured, monitored, and reported in neighborhoods in San Francisco.

A local city level decision-maker in Oakland also commented that the collaborative's research findings and youth involvement shed a lot of light on the nature and urgency of the food security problem among local officials. At the level of state policy, I-SEEED and other members of the M2M collaborative are currently working with the California Public Health Department on the Network for a Healthy California initiative to support healthy food, nutrition, and physical activity efforts throughout the state. To date, the initiative has provided funding for

- 85 local assistance contracts to qualifying school districts, local health departments, food banks, health centers, Indian tribal organizations, and other public and nonprofit entities to increase healthy food consumption, nutrition, and/or physical activity;
- 30 competitive grants for Regional Networks, non-profit organizations, and African-American faith organizations to increase healthy food consumption, nutrition, and/or physical activity;
- 12 grants to leadership and training organizations to increase healthy food consumption, nutrition, and/or physical activity;
- Bilingual advertising and public relations that support community-based health programs;
- Five tailored fruit, vegetable, and physical activity campaigns and programs (African-American, Latino, Worksite, Retail, and Children's campaigns and programs);
- Training and technical assistance to contractors and unfunded partners that serve low-income families;

The M2M collaborative is a community-driven YPAR collaboration that firmly begins to integrate the work of educational and environmental justice, with youth at the epicenter. Our collaboration has made an impressive series of policy-related victories over the past several years. These include youth-led research on the understudied problem of food apartheid in East Oakland, a successful pilot project, community outreach and education to influence community knowledge and behavior change, the development of a farmers' market at Castlemont High School, and state legislation to influence efforts across California. The success of this effort expands the potential for involving youth in participatory action research processes and ground-truthing aimed at improving the health and well-being of low-income communities, where youth of color live, learn, work, and play.

Youth Perspective

The M2M collaborative project also illustrates how principles and methods of YPAR can be adapted for use with youth in an underserved community to increase feelings of empowerment, facilitate the development of critical thinking skills, and promote social justice through social action. As stated by various interventionists and researchers (Catalano, Berglund, Ryan, Lonczak, & Hawkins, 2004), YPAR can lead to the fostering and building of competence (skills and resources for developing healthy options, developmentally appropriate skill-building activities), confidence (opportunities for making decisions, positive self-identity), connection (primary or secondary support, bonding with others, relationships with caring adults and peers), character (a sense of responsibility for self and for others), caring (a sense of belonging), and contribution to the community (participation in meaningful community work). To this list, the M2M collaborative added an emphasis on a participatory strategy of having youth identify their community concerns and then plan and engage in social action to change underlying conditions contributing to food apartheid in their communities.

Over the course of 3 years, we trained three cohorts of students and conducted extensive interviews with youth. The below table summarizes the grade, race, and gender of the students interviewed (all names are pseudonyms to protect the identity of the youth) (Fig. 5).

In student exit interviews and focus groups, youth spoke about how participation in ground-truthing activities with the M2M collaborative increased their awareness of the social and environmental determinants of health that disproportionately affect their communities generally, and themselves personally, and ultimately inspired them to take action.

As one African-American male student notes,

We went to different communities and what really stuck out to me was the huge differences that I've never noticed before in my daily life...we went inside stores and we seen them glorify and promote sales on unhealthy food, while in the wealthier community, they didn't even sell any unhealthy food at all...we, the youth, need to do something to make things more equal...more healthy....for our communities....

—LeShawn (10th Grade)

Summary of Interview Data			
Name	Grade	Race/Ethnicity	Gender
Erika	10th	African American	Female
Justice	11th	African American	Male
LeShawn	10th	African American	Male
Tony	10th	African American	Male
Javonte	10th	African American	Male
Giovanni	12th	Latino	Male
Norma	12th	Latina	Female
Maya	11th	Latina	Female
Juanita	12th	Latina	Female
Lydell	9th	African American	Male
Anthony	10th	African American	Male
Devonne	9th	African American	Female
Latisha	10th	African American	Female
Candice	11th	African American	Female
Alma	12th	Latina	Female
Marisol	9th	Latina	Female
Wilson	9th	African American	Male
Maribel	11th	Latina	Female
Jose	10th	Latino	Male
Carlos	12th	Latino	Male
Dante	10th	African American	Male
Raquel	11th	African American	Female
Carla	10th	Latina	Female
Jordan	9th	African American	Male
Muhammed	9th	Iranian-American	Male
Claudette	11th	Latina	Female
Thomas	10th	African American	Male
Wydell	10th	African American	Male
Tori	12th	African American	Female
Candia	11th	African American	Female

Fig. 5 Summary of interview data of 30 youth participants over 3 years

A Latina student expands on her peer's statement about how the mapping process can crystallize understanding of food apartheid and structural racism. She speaks more specifically about how the processes of ground-truthing and mapping give community-voice and community-driven data a platform to be considered as "valid" as other sources of data and—ultimately—a vehicle for change:

It was very interesting, to finally show people what's actually happening, because if you're not aware of it, then you don't really know what to fix, but once you finally find what the problem is you realize that you can do something to fix it.

—Norma (12th Grade)

Her African-American female classmate also shared her feelings on how the ground-truthing and mapping process not only changed her awareness of food apartheid but also influenced others in her community as well as policymakers:

> It makes people that are oblivious open up their eyes to what's really happening. It's like a wake-up call.

—Candia (11th Grade)

The M2M collaborative stressed principles of relevance—or starting where the youth are—participation, and the importance of creating environments in which individuals and youth become empowered as they increase their community understanding and problem-solving abilities. As evidenced through these stories/quotes from the young people involved in the M2M project—as well as the policy-related outcomes in the earlier section—we believe that YPAR and ground-truthing provide an effective foundation to achieve positive, and participatory, individual and community-change.

Limitations

As YPAR and CBPR scholars have previously noted, there exist constraints with utilizing a YPAR methodological approach (Minkler, 2005). For example, outside researchers committed to a YPAR approach could experience difficulty in moving from the goal of heavy community partner involvement in the research process to the reality of implementation. More specifically, even though researchers may have a strong commitment to involving the most marginalized and vulnerable classes, such individuals often are "least likely to be in a position to donate their time and energy" (Minkler, 2005). Equally problematic is the situation when community desires—in regard to research methods, design, data collection and ownership—conflict with what researchers consider to be "sound science." Importantly, while YPAR (and other CBPR-based methodologies) does not require "abandoning" scientific standards or theoretical bases, it does advocate for a genuine co-development, co-learning, and co-benefiting process through which both local and scientific ways of knowing are valued (Minkler, 2005).

A final issue in community building and organizing specifically with youth involves the key role of older facilitators/researchers, who can both spark participant empowerment and decision making, and provide structure and guidance to help the group and its social action efforts move forward. Advanced training for the facilitators/researchers proved critical to this project's success. Facilitators/researchers also needed a clear understanding of their role and how to serve as the holder of vision of the project when a group was stuck. Ongoing dialogue between facilitators/researchers and youth—as well as frequent opportunities to debrief/discuss how to handle difficult situations—are also essential to effective community-organizing and community-building work with youth (Wilson et al., 2007; Wilson, Minkler, Dasho, Wallerstein, & Martin, 2008).

Our results reinforced the need to take a more holistic approach to environmental equity research, spanning beyond looking at a single indicator of health (i.e., food access). As better data become available, future studies should move away from locational and single-indicator analysis (food access) and toward a cumulative exposure approach (across several assets, challenges, pollutants, and opportunities) that better answers the question of what disparities in exposure mean cumulatively for potential inequities in health and educational risks. Of course, the use of risk assessment, even within an equity analysis framework, remains controversial among the public and policymakers alike. We sought to improve the use of risk assessment by using it comparatively to assess the distribution of risk due to lack of access to healthy food among diverse communities.

Conclusion

In South Africa, pervasive racism, discrimination, and degradation faced by Blacks and other ethnic minorities grew out of a legalized system of governance that discriminated against Black South Africans. Though apartheid has officially ended, there is no doubt that racism is still deeply rooted in the country. Similarly, the American legacy of residential segregation and institutionalized racism is woven into all aspects of daily life for Black and Brown communities. As a direct result of the high degree of racial isolation created by segregation, growing up in a Black or Brown neighborhood today increases the likelihood of dropping out of high school, reduces the probability of persisting through college, lowers employment opportunities, reduces income earned as an adult, lowers access to healthy foods, increases risk of obesity, heart disease, and diabetes, and ultimately leads to death at an early age—or as we call it, death due to "un-natural causes" (Bell & Lee, 2011). But Black and Brown communities are fighting back with resistance, agency, and political contestation through the use of new technology tools designed to engage, integrate, and elevate community voice.

In this chapter, we introduce the concept of food apartheid and use YPAR to demonstrate how the schooling and sustainability movement can better attend to issues of social equity—and how the environmental justice movement can better articulate community-driven, sustainable, alternatives for youth of color inside and outside of urban schools. Moreover, it is our hope that the concept of food apartheid may create stronger and more effective political alliances between the two movements. These theoretical and practical alliances depend on a deeper understanding of how racial and economic inequality affects the production and consumption of food and how the production, distribution, and consumption of food impact educational and environmental health outcomes.

Theoretically, a food apartheid framework links food access to broader questions of race, power, identity, educational equity, and community defense. Access to healthy food is shaped not only by purchasing power—the economic ability to purchase it—but also by the historical processes through which race has come to shape schools, neighborhoods, and access to social services. Because it highlights institutional racism and racialized geographies, food apartheid may therefore encourage the schooling and sustainability movement to embrace more community and culturally responsive approaches to social justice (Tintiangco-Cubales et al., 2014)

Building off the CBPR work of researchers Sadd et al. (2013), our YPAR approach sought to extend the rigor, relevance, and reach of food apartheid research in the following ways (as outlined by Sadd et al. (2013)):

Rigor is the practice of ensuring that a co-production model is utilized in all phases of the research process (Coburn, 2002).

Relevance outlines whether community-driven research involves questions that the community themselves developed in partnership with researchers and scientists; inquiries that community members deem relevant; and research that provides opportunities for collective action.

Reach refers to the degree to which local knowledge is re-introduced back to the community itself as well as more broadly to diverse audiences and is translated into useful tools and products to improve research, practice, policy, and community transformation processes (Sadd et al., 2013)

Both the Streetwyze and Local Ground platforms coupled with ground-truthing seek to achieve rigor, relevance, and reach by using innovative community-driven technology platforms to uncover gaps in regulatory agency data, raise important food security issues at local scales, and provide fuel for preventative policy initiatives. In particular, Streetwyze's community-driven platform supplements regulatory data, which is often riddled with significant geographical inaccuracies and gaps. It also documents and makes real the concept of Eco-Apartheid or cumulative causation—in other words, the extent to which communities are overburdened with multiple environmental health hazards and social stressors (Akom, 2011a). Most importantly, Streetwyze empowers community members to examine and improve the accuracy of regulatory data that facilitates productive "street science" and dialogue between youth researchers, academics, and regulatory officials.

This chapter follows in a long line of CBPR research (Corburn, 2002; Minkler, 2005; Sadd et al., 2013) and demonstrates that validating secondary data through YPAR can be a powerful approach for community transformation and policy change as well as improve the relevance, rigor, and reach of scientific work. Using tools like Local Ground and Streetwyze, ground-truthing was an engaging and effective way to meet the collective goals of building community capacity, improving the accuracy of environmental data, strengthening academic engagement, and developing community-based solutions to environmental and social justice issues.

References

Akom, A. A. (2008). Ameritocracy and infra-racial racism: Racializing social and cultural reproduction theory in the twenty-first century. *Race Ethnicity and Education, 11*(3), 205–230.

Akom, A. A. (2009a). Critical race theory meets participatory action research: Creating a community of youth as public intellectuals. In W. Ayers, T. Quinn, & D. Stovall (Eds.), *Social Justice in education handbook* (pp. 508–521). New York: Erlbaum Press.

Akom, A. A. (2009b). Research for Liberation: Du Bois, the Chicago School, and the Development of Black Emancipatory Action Research. In N. S. Anderson & H. Kharem (Eds.), *Education as a practice of freedom: African American educational thought and ideology* (pp. 193–212). New York: Lexington Press.

Akom, A. A. (2011a). Eco-apartheid: Linking environmental health to educational outcomes. *Teachers College Record, 113*(4), 831–859.

Akom, A. A. (2011b). Black emancipatory action research: integrating a theory of structural racialisation into ethnographic and participatory action research methods. *Ethnography and Education, 6*(1), 113–131.

Akom A. A., Scott, A., & Shah, A. (2013). Rethinking resistance theory through STEM Education: How working class kids get world class careers. In Tuck, E., & Yang, K. W. (Eds.), *Youth Resistance Research and Theories of Change*. Routledge.

Akom, A. A., Shah, A., & Nakai, A. (2014). Visualizing change: Using technology and participatory research to engage youth in urban planning and health promotion. In H. Hall, C. C. Robinson, & A. Kohli (Eds.), *Uprooting urban America: Multidisciplinary Perspectives on race*. Peter Lang. New York: Class and Gentrification.

Akom, A. A., Cammarota, J., & Ginwright, S. (2008). Youthtopias: Towards a new paradigm of critical youth studies. *Youth Media Reporter, 2*(4), 1–30.

Alkon, A. H., & Norgaard, K. M. (2009). Breaking the food chains: An investigation of food justice activism. *Sociological Inquiry, 79*(3), 289–305.

Alter, D. A., & Eny, K. (2005). The relationship between the supply of fast-food chains and cardiovascular outcomes. *Canadian Journal of Public Health/Revue Canadienne de Sante'e Publique*, 173–177.

Anderson, E. (1990). *Streetwise: Race, class, and change in an urban community*. Chicago: Univ.

Balazs, C. L., Morello-Frosch, R., Hubbard, A. E., & Ray, I. (2012). Implications of arsenic contamination in California's San Joaquin Valley: A cross-sectional, cluster-design examining exposure and compliance in community drinking water systems. *Environ. Health, 11*, 84.

Basch, C. (2010). Healthier students are better learners: A mission link in school reforms to close the achievement gap. The Campaign for Educational Equity, Teachers College, Columbia University, p. 50. Retrieved from http://www.equitycampaign.org/i/a/document/12557_equit ymattersvol6_web03082010.pdf.

Bell, J., & Lee, M. M. (2011). Why Place and race matter: Impacting health through a focus on race and place. *Report. Policy Link, Oakland, CA*. http://www.policylink.org/atf/cf/% 7B97c6d565-bb43-406d-a6d5-eca3bbf35af0%7D/WPRM%20FULL%20REPORT,20

Belot, M., & James, J. (2011). Healthy school meals and educational outcomes. *Journal of Health Economics, 303*(3), 489–504.

Black, T. (Producer), & Muccino, G. (Director). (2006). *Pursuit of happyness*. United States: Columbia TriStar Motion Picture Group.

Block, J. P., Scribner, R. A., & DeSalvo, K. B. (2004). Fast food, race/ethnicity, and income: A geographic analysis. *American Journal of Preventive Medicine, 27*(3), 211–217.

Brownell, K. D., & Horgen, K. B. (2004). *Food fight: The inside story of the food industry, America's obesity crisis, and what we can do about it* (p. 69). Chicago: Contemporary Books.

"Building Healthy Communities: East Oakland Health Profile". (2011). UCLA Center for Health Policy Research. Retrieved from http://www.calendow.org/uploadedFiles/Health_Happends_ Here/Communities/Our_Places/BHC%20Fact_Sheet_E%20Oakland.pdf.

Bonilla-Silva, E. (2001). *White supremacy and racism in the post-civil rights era*. Boulder, CO: Lynne Rienner.

Bullard, R. (1990). *Dumping in Dixie: Race, class, and environmental quality*. Boulder, CO: Westview Press.

Bullard, R. D., Johnson, G. S., & Torres, A. O. (Eds.). (2004). *Transportation racism and new routes to equity*. Cambridge, MA: South End Press.

Catalano, R. F., Berglund, M. L., Ryan, J. A., Lonczak, H. S., & Hawkins, J. D. (2004). Positive youth development in the United States: Research findings on evaluations of positive youth development programs. *The annals of the American academy of political and social science, 591*(1), 98–124.

Camino, L. (2005). Pitfalls and promising practices of youth–adult partnerships: An evaluator's reflections. *Journal of Community Psychology, 33*(1), 75–85.

Cammarota, J., & Fine, M. (Eds.). (2010). *Revolutionizing education: Youth participatory action research in motion*. Routledge.

Cohen, B. E. (2002). *Community food security assessment toolkit* (pp. 02–013). Washington, DC: US Department of Agriculture, Economic Research Service.

Coleman-Jensen, et al. (2013). Household Food Security in the United States 2012. US Department of Agriculture Economic Research Service. Retrieved from http://www.ers.usda. gov/publications/err-economic-research-report/err155.aspx#.Uml1LCS4B_k.

Corburn, J. (2002). Combining community-based research and local knowledge to confront asthma and subsistence-fishing hazards in Greenpoint/Williamsburg, Brooklyn. *New York. Environmental Health Perspectives, 110*(Suppl 2), 241.

Corburn, J. (2005). *Street science: Community knowledge and environmental health justice*. Cambridge, MA: MIT Press.

Corburn, J., Osleeb, J., & Porter, M. (2006). Urban asthma and the neighbourhood environment in New York City. *Health & Place, 12*(2), 167–179.

Darden, J. T. (1986). The residential segregation of Blacks in Detroit, 1960–1970. *International Journal of Comparative Sociology, 17*(1–2), 84–91.

Drewnowski, A., & Specter, S. E. (2004). Poverty and obesity: the role of energy density and energy costs. *The American journal of clinical nutrition, 79*(1), 6–16.

Duncan-Andrade, J. M. R., & Morrell, E. (2008). *The art of critical pedagogy: Possibilities for moving from theory to practice in urban schools* (Vol. 285). Peter Lang.

Ecotrust (2011). The Impacts of Seven Cents. Retrieved from http://www.ecotrust.org/farmtosch ool/downloads/Kaiser-ReportFINAL_110630.pdf.

Farley, R., Steeh, C., Krysan, M., Jackson, T., & Reeves, K. (1994). Stereotypes and segregation: Neighborhoods in the Detroit area. *American Journal of Sociology, 100*, 750–780.

Fergus, E., Noguera, P. A., & Martin, M. (2014). *Schooling for resilience: Improving the life trajectory of Black and Latino boys*. Cambridge, MA: Harvard Education Press.

Florence, M., Asbridge, M., & Veugelers, P. (2008). Diet Quality and Academic Performance. *Journal of School Health* 78(4), p. 213. Retrieved from onlinelibrary.wiley.com/doi/10.1111/ j.1746-1561.2008.00288.x/abstract.

French, S. A., Harnack, L., & Jeffery, R. W. (2000). Fast food restaurant use among women in the Pound of Prevention study: dietary, behavioral and demographic correlates. *International journal of obesity and related metabolic disorders: journal of the International Association for the Study of Obesity, 24*(10), 1353–1359.

Freudenburg, W. R. (2005). Privileged access, privileged accounts: Toward a socially structured theory of resources and discourses. *Social Forces, 84*(1), 89–114.

Greene, A. Brain Food for Children. Center for Ecoliteracy. Retrieved from http://www.ecoliteracy. org/essays/brain-food-kids.

Ginwright, S. A., Noguera, P., & Cammarota, J. (Eds.). (2006). *Beyond resistance!: Youth activism and community change: New democratic possibilities for practice and policy for America's youth*. Routledge.

Gottlieb, R., & Fisher, A. (1996). "First feed the face": Environmental justice and community food security. *Antipode, 28*(2), 193–203.

Hacker, A. (1992). *Two Nations: African American and White*. Hostile, Unequal: Separate.

Hall, H., Robinson, C. C., & Kohli, A. (Eds.). (2014). *Uprooting urban America: Multidisciplinary perspectives on race*. New York: Class and Gentrification. Peter Lang.

Hensrud, D. D., & Klein, S. (2006, October). Extreme obesity: a new medical crisis in the United States. In *Mayo Clinic Proceedings* (Vol. 81, No. 10, pp. S5–S10). Elsevier.

Heynen, N. (2009). Bending the bars of empire from every ghetto for survival: The Black Panther Party's radical antihunger politics of social reproduction and scale. *Annals of the Association of American Geographers, 99*(2), 406–422.

Jakle, J. A., & Sculle, K. A. (2002). *Fast food: Roadside restaurants in the automobile age*. JHU Press.

Jackson, C. L., Szklo, M., Yeh, H. C., Wang, N. Y., Dray-Spira, R., Thorpe, R., & Brancati, F. L. (2013). Black-white disparities in overweight and obesity trends by educational attainment in the United States, 1997–2008. *Journal of obesity, 2013*.

Jeffery, R. W., Baxter, J., McGuire, M., & Linde, J. (2006). Are fast food restaurants an environmental risk factor for obesity? *International Journal of Behavioral Nutrition and Physical Activity, 3*(1), 2.

Kaplan, S., & Morris, J. (2000). Kids at risk. Chemicals in the environment come under scrutiny as the number of childhood learning problems soars. *US News & World Report, 128*(24), 46.

Krieger, N. (1999). Embodying inequality: A review of concepts, measures, and methods for studying health consequences of discrimination. *International Journal of Health Services, 29*, 295–352.

Kwate, N. O. A. (2008). Fried chicken and fresh apples: Racial segregation as a fundamental cause of fast food density in black neighborhoods. *Health & Place, 14*(1), 32–44.

LaVeist, T. A. (2003). Racial segregation and longevity among African Americans: An individual-level analysis. *Health Services Research, 38*(6p2), 1719–1734.

Lewis, L. B., Sloane, D. C., Nascimento, L. M., Diamant, A. L., Guinyard, J. J., Yancey, A. K., & Flynn, G. (2005). African Americans' access to healthy food options in South Los Angeles restaurants. *Journal Information, 95*(4).

Link, B. G., & Phelan, J. (1995). Social conditions as fundamental causes of disease. *Journal of Health and Social Behavior*, 80–94.

MacLeod, J. (1995). *Ain't no makin' it: Aspirations and attainment in a low-income neighborhood*. Boulder, CO: Westview Press. (Original work published 1987).

Marable, M. (2000). *How capitalism underdeveloped Black America: Problems in race, political economy, and society* (Vol. 4). Pluto Press.

Massey, D., & Denton, N. (1993). *American apartheid: Segregation and the making of the underclass*. Cambridge, MA: Harvard University Press.

Michman, R. D., & Mazze, E. M. (1998). *The food industry wars: Marketing triumphs and blunders*. Greenwood Publishing Group.

Minkler, M. (2005). Community-based research partnerships: Challenges and opportunities. *Journal of Urban Health, 82*, ii3–ii12.

Morello-Frosch, R., Pastor, M, Jr, & Sadd, J. (2002). Integrating environmental justice and the precautionary principle in research and policy-making: The case of ambient air toxic exposures and health risks among schoolchildren in Los Angeles. *Annals of the American Academy of Political and Social Science, 584*, 47–68.

Morello-Frosch, R., Zuk, M., Jerrett, M., Shamasunder, B., & Kyle, A. D. (2011). Understanding the cumulative impacts of inequalities in environmental health: Implications for policy. *Health Affairs, 30*(5), 879–887.

Morrell, E. (2008). *Critical literacy and urban youth: Pedagogies of access, dissent, and liberation.* New York: Routledge.

Morland, K., Wing, S., Diez Roux, A., & Poole, C. (2002). Neighborhood characteristics associated with the location of food stores and food service places. *American Journal of Preventive Medicine, 22*(1), 23–29.

Morland, K., Diez Roux, A. V., & Wing, S. (2006). Supermarkets, other food stores, and obesity: The atherosclerosis risk in communities study. *American Journal of Preventive Medicine, 30*(4), 333–339.

Nasir, N. I. S., Rosebery, A. S., Warren, B., & Lee, C. D. (2006). Learning as a cultural process: Achieving equity through diversity. *The Cambridge handbook of the learning sciences,* pp. 489–504.

National Center for Health Statistics US. (2013). Special feature on emergency care. Retrieved from: http://www.cdc.gov/nchs/data/hus/hus12.pdf.

Nielsen (2014). Multiplying Mobile: How Multicultural Consumers are Leading Smartphone Adoption. Retreived from http://www.nielsen.com/us/en/insights/news/2014/multiplying-mobile-how-multicultural-consumers-are-leading-smartphone-adoption.html.

Ogden, C. L., Carroll, M. D., Kit, B. K., & Flegal, K. M. (2013). Prevalence of obesity among adults: United States, 2011-2012. *NCHS Data Brief, 131,* 1–8.

Omi, M., & Winant, H. (2004). Racial formations. *Race, class, and gender in the United States, 6,* 13–22.

Parikh, T. S., et al. (2006). *Mobile phones and paper documents: Evaluating a new approach for capturing microfinance data in rural India* (pp. 551–560). Montréal, Canada.

Pastor, M. (2000). *Regions that work: How cities and suburbs can grow together.* University of Minnesota Press.

Pastor, M, Jr, Sadd, J. L., & Morello-Frosch, R. (2002). Who's minding the kids? Pollucion, public schools, and environmental justice in Los Angeles. *Social Science Quarterly, 83*(1), 263–280.

Patel, M., Sotsky, J., Gourley, S., & Houghton, D. (2013). The emergence of civic tech: Investments in a growing field. *The Knight Foundation,* December 2013.

Powell, L. (2014). The Legacy and Future of School Food Reform. *Healthy Schools Campaign.* Retrieved from http://www.healthyschoolscampaign.org/blog/guest-blog-the-legacy-and-future-of-school-food-reform.

Powell, J. A. (2008). Race, place and opportunity. *The American Prospect,* September 22.

Pulido, L. (2000). Rethinking environmental racism: White privilege and urban development in Southern California. *Annals of the Association of American Geographers, 90*(1), 12–40.

Reece, J., Norris, D., Olinger, J., Holley, K., & Martin, M. (2013). Place matters: Using mapping to plan for opportunity, equity, and sustainability. Kirwan Institute at The Ohio State University.

Ruglis, J., & Freudenberg, N. (2010). Toward a healthy high schools movement: strategies for mobilizing public health for educational reform. *American Journal of Public Health, 100*(9), 1565.

Sadd, J., Morello-Frosch, R., Pastor, M., Matsuoka, M., Prichard, M., & Carter, V. (2013). The truth, the whole truth, and nothing but the ground-truth methods to advance environmental justice and researcher–community partnerships. *Health Education & Behavior,* 1090198113511816.

Self, R. O. (2005). *American Babylon: Race and the struggle for postwar Oakland.* Princeton University Press.

Sharkey, J. R., & Horel, S. (2008). Neighborhood socioeconomic deprivation and minority composition are associated with better potential spatial access to the ground-truthed food environment in a large rural area. *The Journal of Nutrition, 138*(3), 620–627.

Smith, L. T. (1999). *Decolonizing methodologies: Research and indigenous peoples.* Zed books.

Stone, M. K., Brown, K., Weiden, W., & Barlow, Z. (2014). *Making the case for healthy, freshly prepared school lunch.* Berkeley, CA: Center for Ecoliteracy.

Sze, J., & London, J. K. (2008). Environmental justice at the crossroads. *Social Compass, 2*, 133–164.

Tintiangco-Cubales, A., Kohli, R., Sacramento, J., Henning, N., Agarwal-Rangnath, R., & Sleeter, C. (2014). Toward an ethnic studies pedagogy: implications for K-12 schools from the research. *The Urban Review*, 1–22.

Tuck, E., & Yang, K. W. (Eds.). (2013). Youth resistance research and theories of change. Routledge.

Van Wart, S., Tsai, K. J., & Parikh, T. (2010). Local ground: A paper-based toolkit for documenting local geo-spatial knowledge. In *Proceedings of the First ACM Symposium on Computing for Development* (p. 11). ACM.

Vásquez, V. B., Lanza, D., Hennessey-Lavery, S., Facente, S., Halpin, H. A., & Minkler, M. (2007). Addressing food security through public policy action in a community-based participatory research partnership. *Health Promotion Practice, 8*(4), 342–349.

Wallerstein, N. B., & Duran, B. (2006). Using community-based participatory research to address health disparities. *Health Promotion Practice, 7*(3), 312–323.

Williams, D. R. (1996). Race/ethnicity and socioeconomic status: Measurement and methodological issues. *International Journal of Health Services, 36*, 483–505.

Williams, D. R. (1999). Race, socioeconomic status, and health: The added effects of racism and discrimination. *Annals of the New York Academy of Sciences, 896*, 173–188.

Williams, D. R., & Collins, C. (2001). Racial residential segregation: a fundamental cause of racial disparities in health. *Public Health Reports, 116*(5), 404.

Wilson, N., Dasho, S., Martin, A. C., Wallerstein, N., Wang, C. C., & Minkler, M. (2007). Engaging young adolescents in social action through photovoice the youth empowerment strategies (YES!) project. *The Journal of Early Adolescence, 27*(2), 241–261.

Wilson, N., Minkler, M., Dasho, S., Wallerstein, N., & Martin, A. C. (2008). Getting to social action: The youth empowerment strategies (YES!) project. *Health Promotion Practice, 9*(4), 395–403.

Wrigley, N., Warm, D., & Margetts, B. (2003). Deprivation, diet, and food-retail access: findings from the Leedsfood deserts' study. *Environment and Planning A, 35*(1), 151–188.

Zenk, S. N., Schulz, A. J., Israel, B. A., James, S. A., Bao, S., & Wilson, M. L. (2005). Neighborhood racial composition, neighborhood poverty, and the spatial accessibility of supermarkets in metropolitan Detroit. *Journal Information, 95*(4).

Part III
Complicating Racial Histories and Racial Categories

Charter Schooling, Race Politics, and an Appeal to History

Lisa M. Stulberg

The November 2013 election of New York City Mayor Bill de Blasio renewed and reenergized a public discussion of the legitimacy, effectiveness, and future of public charter schools in New York City and the country. Yet academics, policymakers, and the general public now seem no more able to have a complex, productive, honest conversation about charter schooling than they were when the reform began. The debate's current iteration is just as contentious, the sides just as deaf to each other's critiques and claims, and the empirical evidence about the experience and impact of charter schools just as likely to be dismissed by both sides. We seem not to have made much progress in developing a nuanced discussion about a politically and educationally complex reform.

I believe that history has much left to teach us as we search for ways of talking about, learning from, and making public policy decisions regarding present-day charter schooling. This is especially the case, as I will detail here, when it comes to understanding the race politics of charter schools, especially for African Americans.

In the mid-1990s I was a political progressive (as I am now); a Ph.D. student in sociology at the University of California at Berkeley; and a strong believer in racial integration, public schooling, and labor rights. I was not predisposed to be sympathetic to the charter school concept, a new reform at the time.

This chapter was adapted with permission from Stulberg, L. M. (2015). African American school choice and the current race politics of charter schooling: Lessons from history. *Race and Social Problems, 7*(1), 31–42. Springer New York.

L.M. Stulberg (✉)
Steinhardt School of Culture, Education, and Human Development,
New York University, 246 Greene Street, 3rd Floor, New York, NY 10003, USA
e-mail: lms9@nyu.edu

Yet, through my work with an afterschool program at a middle school in West
Oakland, California, I came to be involved in the founding of a college preparatory, explicitly African American-centered charter school called the West Oakland
Community School (WOCS). When I was asked to be part of the WOCS founding
group, I decided to study the race and school choice politics as they intersected
at WOCS and in the public debate around charter schooling. I wanted to understand where charter schools came from, both educationally and politically, and
I was surprised to learn about a number of non-desegregation focused efforts in
African American education that I had not encountered in any urban education or
sociology of education courses I had taken. Participating in the building of WOCS
gave me a more nuanced view of charters than I would have had from afar (given
my politics, I would have been quicker to dismiss the reform for many of the reasons I detail below). In addition, learning more about these historical examples of
African American schooling helped me understand the complicated politics of the
charter school that I was a part of building. It also helped me situate the charter
reform in a broader politics of race and schooling for African Americans that did
not allow me to easily dismiss or fully embrace this form of school choice.

In the discussion that follows, drawing on my ethnographic and historical archi-
val data, I will argue that a full understanding of charter schools that serve African
American students requires a look at the historical roots of African American
school choice. While scholarly and public conversations tend to connect school
choice to the evasion of desegregation after the *Brown* decision, there is another,
lesser known historical narrative that is important and illuminating. Particularly
informed by the community-based charter school that I helped to found, the public
school community control movement in New York City in the late 1960s, the
African American independent school movement, and the Council of Independent
Black Institutions (CIBI) in the 1970s, I find that history helps us better understand the dynamics of race and school choice. We can understand that African
American parent and educator commitment to desegregated schooling is complex
and certainly not unwavering; that the distinction between *public* and *private* in
public education is quite murky; that the definition of community for purposes of
building schools is complicated; and that strange bedfellows in African American
education are nothing new.[1]

Charter Schools and Their Historical Predecessors

The West Oakland Community School began as a response to the failure of the
Oakland Unified School District to serve its African American students. WOCS
was also a response to race politics at the time in California, especially a retreat
from race-conscious remedies to inequality, like affirmative action. The WOCS

---

[1]My discussion here draws on data and arguments that I have presented in other places, as well,
in the earlier years of the charter reforms. See Stulberg (2004, 2008).

founding group was convened by Marjorie Wilkes, an African American woman then in her 30s who had started her career at the New York City teachers' union and who did school reform work in the East Bay. The group of, initially, 14 people that Wilkes put together was comprised primarily of professionals who worked in education in the Bay Area in some capacity, as teachers or administrators, founders of youth programs, researchers, policy advocates, or as parents and community activists. The core group was almost entirely African American, except for me and for one Asian American woman, Akiyu Hatano, a teacher who eventually became WOCS's founding principal.

The group worked for 3 years to plan the small charter school. Founders decided that the school should focus explicitly on African American students, and that its mission should be to prepare students for college, to tie academic achievement to community building, and to nurture leaders who would fight for racial and economic justice. The school had an explicit social change mission, reflecting the political commitments of the founders and their assessment that this was needed to disrupt the substantial disempowerment of African American students and families in West Oakland (Task Force, 1996). WOCS opened its doors in September 1999 with 50 sixth-grade students (see Stulberg, 2008).

When the WOCS group came together in 1996, the charter reform was relatively new. The charter mechanism is a *governance* reform, not an endorsement of a particular curriculum or pedagogical approach. Charter schools are independent public schools of choice that gain a certain degree of autonomy in exchange for increased accountability for student achievement, fiscal responsibility, and the fulfillment of their particular missions. State laws vary significantly, but charter schools in most states have flexibility over hiring and firing and are not required to employ unionized teachers and administrators. Charters also are governed by independent boards and have substantial flexibility over budgets and their programming and curricula. The first charter legislation was enacted in Minnesota in 1991, followed by similar legislation in California in 1992 (see, e.g., Nathan, 1996a; National Center for Education Statistics, 2014).

The charter reform has grown substantially in the past two decades. When the WOCS group convened, during the 1996–1997 school year, there were 432 charter schools in the country (RPP International, 2000, p. 11). By 1999–2000, there were 0.3 million students in 1,500 charter schools nationwide (National Center for Education Statistics, 2014). By the 2011–2012 school year, the last year for which I could find data that I consider nonpartisan, there were ~5,700 charter schools, comprising 5.8 % of all U.S. public schools, and there was charter legislation on the books in 42 states plus the District of Columbia (though no operating charters in Maine or Washington state). In 2011–2012, there were ~2.1 million students enrolled in charter schools, ~4.2 % of all students in public schools nationwide (National Center for Education Statistics, 2014). The percentage of public school students in charter schools varies substantially by district and state. As of 2011–2012, compared to the U.S. states, the District of Columbia had the highest proportion of public school students attending charter schools, 39 % or 29,000 students (National Center for Education Statistics, 2014). New Orleans, which experienced a state takeover of most of the city's schools after the devastation of Hurricane Katrina, shifted to an all-charter model in the state-controlled Recovery School District in the fall of 2014. This is the first time that a district is comprised entirely of charter schools (Layton, 2014). Overall, nationwide, (there is substantial state-by-state variation), charter schools serve a greater proportion of African American, Latino, and low-income students than public schools as a whole. There is a particularly large disparity for African American students, who, in 2010–2011, made up 16 % of all U.S. public school students and 29 % of charter school students (Center for Research on Education Outcomes, 2013, p. 16).

Despite overblown claims on all sides of the public conversation, charter schools as a whole are neither a panacea nor a public shame. There is now some "convergence" of opinion, despite complexity and debate in methodological approaches (Henig, 2008, p. 92; also see Carnoy, Jacobsen, Mishel, & Rothstein, 2005), that charter schools tend to look like traditional public schools in the varied way they serve students: some are excellent, some are awful, and many are somewhere in between. National and state-by-state comparative studies find that charter schools report mixed results (e.g., Center for Research on Education Outcomes, 2013, 2013; and for a review of these studies see, e.g., Frankenberg, Siegel-Hawley, & Wang, 2010). Yet an unparalleled national study conducted by the independent Center for Research on Education Outcomes (CREDO), found that charter school performance is improving relative to traditional district schooling. The most recent 2013 CREDO study, which focuses on states that serve 95 % of all charter school students nationwide (p. 15), also indicates that charter school test score benefits are especially pronounced (and growing over time) for some students who are most underserved by traditional public schools: African American students, low-income students, and English language learners (pp. 32–39). These benefits are particularly pronounced for low-income, urban African American and Latino students (pp. 65–69).[2]

While there is substantial district and state variation in charter school demographics and performance (Frankenberg et al., 2010), it may be instructive to look a bit more closely at one example: New York City. In 2012, charter schools served ~47,000 students out of ~1.1 million students total in the district. Charter schools in the city are primarily located in Harlem, the South Bronx, and Central Brooklyn. In 2010–2011, charter school students were 3.9 % of all public school students in the city and 9.2 % of all public school students in these three areas. The proportion for the city as a whole now might be closer to 6 % (Editorial Board, 2014; Kahlenberg & Potter, 2014b). In this same year, 2010–2011, approximately

---

[2]For instance, in its study of 25 states, the District of Columbia, and New York City, a study of more than 95 % of all charter school students in the country, CREDO found that low-income African American students in charter schools make gains that are equivalent to 29 additional days of reading instruction and 36 days of math instruction when compared with their peers in traditional public schools (p. 65). For low-income Latino students in charter schools, the gains are the equivalent of 14 instructional days of reading and 22 days of math–though the pattern is reversed for *non*-low income Latino students, whose academic performance seems to benefit from enrollment in traditional public schools (p. 68).

three-quarters of New York City's charter school students were from low-income backgrounds. The lowest income families, those who qualify for free lunch, were slightly underrepresented in the city's charter schools (65.2 % of all charter students vs. 67.6 % of all students in district schools). African American students are substantially overrepresented in the city's charters. Approximately 30 % of the district's students are African American, yet more than 60 % of the city's charter school students are African American (data from this paragraph, unless otherwise noted, can be found in New York City Charter School Center, 2012).

As is the case nationwide, charter school performance in New York City indicates that the public schools of choice have mixed results relative to traditional district schools. We can look at some comparative data on state tests in the first year that the tests were tied to Common Core State Standards, 2012–2013. In this year, overall 34.8 % of the city's charter school students scored advanced or proficient on math tests in grades 3–8, compared with 29.6 % of students in district schools. On ELA tests, though, in 2012–2013, only 25.0 % of charter school students in grades 3–8 scored advanced or proficient on state tests, compared with 26.4 % of their district counterparts. There is some evidence that charter schools do better on these tests when compared with their "peer" schools (New York City Charter School Center, 2013, p. 1).

How can we understand the origins and development of the charter reform? As I have written about elsewhere (Stulberg, 2004, 2008), charter schooling developed on the heels of a number of forms of public and private school choices: the public and private alternative school movement of the 1970s, the public magnet school efforts also of the 1970s, and the private voucher reforms that were beginning to gain real political traction at the end of the 1980s. In fact, charters, in many states like California, were a political compromise in the face of growing support for private vouchers (Stulberg, 2008, p. 96).[3]

The charter reform also can trace its roots to a number of grassroots movements for social and educational justice. In my work (Stulberg, 2008), I have identified two particular African American-centered school-based movements that I believe are direct historical precursors to charter schools like WOCS. The first is the public school movement for community control in New York City in the late 1960s. A number of excellent books have chronicled this movement, which centered in Ocean Hill–Brownsville, Brooklyn (e.g., Perlstein, 2004; Podair, 2002).

By the mid-1960s, after years of broken promises from New York City leaders on school desegregation and bolstered by a growing Black Power movement, African American and Latino parents and education activists in East Harlem and Ocean Hill–Brownsville, Brooklyn demanded change. They urged that if the city was not going to truly provide desegregated options then it should give them control of their schools—control of budget, staffing, and curriculum and

---

[3]Ravitch (2014) asserts that charter schools made vouchers more politically palatable, writing: "The charter movement paved the way for the resurgence of the voucher movement, as its advocates insisted that 'choice' was far more important than investing in public education" (p. 316). I believe it was primarily the other way around.

programming. With the backing of a politically disparate group of supporters from the Ford Foundation to the Republican mayor John Lindsay, these community control supporters organized three demonstration districts around the city, comprised of intermediate schools and their small groups of feeder elementary schools (e.g., five schools in East Harlem and eight total schools in Ocean Hill–Brownsville). Community-elected governing boards hired new principals and many new teachers who supported this experiment in community control, and set about devising new, culturally relevant, social justice-oriented curricula.

The community control experiment came to a head when the governing board in Ocean Hill dismissed a group of union-affiliated teachers and administrators that they felt were not supportive of the reform. The United Federation of Teachers called citywide teachers strikes that virtually shut down more than 900 city schools for much of the fall of 1968 and garnered substantial national attention (Berube & Gittell, 1969). The controversial experiment did not last long in the city. By the spring of 1969, Albany lawmakers had passed a decentralization bill for New York City that broke the schools into ~30 local districts across the city, effectively subsuming the demonstration districts (Gittell, 1969).

Frustrated with the short-lived nature of the public school community control movement and still feeling stifled by the public nature of this reform, some African American education activists urged a private form of educational self-determination instead. Out of the public school community control movement in places grew the African American independent school movement and one of its primarily organizational actors, the Council of Independent Black Institutions (CIBI), which was founded in 1972 (Shujaa & Afrik, 1996). CIBI and these private alternatives are a second historical antecedent to charter schools like WOCS (Stulberg, 2008). CIBI school founders located their political commitments in, primarily, pan-Africanism and cultural nationalism. They understood white supremacy in largely cultural terms and urged cultural solutions that focused on self-determination and the tying of academic achievement to racial identity-building. These solutions included building African American-centered alternative educational and arts-centered institutions. By 1973, CIBI had 21 small, private, largely tuition-driven member schools that were often part of larger community centers that housed independent bookstores, restaurants, grocery stores, and arts spaces (Doughty, 1973). The number of CIBI schools has declined since the late 1970s, but the organization still exists and has active school members (Council of Independent Black Institutions, n.d.).

The Current Race Politics of Charter Schools

A lot has changed in the landscape of public schooling in general and charter schooling in particular since I joined the WOCS founding group in 1996, including massive federal efforts like No Child Left Behind, Race To The Top, and the Common Core. Yet little has changed in the volume and tenor of the public conversation—the "stale debates" (Kahlenberg & Potter, 2014a, p. SR-12)—about charter schooling. This controversial reform, which serves relatively very few students in any particular state and nationwide, gets an incredible amount of air time around the seminar tables of schools of education, in the school politics blogosphere, in legislative chambers, and in public conversation (Frankenberg et al., 2010). This is, in my view, because charter schooling raises such fundamental questions about the scope and purpose of schooling and the role and responsibility of the state to provide for young people and their families. Particularly with respect to race and the charter reform, supporters and detractors find much to both celebrate and to malign, and their arguments just grow more emphatic—yet not much more nuanced—as the reform persists.

Given tenacious and enduring racial inequality in American schooling and a significant retreat from desegregation in schooling over the past couple of decades (Orfield, Frankenberg with Ee, & Kuscera, 2014) and lack of political will to change course on school segregation (Wells, Holme, Revilla, & Atanda, 2009), it is not surprising that many have claimed that the charter reform is part of a broader movement for racial justice, a new civil rights movement. Enthusiastic supporters of the latest round of school choice reforms in the last two decades, from early charter supporters (Nathan, 1996b) to voucher supporters from across the political spectrum (Holt, 2000; Paige, 2002), have tied choice to civil rights (Stulberg, 2006, 2008). As the Reverend and former New York City U.S. Representative Floyd Flake, a Democrat, said enthusiastically in 1997: "The next wave of the civil rights movement will be a demand for choice in schools" (quoted in LaCayo, 1997, p. 74 and in Stulberg, 2008, p. 97). Republicans have made the same connections. In May 2014, Texas Senator Ted Cruz insisted that "[s]chool choice is the civil rights issue of the twenty first century" (quoted in Key, 2014, n.p.), while the chair of the Republican National Committee, Reince Priebus (2014), used the occasion of the 60th anniversary of the *Brown versus Board of Education* decision in May 2014 to make the connection between civil rights and school choice. He urged that "education remains a civil rights issue—the civil rights issue of our time, and it demands action from all of us." He continued: "Fighting for school choice is one of the ways to take action" (n.p.).

Others have invoked civil rights imagery to blast charter opponents. Fox News contributor and Hoover Institution fellow Deroy Murdock (2014) compared charter opponent de Blasio to arch segregationist, Alabama Governor George Wallace, dubbing de Blasio "George Wallace on the Hudson":

> Just as Alabama's segregationist Democratic governor notoriously stood in the school door to deny quality education to disadvantaged black children in 1963, New York's far-left Democrat mayor stands in the charter-school door to deny quality education to disadvantaged black children in 2014. De Blasio should hang his head in shame. (n.p.)

Charter supporters, in this and many examples over the past two decades, have mobilized the language and symbolism of civil rights to connect choice to racial justice.

Supporters of charter schools also claim that charters are serving students of color by filling in where district schools are failing: by providing safe, rigorous, caring schools that prepare students of color for their adult lives, both academically and socially. This claim has been part of charter advocacy since the beginning of the reform. To draw on examples from just the past couple of years: New York's Democratic Governor Andrew Cuomo, speaking to a large pro-charter school rally of students, parents, teachers, and others in Albany in early March 2014, linked charter schooling to the American Dream, saying: "education is what makes the American dream a reality… And you being here today is a tremendous step in the right direction!" (quoted in Campbell, 2014, n.p; also see Decker, 2014). Uncommon Schools, a high-performing nonprofit charter management organization with 44 college preparatory schools in Massachusetts, New York, and New Jersey, connects charter schooling with college preparation with educational equity:

> College is crucial. We believe a Bachelor's degree should be within reach for every young person in this nation.
>
> Still today, too many students in low-income school districts struggle to get to and through college because they don't have the same opportunities as students in wealthier neighborhoods. Every morning, the doors of our schools open to defy this injustice and to celebrate the achievement we know is possible. (Uncommon Schools, n.d., n.p.)

Charter schools, in this construction, serve to open up life's possibilities to students who are typically underserved by traditional public schools.

Finally, there are some charter advocates who make a cultural argument as to why charter schools succeed for students of color. In 2008, reporter David Whitman published the widely cited and hotly debated book, *Sweating the Small Stuff*, which was published by the conservative and pro-school choice Fordham Institute. In his work, Whitman (2008) makes an unusual argument in favor of a kind of "benevolent" (p. 39) educational and cultural "paternalism," which he defines as the model of the kind of school that is a "highly prescriptive institution that teaches students not just how to think but how to act according to what are commonly termed traditional, middle-class values" (p. 3). Whitman finds that this kind of paternalism is one of the keys to the success of so-called "no-excuses" models: schools that are located in low-income communities and that are sharply focused on preparing students for college. These schools, he asserts, have a cultural project. They are "cultural evangelists" and "culturally authoritative" (p. 38). School founders and staff share values with the students and communities they serve, Whitman argues, but people in these communities face structural barriers to living in accordance with these values (p. 48). "The new breed of paternalistic schools," Whitman urges enthusiastically, "appears to be the single most effective way of closing the achievement gap" (p. 5).[4]

In sum, charter supporters, with disparate politics but a shared enthusiasm for public school choice as a mechanism for educational equity, tie charter schooling

[4]Others do not make an explicitly class- or race-focused argument about culture and charter schooling, but they, too, are taken with the idea that some charter schools focus so explicitly on the teaching of values and character (e.g., Tough, 2012).

to the unfinished business of the civil rights movement and frame charters as the educational and cultural solutions to the failures of traditional public schools to adequately serve students of color and low-income students.

On the other hand, many people have significant concerns about the ability of charter schools to meet the needs of students of color. One primary argument here is that charter schools are more segregated than their district counterparts and that they contribute to the substantial backslide on desegregation in this country. Gary Orfield (2010), Codirector of the Civil Rights Project at UCLA, argues: "The charter school movement has been a major political success, but it has been a civil rights failure.... Though there are some remarkable and diverse charter schools, most are neither" (p. 1). The Civil Rights Project's (2010) recent comprehensive charter school study concluded that students in charter schools are more "intensely segregated" by race and class than traditional public school students (p. 4), that charter schools "intensify patterns of isolation prevalent among traditional public schools" (p. 81), and that "charter schools comprise a divisive and segregated sector of our already deeply stratified public school system" (p. 85).

Others make a related argument that charter schools perpetuate inequality by creating haves and have-nots or by exacerbating existing disparities between students. New York's Mayor de Blasio, for instance, has urged that charter schools encourage division in an already-strained public education system where students and communities are competing for scare resources: "The answer is not to save a few of our children only...The answer is not to find an escape route that some can follow and others can't. The answer is to fix the entire system" (quoted in Hernández, 2014, n.p.). Others argue that charter schools "skim" or "cream" the relatively high-performing and/or most driven students (e.g., Frankenberg et al., 2010, p. 16; Ravitch, 2014, p. 247; Scott & DiMartino, 2009, p. 439) or the most involved parents, while leaving others behind in languishing district schools.

Charter skeptics also make emphatic claims that charter schools, especially those that serve low-income communities and communities of color, are part of a neoliberal attempt at privatization that would undermine public education and teachers unions (for a good definition and discussion of neoliberalism and school choice, see Pedroni, 2007, p. 18). They point to the charter movement's backing by some wealthy private donors as evidence that the reform is part of the corporatization of public education and part of a broader assertion of will and control by the country's one percenters. As Mayor de Blasio asserted on one of New York City's local hip hop stations in March 2014: "a lot of [charters] are funded by very wealthy Wall Street folks and others—that doesn't mean the schools don't do good work—but absolutely, there's a very strong private sector element here" (quoted in Gonen, 2014, n.p.). Many others echo this critique. Columnist Margaret Kimberley (2014), writing for the *Black Agenda Report*, insisted: "Charter schools are the inventions of rightwing corporations and foundations, and serve as profit centers for the filthy rich." She continued: "Charter schools are a scam inflicted on black and Latino children and are meant to turn education into just another profit center" (n.p.).

With this analysis, as well, critics lump charter schooling with other education reforms of the last 15 years, like No Child Left Behind and the Common Core.

Diane Ravitch, a historian of education and former school choice enthusiast who served as Assistant Secretary of Education in President George H.W. Bush's administration in the early 1990s, has become one of the most prolific, fervent, and visible school choice critics in recent years. Connecting charter schooling to a broader movement for privatization and an "unnatural focus on testing" (p. 13), Ravitch (2014) responds directly to those who associate school choice with civil rights:

> It defies reason to believe that Martin Luther King Jr. would march arm in arm with Wall Street hedge fund managers… to lead a struggle for the privatization of public education, the crippling of unions, and the establishment of for-profit schools. Privatization inevitably means deregulation, greater segregation, and less equity, with minimal oversight by public authorities. Privatization has typically not been a friend to powerless groups. (p. 55)

In linking privatization to testing to charter schools, Ravitch sees charter schools as part of a larger historical movement in American education to aggressively undermine public, democratic schooling.

Relatedly, charter skeptics offer strong critiques of independent groups that start and manage charter schools across the country: nonprofit charter management organizations (CMOs) and their less-prolific and struggling cousins (Scott & DiMartino, 2010), for-profit education management organizations (EMOs). Charter critic Ravitch (2014), for instance, estimates—citing data from 2010–2011—that ~35 % of charter schools are affiliated with CMOs or EMOs, and that these schools serve almost half of all charter school students (p. 165).[5] CREDO (2013) however, which also does not seem to distinguish between CMOs and EMOs in its accounting, estimates that the proportion of students in CMO schools is smaller: at about 26 % by the end of the 2010–2011 academic year (p. 20). "The remaining 74 percent" of students, CREDO reports, "attended independent charter schools" (p. 20). Exact accounting is difficult, and there is significant state-by-state and district-by-district variation in CMO/EMO involvement in the charter sector (Scott & DiMartino, 2010). They do tend to have a "significant presence" in urban districts (Scott & DiMartino, 2010, p. 185; also see Scott, 2009). CREDO (2013) also reports that CMO schools' test scores do not differ significantly from those of unaffiliated charter schools (p. 51).

Ravitch (2014), however, argues that CMOs and EMO "charter chains" represent the "Walmartization of American education" (p. 248, p. 321) and are disconnected from communities of color and ostensibly offer a one-size-fits-all approach that does not serve these communities well. She writes:

> Charter schools should be managed by local educators and nonprofit organizations, not by charter chains. They should be stand-alone, community-based schools designed and managed by parents, teachers, and members of the local community for the children of that district. They should not be run like Walmart or Target. By allowing schools to operate like chains stores, states have encouraged a chain-store mentality, with standardized

---

[5]Ravitch (2014) here does not disaggregate this data by nonprofit/for-profit status. She is not alone in employing this rhetorical device that elides nonprofit and for-profit charter organizations (e.g., Scott, 2009, 2012).

management and standardized practices... Schooling is not a commodity that can be packaged and distributed across the nation, a standard product that is not responsive to individual children and local needs. (pp. 250–251)

Charter skeptic and researcher, Janelle T. Scott, offers, in an article with a colleague, a similar critique:

Although uniform practices are common in corporate settings, in public school settings, tension can emerge when brand homogeneity conflicts with local desires to shape the schooling environments according to the needs of particular students or communities, or to reflect particular racial, cultural, or linguistic identities. (Scott & DiMartino, 2009, p. 440)

In their view, the ambitions of these management organizations and their ostensible desire to build an "identifiable brand" (p. 440) can supercede local community needs and input. This critique draws on the claim that management organization leaders tend not to come from the communities they serve. Scott (2013), for instance, writes that: "a new generation of privatized charter schools has emerged, largely advocated by a network of elite, white, and male philanthropists, entrepreneurs, and policy makers" (p. 12).

Finally, charter skeptics and opponents claim that charter schools advance "white middle class" values and that this is disastrously detrimental to students and communities of color. This is an argument that can be heard quite frequently in informal ways, for instance, in students' class comments at schools of education; it is much more difficult to find it in print, especially by scholars. The example I offer here is from the annual meeting of the American Educational Research Association (AERA) in the spring of 2011. During the New Orleans gathering of thousands of education scholars, I attended a session on neoliberalism. As the session began, the panelists, quite predictably, launched into their abundant critiques of charter schools. Finally, an audience member raised his hand and said that he had conducted research on a number of schools in the KIPP network and that the panelists' comments did not ring true to his experience in these schools. He asked if any of the panelists had been inside one of the schools they spoke so knowingly about. One of the panelists responded (and I am paraphrasing here), without any irony whatsoever, that he did not need to witness Nazi concentration camps to know that Hitler was a bad man. In this researcher's reckless analogy between Hitler and KIPP's cofounders Dave Levin and Mike Feinberg was an implicit argument that charter schools were perpetrators of cultural genocide. This example from AERA is not an extreme outlier in the way that charter critics understand the cultural project of charter schools, especially those associated with so-called "no excuses" models.

Complicating the Current Conversation: An Appeal to History

My most significant frustration with the current scholarly and public conversation on charter schools is that it does not allow for complex analysis and nuanced discussion.

To be sure, many have done careful research on school choice and do not have a political ax to grind. But, many—including those whose livelihood should rest on their ability to do careful research and make grounded claims—have been irresponsible and anti-intellectual when it comes to school choice research. Many speak publicly from a place of ideology rather than inquiry, and many let their colleagues and students get away with shoddy reasoning and substandard research. The example I cite above at the annual AERA meeting is a perfect illustration of this: In a room full of education researchers, the speaker who invoked Hitler made clear that he did not need data in order to speak as an expert in this case.

More than two decades into the charter school reform, we still cannot get to a place where the standard is rigorous, responsible, measured, complicated public conversation, or scholarship about this complex reform. This needs to end. I think that an appeal to history can help (Stulberg, 2004).[6]

First, we need to draw a more complicated historical connection between school choice and desegregation. While it is an easy political win and a nice rhetorical move for choice skeptics to say that charter schools can be connected to the kind of school choice maneuvers that were the last-gasp attempts of segregationists in the South after *Brown* (e.g., Bonastia, 2012), this does not represent the only way that school choice was mobilized in the years following *Brown*. Nor is it historically accurate to suggest that African American communities have sought school desegregation at all costs. They have not. From the community control movement and the African American independent school movement (among other examples), we can see that African Americans have advocated for alternatives, especially when facing an extreme lack of public political will for desegregation. This does not mean that racial integration in school is not important. It is clearly for a number of short- and long-term educational, social, political, and economic reasons (Brief of…, n.d.; Wells et al., 2009). But integration has never been the full metric by which African Americans and other communities of color have measured their educational progress and success, in the years preceding (e.g., Du Bois, 1935; Walker, 1996; Woodson, 1933) or following *Brown*. It is important to broaden the desegregation framework if we are to fully understand the experience of students and communities of color in public schools—including schools of choice (also see Rofes & Stulberg, 2004).

Drawing on the historical cases I have studied, we can see that African American communities after *Brown* have used school choice for their own purposes, where their focus was generally not desegregated schooling. These examples demonstrate that we need to move beyond an easy connection of choice to white supremacy after *Brown*. African Americans and Latinos in New York after *Brown* turned to community control only when they knew there was virtually no political will for a broad desegregation movement. Many had fought for years for desegregated schooling for their children and their communities. When it was clear that the city was not going to fulfill its desegregation promise, school advocates

---

[6]Empirical discussion in this section draws on my work in Stulberg (2008).

shifted gears. As an East Harlem education activist said in 1966, parents who demanded community control were essentially saying to New York school leaders:

> We recognize, that though your policy is quality integrated education, you cannot deliver. Therefore, we know we will have segregated school. In that case we want a segregated school that will deliver quality education, the kind that will assure our children the opportunity to advance in the world. (quoted in Stulberg, 2008, p. 42)

Others who supported community control, like activist Stokely Carmichael and his coauthor, historian Charles V. Hamilton (1967), saw Black control of community institutions as a step on the way to more meaningful integration: "Before a group can enter the open society," they wrote, "it must first close ranks" (p. 44; quoted in Stulberg, 2008, p. 44. Italics omitted).

The African American independent school movement was also a form of post-*Brown* African American school choice that was decidedly non-desegregation focused in its approach to schooling and that was, like public school community control, a response to the failure of public schooling to serve African American students. The schools themselves often excluded white staff members (Bowers, 1984), took an African-centered approach to curriculum and programming, and taught a strong connection between racial identity and academic identity by teaching children that their Blackness was intricately connected to their ability to love learning and excel at it. The CIBI model was grounded in the concept of educational self-determination. As students in CIBI schools recited every day in a pledge that was written in 1980: "We are an African people struggling for national liberation…. Our commitment is to self-determination, self-defense and self-respect for our race" (quoted in Stulberg, 2008, p. 63).

Turning to history also teaches us that the distinction between public and private education is messy. It teaches us that private involvement has always been a part of American public education, often in the form of private for-profit interests in education (Scott & DiMartino, 2009, 2010; Tyack & Cuban, 1995). It also teaches us that African American activists have never been dedicated to public schooling at all costs. The state has always played a complicated role—and abdicated its responsibility in serious ways—in African American education.

Charter schools certainly have no monopoly on the substantial involvement of private wealth in public education. This observation is not meant to let charter schools off the hook; it is simply meant to point out that charter schools are part of a much broader trend. We *should* have a strong, progressive state that truly takes responsibility for the education of all children and does not rely on targeted private subsidy in the way it does now (Stulberg, 2008). Yet, these examples of private involvement abound in public schooling. Parents themselves supplement public school budgets with their private donations. As a 2011 report by the New York City Charter School Center compared:

> Bronx Community Charter School, for example, reported over $380,000 in fundraising in fiscal year 2008–2009, while the parents' organization at PS 334, a gifted and talented district school on the Upper West Side, reported over $500,000 in revenue during that same year. (p. 7)

School auction fund-raisers at district schools, too, can raise hundreds of thousands of dollars at a time (Medina, 2008). For-profit companies and commercial brands, as well, are heavily enmeshed in public education. Janelle Scott and Catherine DiMartino (2009), for instance, reported: "In 2003, Mayor Bloomberg signed a contract with Snapple, making it the only beverage brand sold in the city's public schools. In exchange... New York City received a 30 % commission and $3 million donated annually to school sports programs" (p. 445). So, too, as urban districts across the country struggle to support high-quality education for their students, individual private donors have stepped in to fill the financial gap. Facebook mogul Mark Zuckerberg's $100 million challenge pledge in 2010 to the Newark public school district—also intricately connected to charter school politics there—is perhaps the most substantial example here (see, e.g., Russakoff, 2014).

Historically, and with respect to African American education, both public school community control and IBIs were an acknowledgement that the state was relinquishing its responsibility to educate African American children. Private involvement came in the form of foundation support, from the Ford Foundation and others, and tuition-driven schooling. Yet even the independent schools that were the most critical of the state to serve African American communities sometimes needed public support to stay solvent, like federal Title I support and public funds for youth programming (Gittell, 1970; Parsons, 1970).

So, when charter skeptics bemoan the involvement of private interests in public education, it is important to remember that it has always been there: in public education in general and African American education in particular, there has always been a messy connection between the public and the private sphere. If we hope to get private interests and actors out of public education, we should be engaged in a much broader conversation. We also should learn from history that African American communities have never wholly trusted the public sphere to meet their educational needs and interests.

Third, turning to history, we see that the cultural debates about so-called "no excuses" charter models and CMOs/EMOs and the involvement of charter leaders who are not "from the community" are part of a longer historical conversation about culture and African American schooling and about who counts as a legitimate ally in racial justice movements.

African American critics of public schooling have always included cultural analyses of the impact of these schools on racial identity (e.g., Woodson, 1933). They have sought to build intentional communities around alternative visions of education, ones that take seriously that culture and values matter and must be taught in alternative ways through schools. This has always involved conversations about how this community was defined: about the role that white people could play in these movements either at the center, as allies, or coalition partners, for instance (see, e.g., Van Deburg, 1992); or the harm that African American leaders who did not have community interests at heart could cause to Black communities (Carmichael & Hamilton, 1967). The public school community control movement and the Council of Independent Black Institutions resolved these questions in different ways. For instance, there were a substantial number of white teachers involved in the New York community control movement. These historical examples raise questions about how we define community for purposes of involvement in and leadership of African American school choice efforts.

From history we can understand, too, that choice efforts led by African Americans to improve African American education have always involved strange bedfellows. New York's community control movement had the backing of a Republican mayor, the Ford Foundation, and Black Power activists like Carmichael and others. CIBI-affiliated African American independent schools occasionally needed foundation and state support, even as their founders doubted that the American state could ever serve African American interests. One of the reasons why the Ocean Hill–Brownsville conflict was so painful for so many liberals is that it seemed to break up the alliance between organized labor and civil rights activists (see Kahlenberg, 2007; Perlstein, 2004). Certainly, African Americans looking for educational excellence and self-determination have not been union supporters at any cost. This same split between unions and African American choice advocates is echoed in the modern choice movement (see, e.g., Pedroni, 2007, p. 39).

Finally, history helps us have a more complicated conversation about parent agency and school choice. In the current debate on charter schools—and vouchers, for that matter—choice skeptics often talk about parents who choose charter schools as if they have been duped by corporate interests and neoliberals into making choices that are against their best interests. Reporting on the Albany March 2014 charter school rally attended by Governor Cuomo and the pro-charter local television ads that began to air around the same time, for example, focused on their wealthy advocates and backers (Lewis, 2014). Charter critics targeted the organization that funded the ads, Families for Excellent Schools, calling its grassroots connections into question. Steve Nelson (2014), head of a selective private school in Manhattan, wrote: "The campaign is calculated propaganda. The only 'family' materially involved in this organization is the Walton family…" of Walmart fortune. He continued by framing the involvement of pro-charter families this way: "The parents and children who appear in these ads may well be sincere, but they are pawns in a much larger game" (n.p.). Ravitch (2014), too, characterizes parents this way, writing:

> When public hearings are conducted about charter schools in New York City and Los Angeles, charter operators send busloads of their students and parents wearing identical T-shirts to the hearings to demand more charter schools, more funding, and less regulation and oversight. When New York City held public hearings about closing public schools, the same brigades of charter students and parents arrived in buses to support the school closing to provide more free space for charters. If public schools used their students to engage in the same political lobbying, their principals would be brought up on charges and fired. (p. 307)

Writing that choice does not have a "popular base" (p. 317), Ravitch describes the millions of parents who chose charter schools for their children or who advocate for these schools of choice as if they have no agency.

The community control and African American independent school movements remind us that parents and education advocates of color have always made strategic choices about schooling, assessing political will and structural constraints and backing efforts that work best for them within what seems possible. To offer another example from more recent history: Scholar Thomas C. Pedroni (2007), who is not a school voucher enthusiast by any means, nevertheless provides one of the most nuanced accounts of African American parents' embrace of some current school choice reforms. Using the case of the Milwaukee voucher movement, begun in the early 1990s, Pedroni seeks to understand why parents might align with political actors with whom they share very little, like the conservative foundations, politicians, and scholars who enthusiastically backed private vouchers in Milwaukee and elsewhere. His argument is that these parents and activists exercise substantial agency in this choice, making "tactical" decisions (p. 40) about the education of their children and their communities. He writes:

> This movement to vouchers, like other historical struggles for quality education in which communities of color have engaged, is a product of parents' agency on a social and educational terrain over which they have had little control. I argue that African American investment in vouchers is a momentary strategy chosen in the context of a largely correct reading of the powerful political and educational dynamics currently driving educational reform in the United States. (p. 4)

Pedroni's reading is in line with historical examples of the ways in which African American parents and education advocates have made strategic choices. It is not, however, in line with the current popular discourse on the role (or lack thereof) that charter school parents of color play in the choices they make for their children.

Conclusion

Many legitimate questions about race and charter schools remain. These require empirical investigations and reasoned conversations. Most of these are questions we should be asking of public education more broadly. These questions include: How can we increase political will for true school integration and how do parents' school choices help or undermine this? How can public support for and involvement in the education of our nation's children increase rather than detract from the democratization of American schooling? How do schools "teach" culture and racial identity and connect it to educational achievement? How can parents and communities feel invested in and ownership of their schools? How can higher education become affordable enough and teaching and educational administration become high-prestige enough so that low-income college graduates and graduates of color are inclined to commit to education as a profession? How do the demographic backgrounds of teachers and school leaders impact their orientation to teaching and learning?

We are not yet, even more than 20 years into the charter reform, at a place where we can have these conversations in a productive way. The current polarized public debate is not helping us build a responsible, rigorous, complicated research agenda. As education writers Kahlenberg & Potter (2014b) recently argued, these "charter schools wars" are not helping us build better public schools, either, and both "sides" are to blame. In my view, charter supporters often feel threatened by any criticism, and charter critics often refuse to give up any ground and to seek empirical evidence for the claims they make. Hopefully, turning to history can help.

References

Berube, M. R., & Gittell, M. (Eds.). (1969). *Confrontation at Ocean Hill-Brownsville: The New York school strikes of 1968*. New York, NY: Frederick A. Praeger.

Bonastia, C. (2012, March 9). Why the racist history of the charter school movement is never discussed. *AlterNet*. Retrieved from http://www.alternet.org/story/154425/why_the_racist_history_of_the_charter_school_movement_is_never_discussed.

Bowers, M. A. (1984). *The independent black educational institution: An exploration and identification of selected factors that relate to their survival*. Ed. dissertation. Atlanta: Atlanta University.

Brief of 553 social scientists as *amici curiae* in support of respondents. (n.d.). Amicus brief nos. 05–908 & 05–915. *Parents Involved in Community Schools v. Seattle School District No. 1*.

Campbell, C. (2014, March 4). Cuomo joins charter advocates at rally critical of de Blasio. *New York Observer*. Retrieved from http://observer.com/2014/03/cuomo-joins-charter-advocates-at-rally-critical-of-de-blasio/.

Carmichael, S., & Hamilton, C. V. (1967). *Black power: The politics of liberation* (1992). New York, NY: Vintage Books.

Carnoy, M., Jacobsen, R., Mishel, L., & Rothstein, R. (2005). *The charter school dust-up: Examining the evidence on enrollment and achievement*. Washington, DC: Economic Policy Institute and Teachers College Press.

Center for Research on Education Outcomes. (2009, June). *Multiple choice: Charter school performance in 16 states*. Stanford, CA: Center for Research on Education Outcomes (CREDO), Stanford University. Retrieved June, 2009, from http://credo.stanford.edu/reports/MULTIPLE_CHOICE_CREDO.pdf.

Center for Research on Education Outcomes. (2013). *National charter school study 2013*. Stanford, CA: Center for Research on Education Outcomes (CREDO), Stanford University. Retrieved from http://credo.stanford.edu/documents/NCSS%202013%20Final%20Draft.pdf.

Council of Independent Black Institutions. (n.d.). *Who we are*. Retrieved from http://www.cibi.org/newsite/index.html#/about-us.

Decker, G. (2014, March 4). Cuomo touts charter schools in surprise rally appearance, clouding de Blasio's pre-k lobby day. *Chalkbeat New York*. Retrieved from http://ny.chalkbeat.org/2014/03/04/cuomo-touts-charter-schools-in-surprise-rally-appearance-clouding-de-blasios-pre-k-lobby-day/#.U6Mp-ah763M.

Doughty, J. J. (1973). *A historical analysis of Black education—Focusing on the contemporary independent Black school movement*. Ph.D. dissertation Ohio State University.

Du Bois, W. E. B. (1935). Does the Negro need separate schools? *Journal of Negro Education, 4*(3), 328–335.

Editorial Board. (2014, March 10). Why is New York Mayor Bill de Blasio undermining charter schools? *The Washington Post*. Retrieved from http://www.washingtonpost.com/opinions/why-is-new-york-mayor-bill-de-blasio-undermining-charter-schools/2014/03/10/2a1f02f0-a3db-11e3-8466-d34c451760b9_story.html.

Frankenberg, E., Siegel-Hawley, G., & Wang, J. (2010). *Choice without equity: Charter school segregation and the need for civil rights standards.* Los Angeles, CA: The Civil Rights Project/Proyecto Derechos Civiles at UCLA.

Gittell, M. (1969). New York City School Decentralization. *Community, 1,* 1–2.

Gittell, M. (1970, February). The community school in the nation. *Community Issues, 2*(1).

Gonen, Y. (2014, March 6). De Blasio: Charter school funding has "strong private sector element." *New York Post.* Retrieved from http://nypost.com/2014/03/06/de-blasio-charter-school-funding-has-strong-private-sector-element/.

Hernández, J. C. (2014, March 23). Gentler words about charter schools from de Blasio. *The New York Times.* Retrieved from http://www.nytimes.com/2014/03/24/nyregion/de-blasio-strikes-conciliatory-tone-on-charter-schools.html.

Henig, J. R. (2008). *Spin cycle: How research is used in policy debates: The case of charter schools.* New York, NY: Russell Sage Foundation and The Century Foundation.

Holt, M. (2000). *Not yet "free at last": The unfinished business of the Civil Rights Movement: Our battle for school choice.* Oakland, CA: Institute for Contemporary Studies Press.

Kahlenberg, R. (2007). *Tough liberal: Albert Shanker and the battle over schools, unions, race, and democracy.* New York: NY Columbia University Press.

Kahlenberg, R., & Potter, H. (2014a, August 13). The original charter school vision. *The New York Times,* p. SR-12.

Kahlenberg, R., & Potter, H. (2014b, September 28). End the charter school wars. *New York Daily News.* Retrieved from http://www.nydailynews.com/opinion/kahlenberg-potter-charter-school-wars-article-1.1954490.

Key, P. (2014, May 7). *Cruz slams "affluent," "apathetic" GOP for not making school choice "civil right issue of the 21st century."* Retrieved from http://www.breitbart.com/Breitbart-TV/2014/05/07/Cruz-Slams-Affluent-Apathetic-GOP-For-Not-Making-School-Choice-Civil-Right-Issue-Of-The-21st-Century.

Kimberley, M. (2014, April 9). Charter school corruption. *Black agenda report.* Retrieved from http://www.blackagendareport.com/content/freedom-ridercharter-school-corruption.

LaCayo, R. (1997). They'll vouch for that. *Time, 150*(17), 72–74.

Layton, L. (2014, May 28). In New Orleans, traditional public schools close for good. *The Washington Post.* Retrieved from http://www.washingtonpost.com/local/education/in-new-orleans-traditional-public-schools-close-for-good/2014/05/28/ae4f5724-e5de-11e3-8f90-73e071f3d637_story.html.

Lewis. R. (2014, March 6). Who is behind the pro-charter schools group fighting de Blasio? *WNYC.* Retrieved from http://www.wnyc.org/story/behind-pro-charter-school-group-fighting-de-blasio/.

Medina, J. (2008, May 3). Bids for Botox? Auctions go deep to aid schools. *The New York Times.* Retrieved from http://www.nytimes.com/2008/05/03/nyregion/03auctions.html?pagewanted=all&_r=0.

Murdock, D. (2014, March 18). Bill de Blasio: George Wallace on the Hudson. *National Review.* Retrieved from http://www.nationalreview.com/article/373581/bill-de-blasio-george-wallace-hudson-deroy-murdock.

Nathan, J. (1996a). *Charter schools: Creating hope and opportunity for American education.* San Francisco, CA: Jossey-Bass Publishers.

Nathan, J. (1996b). Possibilities, problems, and progress: Early lessons from the charter movement. *Phi Delta Kappan, 78*(1), 18–23.

National Center for Education Statistics. (2014, April). *Charter school enrollment.* Retrieved from http://nces.ed.gov/programs/coe/indicator_cgb.asp.

Nelson, S. (2014, March 28). Bill de Blasio versus charter schools—a pointless battle. *Huffington Post.* Retrieved from http://www.huffingtonpost.com/steve-nelson/charter-schools-bill-de-blasio_b_5045454.html.

New York City Charter School Center. (2011). *The profit myth: Understanding the structure of New York Charter Schools.* New York, NY: New York City Charter School Center.

New York City Charter School Center. (2012). *The state of the NYC charter school sector.* New York, NY: New York City Charter School Center.

New York City Charter School Center. (2013). *Data brief: NYC charter school performance on the 2012–2013 state exams for Math and English.* New York, NY: New York City Charter School Center.

Orfield, G. (2010). Foreword. In E. Frankenberg, G. Siegel-Hawley, & J. Wang (Eds.), *Choice without equity: Charter school segregation and the need for civil rights standards* (pp. 1–3). Los Angeles, CA: The Civil Rights Project/Proyecto Derechos Civiles at UCLA.

Orfield, G., Frankenberg, E., Ee, J., & Kuscera, J. (2014). *Brown at 60: Great progress, a long retreat and an uncertain future.* Los Angeles, CA: The Civil Rights Project/Proyecto Derechos Civiles at UCLA.

Paige, R. (2002, June 28). A win for America's children. *The New York Times*, (p. A29).

Parsons, T. (1970, December). The community school movement. *Community Issues, 2.*

Pedroni, T. C. (2007). *Market movements: African American involvement in school voucher reform.* New York, NY: Routledge.

Perlstein, D. H. (2004). *Justice, justice: School politics and the eclipse of liberalism.* New York, NY: Peter Lang.

Podair, J. E. (2002). *The strike that changed New York: Blacks, whites, and the Ocean Hill-Brownsville crisis.* New Haven, CT: Yale University Press.

Priebus, R. (2014, May 17). *Why school choice is a civil rights issue.* Retrieved from http://www.cnn.com/2014/05/17/opinion/priebus-school-choice/.

Ravitch, D. (2014). *Reign of error: The hoax of the privatization movement and the danger to America's public schools.* New York, NY: Alfred A. Knopf.

Rofes, E., & Stulberg, L. M. (2004). Conclusion: Toward a progressive politics of school choice. In E. Rofes & L. M. Stulberg (Eds.), *The emancipatory promise of charter schools: Toward a progressive politics of school choice* (pp. 263–302). Albany: SUNY Press.

RPP International. (2000, January). *The state of charter schools 2000: Fourth-year report.* Washington, DC: Office of Educational Research and Improvement, US Department of Education.

Russakoff, D. (2014, May 19). Schooled. *The New Yorker.* Retrieved from http://www.newyorker.com/magazine/2014/05/19/schooled.

Scott, J. (2009). The politics of venture philanthropy in charter school policy and advocacy. *Educational Policy, 23*(1), 106–136.

Scott, J. T. (2012). When community control meets privatization: The search for empowerment in African American charter schools. In D. T. Slaughter-Defoe, H. C. Stevenson, E. G. Arrington, & D. J. Johnson (Eds.), *Black educational choice: Assessing the private and public alternatives to traditional k-12 schools* (pp. 191–204). Santa Barbara, CA: Praeger.

Scott, J. T. (2013). A Rosa Parks moment?: School choice and the marketization of civil rights. *Critical Studies in Education, 54*(1), 5–18.

Scott, J., & DiMartino, C. (2009). Public education under new management: A typology of educational privatization applied to New York City's restructuring. *Peabody Journal of Education, 84*, 432–452.

Scott, J. T., & DiMartino, C. C. (2010). Hybridized, franchised, duplicated, and replicated: Charter schools and management organizations. In C. A. Lubienski & P. C. Weitzel (Eds.), *The charter school experiment: Expectations, evidence, and implications* (pp. 171–196). Cambridge, MA: Harvard Education Press.

Shujaa, M. J., & Afrik, H. T. (1996). School desegregation, the politics of culture, and the Council of Independent Black Institutions. In M. J. Shujaa (Ed.), *Beyond desegregation: The politics of quality in African American schooling* (pp. 253–268). Thousand Oaks, CA: Corwin Press.

Stulberg, L. M. (2004). What history offers progressive choice scholarship. In E. Rofes & L. M. Stulberg (Eds.), *The emancipatory promise of charter schools: Toward a progressive politics of school choice* (pp. 7–51). Albany: SUNY Press.

Stulberg, L. M. (2006). School choice discourse and the legacy of Brown. *Journal of School Choice, 1*, 23–45.

Stulberg, L. M. (2008). *Race, schools, and hope: African Americans and school choice after Brown*. New York, NY: Teachers College Press.

Task Force on the Education of African American Students. (1996, December 19). *Resolution of the Board of Education*. Oakland, CA: Oakland Unified School District.

Tough, P. (2012). *How children succeed: Grit, curiosity, and the hidden power of character*. New York, NY: Houghton Mifflin Harcourt.

Tyack, D., & Cuban, L. (1995). *Tinkering toward utopia: A century of public school reform*. Cambridge, MA: Harvard University Press.

Uncommon Schools. (n.d.). The opportunity gap. Retrieved from http://www.uncommonschools.org/our-approach/the-opportunity-gap.

Van Deburg, W. L. (1992). *New day in Babylon: The Black Power movement and American culture, 1965–1975*. Chicago, IL: The University of Chicago Press.

Walker, V. S. (1996). *Their highest potential: An African American school community in the segregated South*. Chapel Hill, NC: The University of North Carolina Press.

Wells, A. S., Holme, J. J., Revilla, A. T., & Atanda, A. K. (2009). *Both sides now: The story of school desegregation's graduates*. Berkeley, CA: University of California Press.

Whitman, D. (2008). *Sweating the small stuff: Inner-city schools and the new paternalism*. Washington, DC: Thomas B. Fordham Institute Press.

Woodson, C. G. (1933). *The mis-education of the Negro* (1990th ed.). Trenton, NJ: Africa World Press.

An Asian American Perspective on Segregated Schooling, *Brown v. Board*, and Affirmative Action

Evelyn Hu-DeHart

Most Americans are at least dimly aware of the "separate but equal" doctrine, the notorious chapter in U.S. history that the *Brown v. Board of Education* decision intended to end, and are occasionally reminded of persistent difficulties faced by African-American students when using education in a bid for upward social mobility. Meanwhile, another group of minority Americans, those of Asian descent, have been extolled for some four decades as whiz kids, dubbed the "model minority" because of their impressive academic achievement in K-12 and on through college, graduate, and professional schools. Accompanying this seemingly benign model minority construction is the stereotype of docile, compliant, and studious Asian American students who seldom stray from their books to complain or protest.

Thus, an invidious comparison has been set up among different groups of U.S. minorities that showcases a "successful" minority, Asian Americans, for the apparent purpose of denigrating the character of "failed" minorities, in so doing also mitigating societal responsibility for the consequences of institutionalized racism, such as segregated schooling, that the *Brown* decision aggressively addressed. It is important to deconstruct this dangerous setup and recall some history that has been largely erased, namely that Asian American children in the early twentieth

---

This chapter is an adaptation of a chapter by the author entitled "An Asian American Perspective on Brown" in *The Unfinished Agenda of Brown v. the Board of Education* by the Editors of Black Issues in Higher Education. © 2004 by Black Issues in Higher Education. Adapted by permission from Turner Publishing Company. ALL RIGHTS RESERVED.

E. Hu-DeHart (✉)
American Studies and Ethnic Studies, Brown University, 150 Power St, Providence, RI 02912, USA
e-mail: evelyn_hu-dehart@brown.edu

© Springer International Publishing Switzerland 2016
P.A. Noguera et al. (eds.), *Race, Equity, and Education*,
DOI 10.1007/978-3-319-23772-5_6

century were also forced to attend segregated schools in California. In addition, careful analysis of the composition of the current generation of Asian American high academic achievers and concrete explanations for their success are needed without resorting to facile culturalist arguments.

School Segregation and Asian American Students

It is generally not known in American public opinion, not even in educational circles, that in the late nineteenth, early twentieth century California, where most Chinese and Japanese immigrants had settled, Asian American children were sometimes forced into segregated schools. Although the practice was uneven and sporadic, and nowhere approached the near universal extent and persistence of segregated schooling imposed on black children in the country, Chinese and Japanese families fought hard against what they correctly perceived as blatant and illegal discrimination. Asian immigrant parents understood that their American-born children were automatic birthright citizens by virtue of the equal protection clause of the Fourteenth Amendment, even as they themselves, as immigrants born abroad, were denied access to citizenship by the U.S. Naturalization Law of 1790, which restricted citizenship to "white" newcomers (Odo, 2002, pp. 13–14).

By the late 1870s, there were some 3000 Chinese children and youth, ages 5 to 17; many were still of school age, while others, not surprisingly, were already in the workforce. Around 1878, a group of 1,300 California Chinese merchants, mostly in the San Francisco and Sacramento areas, noting that they had paid more than $42,000 in state taxes, petitioned the state Senate and Assembly to establish "separate schools" if the state was unwilling to admit these children into schools for whites (Odo, 2002, pp. 49–50). This move represented an explicit desire on the part of Chinese community leaders for their children to be educated in America and to learn English, as well as a tacit acceptance of racial segregation already in practice in California and that included the public schools. Up to then, the only schools available to the Chinese were those operated by missionaries, some of which actually operated with public money. These schools were primarily interested in teaching English to youth and young adults as a conversion strategy, while Chinese merchants saw the acquisition of some English by their adult sons as an essential business strategy.

But many of these students did not relish the long hours praying and reading the Bible, leading some community leaders to push for nonreligious schools in the public education system. This initial request encountered strenuous opposition in local public opinion, as the movement for Chinese exclusion was already gathering momentum in the late 1870s, and would culminate in the Chinese Exclusion Act of 1882. A San Francisco newspaper, the *Daily Morning Mail*, warned the public about giving Chinese access to public education, noting that the "Chinese race," is "striving to take root in the soil. They desire or profess to desire, to mingle their youth with ours, with a view, doubtless, to more thorough assimilation in the body politic" (Ngai, 2010, p. 48). In other words, acculturation and assimilation of the Chinese via the public schools was seen as anathema to the goal of Chinese exclusion, the end game of the mounting racist, anti-Chinese movement.

The bid for a public education for Mamie and Frank Tape of San Francisco, captured by historian Mae Ngai in her family biography, illustrates the story of one Chinese American family's struggle to overcome racial segregation in schooling in the late nineteenth century (Ngai, 2010, pp. 43–57). By 1884, Mamie was eight, her brother Frank six. Initially, they were tutored at home in arithmetic and reading by a young white American woman who had befriended her neighbor and the children's parents, Joseph and Mary Tape. This was a totally atypical Chinese family for the times: Joseph, who had arrived in California as a penniless kid of 12 from a south China village in 1864, worked in transportation for the Pacific Mail, while Mary, a young runaway from her penurious Chinese home and raised by white missionary parents, was an artist and photographer. They were practicing Christians and self-described as totally Americanized (that is, white acculturated). Joseph bragged about cutting his queue, and hence his ties to China and perceived heathenness, while Mary had long forsaken the Chinese name she must have received from her birth parents, preferring to identify as white-sounding Mary McGladery. A fluent English speaker, Mary also wrote English with ease. In short, they built a comfortable, prosperous, bourgeois, English-speaking home for their family, soon to include two more siblings for Mary and Frank. The Tapes lived near but not in Chinatown, often in mixed-race neighborhoods. But the Tapes did not entirely distance themselves from other Chinese; after all, Joseph occasionally did interpreting work for the Chinese consulate after it was established in 1878, and Mary knew in her heart that, given the prevailing racism of society, her Chinese children would probably have to find Chinese mates.

One fine day in September 1884, Mary took Mamie to register for school at the Spring Valley Primary School on Union Street. Perhaps she believed that her highly acculturated, English-speaking family, Americans "except in features" in Mary's own inimitable phrasing, would protect them from Chinese exclusion, the act passed just 2 years prior. But Miss Hurley, the principal, refused to admit little Mamie, who, despite speaking fluent English and being dressed in a pretty checkered pinafore with a ribbon in her braids, had features that marked her as Chinese. The principal seemed undeterred by the new state law that entitled all children in the state to a public education, confident, indeed, that she was upholding the views of her boss, school superintendent Andrew Jackson Moulder, already known for his racist views "to resist, to defeat and to prohibit... the admission of Africans, Chinese and Diggers [Miwok Indians] into our white schools" (Ngai, 2010, p. 50). At this time, when an estimated 1000 Chinese were of school age, the San Francisco superintendent of public schools was digging his heels in deeper.

Joseph first appealed to the Chinese consulate for help in protesting the illegal exclusion of his children from public schools, and won the attention of vice consul Fredrick A. Bee, a white attorney who often sued on behalf of Chinese individuals and organizations against discriminatory immigration laws and civil rights violations. In the protest he lodged with the San Francisco school board, he pointedly noted that the exclusion of Mamie from Spring Valley Primary School was "inconsistent with the treaties, Constitution and laws of the United States, especially so in this case as the child is native-born," and hence, a U.S. citizen (Ngai, 2010, p. 51). When the city school board, backed by the state superintendent of education, not only upheld the exclusion, but reiterated to other principals to follow Hurley's example "under pain of dismissal," it left Joseph no further option but to retain prominent lawyer William Gibson to sue on behalf of Mamie, who became famous in the local press as "That Chinese Girl" in the well-covered *Tape v. Hurley* case.

Lawyer Gibson argued that excluding Mamie violated California's 1880 education law as well as the Fourteenth Amendment of the U.S. Constitution. Joseph argued that his family members were in fact so Americanized—in language, dress, daily habits—that they could hardly be equated with excludable Chinese of "filthy habits" and "contagious diseases." Despite widespread public opinion against school integration for the Chinese, some white Americans did come out publicly in support of those, like Mamie, who were citizens by birth and entitled to all citizenship's benefits and privileges, including a free public education.

Citing the equal protection clause of the Fourteenth Amendment, state law, and the taxes Chinese residents paid, California Superior Court and Supreme Court both ruled in Mamie's favor. But it was a pyrrhic victory, because the courts also tacitly acknowledged the validity of "separate but equal" that undergirded racial segregation in American public life, soon to be legitimated constitutionally in *Plessy v. Ferguson* in 1896. California politicians quickly responded by passing legislation to establish separate schools for "children of Chinese and Mongolian descent," setting the stage for opening the Chinese Primary School on the edge of Chinatown. After being rebuffed again by Principal Hurley at Spring Valley as well as by the ever racist Superintendent Moulder, after Mary's clearly agitated protestation to the American public via a newspaper letter that "Mamie Tape will never attend any of the Chinese schools of your making!", the Tapes relented and sent Mamie as well as younger brother Frank to the Chinese Primary School when it opened at the edge of Chinatown on April 15, 1885, the first two students to arrive.

Five years later, in 1890, the Chinese Primary School had more than 100 students, almost all male, except for Mamie and one other girl, who soon dropped out. Although these highly acculturated siblings continued to stand out from their peers, they were also becoming more Sinicized, finding it necessary to learn the Cantonese of their classmates. Occasionally, they even wore Chinese-style clothes to school, though not the shabby wear of poor classmates; rather, they boasted the latest styles from cosmopolitan Shanghai. In this way, Mamie and Frank finished primary school, while younger siblings Emily and Gertrude were poised to follow suite to attend the segregated Chinese school. Mamie and Frank probably could have gone on to attend a public high school, as a few Chinese teens were already doing, but their parents thought otherwise. They moved the family to nearby Berkeley, where Chinese could buy property and attend regular public schools.

In California at the end of the nineteenth century, a few other municipalities like Sacramento followed San Francisco's example of compelling Chinese children to attend segregated Chinese schools, along the model of what was imposed on black and Native American children. Others like Berkeley, as the Tapes discovered, had moved on toward integration. Meanwhile, in San Francisco, some Chinese children attended mandated, then *de facto*, segregated schools through World War II. A school study in 1947 concluded that while formal segregation for the Chinese had ended, residential segregation rendered one public school 100 % Chinese (Wollenberg, 1995a, p. 9).

Like the Chinese at the dawn of the twentieth century, Japanese children in San Francisco were also compelled into segregated schooling. In 1907, when 10-year-old Keikichi Aoki, with the help of the U.S. Attorney's office, attempted to enroll in a San Francisco elementary school, he was rebuffed by the Board of Education. The board president explained that "because of state law providing for an Oriental school, this boy cannot be admitted" (Wollenberg, 1995b, p. 13). He further cited Section 1662 of the California Education Act, which allowed school districts to establish separate schools for "children of Mongolian or Chinese descent," the term Mongolian apparently standing in for Japanese and all other Asians (p. 13). The lawyer's insistence that Japanese were not Mongolian, hence Aoki should not be forced into segregated schools, went unheeded.

Aoki's parents were protesting because the board had decided in October 1906 to concentrate all Chinese, Japanese, and Korean children in the "Oriental Public School" located in Chinatown. Only two of the city's 93 Japanese families complied, while all the handful of Koreans showed up. Eventually, President Teddy Roosevelt himself intervened to forestall a brewing international crisis, because Japan, which had just defeated Russia, a Western power, was in no mood to have its citizens pushed around in the U.S. By the 1920s, apart from the few small districts in Sacramento County that still maintained "Oriental schools," all but 575 of the 30,000 or so Japanese *nisei* children (*nisei* meaning U.S. born, hence U.S. citizens) in California were attending regular public schools (Wollenberg, 1995b, p. 26).

Ironically, having escaped segregated schools, *nisei* children were rudely yanked back into *de facto* segregated schools when they had to accompany their *issei* (immigrants denied citizenship) parents into the concentration camps set up by the federal government for all West Coast Japanese families during the war years. The War Relocation Authority (WRA), which operated the camps, found itself suddenly responsible for the education of some 25,000 Japanese American schoolchildren, almost all U.S. citizens. By the very nature of relocation and internment, of course, the WRA schools were racially segregated, operating behind barbed wire and often in unheated, flimsy classrooms, with severe short-ages of textbooks, supplies, and teachers. The ever-resourceful Japanese parents soon found ways and means to improve these schools, so that when the camps closed after the war, their children returned to integrated public schools and began to thrive (Hirabayashi, 1991; Wollenberg, 1995b, pp. 24–27).

In this brief historical survey of Chinese and Japanese American experience with U.S. public education, certain facts stand out: many Asian Americans are intensely interested in education and will resort to any means at their disposal to obtain it, and, at the same time, fight discriminatory practices and policies, notably segregated schools. Nevertheless, as a group they were pragmatic enough to accept segregated schools if that was all they had.

History is full of twists and turns, and so it was with the trajectory of Asian Americans and education. By the late 1960s, when segregated schooling was long behind them, high-achieving Japanese and Chinese students in American schools began to attract attention from educators, media, and the general public. These longtime Asian Americans were soon joined by waves of new Asian immigrants arriving after the 1965 reforms that finally ended the long exclusion of Asian immigrants (for the Chinese in 1882, for all the other Asians since 1924). Collectively, Asian American students boosted test scores, graduation rates, and matriculation at the nation's most selective public and private universities, and soon in medical, law, business, and other professional schools as well. Within 10 years of bursting on the scene, the Asian American "model minority" had saturated the media, with every major outlet from print to television vying to sing their praises (Chun, 1995; Suzuki, 1995). The attention continues unabated to this day. In the 2003 *USA Today*'s Academic High School All-Stars, for example, 12 of the top 20 students were Asian Americans (2003 All-USA, 2003). While many Asian American community leaders and activists, students, and educators are understandably wary of the "model minority" label, given this country's unsavory use of stereotypes against the interests of minority groups, it would also be disingenuous to dismiss irrefutable evidence of Asian American academic achievements that underlie this new social construction and fail to examine this phenomenon dispassionately.

Asian Americans and Contemporary Education

Dramatic and profound changes to the Asian American population have occurred since the immigration law reforms of 1965. Today it is the fastest growing non-white population (U.S. Census Bureau, 2013a), at a rate of more than 100 % per decade since the 1970s. This population has exceeded 18 million, from barely one million in total when the reforms were enacted, to more than 5 % of the total U.S. population in 2013 (U.S. Census Bureau, 2014). Distributed not just bi-coastally but all over the United States, this category has also become incredibly diverse, ranging from the early Chinese and Japanese to now well over 20 ethnicities[1] (U.S. Census Bureau, 2012), with more religions, languages, and cultural frameworks. Over 90 % of this population is comprised of immigrants or children of immigrants (Zhou & Xiong, 2007), so transnational ties with homeland cultures and places remain strong. English is not necessarily the preferred language at

[1]The most populous dozen of these ethnic groups are Chinese, Filipino, Asian Indian, Vietnamese, Korean, Japanese, Other Asian, Pakistani, Cambodian, Hmong, Thai, and Laotian (U.S. Census Bureau, 2012, Table 6).

home. Although most have come as voluntary immigrants after the civil rights movement, usually as families and eligible to become citizens regardless of race, nearly half of U.S. refugee arrivals between 2000 and 2010 were Asian born (Batalova, 2011). The gender ratio of Asian Americans favors women; the median age is young; and the average family size is larger than the national average (Batalova, 2011; Hune & Chan, 1997). Unlike immigrants of the last century, who were mostly men arriving without families for manual labor and small businesses, today, families are the norm. While laborers continue to arrive for menial jobs in restaurants and sweatshops, many more come armed with high levels of education, acquire more degrees upon arriving in America, and expect their children to aim even higher.

Among these new Asian immigrants, the Chinese present a specially nuanced picture. Beginning with a trickle in the late 1950s and early 1960s, they grew into a veritable rush in the eighties and nineties. No longer just from a few counties in south China, they came from all over China as well as from the vast Chinese diaspora in Hong Kong, Taiwan, Southeast Asia, Central and South America, the Caribbean and Canada, the Asia-Pacific, Africa, and Europe, destined to all parts of the United States. Many came as students and as professionals, already highly educated in their home country. The transformation began immediately after the postwar years, when U.S. policy-makers articulated a new approach to selecting Chinese immigrants as the Cold War emerged. They argued that well-educated Chinese refugees fleeing communism who were stranded in Hong Kong or had relocated to Taiwan—so-called "intellectuals"—constituted "the best type of Chinese" to welcome as immigrants to the U.S. (Hsu, 2015; see also Hu-DeHart, 2015).

These basic characteristics alone underscore the fundamental differences between today's immigrants and the male manual laborers of yesteryear some 150 years ago. Another stark contrast is in the social environment of the two periods. Nineteenth-century Asian immigrants came into an America that was being defined by the Civil War and the end of slavery, which then quickly morphed into a century of racial segregation designed primarily for former slaves, but which also swept in the racialized Asians. However, late twentieth century immigrants like the Chinese benefitted from the Civil Rights movement that dismantled American apartheid and devised policies such as affirmative action to force open access to education, business, and good jobs.

Because of immigration preferences for well-educated, highly skilled workers and professionals, many of the Asian newcomers brought with them sufficient cultural capital, even if not always financial capital, to immediately claim and invest in the opportunities opened up by affirmative action. It is not unusual to arrive in the U.S. with a college or advanced or professional degree, or remain in the U.S. after having obtained these degrees. Given their income, many Asian newcomers can afford to live in middle class and affluent suburbs, and attend school with mostly white and other Asian students, or opt for private or parochial schools. Not surprisingly, these students take a large load of college prep courses, piling on Advanced Placement courses as fast as the College Board can invent them.

Since the 1970s, Asian Americans have consistently scored higher than whites and all other groups in SAT Math, and they pulled alongside whites in SAT Verbal by the 1990s (see College Board, 2014). By the century's end, these students had the lowest absenteeism and the lowest dropout rates. Only 6 % of 19-year-old Asian Americans were not in school, compared to 26 % of Latinos, who were at the other extreme (Kao & Tienda, 1995; Kao, Tienda, & Schneider, 1996, p. 271; Ong, 2000, p. 324, Pang, 1995, p. 418; Wong, 1990, p. 362). These patterns have continued to prevail into the new century.

With this kind of high school background, no wonder Asian Americans had by far the highest college enrollment rate entering the twenty-first century, at 55 %, compared to only 36 for whites, 30 for African-Americans, and 22 for Latinos. Even more impressive were the figures for the most selective public and private universities: by the early twenty-first century, Asian Americans constituted 39 % of all students at Berkeley, 22 % at Stanford, 19 % at Harvard, 17 % at Yale, and 28 % at MIT. It follows that Asian Americans have by far the highest percentage of B.A. degrees, more than even for whites, and, at more than 10 %, earn more than their 5 % proportion of the national population in degrees earned in science and engineering, 40 % or more in medicine, and at least 30 % in law (Hune & Chan, 1997, pp. 45, 53−55; Hsia, 1988a, p. 165, 1988b, p. 119; Ong, 2000, pp. 326–328).[2] Together with graduate students from Asia, they earn 25 % of all research doctorates granted in the United States (Pew Research Center, 2012). This is important because many of these newly minted Ph.D.s apply for U.S. residency and eventually citizenship; their children swell the ranks of the Asian American high achievers in high school and college.

Characteristics associated with the model minority construction can be found primarily among the five largest groups of Asian Americans. These are Chinese, Filipino, Asian Indian, and Korean, all post 1965 voluntary immigrants, as well as the children of Vietnamese refugees (U.S. Census Bureau, 2012; see also Caplan, Choy, & Whitmore, 1991). In these families, the immigrant ethos predominates; together with parents' high socioeconomic status (SES) measured by income and education, these two factors together and separately explain much of the students' success.

At the other end of the spectrum are the rest of the refugees—Cambodians, Laotians, Hmong, whose experiences with schooling resemble those of many other urban minorities, black and Latino, except that these Asian refugees' low academic attainment and general poverty are rarely noticed (see Teranishi, Nguyen, & Alcantar, this volume). In short, Asian Americans today exhibit a bimodal pattern, but the low end has been rendered practically invisible by the big brush that problematically paints the broad "model minority" canvas that covers this very diverse category (Hune & Chan, 1997, p. 60; Pang, 1995, pp. 412–416; Wong, 1990, p. 357).

Intrigued by the highest-achieving Asian American groups plus the fast-rising Vietnamese, the Educational Testing Service conducted a survey in 1997 to

---

[2]For comparative statistics on undergraduate degrees earned see Top 100 degree producers, 2003. Part I: Undergraduate Degrees (2003, 5 June). *Black Issues in Higher Education, 20(8)*.

uncover specific factors that could explain their impressive academic achievement. The South Asian community is perhaps most revealing. Almost all of them are recent immigrants, and the parents' pre-migration educational attainments and professional skills are reinforced by English proficiency, the result of an educational system derived from centuries of British colonialism. (A similar advantage can be found in well-educated Filipino immigrants, whose families became English proficient under American colonialism in the first half of the twentieth century.) At the end of the twentieth century, a survey conducted by the Educational Testing Service disclosed that fully 87 % of South Asian fathers had a college degree or higher, and an astounding 41 % of them had Ph.D.s. Another 32 % had a master's degree. Of South Asian mothers, 70 % had a bachelor's or master's, and 10 % had Ph.D.s. Not surprisingly, fully 100 % of these parents expected their children to earn college degrees or higher, making no distinction among sons or daughters (Kim, 1997, pp. 8–10).

Psychologists Stanley Sue and Sumi Okazaki argue that because Asian immigrants are cognizant of American discrimination against racialized minorities, including themselves, they respond by using educational credentials to optimize opportunities in education-dependent careers in science and technology, engineering, and accounting, eschewing those that require more proficient English communication and writing abilities. In other words, Asian immigrants stress education because of its "relative functionalism" for upward mobility. It works because it enables them to circumvent the effect of exclusion in non-education-dependent pursuits (e.g., sports, entertainment, politics) (Sue & Okazaki, 1995). Sociologist Grace Kao further notes that "relative functionalism" is the other side of the "blocked opportunity" theory often used to explain why longtime U.S. minorities, such as African-Americans and Chicanos, do not place the same faith in education, given their lengthy past experience with racism (Kao, 1998; Kao & Tienda, 1995; Kao et al., 1996). Contrary to popular assumptions embedded in the model minority construction, these scholars suggest that the "centrality of education for success" is not primarily an expression of Asian cultural values as much as it is a response to a perceived hostile environment (Ong, 2000, p. 325). In the words of Hsia, "Cultural values certainly play a role, but economic survival remains the driving force" (1998b, p. 119).

Scholars mentioned above—Sue, Okazaki, Kao, Hsia—explicitly address the issue of "culture" because it is so often used as a facile explanation for Asian American success in education, especially by those pundits and even educators who want to denigrate less successful minorities as being somehow culturally deficient. These thoughtful scholars emphasize that many factors other than "culture," which is difficult to define and test, play important roles. Sue and Okazaki (1995) argue that cultural practices in and of themselves, devoid of a context in which they are deployed, carry little meaning. But when they "interact with conditions in any particular society" at a particular time in history, these values and practices can become significant (p. 140). To those who assert that cultural differences explain Asian American superior academic standing (Steinberg, 1996, p. 92), Sue and Okazaki would counter that although Asian family values and socialization emphasize the need to succeed educationally, culture gains real meaning when Asian immigrants adopt education as the major strategy to respond to a peculiarly American phenomenon of institutional and individual discrimination against those defined as a "minority" in U.S. society (Sue & Okazaki, 1995, pp. 137–140).

Now some 60 years after *Brown*, many of the intended beneficiaries still languish in our public education system, for reasons discussed cogently and extensively in other chapters in this volume. One minority group, however, has seemingly defied the odds by surging ahead of even white Americans in their pursuit of academic excellence. However, by crowning these largely new immigrant groups from Asia a "model minority," political pundits, commentators, and misguided educators have done them no favor. By highlighting their success, they have helped create a backlash against Asian Americans. Although originally included in affirmative action plans, once they were deemed "over-represented" because their numbers in higher education and professional schools exceeded their percentage in the larger population, all Asian Americans, including refugee Southeast Asians who have not been thriving to nearly the same extent, were quietly excluded from further consideration.

Even more insidious, it was discovered in the 1980s and 1990s that elite institutions such as Stanford, Brown, and UCLA, had quietly imposed a top-down quota on Asian American admissions, similar to the quotas imposed on Jewish immigrant students at the front end of the twentieth century (Nakanishi, 1995, pp. 688–692; Takagi, 1992). In other words, when Asian American students were able to compete as individuals against white students on the basis of traditional meritocratic criteria such as high school grades and standardized test scores (SAT, ACT), and without the benefit of affirmative action considerations, they were subject to a higher set of standards and expectations in the very competitive process of college admissions. Critics charge that this was done in order to hold down Asian American numbers in competition with white students. Justifiably viewed as backlash against the relative functionalism of education as practiced by many Asian immigrants, their worst fear, racism—which they thought they had so cleverly dodged—has come around to haunt them after all. Aggressive community organizing against these patently discriminatory practices—by exposing and thus embarrassing the elite institutions— has apparently curtailed, if not ended, such cynical maneuvers.

It might appear that the sense of grievance can be taken to extremes by some Asian Americans, such as in the case of Chinese immigrant and Yale freshman Jian Li, who filed a civil rights complaint against Princeton in 2006 for having rejected him. He pointedly compared his stellar high school academic record to those of black and Latino admits with lesser credentials, implying that Asian Americans had become victims of preferences for blacks and Latinos; significantly, he made no similar charge against less meritorious white admits who also enjoyed preferences, such as athletes and legacies. Hardly disadvantaged by not attending Princeton, he subsequently transferred from Yale to Harvard. Given the strong support he received from anti-Affirmative Action organizations such as the Center for Equal Opportunity, Jian Li might have, inadvertently or otherwise, lent his compelling immigrant story to the political movement to dismantle affirmative action for still under-represented minorities in American education.

Nevertheless, the perspective that Jian Li helped launch with his complaint against Princeton—that affirmative action has unfairly reduced educational opportunities for high-achieving Asian Americans—has hardly receded. If anything, it has only gathered steam, goaded by political activists only too happy to have found in rejected Asian American applicants to elite universities the perfect mascots in their relentless march against affirmative action. In Jian Li *redux*, anti-affirmative activist litigator Edward Blum and plaintiff *Students for Fair Admissions* sued Harvard University in federal court in late 2014 for violation of the 1964 Civil Rights Act because of its "diversity initiatives," meaning the use of race and ethnicity as factors in admissions (Giambrone, 2014).

But even before Jian Li and these other complaints and law suits were filed, American higher education had already begun to shrink in the face of challenges to affirmative action, opening the door to efforts to dismantle it totally. I end with this cautionary tale about justice, merit, and racism in American schooling and education. When the University of Michigan found its affirmative action practices challenged by outside forces led by neoconservatives, it veered from the compensatory justice arguments initially advanced to support the need for affirmative action, toward embracing an assertion of "diversity" as an educational value, but leaving the meaning and parameters of "diversity" vague and fuzzy (Gurin, Dey, Hurtado, & Gurin, 2002). Some Asian American families today have a hard time accepting the diversity rationale, perhaps because they are not sure if they are included or excluded. If a century ago Chinese parents in San Francisco protested the imposition of segregated schools for their children, today, in the twenty-first century, some of the mostly immigrant Chinese American parents of high-achieving children threaten to undo racial harmony and exacerbate racial tension by successfully challenging Lowell High School's desegregation plan designed 30 years ago to achieve some balance among the students in a multicultural, multiracial city and its public school system. They do not buy into the argument that "diversity" carries educational value.

The story of Asian Americans and the struggle for racial equality in American education is complex and contradictory. On the surface, their struggle for racial justice—expressed as being fairly rewarded for academic achievement—is entangled with other minority groups' bid for greater balance in representation. Today this group is largely composed of postwar immigrants and their Asian and American-born children, and perhaps more damaging than anything that has been thrown their way is the "model minority" construction. Reduced to its basest expression, the model minority renders all Asian Americans as an amorphous cultural mass of featureless, interchangeable parts who all do the same thing in the same way, marching inexorably to the relentless beat for excellence, best captured and problematically promoted by the self-parodying Yale law school professor Amy Chua (2011) of "Tiger Mother" fame. Who will control and write the script of the next or last chapter in this still evolving story? (Havana 31 January 2015)

References

All-USA High School Academic Team. (2003, May 15). *USA Today*, Section D, pp. 1–2, 8–9.

Batalova, J. (2011, May 24). *Asian immigrants in the United States*. Migration Policy Institute. Retrieved from http://www.migrationpolicy.org/article/asian-immigrants-united-states.

Caplan, N., Choy, M. H., & Whitmore, J. K. (1991). *Children of the boat people*. Ann Arbor, MI: University of Michigan Press.

Chua, A. (2011). *Battle hymn of the Tiger Mother*. New York, NY: Penguin.

Chun, K. (1995). The myth of Asian American success and its educational ramifications. In D. T. Nakanishi & T. Y. Nishida (Eds.), *The Asian American educational experience: A source book for teachers and students* (pp. 95–112). New York, NY: Routledge.

College Board. (2014). *The 2014 SAT Report on College and Career Readiness*. Retrieved from http://research.collegeboard.org/programs/sat/data/cb-seniors-2014.

Giambrone, A. (2014, December 26). Do diversity initiatives indirectly discriminate against Asian Americans? *The Atlantic*. Retrieved from http://www.theatlantic.com/education/archive/2014/12/do-diversity-initiatives-indirectly-discriminate-against-asian-americans/384054/.

Gurin, P., Dey, E. L., Hurtado, S., & Gurin, G. (2002). Diversity and higher education: Theory and impact on educational outcome. *Harvard Educational Review, 72*(3), 330–366.

Hirabayashi, L. R. (1991). The impact of incarceration on the education of *nisei* schoolchildren. In R. Daniels, S. C. Taylor, & H. H. L. Kitano (Eds.), *Japanese Americans: From relocation to redress* (pp. 44–51). Seattle, WA: University of Washington Press.

Hsia, J. (1988a). *Asian Americans in higher education and at work*. Hillsdale, NJ: Lawrence Erlbaum.

Hsia, J. (1998b). Limits of affirmative action: Asian American access to higher education. *Educational Policy, 2*(2), 117–136.

Hsu, M. Y. (2015). *The good immigrants: How the yellow peril became the model minority*. Princeton, NJ: Princeton University Press.

Hu-DeHart, E. (2015). Yellow peril, model minority, honorary white, tiger nation: Chinese in America, Global China and the United States. In J. B. Antolín, A. S. López, & F. H. Navejas (Eds.), *Imágenes y percepciones de China en las Américas y en la Península Ibérica*. Edicions Bellaterra: Barcelona, Spain.

Hune, S., & Chan, K. S. (1997). Special focus: Asian Pacific American demographic and educational trends. In D. Carter & R. Wilson (Eds.), *Minorities in higher education 15* (pp. 39–63). Washington, D.C.: American Council on Education.

Kao, G. (1998). Educational aspirations of minority youth. *American Journal of Education, 106*, 349–384.

Kao, G., & Tienda, M. (1995). Optimism and achievement: The educational performance of immigrant youth. *Social Science Quarterly, 76*(1), 1–19.

Kao, G., Tienda, M., & Schneider, B. (1996). Racial and ethnic variation in academic performance. *Research in Sociology of Education and Socialization, 11*, 263–297.

Kim, H. (1997). *Diversity among Asian American school students*. Princeton, NJ: Policy Information Center, Educational Testing Service.

Nakanishi, D. T. (1995). Asian Pacific Americans and colleges and universities. In J. A. Banks (Ed.), *Handbook of research on multicultural education*. New York, NY: Macmillan.

Ngai, M. (2010) *The lucky ones: One family and the extraordinary invention of Chinese America*. New York, NY: Houghton Mifflin.

Odo, F. (Ed.). (2002). *The Columbia documentary history of the Asian American experience*. New York, NY: Columbia University Press.

Ong, P. (2000). The affirmative action divide. In P. Ong (Ed.), *The state of Asian Pacific America: transforming race relations. A public policy report* (Vol. IV). Los Angeles, CA: LEAP Asia Pacific American Public Policy Institute and UCLA Asian American Studies Center.

Pang, V. O. (1995). Asian Pacific American students: A diverse and complex population. In J. A. Banks (Ed.), *Handbook of research on multicultural education* (pp. 412–424). New York, NY: Macmillan.

Pew Research Center. (2012). *The rise of Asian Americans: Chapter 1: Portrait of Asian Americans*. Retrieved from http://www.pewsocialtrends.org/2012/06/19/chapter-1-portrait-of-asian-americans/.

Steinberg, L. (1996). *Beyond the classroom: Why school reform has failed and what parents need to do*. New York, NY: Simon & Schuster.

Sue, S., & Okazaki, S. (1995). Asian American educational achievements: A phenomenon in search of an explanation. In D. T. Nakanishi & T. Y. Nishida (Eds.), *The Asian American educational experience: A source book for teachers and students* (pp. 133–145). New York, NY: Routledge.

Suzuki, B. H. (1995). Education and the socialization of Asian Americans: A revisionist analysis of the "model minority" thesis. In D. T. Nakanishi & T. Y. Nishida (Eds.), *The Asian American educational experience: A source book for teachers and students* (pp. 113–132). New York, NY: Routledge.

Takagi, D. Y. (1992). *The retreat from race: Asian American admissions and racial politics*. New Brunswick, NJ: Rutgers University Press.

U.S. Census Bureau. (2012, March). The Asian population: 2010 (C2010BR-11). Retrieved from http://www.census.gov/prod/cen2010/briefs/c2010br-11.pdf.

U.S. Census Bureau. (2013, June 13). *Asians fastest-growing race or ethnic group in 2012, Census Bureau reports (Release Number: CB13-112)*. Retrieved from http://www.census.gov/newsroom/press-releases/2013/cb13-112.html.

U.S. Census Bureau. (2014). *State and County QuickFacts* (Data derived from Population Estimates, American Community Survey, Census of Population and Housing, State and County Housing Unit Estimates, County Business Patterns, Nonemployer Statistics, Economic Census, Survey of Business Owners, Building Permits). Retrieved from http://quickfacts.census.gov/qfd/states/00000.html.

Wollenberg, C. M. (1995a). "Yellow peril" in the schools (I). In D. T. Nakanishi & T. Y. Nishida (Eds.), *The Asian American educational experience: A source book for teachers and students* (pp. 1–12). New York, NY: Routledge.

Wollenberg, C. M. (1995b). "Yellow peril" in the schools (II). In D. T. Nakanishi & T. Y. Nishida (Eds.), *The Asian American educational experience: A source book for teachers and students* (pp. 13–29). New York, NY: Routledge.

Wong, M. G. (1990). The education of White, Chinese, Filipino, and Japanese students: A look at "high school and beyond". *Sociological Perspectives, 33*(3), 355–374.

Zhou, M., & Xiong, Y. S. (2007). The multifaceted American experiences of the children of Asian immigrants: Lessons for segmented assimilation. *Ethnic and Racial Studies, 28*(6), 1119–1152. doi:10.1080/01419870500224455.

The Data Quality Movement for the Asian American and Pacific Islander Community: An Unresolved Civil Rights Issue

Robert T. Teranishi, Bach Mai Dolly Nguyen and Cynthia M. Alcantar

Despite a large and growing body of research on inequality in the American education system, Asian Americans and Pacific Islanders (AAPIs) continue to be an outlier in our national conversation about race. In the rare instance when AAPIs are included in the racial discourse about America's equity agenda, they have been reduced to a single, stubbornly persistent narrative as a group that does not have needs or concerns worthy of attention by researchers, policymakers, or practitioners. A key factor that contributes to the exclusion and misrepresentation of AAPI students is the lack of disaggregated data available to inform a deeper understanding of the population. Data that aggregates information on all AAPIs as a single category provides a misleading statistical portrait of a diverse AAPI population. As a result, aggregated data becomes a barrier to policy and program development that can advance the equitable treatment for the AAPI community.

In this chapter, we call for a deeper understanding of the AAPI population through a proactive—as opposed to reactive—stance to the model minority frame. Specifically, we demonstrate how aggregated data is a barrier to policy and program development that can advance the equitable treatment for the AAPI community, and we address the steps the National Commission on Asian American Research in Education (CARE) has taken to encourage better data practices that

R.T. Teranishi (✉) · B.M.D. Nguyen · C.M. Alcantar
UCLA Institute for Immigration, Globalization, and Education, University of California,
1041C Moore Hall, 405 Hilgard Avenue, Los Angeles, CA 90095, USA
e-mail: robert.teranishi@ucla.edu

B.M.D. Nguyen
e-mail: dollynguyen@ucla.edu

C.M. Alcantar
e-mail: cynthia.alcantar@ucla.edu

© Springer International Publishing Switzerland 2016
P.A. Noguera et al. (eds.), *Race, Equity, and Education*,
DOI 10.1007/978-3-319-23772-5_7

provide a more nuanced perspective on ethnic subgroup differences within the AAPI community. Ultimately, we argue that the data disaggregation movement is one of the most important civil rights issues for the AAPI community.

We focus specifically on the work of CARE's *iCount* initiative, which is a data quality movement that aims to tailor institutional data systems so they can effectively reflect an increasingly complex and heterogeneous student population; for AAPI students, this requires data that can reflect the ethnic diversity of the population. The focus of this chapter centers on the work of iCount in the state of Washington, which is historically a very important state for the migration of AAPIs, and today a vibrant site for community activism and political activity to address the needs of a large and growing AAPI population.

We begin the chapter with a historical context of how AAPIs have been positioned in education research. We then shift to discussing the ways in which heterogeneity in the population has emerged as a key concept through which we must understand the unique experiences and outcomes of AAPI students. Next, we highlight CARE's effort to build on the heterogeneity movement to work toward data systems that adequately collect information about and report on AAPI subgroups, and we address the status of the data disaggregation movement in Washington and how it has yielded new and unique insight into the AAPI population. We conclude with a discussion about the implications for broader society, spotlighting the need for data that is tailored to inform efforts that effectively support an increasingly complex and heterogeneous student population. Without disaggregated data for AAPIs, the most marginalized and vulnerable subgroups will remain overlooked and underserved.

A Historical Context

The history of the American education system for minorities can be characterized by the juxtaposition of opportunities and barriers. These contrasting experiences are especially complicated for the AAPI student population, which has been plagued by the "model minority" frame. Coined in 1966, this term appeared in a *New York Times* article (Peterson, 1966) and set into motion a stubborn and persistent stereotype that continues to characterize the Asian American educational landscape. Over the course of the two decades following Peterson's article, scholars countered the conceptualization of universal Asian American success by tacking on the word "myth" to denote that the model minority was an inaccurate and disingenuous portrayal of a heterogeneous population with unique and varying histories, cultures, experiences, and outcomes. Kitano and Sue (1973), for example, asserted:

> The widespread belief that Asian Americans have somehow overcome prejudice and discrimination has given them a low priority in terms of attention and aid. For example, in hiring, in admission to institutions of higher education, and in financial aid, Asians are often regarded as whites (p. 1).

Over the past three decades, despite calls by AAPI scholars like Kitano and Sue to challenge the model minority myth and other forms of discrimination experienced by AAPIs, sweeping generalizations about universal academic success among AAPI students continue to define their treatment in the twenty-first century. The dominant narrative about AAPIs in education is that they continue to experience disproportionately high enrollment in highly selective, 4-year institutions in such academic fields as science, technology, engineering, and mathematics (STEM) and are a population that does not face challenges similar to its non-White counterparts (National Commission on Asian American and Pacific Islander Research in Education [CARE], 2008). Unfortunately, the state of research on AAPIs demonstrates that a considerable amount of what is known about the population continues to be heavily influenced by racial stereotypes and false perceptions, rather than by empirical evidence.

The misrepresentation of the AAPI community deeply impacts the most marginalized AAPI subgroups as they struggle to succeed academically, balance the stigma of a predisposed success, and struggle to gain access to resources necessary to realize their educational aspirations. Compounding this problem is the literature on race and racism that omits AAPI students, as though they have achieved a non-minority, minority status (Teranishi, 2010). These practices have largely gone unchecked in policy arenas, leaving the impression that AAPI students face no academic challenges associated with educational mobility.

Race and the Heterogeneity Movement

The racialization of minority groups is not unique to any one particular group. Racial categories in the United States have been used to explain differences in social outcomes, such as wealth and poverty, on the basis of race. For example, like AAPIs, Latino subgroups are lumped together into one Latino category without consideration of ethnic differences in immigration patterns, culture, and economic and educational outcomes. Contrary to the AAPI model minority myth, Latinos are often depicted as poor, underachieving, criminals, and "illegal" Mexican immigrants (Contreras, Malcom, & Bensimon, 2008). Thus, racial stereotypes influence the way each minority group is treated in the U.S. For AAPIs, the grouping of all students into one pan-ethnic group and the perpetuation of the "model minority" is rooted in the sociohistorical and political context of our society that reinforces outcomes attached to race.

To understand the racialization of AAPIs and its impact on the outcomes of racialized social structures, we converged two sociological theoretical lenses for understanding race: Omi and Winant's (1994) theory of racial formation and Tilly's (1998) exploration of categorical inequality. The nexus of these frameworks allows for a deeper understanding of how race functions and sustains its permanency in society, but also for exploring how race is fluid and ever evolving (Teranishi, 2010). Omi and Winant (1994) offer a critical theory for understanding the evolution of race. They write, "Racial formation is a process of historically situated *projects* in which human bodies and social structures are represented and organized" (pp. 55–56). Further, Omi and Winant (1994) offer an explanation for an evolution of race "as the socio-historical process by which racial categories are created, inhabited, transformed, and destroyed" (p. 55). The key concept relative to our project is transformation and the opportunity for better capturing current social demands and the recognition that race can and will continue to change as it has historically.

Tilly offers a second lens that is helpful for understanding the racialization of AAPIs. Tilly's (1998) categorical inequality is important for understanding why racial categories (the five aggregate race groups) have been persistently durable. He explains that "much of what observers ordinarily interpret as individual differences that create inequality is actually the consequence of categorical organization" (Tilly, 1998, p. 9). This advances the need to reform racial statistics because while racism and discrimination can occur at the individual level, inequality functions at systemic and organizational levels and must be addressed in that way. Thus, the foundational underpinnings of categorical inequality not only help shape our understanding of the functionality of inequality, but they also support the need for examining these injustices as organizational issues. As race is inherently categorized in our current social and political landscape, racial inequality must be addressed as a categorical injustice.

Given the context of race as an evolving concept and the need for attacking it at the systemic level, a major effort by contemporary scholars of AAPI education issues is focused on the better representation of the heterogeneity of the AAPI population, which has been evolving demographically while the population has simultaneously been growing exponentially. For example, in the 20-year period between 1990 and 2010, while AAPIs in the aggregate doubled in size, this rate of growth was most representative of East Asians (Chinese, Japanese, and Koreans). However, Southeast Asians (Vietnamese, Hmong, Cambodians, and Laotians) tripled in size, and South Asians (Asian Indians, Bangladeshis, and Pakistanis) quadrupled in size (CARE, 2013). These differential growth rates are altering the face of the AAPI community.

Given these dramatic shifts, disaggregated data on the AAPI population reveal a wide range of demographic characteristics that are unlike those of any other racial group in America with regard to their heterogeneity. According to the U.S. Census Bureau, the AAPI racial category consists of 48 different ethnic groups that occupy positions along the full range of the socioeconomic spectrum, from the poor and under-privileged, to the affluent and highly skilled. AAPIs also vary demographically with regard to language background, immigration history, culture, and religion (CARE, 2008). Yet, these and other very unique circumstances are often overshadowed by the grouping of AAPIs in the aggregate. Thus, while the AAPI population represents a single entity in certain contexts, such as for interracial group comparisons, it is equally important to understand the ways in which the demography of the population is comprised of a complex set of social realities for individuals and communities that fall within this category.

Data that better represents AAPI subgroups is an essential need for this heterogeneous and unique population, but more importantly, it is vital to move one step further in utilizing disaggregated data to reveal the educational realities of AAPI students and better target interventions to improve their social outcomes. For example, trends in educational attainment for a number of AAPI subgroups are representative of the heterogeneity that exists within the population. Consider that 51.1 % of Vietnamese, 63.2 % of Hmong, 65.5 % of Laotian, and 65.8 % of Cambodian adults (25 years or older) have not enrolled in or completed any postsecondary education (CARE, 2013). For those students who do continue on to college, their pathway to a postsecondary degree is far from certain. For example, while more than four out of five East Asians (Chinese, Japanese, and Korean) and South Asians (Asian Indian and Pakistani) who entered college earned at least a bachelor's degree, large proportions of other AAPI subgroups are attending college, but not earning a degree. Among Southeast Asians, 33.7 % of Vietnamese, 42.9 % of Cambodians, 46.5 % of Laotians, and 47.5 % of Hmong adults (25 years or older) reported having attended college, but not earning a degree (CARE, 2013).

For Southeast Asians, there is actually a high concentration of adults who face attrition at the elementary and secondary education levels. For example, 34.3 % of Laotian, 38.5 % of Cambodian, and 39.6 % of Hmong adults do not even have a high school diploma or equivalent (CARE, 2013). In the Hmong community, nearly a third of the adults have less than a fourth grade education (CARE, 2013). There are a number of factors that contribute to low educational attainment for Southeast Asians and other subgroups experiencing similar educational outcomes. Some AAPI students face disparate language barriers as many are new immigrants (e.g., first generation students who solely speak a language other than English at home versus third generation students who primarily speak English) whereas others confront a lack of access to effective counseling to address high levels of academic pressure or challenges associated with traversing contrasting cultural norms. A significant common denominator tends to be poverty and a lack of access to quality schooling and other resources and opportunities. These challenges are compounded by a general assumption that AAPIs are universally successful, which results in the population being overlooked and underserved.

Given the unique racial position of AAPIs, the heterogeneity movement has been a necessary effort, albeit slow in progress. As the demography of this population continues to experience rapid growth and shifts, however, the urgency for representing the dynamic subgroups included in the AAPI racial category has heightened. Our approach for addressing this issue seeks to reform data practices and the utility of racial categories.

iCount: A Data Quality Movement for Asian Americans and Pacific Islanders

In 2013, CARE launched *iCount: A Data Quality Movement for Asian Americans and Pacific Islanders in Higher Education*. The iCount initiative, a collaborative effort with the White House Initiative on Asian Americans and Pacific Islanders (WHIAAPI) and with generous support from ETS and Asian Americans and Pacific Islanders in Philanthropy (AAPIP), is centered on three interrelated goals. First, the initiative aims to raise awareness about and bring attention to the ways in which aggregate data on AAPI students conceal significant disparities in educational experiences and outcomes between AAPI subgroups, and thus provide an empirical rationale for the collection of disaggregated data. Second, iCount offers models for how postsecondary institutions, systems, and states can respond to this problem by identifying opportunities for data reform. Finally, it aims to work collaboratively with the education field to encourage broader reform in institutional practices related to the collection and reporting of disaggregated data.

The project began with the release of the ETS-published iCount report, which focuses on our first two goals: provide the rationale for disaggregated data and offer institutional models to reform data practices (CARE, 2013). More specifically, we discuss the extent to which AAPI students are a dynamic, heterogeneous, and evolving population and the implications of how measurement standards and techniques are a factor in the representation of their educational needs, challenges, and representation. We build on this discussion and provide institutional, system-, and state-level examples for collecting and reporting disaggregated data and highlight how access to and use of this data increases higher education's ability to be more responsive to the needs of AAPI subgroups.

The 2013 iCount report was released in conjunction with a symposium co-hosted by CARE and WHIAPPI at the U.S. Department of Education. The symposium brought together leaders from K-12 and higher education sectors and experts in demography, institutional research, and philanthropy to engage in an open dialogue about ways to develop data systems that are responsive to the needs of AAPI students and families. Coupled with the report, the iCount convening offered a forward-looking perspective on the need for and benefits of collecting and reporting disaggregated data, and afforded institutions a pathway for implementing methods for collecting data that reflects the heterogeneity in the AAPI population—institutional data practices that are necessary for a more effective and responsive system of education. Several themes emerged from the convening, two of which shaped our continued work to date.

First, the convening brought to the surface the inherent need for data disaggregation, which was well acknowledged by educational stakeholders representing entities from institutional research offices in postsecondary institutions to K-12 focused community organizations. The attendance of over 200 participants reinforced this conclusion. Second, and most importantly, the convening revealed that despite this recognition, practitioners, administrators, and community organizers lacked the political will to pursue changes to their data practice. In other words, with a lack of administrative support or mandated policy incentives, data reform was difficult to achieve, even for those who acknowledged that it was a critical need.

Thus, iCount has evolved to address these very concerns in the pursuit of data reform through localized efforts. Since the 2013 convening, iCount has developed five partnerships with institutions and community and state organizations that have demonstrated a commitment to improving the academic experiences and outcomes of their AAPI students. Each of these five efforts is at a different stage in regard to their data reform process. For example, whereas one higher education system has collected disaggregated data for a number of years and is now exploring how to effectively utilize the subgroup data, another cluster of institutions is conducting a needs assessment to determine what is known (and unknown) about its AAPI students. To further demonstrate the effort to advance data disaggregation through localized efforts and its functionality in providing rationale and building political will, we will turn to a discussion of one of our five partnerships.

iCount and the Data Disaggregation Movement in the State of Washington

The state of Washington has been a critical space for the data disaggregation movement considering the rich history of AAPIs in the state that dates back two centuries. In the eighteenth century, for example, Pacific Islanders began migrating to the Pacific Northwest as staff in merchant ships (Kopple, 1995) and were critical to laying the foundation of Washington as workers who provided shelter for missionaries and contributing to the early economy (Takumi, 1989). In the nineteenth and early twentieth centuries, Asian Americans arrived in the Pacific Northwest as laborers in railroad construction, mining, agriculture, and fishery (Hune & Takeuchi, 2008). The migration to the Northwest broadly, and Washington specifically, drew in a diversity of AAPI ethnic subgroups, each with its own culture, language, and immigration story. Their transition into Washington, however, was one marred by racial discrimination (Takumi, 1989).

For example, Seattle's history is deeply embedded with racial segregation and exclusion of communities of color including AAPIs (Seattle Civil Rights & Labor History Project, 2014). As early as the 1800s, Chinese Americans faced resentment and discrimination by way of the Chinese Exclusion Act. Japanese Americans in the post-war era worked tirelessly as farmers and in other businesses to establish home and community despite efforts to push them out (Spikard, 2009). It was not until the early 1960s that pushback on school segregation occurred. With the threat of a federal lawsuit, Seattle implemented a mandatory busing system in the mid-1970s to desegregate public schools (Dumas, 2011). Black leaders were prominent in their advocacy against busing, as it did not lead to advancements in closing the educational achievement gap and "placed a disproportionate burden on children of color" (Dumas, 2008, p. 84). In Rainer Beach, a neighborhood in Seattle with a particularly high concentration of communities of color (60 % Black and 25 % Asian), the historical implications of segregation continue to take hold as schools are deeply under-resourced as compared to other Seattle schools with smaller minority populations (Dumas, 2008). Although a large part of the Rainier Beach community, Asian Americans are largely absent from the historical narratives on advocacy for and against such issues.

Actually, AAPI community activism in Washington experienced a sharp increase in the 1960s as community organizations, churches, and community centers formed in areas with high AAPI concentration. In 1973, Ruby Chow became the first Asian American elected to a Seattle County seat (Chu, 1991). AAPIs in Washington today face a different set of challenges that continue to demonstrate the strong AAPI activism in the state. Gentrification of Southeast Seattle, for example, where many AAPIs who came upon their arrival to the state now live, is a constant concern. Community organization and advocacy groups have been fighting for claim of their land for a number of years and have made progress, as several capital projects including the Refugee Women's Alliance (ReWa) and the Asian Counseling and Referral Service (ACRS) have been established in Southeast Seattle. In 2009, the AAPI community also celebrated the opening of Samaki Commons, a 40-unit housing complex for immigrant and refugee families. AAPIs have also worked endlessly to resolve issues related to the light rail construction, which has closed down a number of AAPI-owned businesses. The challenges faced by these communities have been further exacerbated by low educational attainment rates and minimal resources for improving academic access and success (Hune & Takeuchi, 2008). Recognizing this, groups such as the Southeast Asians in Education (SEAeD) and the Pacific Islander student coalition, UPRISE, have advocated for the collection of better data. Supported by the efforts from groups like these, Representative Tomiko-Santos submitted House Bill 1680, which included a data disaggregation clause. It did not pass; however, these efforts have continued to move forward with the hopes of reforming data to better represent their communities.

The political and community efforts on the ground in Washington have been joined by national organizations, such as the National Education Association (NEA) and Asian American Legal Defense and Education Fund (AALDEF), which have emerged as outspoken proponents of school integration with a particular focus on the isolation of many Southeast Asian subgroups. Today's AAPI population is a testament to their resilience, as each of these communities has faced a number of challenges in their story of contending with issues of race, place, and space. Thus, in addition to the robust size and growth of AAPIs, Washington is an excellent partner for the work of iCount because of the historical efforts to improve the educational experiences and outcomes of its vulnerable AAPI subgroups.

In the next section, we discuss findings from data provided by the Washington Office of Superintendent of Public Instruction (OSPI), which is charged with the collection of all K-12 enrollment and state assessment data. In 2010, OSPI began collecting disaggregated AAPI data, including information about 16 Asian American and 9 NHPI subgroups featured in this chapter. Data from the 2012–2013 school year on all students enrolled in any one of the K-12 public schools in Washington State are included. In addition to enrollment in K-12 public schools, variables on enrollment in the Free or Reduced Lunch Program, unexcused absences, and disciplinary action (i.e., suspensions and expulsions) are included. To examine the differences that emerged across racial and ethnic subgroups, descriptive analysis was conducted on the above variables.

The framework of disproportionality (Ahram, Fergus, & Noguera, 2011) allowed us to narrowly target our focus on within-group difference, which brought to the surface the nuances and disparities across AAPI ethnic subgroups. Further, it offered a lens for understanding disproportionality not as a symptom of individual performance but a systemic issue of deficit thinking and the application of quick "fixes" by schools that did not do well to mitigate disparities (Ahram et al., 2011). This framework helps shape our understanding of group difference and reinforces the need for "a culturally responsive framework [that] can produce a shift" in addressing educational gaps (Ahram et al., 2011).

What Disaggregated Data Reveals About AAPI Students in Washington

There are 81,788 AAPI students enrolled in Washington's public system of education, which constitutes 8.1 % of the total enrollment. The significant number and proportional representation of AAPIs in Washington's education system is representative of their presence in the state. Between 2000 and 2010, AAPIs were the fastest growing racial group in the state (U.S. Census, 2010). In terms of their AAPI population relative to other states, Washington ranks seventh in the nation for states with the largest AAPI population (U.S. Census, 2012). However, it is important to note that Washington has the third largest concentration of Native Hawaiians and Pacific Islanders after Hawai'i and California (U.S. Census, 2012).

The Demography of AAPI Students in Washington

In Washington's public system of education, the AAPI student population is a vastly heterogeneous representation of different ethnic subgroups. Among Asian Americans, the largest ethnic subgroups are Chinese, Filipino, and Vietnamese, which make up 55.8 % of the Asian American students (Fig. 1). Asian Indians

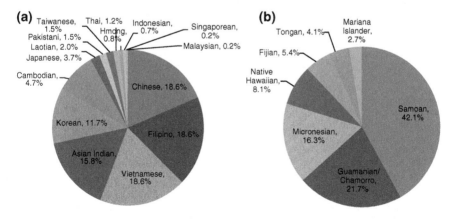

Fig. 1 Washington state 2012–2013 K-12 fall enrollment by AAPI ethnicity (Disaggregated). **a** Asian American subgroup representation. **b** Pacific Islander subgroup representation

and Koreans make up another sizeable group of Asian American students (15.8 and 11.7 %, respectively). Other Asian American ethnic subgroups include Cambodians, Japanese, Pakistani, Taiwanese, Thai, Hmong, Indonesians, Singaporeans, and Malaysians. Among Pacific Islanders, the largest ethnic subgroup is Samoans, which constituted 42.1 % of the Pacific Islander student population. Guamanians and Micronesians also make up a sizeable concentration of Pacific Islander students (21.7 and 16.3 %, respectively). Other Pacific Islander groups include Native Hawaiians, Fijians, Tongans, and Mariana Islanders. Disaggregated data not only identifies the composition of this student population, it also reveals useful insight into the educational experiences that vary between AAPI ethnic subgroups.

AAPI students in Washington also range with regard to their socioeconomic backgrounds. Data on the Free or Reduced Lunch (FRL) program, for example, indicates the rate of students eligible for the National School Lunch Program, a federally assisted meal program based on federal income poverty guidelines (U.S. Department of Agriculture, 2014). To be eligible for the FRL program, students must meet the household income poverty threshold at or below 130 % for *Free* lunch, and between 130 and 185 % for *Reduced* price lunch (USDA, 2014). Our analysis revealed, in the aggregate, 7.0 % of AAPI students participate in the FRL program, indicating a low poverty rate among this population. However, there are some AAPI ethnic subgroups that are disproportionately represented among FRL eligibility. For example, while Southeast Asians make up 24.1 % of the AAPI enrollment, they are 33.7 % of the FRL eligible AAPI students (Fig. 2). Additionally, while Native Hawaiians and Pacific Islanders make up 11.1 % of the AAPI student enrollment, they constitute 20.7 % of the FRL eligible AAPI students. Conversely, East Asians and South Asians have a lower proportional representation in this program relative to their representation in total AAPI enrollment.

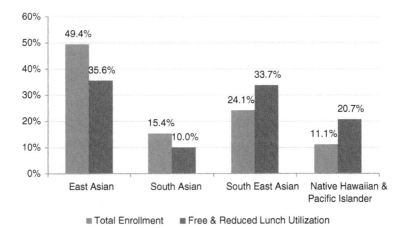

Fig. 2 Proportional representation of ethnic subgroups in total enrollment and free or reduced lunch utilization among AAPIs

Distribution of AAPIs in Bilingual Education and Special Education

AAPI students are disproportionately enrolled in bilingual education in Washington State. Southeast Asian students have the largest proportional representation in bilingual education at 28.4 %, which is nearly twice the proportional representation of East Asians and more than three times the likelihood of being enrolled in bilingual education compared to the statewide average (8.8 %) (Fig. 3). South Asians (19.6 %) and Native Hawaiians and Pacific Islanders (19.4 %) also have a high proportional representation in bilingual education. These data are driven, in part, by a significant proportion of AAPI students with immigrant-origin backgrounds, which accounts for 44.7 % of the total immigrant student population. This is important to note considering Spanish-language programs typically dominate the bilingual education programs in public schools (Ovando, 2003), while AAPI students are actually bringing to their classrooms a number of different languages and dialects. National data indicates that AAPIs utilize over 300 different languages as a primary language spoken at home.

AAPIs also varied in the likelihood they were placed in special education programs. Although nationally, AAPIs make up the lowest proportional enrollment in special education or the Individuals with Disabilities Education Act (IDEA) programs at 4.2 % for ages 3–5 years and 4.8 % for ages 6–21 years (DOE, OSERS, & OSEP, 2012), as compared to 5.7 and 9.0 % nationally, studies have called attention to the variability among AAPI ethnic subgroups. So while some studies have recognized that there are disproportional enrollments of particular AAPI subgroups in special education (Artiles, Harry, Reschly, & Chinn, 2002), the overall "underrepresentation" that is portrayed by aggregate data remains a matter of concern. This issue is exacerbated by the fact that English Language Learners (ELLs) are more likely to be placed in special education (Rueda & Windmueller, 2006), which is particularly relevant to AAPIs who are largely ELLs (CARE, 2008).

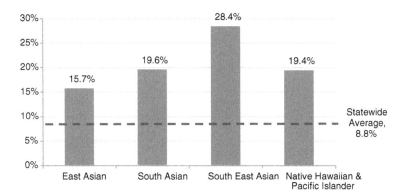

Fig. 3 Enrolled in bilingual education

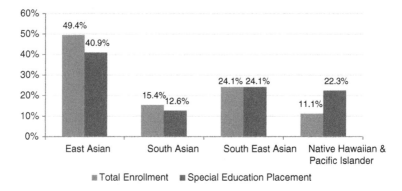

Fig. 4 Proportional representation of ethnic subgroups in total enrollment and special education placement among AAPIs

Disaggregated data in Washington public schools reveals that a higher likelihood of placement in special education for particular AAPI ethnic subgroups warrants attention. As Fig. 4 demonstrates, placement in special education is particularly high for NHPIs who make up twice their proportional total enrollment in special education. Southeast Asian ethnic subgroups should also be considered when thinking about special education placement and culturally sensitive assessments, as their placement in special education matches their proportional total enrollment in Washington State.

Truancy and Disciplinary Action Cases Among AAPI Students

Studies have found that truancy puts students at greater risk for not doing well academically (Gottfried, 2009), dropping out or being pushed out, substance abuse, and living in poverty later in life (Yeide & Korbin, 2009). Various factors put students at greater risk of unexcused absences such as unsafe schools, poor school climate, poor relations with teachers, financial, social, or medical problems that may require students to stay home, and violence near home, among other factors (Yeide & Korbin, 2009). Studies done in the state of Washington in particular have found school factors contributing to poor academic achievement of students of color (Bailey & Dziko, 2008; Contreras & Strikus, 2008; Hune & Takeuchi, 2008).

In our analysis, we found in the aggregate, Asian American students had the lowest rates of unexcused absences (6.7 %) compared to other racial groups (9.1 % White, 17 % Latino, 20.3 % Black, 21.0 % NHPI) (Fig. 5). The high rate of absences among NHPI students is particularly problematic as a large proportion of school-age students in Washington are NHPI.

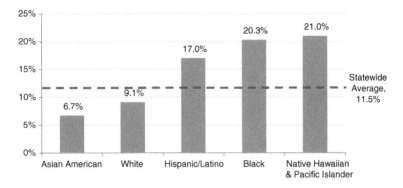

Fig. 5 Five or more unexcused absences

Equally important to consider is school disciplinary action. School discipline has come to the forefront of the American consciousness, which has led to an increase in different forms of zero-tolerance policies. Racial disproportionality in school discipline has been well documented, especially for Black and Latino students (United States Department of Education Office of Civil Rights, 2014). Studies which have examined school discipline by race have found Black and Latino students are disproportionately more likely to be targeted for suspension and expulsion than White and Asian students (OCR, 2014). When Asian American students are included in these studies, they have been characterized as the least likely to be disciplined (Hoffman & Llagas, 2003). In most cases, Pacific Islanders have been left out of these studies. No studies have examined the ethnic representation within racial categories to examine suspensions and expulsions.

Utilizing data from Washington State, we examined school discipline among AAPI subgroups. First, we found that NHPI students were disproportionately likely to be disciplined, relative to their proportional representation among AAPI students (see Fig. 6). While NHPI students represent 11.1 % of all AAPI students

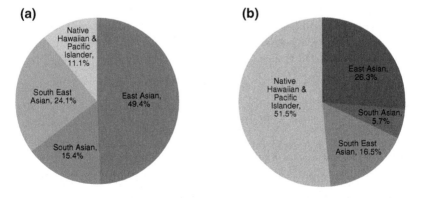

Fig. 6 a Distribution of enrollment for ethnic subgroups among AAPIs. **b** Distribution of disciplinary action for ethnic subgroups among AAPIs

in Washington, they comprise 51.5 % of the cases of discipline in 2013. Thus, NHPI students are an important population for examining differential academic experiences relative to disciplinary action. These findings need closer attention in future research considering the differential academic experiences that are correlated with disciplinary action and the extent to which particular student populations are disproportionately affected by such school policies and practices (Skiba, Michael, Nardo, & Peterson, 2002).

Conclusion and Implications

In this chapter, we provide empirical perspectives on aggregated and disaggregated data for AAPI students in the state of Washington. We discuss the extent to which aggregated data conceals significant differences between AAPI ethnic subgroups with regard to their demographic backgrounds, placement in academic programs, and disciplinary action. We assert that these issues of disproportionality are associated with significant disparities in educational attainment. Future studies should utilize disaggregated data to further an understanding of the ways in which AAPI subgroups have differential access to educational resources and opportunities.

Through a focus on Washington, which has recently begun collecting and reporting on disaggregated data, we believe there are important lessons for other states and education systems. First, this case study sheds light on the importance of involving a broad group of constituents, including community organizations, elected officials, and education constituents. The steps that were taken to achieve more refined data were the result of a clear set of goals and having a collaborative effort to support and monitor progress. Second, the study supports the need for political will in order to achieve data reform, thus reinforcing change that is driven by individuals, but ultimately occurs at organizational and systemic levels. Finally, the Washington effort demonstrates how both the collection and utilization of disaggregated data must come together to identify *and* address the barriers facing AAPI students. This is one of the most important civil rights issues for the AAPI community. Without disaggregated data, AAPI students will remain overlooked and underserved, which is a problem especially for the most marginalized and vulnerable AAPI subgroups.

References

Ahram, R., Fergus, E., & Noguera, P. (2011). Addressing racial/ethnic disproportionality in special education: Case studies of suburban school districts. *Teachers College Record, 113*(10), 2233–2266.

Artiles, A. J., Harry, B., Reschly, D. J., & Chinn, P. C. (2002). Over-identification of students of color in special education: A critical overview. *Multicultural Perspectives, 4*(1), 3–10.

Bailey, M. H., & Dziko, T. M. (2008). *A plan to close the achievement gap for African American students*. Olympia, WA: Superintendent of Public Instruction.

Contreras, F. E., & Stritikus, T. (2008). *Understanding opportunities to learn for Latino students in Washington*. Seattle, WA: University of Washington, Report Submitted to the Washington State Commission on Hispanic Affairs.

Contreras, F. E., Malcom, L. E., & Bensimon, E. M. (2008). Hispanic-serving institutions: Closeted identity and the productions of equitable outcomes for Latino/a students. In M. Gasman, B. Baez, & C. S. V. Turner (Eds.), *Understanding minority-serving institutions* (pp. 71–90). Albany, NY: State University of New York Press.

Chu, C. N. (1991). *Asian mind game*. New York, NY: Simon and Schuster.

Dumas, M. J. (2008). Theorizing redistribution and recognition in urban education research. In J. Ayon (Ed.), *Theory and educational research: Toward critical social explanation* (pp. 81–102). New York, NY: Routledge.

Dumas, M. J. (2011). A cultural political economy of school desegregation in Seattle. *Teachers College Record, 113*(4), 703–734.

Gottfried, M. A. (2009). Excused versus unexcused: How student absences in elementary school affect academic achievement. *Educational Evaluation and Policy Analysis, 31*(4), 392–415.

Hoffman, K., Llagas, C., & Snyder, T. D. (2003). *Status and Trends in the Education of Blacks*. Washington, DC: NCES.

Hune, S., & Takeuchi, D. T. (2008). *Asian Americans in Washington State: Closing their hidden achievement gaps*. Seattle, WA: University of Washington.

Kitano, H., & Sue, S. (1973). The model minorities. *Journal of Social Issues, 29*, 1–9.

Koppel, T. (1995). *Kanaka: The untold story of Hawaiian pioneers in British Columbia and the Pacific Northwest*. Vancouver, BC: Whitecap Books.

National Commission on Asian American and Pacific Islander Research in Education. (2008). *Facts not fiction: Setting the record straight*. New York, NY: CARE Project.

National Commission on Asian American and Pacific Islander Research in Education. (2013). *iCount: A data quality movement for Asian Americans and Pacific Islanders in Higher Education*. New York, NY: CARE Project.

Omi, M., & Winant, H. (1994). *Racial Formation in the United States: From the 1960s to the 1990s*. New York, NY: Routledge.

Ovando, C. J. (2003). Bilingual education in the United States: Historical development and current issues. *Bilingual Research Journal, 27*(1), 1–24.

Petersen, W. (1966, January 9). Success story: Japanese american style. *The New York Times*. pp. 20–43.

Rueda, R., & Windmueller, M. P. (2006). English language learners, LD, and overrepresentation a multiple-level analysis. *Journal of Learning Disabilities, 39*(2), 99–107.

Skiba, R. J., Michael, R. S., Nardo, A. C., & Peterson, R. L. (2002). The color of discipline: Sources of racial and gender disproportionality in school punishment. *The Urban Review, 34*(4), 317–342.

Spickard, P. R. (2009). *Japanese Americans: The formation and transformations of an ethnic group*. New Brunswick, NJ: Rutgers University Press.

Takumi, D. (1989). *Shared dreams: A history of Asians and Pacific Islanders in Washington state*. Seattle, WA: Washington Centennial Commission.

Teranishi, R. T. (2010). *Asians in the ivory tower: Dilemmas of racial inequality in American higher education*. New York, NY: Teachers College Press.

Tilly, C. (1998). *Durable inequality*. Berkeley, CA: University of California Press.

U.S. Department of Education (DOE), Office of Special Education and Rehabilitative Services (OSERS), & Office of Special Education Programs (OSEP) [DOE, OSERS, & OSEP] (2012). *31st annual report to Congress on the implementation of the Individuals with Disabilities Education Act, 2009*. Washington, DC: US Department of Education.

U.S. Department of Agriculture, Food and Nutrition Service [USDA]. (2014). *Child nutrition programs: Income eligibility guidelines, 2013–2014*. Retrieved from http://www.fns.usda.gov/sites/default/files/IEG_Table-032913.pdf.

United States Census. (2010). *The Asian Population: 2010*. Washington, DC: US Census. Retrieved from http://www.census.gov/prod/cen2010/briefs/c2010br-11.pdf.

U.S. Census. (2012). *Asian/pacific American heritage month: May 2012. Profile America Facts or Features*. Retrieved from http://www.census.gov/newsroom/releases/archives/facts_for_features_special_editions/cb12-ff09.html.

United States Department of Education Office of Civil Rights [OCR]. (2014). *Civil Rights Data Collection: Data Snapshot (School Discipline)*. Retrieved from http://www2.ed.gov/about/offices/list/ocr/docs/crdc-discipline-snapshot.pdf.

Yeidee, M., & Korbin, M. (2009). *Truancy literature review: Prepared for U.S. department of justice*. Retrieved from http://www2.dsgonline.com/dso/truancy%20literature%20review.pdf.

Race and Education in the Mountain West: Charting New Territory in America's Racial Frontier

Sonya Douglass Horsford

On matters of education policy and reform, the Mountain West remains one of the least studied regions in the country (Horsford, Sampson, & Forletta, 2013). Comprised of Arizona, Idaho, Montana, Nevada, New Mexico, Utah, and Wyoming, and located within the more expansive American West (see Fig. 1), between 2001 and 2011, the Mountain West[1] experienced more population growth and demographic change than anywhere else in the country (Teixeira, 2012). In 2012, the region's 1134 school districts and 8,838 traditional public schools enrolled more than 3.8 million children and youth (see Table 1), a growing share of whom are Latino, Asian, English learners (ELs), and/or living in poverty. Such trends are not limited to the West, yet provide an ideal starting place from which to revisit, reconsider, and recast questions of race, equality, integration, and justice in education within this dynamic and complex multiracial context. To borrow an adage from one of the region's most popular and populous cities—Las Vegas, Nevada—what happens in the West is not likely to stay there.

Mountain Western trends reflect, albeit in slightly exaggerated fashion, larger U.S. public enrollment trends in the twenty-first century. From 2001 to 2011, the nation's school population grew from 47.7 to 49.5 million, and by 2014, became "majority-minority" with white students making up only 49.8 % of the overall

---

[1]In this chapter, the Mountain West region refers to Arizona, Colorado, Idaho, Montana, Nevada, New Mexico, Utah, and Wyoming; although some parts of the chapter do not include the smaller states of Montana and Wyoming in their discussion.

S.D. Horsford (✉)
Graduate School of Education, College of Education and Human Development, George Mason University, 4400 University Drive, Fairfax, VA, MS 4C2, 22030, USA
e-mail: shorsfor@gmu.edu

© Springer International Publishing Switzerland 2016
P.A. Noguera et al. (eds.), *Race, Equity, and Education*,
DOI 10.1007/978-3-319-23772-5_8

Fig. 1 Map of American West, Mountain West, and U.S. by region. *Source* http://proviacorp. com/

Table 1 School/District characteristics in mountain west states

	# of school districts	# of schools	# of charter schools	Per pupil expenditures	Pupil/ teacher ratio	# of FTE teachers
Arizona	227	2421	567	$7,737	21.2	50,800
Colorado	178	1843	178	$8,901	17.7	48,078
Idaho	116	774	46	$6,810	17.5	15,900
Montana	417	827	0	$10,710	14.0	10,153
Nevada	17	683	42	$8,572	20.8	21,132
New Mexico	89	868	84	$9,351	15.3	21,957
Utah	41	1052	97	$6,575	23.0	25,970
Wyoming	49	370	4	$15,960	11.4	7,487

Source NCES Common Core of Data, 2011–2012 school year

student population followed by Hispanics at 25.8 %, Blacks at 15.4 %, Asian/ Pacific Islanders at 5.2 %, Indian/Alaska Natives at 1.1 %, and two or more races at 2.8 % (NCES, 2014). These enrollment trends and their shifting distribution by race/ethnicity and region are not expected to slow down any time soon. By 2023, total student enrollment is projected to reach 52.1 million—a racial, cultural, and political transformation that will forever change the racial make-up and balance of American education. This demographic shift in school age population is a reality that school leaders and policymakers must understand in order to effectively address the educational needs of all children. For the nearly 180,000 school teachers in the Mountain West working with administrators, parents, and policymakers in an era of top-down, high-stakes accountability for performance, to educate a growing share of children and youth of color who are poor, attend resegregated schools, and may or may not speak English at home; the future is now (Table 2).

This chapter explores the growing racial, cultural, and linguistic diversity in the Mountain West and its implications for racial integration and equality in the post-Civil Rights Era. Animated by the region's rapidly growing number and share of students who are racial and linguistic "minorities," and emerging political clout as America's New Heartland, I argue there is much to learn about the future of American education from the Mountain West based on its (a) distinctive racial history, (b) changing demography and politics, and (c) widening opportunity gaps in education. I begin with a discussion of the region's unique racial and multicultural

Table 2 Population growth, demographic, and political indicators for the Mountain West states

Indicator	U.S.	AZ	CO	ID	NV	NM	UT
Growth and economic indicators							
Population growth rate, percent 2000–2010 (state rank)	9.7	24.6 (2)	16.9 (9)	21.1 (4)	35.1 (1)	13.2 (15)	23.8 (3)
Median household income (state rank)	50,046	46,789	54,046	43,490	51,001	42,090	53,744
Percent of persons in poverty, 2010 (state rank)	15.3	17.4 (13)	13.4 (32)	15.7 (20)	14.9 (24)	20.4 (2)	13.2 (34)
Demographic indicators							
2000–2010 change in share of eligible voters							
White		−5.9	−2.9	−2.5	−10.3	−3.9	−2.9
All minorities		5.9	2.9	2.5	10.3	3.9	2.9
Black		1.0	0.0	0.0	-0.1	0.7	0.2
Hispanic		4.2	2.2	2.4	5.5	3.0	2.2
All other		0.7	0.7	0.1	3.1	3.2	1.4
State political indicators							
Democratic or Republican governor		R	D	R	R	R	R
Democratic margin, 2008 presidential election		−9	9	−26	12	15	−29

Source Adapted from Frey and Teixeira (2012)

history and libertarian ethos as part of the American West (Flamming, 2009; Limerick, 1988; Taylor, 1998), followed by a description of its demographic transformation and anticipated political rise as "America's New Heartland" (Lang & Sanchez, 2012). I then present selected Mountain West state-level education enrollment and achievement data and education reform efforts in Nevada, as representative of the region, and ways to expand opportunity for the Mountain West's racially, culturally, and linguistically diverse student population.

The chapter concludes with a call for a political race project (Guinier & Torres, 2002) in education—comprised of cross-racial solidarity, strategic linkages between black, white, Latino, Asian, and indigenous communities around racial and social justice issues, and a democratic politics of practice that advances the freedom struggle for equal education in the post-Civil Rights Era. Using the Las Vegas Promise Neighborhood Initiative as an example, I consider how shared visions of educational equality, integration, and opportunity for students of all races and backgrounds can be achieved through a political race project in education, grounded in grass-roots, community-based education reform efforts that seek to leverage demographic and political power through cross-racial (and multigenerational) cooperation.

The Mountain West: America's New Heartland

Less than 30 years ago, much of the Mountain West still satisfied the nineteenth-century definition of *frontier* due to its sparsely populated counties (Lang & Sanchez, 2012). Just one generation later, the region leads the nation in population growth and demographic change with projections that it will continue to do so through 2030 (Teixeira, 2012). Its increasing diversity, urbanization, and growing Millennial population, coupled with a declining number of working-class whites, forecasts a shift away from its independent and libertarian ethos and toward a more left-leaning electorate that has the potential to shape education policy at the local, state, and federal levels. Scholars at the Brookings Institution have characterized the Mountain West as America's "new swing region" (Teixeira, 2012) and "New Heartland" (Lang, Muro, & Sarzynski, 2008)—given its emergent centrality in national politics—a position previously enjoyed by the Old Heartland states of the Midwest (Lang & Sanchez, 2012). Such dramatic growth and demographic change are influencing not only the region's politics, but also the nature of schools and schooling: sadly, with troubling academic results for the growing share of students of color, ELs, and those living in poverty. Although the New Heartland's racial diversity is remarkably different now in terms of sheer population density and distribution, its legacy and distinctiveness as a multiracial, multicultural region where many different groups coexisted for more than 500 years is instructive in considering both the histories and possibilities of cross-racial cooperation for shared causes and agendas.

Racial Distinctiveness

As Quintard Taylor (1998) lamented in his groundbreaking work, *African Americans in the West: In Search of the Racial Frontier*, the American West conjures up images of "Frederick Jackson Turner's rugged Euro-American pioneers constantly challenging a westward-moving frontier, bringing civilization, taming the wilderness, and, in the process, reinventing themselves as 'Americans' and creating an egalitarian society that nurtured the fundamental democratic values that shaped contemporary American society" (p. 313). Historians have defined the West as a frontier movement, a region, and "an ideal" associated with freedom, equality, and opportunity (Flamming, 2009, p. 11), but until the 1960s, the region's historiography included very little about the centrality of multiracial and multiethnic communities that coexisted for centuries throughout the region. As the historical record now reflects, American Indians, Asians, blacks, Hispanics, and Anglos were always part of western history. They persisted through "external pressures and internal ties," experienced life in the West differently from each other, and "influenced western history even as they were being shaped by it" (Flamming, p. 11). Despite coexisting for five centuries, however, Limerick (1988) observed, "Indians, Hispanics, Asians, blacks, Anglos, businesspeople, workers, politicians, bureaucrats, native, and newcomers, we share the same region and its history, *but we wait to be introduced*" [emphasis added] (p. 359).

According to Taylor (1998), "There is a striking ambiguity about race in the West" (p. 18). He explained, "The idea of race as understood in the South and East had since been reconceptualized as a result of the West's racial diversity" (p. x). This distinction is not limited solely to the concept of race, but also the practice of racism. According to Limerick (1988), "The diversity of the West put a strain on the simpler varieties of racism. In another setting, categories dividing humanity into superior white and inferior black were comparatively easier to steer by." She wrote, "The West, however, raised questions for which racists had no set answers. Western diversity forced racists to think—an unaccustomed activity" (p. 260). As such, the West should be viewed in light of its "complex, varied, paradoxical history rather than as a collage of stereotypes" (Limerick, 1988 p. xx).

Indeed, as part of the West—"the most mythologized region in the country"—the Mountain West states of Arizona, Colorado, Idaho, Nevada, New Mexico, Utah, Montana, and Wyoming are probably less commonly associated with people of color than the Deep South and urban centers of the Northeast. Yet, as African Americans and many other groups "in search of the racial frontier" (Taylor, 1998) dreamed of unprecedented opportunity for land, freedom, and equality, the Mountain West's brand of *de facto* segregation still governed much of business and public life. In a 1925 article in the *Denver Post*, NAACP national secretary James Weldon Johnson argued, "Your West is giving the Negro a better deal than any other section of the country .... I cannot attempt to analyze the reasons for this, but the fact remains that there is more opportunity for my race, and less prejudice against it in this section of the country than anywhere else in the United

States" (Taylor, 1998, p. 18). 90 years later, racially discriminatory practices in employment, housing, and schools have worked to undermine this once held belief.

Changing Demography and Politics

In the Mountain West, this dynamic blend and shifting distribution of racial groups would continue well into the twenty-first century. Between 2000 and 2010, the Mountain West region was home to the top four fastest-growing states in the country with Nevada's population increasing by 35 %, Arizona by 25 %, Utah by 24 %, and Idaho by 21 % (Frey & Teixeira, 2012). Much of this growth has been centered in what Lang and Sanchez (2012) described as the "Mountain Mega" metropolitan areas of Phoenix (66 % of the state population); Denver (51 %); Las Vegas (72 %); Albuquerque (43 %); and Salt Lake City (41 %), making the Mountain West, counterintuitively, one of the most urbanized areas in the U.S (Lang & Sanchez, 2012, p. 70).

Illustrating the explosive growth of this urbanization, between 2000 and 2010, Albuquerque grew by 24 %, Phoenix-Mesa-Glendale by nearly 29 %, Boise-Nampa by 33 %, and the Las Vegas-Paradise metropolitan statistical area by 41 % (Damore, 2012). In terms of population diversity, the region's nonwhite population, and more specifically, its Hispanic population, is outpacing all others. With the exception of Idaho and Utah, in 2010, the Hispanic populations in Mountain West states exceeded 20 %, ranging from a low of 20.7 % in Colorado, 26.5 % in Nevada, 29.6 % in Arizona, and a high of 46.3 % in New Mexico (Damore, 2012).

Naturally, such changes in population density and diversity shake up the region's politics, which in the case of the Mountain West have resulted in increased, albeit fragile, support for the Democratic Party (Damore, 2012). For centuries, the Old Heartland states of Illinois, Indiana, Michigan, Ohio, and Wisconsin served as the bellwether for presidential elections, but in light of the Mountain West's anticipated growth and changing demography, the political emergence of this region as America's New Heartland is palpable (Lang & Sanchez, 2012). Despite midterm elections that resulted in setbacks for Democrats in both 2010 and 2014, the region's record-breaking growth and urbanization and increasingly Latino population created a new demographic and political landscape where "the urban and minority vote offset a wave of white rural voters" (Lang & Sanchez 2012, p. 71). According to Lang and Sanchez, "minority voters, especially Hispanics .... are to the New Heartland of the twenty-first century what white ethnic voters from southern and eastern Europe were to the Old Heartland in the twentieth century" and have become "the potential deciding voters in any toss-up presidential election" (p. 71).

Although such trends may bode well for the region by elevating its profile and influence in national politics (less so for those who prefer the Mountain West's conservative, independent, and libertarian roots), their impact on districts, schools, and students is substantial. The sheer challenge of constructing new schools quickly enough to accommodate growing enrollments is significant. Add to this the task of securing the best teachers and administrators to serve a racially, ethnically, and linguistically diverse student population amidst state budget shortfalls, increased state and federal accountability frameworks, and federal support for competition-based funding over needs-based funding.

Education Trends and Conditions

U.S. public school enrollment is projected to set new records each year until 2021 (NCES, 2013). With the exception of slowed growth due to the Great Recession of 2009, the Mountain West continues to expand, especially its Hispanic and Asian/Pacific Islander student populations. During the 2011–2012 school year, as noted in Table 3, Hispanic students made up nearly one-fourth of the nation's total school enrollment (23.7 %), but comprised a much higher proportion of students in Colorado (56.1 %), Nevada (39.6 %), Arizona (42.8 %), and New Mexico (59.4 %).

The region's American Indian/Alaskan Native population declined by 4,935 students, with decreases in all but the "whitest" Mountain Western states of Idaho, Utah, and Wyoming (Frey, 2012). And while Hispanic enrollment increased by 452,750 students, Asian/Pacific Islanders by 41,031, and African Americans by 32,003; the total number of white students declined from 2,100,231 to 2,056,994, mirroring the larger demographic and political trends contributing to the region's rise as the New Heartland. These sharp enrollment increases among racial minorities, ELs, and students living in poverty have certainly changed the landscape of public education in the Mountain West (Tables 4 and 5).

As local school districts and states competed for Race to the Top Grant funds during the Great Recession, these same entities were reeling from the effects of

Table 3 Student racial/ethnic background in Mountain West states

	Total	White (%)	Hispanic (%)	Black (%)	Asian (%)	PI (%)	A I/AN (%)
Arizona	1,080,319	42.1	42.8	5.3	2.7	0.2	5.0
Colorado	854,265	56.1	31.9	4.7	3.1	0.2	0.8
Idaho	279,873	78.0	16.2	1.0	1.3	0.3	1.3
Montana	142,349	80.9	3.6	1.0	0.8	0.2	11.6
Nevada	439,634	37.4	39.6	9.6	5.6	1.2	1.1
New Mexico	337,225	25.9	59.4	2.0	1.2	0.0	10.1
Utah	598,832	77.4	15.3	1.3	1.7	1.5	1.2
Wyoming	90,099	80.4	12.5	1.0	0.7	0.1	3.2
U.S.	49,522,00	51.7	23.7	15.8	5.1 % combined		1.1

Source NCES Common Core of Data, 2011–2012 school year

Table 4 Other student characteristics in Mountain West states

	Total	Percent in Title I schools (%)	With IEP (%)	Percent in LEP (%)	Percent FRL eligible (%)
Arizona	1,080,319	95.6	11.7	7.0	47.4
Colorado	854,265	27.4	10.2	12.0	40.8
Idaho	279,873	77.3	9.6	5.4	48.5
Montana	142,349	82.2	11.2	2.3	40.2
Nevada	439,634	–	11.1	19.1	54.0
New Mexico	337,225	90.2	13.8	15.9	68.0
Utah	598,832	23.3	11.9	5.6	47.6
Wyoming	90,099	39.9	14.2	3.0	36.8

Source NCES Common Core of Data, 2011–2012 school year

its economic crisis and budget shortfalls that were equally stark. In the case of Nevada, which was leading the country in unemployment and home foreclosures, as well as some of the worst indicators for children and young people, the role of education became a growing area of concern and priority. For those education leaders and policymakers who had long been fighting to close achievement gaps, raise test scores, and prepare every student for college or career, a new demographic and political landscape was emerging. In the midst of this rapid diversification and urbanization, Nevada experienced the largest budget decline as a percentage of its budget than any other state in the nation that resulted in decreased funding for public education. Moreover, the state pursued but was not selected for Race to the Top grants in large part because it failed to have adequate capacity and structural reforms in place to be competitive with other states. Although state-level trends offer much needed information concerning how states could structure, support, and improve the overall quality of education in their respective counties and communities, the implications of such trends at the school and district levels are especially relevant to students, educators, parents, advocates, and others concerned with the degree to which schools and school systems are equipped to provide an adequate and equitable education for their current and future students. And as my colleagues and I have argued elsewhere, no city better illustrates these dramatic Mountain Western shifts than Las Vegas, Nevada (Horsford, Sampson, et al., 2013).

Learning in Las Vegas: The Mississippi of the West

Located in Clark County, where 77 % of the state's population resides, Las Vegas is home to Clark County School District, which serves more than 311,000 students, making it the largest school district in the Mountain West and fifth largest in the country. Founded in 1956, just 2 years after the landmark *Brown v. Board* decision of 1954, CCSD served a majority white student population, with African

Table 5 Student enrollment by race/ethnicity in Mountain West states, 2000–2001 and 2010–2011

State Abbr (School)	Total students- White (State) [2000–2001]	Total students- White (State) [2010–2011]	Total students- Hispanic (State) [2000–2001]	Total students- Hispanic (State) [2010–2011]	Total students- Black (State) [2000–2001]	Total students- Black (State) [2010–2011]	Total students- Asian/Pac. Isl. (State)[a] [2000–2001]	Total students- Asian/Pac. Isl. (State)[a] [2010–2011]	Total students- Amer. Ind./Alask. (State) [2000–2001]
AZ	463,302	459,348	297,703	452,283	40,483	59,549	18,049	32,427	58,159
CO	494,308	479,327	159,600	266,098	40,967	40,537	20,932	26,337	8,701
ID	210,746	216,683	26,121	43,795	1,827	2,819	3,005	4,553	3,310
MT	133,574	115,827	2,658	4,996	877	1,378	1,473	1,561	16,293
NM	112,920	88,009	160,708	200,774	7,622	7,151	3,461	4,397	35,595
NV	193,215	169,220	87,696	169,236	34,591	43,225	19,282	31,209	5,922
UT	413,118	456,510	42,932	88,285	4,684	8,468	13,250	19,942	7,501
WY	79,048	72,070	6,231	10,932	1,095	1,022	780	837	2,786

Numbers reported represent valid responses

† indicates that the data are not applicable

– indicates that the data are missing

‡ indicates that the data do not meet NCES data quality standards

[a]Data with Asian/Pacific Islander Summation

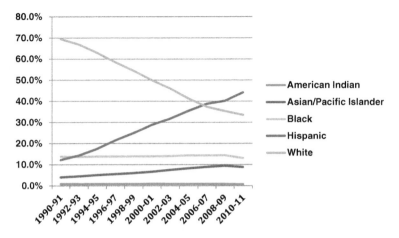

Fig. 2 CCSD student racial composition, 1990–2010

Americans constituting the second largest racial group. By 1970, 80 % of CCSD students were white, 16 % were black, 3 % were Latino, 1 % was "other," and less than 1 % were American Indian. Fast forward to 2010, where the district's new Latino majority comprises 42 % of student enrollment, followed by 32 % white, 12 % black, 8 % Asian/Pacific Islander, and 0.06 % American Indian (Horsford, Sampson, et al., 2013) (see Fig. 2).

Drawing from previous studies of education in Las Vegas and Nevada (Horsford, 2008; Horsford, Mokhtar, & Sampson, 2013; Horsford & Sampson, 2014; Horsford, Sampson, et al., 2013), I provide some state context of education policy and reform in Nevada, a discussion of CCSD's "Prime 6 Schools"—the product of a voluntary desegregation plan developed in response to the district's failed mandatory one (Horsford, 2008; Horsford, Mokhtar, et al., 2013)—and an overview of Nevada's growing EL population and CCSD's efforts to expand opportunity for this growing share of students (Horsford, Mokhtar, et al., 2013). My aim here is to provide some additional district and local community perspectives on racial diversity, educational equality, and expanding opportunity within the larger context of federal and state accountability pressure, state funding formulas, and market-based reforms that do not account for the region's changing student population.

State Context: Education Policy and Reform in Nevada

Nevada has consistently ranked last or near last nationally on indicators from early childhood access, per pupil funding, and high-school graduation rates to economic opportunity and social mobility (The Annie E. Casey Foundation, 2010). Since 1993, when the state's original education reform package, Nevada Education Reform Act (NERA), was introduced, Nevada has struggled to improve its educational outcomes, despite the continued support for high-stakes accountability. Nevada's poor national rankings and their implications for attracting business and industry have led many of the state's business, gaming, development, and philanthropic elite to express their dissatisfaction with schools and devise ways to improve them (Horsford & Sampson, 2013).

In 2010, then Republican Governor Jim Gibbons established the Nevada Education Reform Blue Ribbon Task Force for its twofold purpose: (1) prepare the state's Race to the Top application and (2) "facilitate public and private discussion and consensus for overall reform of public education for Nevada's children" (Nevada Education Reform Blue Ribbon Task Force, 2010). Given the state's poor record of educational performance and insufficient capacity to institute its proposed reforms, not receiving the grant was not surprising. Nevertheless, the federal intent of Race to the Top was accomplished, since Nevada, in order to be competitive for the grant, passed legislation aligned with the Department of Education's reform agenda, which included college and career readiness benchmarks, student growth models, teacher and leader quality indicators, and school turnarounds, to include incentives for new charter schools.

Regretfully, while education reformers were competing for Race to the Top funds, largely intended to fill state budget holes and attempt to meet "maintenance of effort" levels of funding for education, they missed the opportunity to chart new territory as America's new racial frontier in addressing education reforms that would meet the local and state needs of a rapidly changing, burgeoning student population that reflects the faces of the New West.

Amidst the major population changes taking place, reformers must engage in critical conversations about the source of Nevada's poor educational outcomes and how an education policy focused on meeting the needs of its changing student body (and future workforce and electorate) must be the state's priority. The complex contemporary challenges facing today's schools and school systems concern matters of race, diversity, geography, equality, and achievement, which is why there is much to be gained from reflecting on histories of educational inequality. In the next section, I draw from previous work on the history of desegregation in CCSD to better understand linkages between a community's educational history and its present condition.

School Desegregation and Resegregation: Prime 6 Schools

In the West, the freedom struggle for equal education for nonwhite children, whether Native American, African American, Hispanic, or Asian, was often initiated through legal and direct action, and Las Vegas was no exception. In their historical case study of school desegregation and resegregation in Las Vegas from 1968 to 1994, Horsford, Sampson, et al. (2013) described the events surrounding the Clark County's school desegregation case, *Kelly v. Guinn* (1972), which led to CCSD's mandatory *Sixth Grade Center Plan of Integration* in 1972, and ultimately, a voluntary desegregation plan launched in 1993 known as the *Prime 6 Schools Plan*. Findings revealed a community narrative characteristic of the American West—one of legal challenges to school segregation coupled with direct action (Taylor, 1998).

One of the more interesting findings from this case study was the return to neighborhood schools initiated by African American community leaders, educators, parents, and activists who were displeased with the results of CCSD's forced busing plan as the *Sixth Grade Center Plan of Integration*. After 20 years of the Westside's predominately black student population bearing the burden of busing for 11 of the 12 years of their schooling, community protests of the *Sixth Grade Center Plan of Integration* and the broader community's desire for a return to its neighborhood elementary schools led to CCSD's creation of the Educational Opportunities Commission, which recommended the sixth grade centers in West Las Vegas be converted back into elementary schools. Implemented at the start of the 1993–1994 school year, this voluntary desegregation plan known as the *Prime 6 Schools Plan* would grant Westside students the option of attending their neighborhood school or school of choice outside of the Prime 6 Attendance Zone. According to CCSD, the *Prime 6 Schools Plan* reflected the district's commitment to "the educational benefits of cultural and racial diversity for all students" and "increasing the opportunities for parents to have options regarding the schools their children will attend." This focus on the benefits of diversity, equitable resources, and opportunities for parental choice over racial balance marked an interesting shift regarding both the district and the black community's conceptualizations of educational equality and opportunity. Investments and improvements into the Prime 6 Schools included increased support for staffing, parent engagement, and pre-kindergarten and summer learning programs, along with a community involvement component, multicultural education, extended school days, and resource rooms for students with special needs. The original plan of 1993 consisted of seven traditional K-5 schools and one magnet school. By 2014, six traditional public schools and three magnet schools comprised the Prime 6 Schools, but with a much different student population in terms of race and home language. Beyond issues of race, culture, and segregation, the area's concentrated poverty contributes to gaps in opportunity and achievement as uniquely experienced by black and Latino students attending Prime 6 Schools even when compared to their black and Latino peers attending non-Prime 6 Schools (Terriquez, Flashman, Schuler-Brown, & Orfield, 2009).

Expanding Opportunity for English Learners: Zoom Schools

In addition to outpacing the rest of the U.S. in population growth, Nevada has also led the nation in the number of its ELs, many of whom are from families who are disproportionately poor, unemployed, and more likely to have a parent without a high-school diploma (Horsford, Mokhtar, et al., 2013). One in three Nevada children speak a language other than English at home, and sadly, are struggling academically when compared to their native English-speaking peers. For CCSD students, the figures are even more staggering, given the sheer number of students and their racial distribution.

Based on a review of math and reading achievement data on the Nevada Criterion Referenced Test and High School Proficiency Examination (both of which are no longer in use), although Nevada's students regardless of race and across grade levels are achieving at rates lower than the national average, ELs are faring particularly poorly (Horsford, Mokhtar, et al., 2013). In 2011, only 69 % of CCSD's third graders met the state grade-level standard in reading: but only 61 % of ELs. Eighth graders overall performed even worse with only 58 % meeting the math standards, with only 28 % of ELs meeting the standard. Reading scores were even worse, with only 44 % of CCSD eighth graders meeting the standards, and only 10 % of ELs meeting the standards that year (Horsford, Mokhtar, et al., 2013). At the high school level, EL students lag even further behind with only 31 % deemed proficient in math compared to 71 % of students overall.

Many states and districts in the Mountain West and throughout the country struggle to manage rapid growth and/or a diversifying student body without the research, funding, or leadership capacity to serve its growing EL population, which requires hiring skilled teachers, administrators, and staff to meet its unique educational needs. A review of EL enrollments and education in Nevada revealed a critical demand for EL-related research in not only Nevada, but also the nations' states experiencing increasing numbers of ELs in high-growth states. As noted before, "The lack of EL-related research is not only stunning, but also explains the absence of meaningful policy discussions and the inability for educational leaders and policymakers to craft and implement evidence-based policy solutions designed to improve educational opportunities for the state's ELs" (Horsford, Mokhtar, et al., 2013).

Fortunately, research on Nevada's ELs (i.e., Horsford, Mokhtar, et al., 2013) generated enough policy discussion to lead to the passing of Senate Bill 504, which granted for the first time in Nevada's history monies allocated specifically to EL education. Until this recent investment, Nevada was one of the only eight states in the country that did not have EL funding included as a part of their formula funding, despite the fact that nearly a third of the students were Latino, and half of them were limited ELs. The majority of this one-time allocation of $50 million was directed to fund fourteen CCSD elementary schools with the highest shares of EL students. These newly designated "Zoom Schools" received nearly $40 million to fund pre-kindergarten and full-day kindergarten programs, smaller class sizes, summer learning, and reading skills centers, along with extra supplies, textbooks, and learning technologies (Mokhtar, 2013). Although this step was a big one for the state, expectations by lawmakers that EL test scores will rise quickly enough in 2 years to justify additional funding is problematic, since it takes between 4 and 7 years for ELs to become proficient enough in English to learn content (Mokhtar, 2013). As Mokhtar concluded, "Although Senate Bill 504 is a big win for ELLs [English Language Learners] in CCSD, the district's strategy should involve adequate time, evidence-based programs and practices, and a more permanent solution that is not tied to the legislative process" (para 10).

The similarities between the African American quest for equal education in Las Vegas between 1968 and 1994 (resulting in the Prime 6 Schools) and the more recent push for expanded educational opportunities for the region's increasing Latino, EL population (through the designation of 14 Zoom Schools) in 2013, are striking, as is CCSD's response to these respective communities. Both the Prime 6 Schools and Zoom Schools resulted in additional funding and support for early learning and full-day kindergarten, multicultural and culturally relevant curriculum, parent and family engagement, and additional classroom resources. A troubling disconnect, however, exists between the community-based supports and opportunities provided at the school and district levels that hold the potential to advance educational equality and opportunity for Las Vegas' black and Latino students living in neighborhoods of concentrated poverty, and the federal and state-level push for greater accountability for results regardless of who is in the classroom.

Further, implementing these additional education resources at Prime 6 and Zoom Schools only serves a small percentage of the African American and Latino students who need this support. A much larger commitment of resources needs to be made beyond these initial schools in order to reach all students who could benefit from improved education outcomes. In order for this to be achieved, however, African American and Latino communities and other education and community leaders who support these kinds of community-based approaches must find new and more effective ways to establish coalitions to apply pressure on decision makers and policymakers. Building capacity for this kind of community-based decision-making will require strong leadership, mutual understanding, and a sense that more can be achieved by working together than forging this effort alone (Fig. 3).

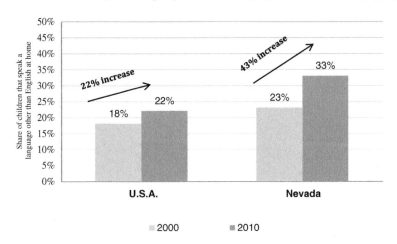

Fig. 3 English learner enrollment growth in U.S. and Nevada. *Source* Horsford, Mokhtar, et al. (2013)

Charting New Territory: Building Community Capacity and Cross-Racial Coalitions to Expand Educational Opportunity

As discussed previously, the Mountain West's rapid expansion, urbanization, and racial diversity reflect America's larger demographic and political transformation. Shaped by major changes in population density and diversity, the region's past and present represent an underexplored legacy and tradition of multiracial competition and collaboration unique to the West. Its future suggests an opportunity to chart new territory by forging real education reforms that meet the unique needs of its people, rather than narrow conceptions of student achievement and school performance that disregard the demographic realities of the Mountain West. In response to the top-down, high-stakes accountability approaches to school improvement that continue to prove unsuccessful in closing opportunity gaps for the region's historically underserved students, in this section, I suggest a community-based political race project in education grounded in democratic ideals of educational equality and opportunity and operationalized through cross-racial, community capacity building for improved educational experiences and learning outcomes for students of color.

From "Presumed Alliance" to "Political Race"

In his book, *The Presumed Alliance: The Unspoken Conflict between Latinos and Blacks and What it Means for America*, California attorney Vaca (2004) challenged the assumption that a "presumed alliance" should exist between blacks and Latinos given their shared minority status. His exploration of the complicated political relationship between these two groups on a variety of issues, especially competition for jobs and resources, reflects the historically complex nature of multiracial relations in the West, particularly around civil rights. His critique of suggestions that blacks and Latinos can and should leverage their political power through cooperation but that fail to provide direction on how this could be accomplished was in some ways answered by the work of Lani Guinier and Gerald Torres 2 years prior in their 2002 book, *The Miner's Canary: Enlisting Race, Resisting Power, Transforming Democracy*. According to Guinier and Torres (2002), *political race* is located at the intersection of race, politics, culture, and economics and "is not something you are," but rather "something you do" (p. 107). Thus, they describe a political race project as one that (1) recognizes, as an asset, the potential solidarity and connection that those who have been raced often experience; (2) articulates a broader social justice agenda that includes discovering "how the construction and uses of race have historically operated to prevent authentic and strategic linkages between communities that have more in common than is normally supposed"; and (3) demonstrates a willingness to experiment with new democratic practices (pp. 95–96).

Using this theory of political race as a guide, I consider here the viability of a political race project in education in Las Vegas, fueled by an existing community-based education reform effort known as the Las Vegas Promise Neighborhood Initiative, which aims to provide a cradle-to-college and career continuum of solutions for the target neighborhood's predominately African American and Latino student population.

Las Vegas Promise Neighborhood Initiative

As discussed earlier, the Prime 6 Schools located in Las Vegas' historic West Las Vegas neighborhood enjoy a rich history, and the African American community's connections to its schools run deep. Rapid growth and demographic change, however, has transformed this formerly black neighborhood into one that is now just as Latino as it is African American. With a student population that is 45 % black and 45 % Latino, 30 % EL, and where 86–100 % qualify for Free and Reduced Lunch, the Prime 6 Schools serve as a microcosm of how racial, cultural, economic, and political forces have converged to create new challenges and questions for rapidly changing schools. Additionally, the disproportionate number of charter schools in the area (which serve predominately black student populations) has resulted in decreased enrollment and further racial segregation in the community that suffered most from school segregation, and according to some community members, desegregation (Horsford, Sampson, et al., 2013). For these reasons and more, the proposed Las Vegas Promise Neighborhood (LVPN) became the focus of a Promise Neighborhoods planning grant application with a mission "to provide cradle-to-college and career support services to children and families in Historic West Las Vegas through strong schools, leveraged resources, and coordinated community-building efforts that would allow all children in the LVPN to have a safe, healthy, and strong academic start in life" (Horsford & Sampson, 2013, p. 11).

Through a large collaborative of community partners (e.g., Clark County School District, City of Las Vegas, Clark County, Nevada Partners, Head Start, United Way of Southern Nevada, Las Vegas Urban League, Communities in Schools, Clark County Department of Juvenile Justice Services, Las Vegas-Clark County Library District, Southern Nevada Health District, Southern Nevada Regional Housing Authority, Culinary Academy of Las Vegas, and The Smith Center for the Performing Arts), the LVPN Initiative would focus on improving student achievement in the neighborhood's persistently low-achieving schools. LVPN's goals, however, were not limited to school improvement, but also involved a larger community capacity building effort designed to "integrate programs, break down agency silos, enhance partner capacity, develop a local infrastructure of systems and resources, and scale up effective solutions" (Horsford & Sampson, 2013, p. 11) in ways that supported project success and sustainability.

As Horsford and Sampson (2014) concluded, "community capacity building in economically distressed and racially minoritized communities should prioritize community organizing as a key function and strategy for future capacity building efforts, particularly around urban school improvement (c.f., Mediratta, Shah, & McAlister, 2008; Stone, Doherty, Jones, & Ross, 1999; Warren, 2005)." The authors also underscored the need, particularly in low-capacity metros like Las Vegas, to mobilize parents, students, residents, and community stakeholders in ways that build their capacity and political power to "sustain democratically-controlled schools committed to equity and improved achievement outcomes for all students."

Building Coalitions and Community to Expand Opportunity

As the West's racial and ethnic groups "wait to be introduced" (Limerick, 1988, p. 359), a political race project grounded in community capacity and cross-racial coalition building can help to shift education policy and reform efforts from a top-down approach, to a more inclusive, democratic politics of practice. The historical legacy of exclusion, segregation, and discrimination experienced by Black and Latino children, families, and communities creates opportunities to build coalitions and community support for an education agenda that holds schools, educational leaders, and policymakers accountable for the quality of education they provide students of color. As Gándara (2010) warned, "Although the problem of school segregation has traditionally been cast as a black/white issue, today Latinos are more likely than African Americans to attend segregated schools" (Gándara, 2010, p. 60). The emergence of triple segregation, or segregation by race, poverty, and language (Gándara, 2010; Terriquez et al., 2009), in historic West Las Vegas does not bode well for either community and underscores the need for community capacity building for school reform.

This is not to suggest a presumed alliance between African American and Latino communities. In fact, it acknowledges critical points of departure on issues such as immigration, employment, and competition for scarce resources (Vaca, 2004). Nevertheless, the changing demography and politics of Las Vegas and the Mountain West region present an opportunity that must be leveraged through strategic cross-racial linkages and political coalitions. Such a project could create space for communities that are presumed to be allies but do not leverage the democratic power that is possible by sharing knowledge of their backgrounds, values, struggles, and dreams for educational opportunity for their children. This democratic politics of practice would serve as the counter balance to an education policy dominated by corporate interests by making room for the voices and demands of everyday parents, students, teachers, and constituents. Such connections, mobilization, and experimentation would serve as a basis for efforts to reclaim power and agency for parents, restore advocacy to students, and ignite the political activism and politics of practice required in today's overly politicized education policy environment.

Conclusion

As education observers grapple with questions of diversity and equity within today's top-down, high-stakes accountability policy environment, a shifting racial, cultural, economic, political, and demographic landscape complicates the already shaky discourse around issues of race and educational equality. Fortunately, the Mountain West region provides an informative context by which to examine such issues and reimagine new approaches to educational advocacy and a politics of practice. As Lang and Sanchez (2012) explained, "The Mountain West is transitioning from a once solid and reliable Republican region into a more contested space" (p. 79)—a space that, I argue, makes room for building civic capacity for education advocacy and reform. The region's contemporary dynamics and rich cultural history represent the intersection of race, politics, economics, and culture in ways that personify *political race* and its potential to transform democracy (Guinier & Torres, 2002). Its legacy of interracial competition and cooperation serves as a natural backdrop for a political race project that leverages the political power of an increasingly young, minority voting population in partnership with allies for change. This growing electorate of young, urban, and diverse voters—today's public school students—can leverage their political voice and agency in ways that transform schools and chart a new frontier for educational equality, opportunity, and social justice in America's New Heartland and beyond.

References

Annie E. Casey Foundation (2010). *The 2010 Kids Count data book: State Profiles of child well-being*. Baltimore, MD. Retrieved from http://www.aecf.org/m/resourcedoc/AECF-2010 KIDSCOUNTDataBook-2010.pdf

Damore, D. F. (2012). Reapportionment and redistricting in the Mountain West. In R. Teixeira (Ed.), *America's new swing region: Changing politics and demographics in the Mountain West*. Washington D.C.: Brookings.

Flamming, D. (2009). *African Americans in the West*. Santa Barbara, CA: ABC-CLIO LLC.

Frey, W. H. (2012). Hispanics, race, and the changing political landscape of the United States and the Mountain West. In R. Teixeira (Ed.), *America's new swing region: Changing politics and demographics in the Mountain West*. Washington D.C.: Brookings.

Frey, W. H., & Teixeira, R. (2012). America's new swing region: The political demography and geography of the Mountain West, (pp. 11–68). In R. Teixeira (Ed.), *America's new swing region: Changing politics and demographics in the Mountain West*. Washington D.C.: Brookings.

Gándara, P. (2010, November). Overcoming triple segregation. *Educational Leadership*. ASCD.

Guinier, L., & Torres, M. (2002). *The miner's canary: Enlisting race, resisting power, transforming democracy*. Cambridge: Harvard University Press.

Horsford, S. D. (2008). *A history of school desegregation in the Mississippi of the West: Implications for educational leaders*. Paper presented at the University Council for Educational Administration.

Horsford, S. D., & Sampson, C. (2013, May). *The Las Vegas Promise Neighborhood Initiative: A community-based approach to improving educational opportunity and achievement*. Las Vegas, NV: The Lincy Institute at UNLV.

Horsford, S. D., & Sampson, C. (2014). Promise Neighborhoods: The politics and promise of community as urban school reform. *Urban Education, 49*(8), 955–991.

Horsford, S. D., Mokhtar, C., & Sampson, C. (2013, March). *Nevada's English language learner population: A review of enrollment, outcomes, and opportunities.* The Lincy Institute at The University of Nevada, Las Vegas. Retrieved from http://www.unlv.edu/sites/default/files/24/Lincy-EducationSector-ELL-FullReport.pdf.

Horsford, S. D., Sampson, C., & Forletta, F. M. (2013). School resegregation in the Mississippi of the West: Community counternarratives on the return to neighborhood schools in Las Vegas, Nevada, 1968–1994. *Teachers College Record, 115*(11), 1–28.

Kelly v. Guinn, 456 F. 2d 100 (1972) Cert. Denied. 413 U.S. 919

Mediratta, K., Shah, S., & McAlister, S. (2008). *Organized communities, stronger schools: A preview of research findings.* Providence, RI: Annenberg Institute for School Reform at Brown University. Retrieved from http://annenberginstitute.org/pdf/OrganizedCommunities.pdf

Mokhtar, C. (2013, November). *An increase in ELL funding for Nevada's Clark County positions district as state and national model.* AISR Speaks Out: Commentary on Urban Education. Retrieved from http://annenberginstitute.org/?q=commentary/2013/11/increase-ell-funding-nevadas-clark-county-positions-district-state-and-national-m.

Nevada Education Reform Blue Ribbon Task Force (2010). *Nevada's Promise: Excellence, rigor, and equity.* Retrieved from http://www.nevadaracetothetop.org/pdfs/nevada-promise-complete100.pdf

Lang, R. E., & Sanchez, T. W. (2012). Metropolitan voting patterns in the Mountain West: The new and old political heartlands. In R. Teixeira (Ed.), *America's new swing region: Changing politics and demographics in the Mountain West* (pp. 69–80). Washington D.C.: Brookings.

Lang, R. E., Muro, M., & Sarzynski, A. (2008). *Mountain megas: America's newest metropolitan places and federal leadership to help them prosper.* Retrieved from: http://www.brookings.edu/research/reports/2008/07/20-mountainmegas-sarzynski

Limerick, P. (1988). *The legacy of conquest: The unbroken past of the American West.* New York: W.W. Norton & Company.

Stone, C. N., Doherty, K., Jones, C., & Ross, T. (1999). Schools in disadvantaged neighborhoods: The community development challenge. In R. Ferguson & W. Dickens (Eds.), *Urban problems and community development* (pp. 339–380). Washington, DC: Brookings Institution Press.

Taylor, Q. (1998). *In search of the racial frontier: African Americans in the American West, 1528–1990.* New York: W.W. Norton & Company.

Terriquez, V., Flashman, J., Schuler-Brown, S., & Orfield, G. (2009). *Expanding student opportunities: Prime 6 Program review.* Clark County School District, Las Vegas, Nevada. *Civil Rights Project at UCLA.* Retrieved from http://civilrightsproject.ucla.edu.

Teixeira, R. (Ed.). (2012). *America's new swing region: Changing politics and demographics in the Mountain West.* Washington D.C.: Brookings.

Vaca, N. C. (2004). *The presumed alliance: The unspoken conflict between Latinos and Blacks and what it means for America.* New York: HarperCollins.

Warren, M. R. (2005). Communities and schools: A new view of urban school reform. *Harvard Educational Review, 75*, 133–173.

Part IV
Students', Teachers', and Families' Educational Experiences

Critical Ethnic Studies in High School Classrooms: Academic Achievement via Social Action

Cati V. de los Ríos, Jorge López and Ernest Morrell

The 60th anniversary of the *Brown* decision offers an opportunity to reflect on the current state of race and education in the United States. Along with scholars, advocates, and educational leaders, we pondered this question at the NYU Metropolitan Center for Research on Equity and the Transformation of Schools' *Brown: 60 and Beyond* conference held on that campus in May 2014. The focus of our talk and this article is the potential use of what we call a critical pedagogy of race to increase academic achievement and social awareness for students of color, whose voices and perspectives are often absent from contemporary pedagogical and curricular approaches. One explanation for this absence is that an approach that centers upon race detracts from the development of core academic competencies. To the contrary, we argue that a critical approach to the teaching of race not only has the potential to make curricula more relevant and engaging, but such an approach also has the potential to foster standards-based academic development across the disciplines. We explore these possibilities through the study of three case studies of projects involving high-school students.

A version of this chapter was originally published as an article with the following citation: de los Ríos, C. V., López, J., & Morrell, E. (2015). Toward a critical pedagogy of race: Ethnic Studies and literacies of power in high school classrooms. *Race and Social Problems, 7*(1), 84–96.

C.V. de los Ríos (✉)
Teachers College, New York, NY, USA
e-mail: cvdelosrios@gmail.com

J. López
Claremont Graduate University, Claremont, CA, USA
e-mail: mrlopez.rhs@gmail.com

E. Morrell
Teachers College, Columbia University, New York, NY, USA
e-mail: ernestmorrell@gmail.com

© Springer International Publishing Switzerland 2016   177
P.A. Noguera et al. (eds.), *Race, Equity, and Education*,
DOI 10.1007/978-3-319-23772-5_9

We begin with an explanation of the new demographic reality in American education. In doing so, we make the case that the new non-White majority in US schools demands a rethinking of curriculum and teaching. We next introduce our conception of a critical pedagogy of race, which draws from the fields of critical pedagogy and Ethnic Studies. We then explore the limitations of a race-neutral curriculum and situate our focus on high school Ethnic Studies within a tradition that dates back to the late 1960s. The article then presents three cases of critical race pedagogy with high-school students. We conclude with implications for curriculum development, educational policy, and praxis.

The Demographic Reality of American Education

When looking at recent data gathered from the Council of Great City Schools on the largest school districts in the country (Council of Great City Schools, 2012), the necessity for a critical pedagogy of race becomes salient. Of the 6.9 million students who are enrolled in the nation's largest 60 school districts, 71 % of them are either African American or Latino (as opposed to approximately 35 % for the nation as a whole), 69 % are eligible for free or reduced lunch as determined by household income, and 17 % are classified as an English Language Learners (ELLs), while many, many more come from homes where languages other than English are spoken. Nationwide, the largest central city school districts are home to 28 % of all African American students, 24 % of all Latino students, 19 % of all Asian American students, and 25 % of all ELLs (Council of Great City Schools, 2012). It is interesting to note that only 5 % of White students in the United States attend schools in these larger city districts.

What do these numbers tell us? At one level, they speak to a large demographic shift in the ethnic population across the nation. While a generation ago, America's schools could have been identified as predominantly White, this group now comprises just 52 % of the national public school population (National Center for Education Statistics, 2014), and by 2023 it is projected that nationwide White students will only comprise 45 % of the US public school population. In 2014, there were already several states with a non-White majority such as California, New Mexico, and New York. These numbers also speak to the intense segregation of students of color in America's central cities. A recently published report by the UCLA Civil Rights Project (Kucsera & Orfield, 2014) shows that 60 % of all of the African American students in the state of New York are contained within the five boroughs of New York City, while only 10 % of White students are found in this same geographic area. While a growing non-White student population should bring forward important conversations about diversifying curriculum for all students, what we have instead are hypersegregated non-White educational spaces where students are still provided a curriculum and a set of pedagogical practices representative of an ethnically homogenous America that never existed.

Unfortunately, while there are many exceptions, in the aggregate it is possible to make strong correlations nationally between hypersegregated non-White schools and systems and academic underachievement. Many of these school districts have higher dropout rates and lower standardized test scores than their suburban counterparts. As a nation, it appears that we have come to expect schools serving large numbers of African American and Latino students to fail: that they will have fewer educational resources and substandard academic performance. How is it, in such a wealthy nation (with a GDP north of 15 trillion dollars), that we have allowed ourselves to become so comfortable with so much racialized educational failure?

In 2010, the United States Department of Education released a report entitled *A Blueprint for Reform: The Reauthorization of the Elementary and Secondary Education Act*. The report begins by outlining the relative decline in college completion rates for the United States. In one generation, the US has fallen from second to eleventh worldwide in the percentage of 25–34 year olds who have completed a college degree. The slide represents challenges we are facing in our educational system to provide adequate and equitable college access for all of our students. In particular, these problems are most acute for historically marginalized populations: those who are poor, those who are non-White, and those who attend schools in our nation's central cities. The lack of college access for students of color represents a problem for the US, which wants to maintain its global economic hegemony; however, we argue that the lack of college access among historically marginalized populations holds tremendous implications for our ability to increase the pipeline of educator–advocates who will lead the next generation of educational reform. The nation's teaching force is becoming increasingly homogenous even as K-12 classrooms and schools are becoming increasingly diverse (Feistritzer, 2011; National Collaborative on Diversity in the Teaching Force, 2004).

Students who do not finish high school are more likely to be underemployed, to go to prison, and to have children at a young age; they are less likely to vote and they are more likely to have children who do not finish high school (Rumberger, 2011). When the *Blueprint* identifies that fewer than 20 % of African American and Latino students in the 25–34 age group are completing college, it reveals a problem of epic proportions; a problem that would be mitigated by a critical pedagogy of race in American education.

Toward a Critical Pedagogy of Race in American Education

Without access to a critical global education, there is little that ordinary individuals will be able to offer to the twenty-first century, with its high demands for academic literacy and technological competency needed both for professional opportunities in the knowledge economy and civic responsibilities in our expanding and complex democracies. There is no question that a high-quality education is invaluable to the future of our nation and to the individuals who will shape that future. As the president, the secretary of education, and numerous members of Congress and the business community have reminded us, an educated citizenry is essential for our economic growth and our national security (USDOE, 2010); but, more importantly, a critically educated population is a nonnegotiable for the strength of our multicultural democracy and our national character. How might we rethink the philosophy and practice of American education to ensure the eradication of institutional racism, low expectations, and the general moral disinvestment in our nation's most impoverished schools?

Critical pedagogy is an educational process that engages members of historically underserved groups in humane and problem-posing dialog to name and ultimately transform oppressive social and structural conditions within schools and the larger society (Freire, 1970). Critical pedagogy is an approach to formal and informal education that challenges the concept of "culture-free" learning (Grant & Sleeter, 1990) and seeks instead to build authentic educational experiences that begin with the local experiences of students, families, and communities (Freire & Macedo, 1987; Yosso, 2005). In addition, proponents of this approach desire to foster an awareness of the structural conditions and societal norms that perpetuate inequity and oppression (McLaren, 1994). Moving beyond critique, however, the goals of critical pedagogy are to develop powerful readers and writers who can draw upon their literacy skills and their concern for justice to facilitate action for change (Darder, 2002; Freire, 1970). The very premise of critical pedagogy seeks to move away from the banking model of education that is based on a one-way transmission (or deposit) of knowledge to students' minds to an approach where teachers and students pose questions of the world (Freire, 1970) and engage in a process of inquiry and action (Duncan-Andrade & Morrell, 2008).

The project of critical pedagogy is a humanizing one in that it aims to help historically marginalized groups to obtain an education that will in turn lead to attaining a fuller humanity (Bartolome, 1994). Critical pedagogy is committed to democratizing power and access through collective action that involves those who have been muted, disregarded, or even worse targeted as objects of scorn, hate, or rejection (McLaren, 1994). Critical pedagogy is a belief in the potential of everyday people to function as catalysts of change; it is a dialogic and mutually constitutive process between educators and students that develops skills, sensibilities, and identities; and it holds the promise to become one of the most relevant and revolutionary tools in urban education today (Duncan-Andrade & Morrell, 2008).

While critical pedagogy has much to offer, it lacks an explicit attention to race and racial relations that is at the center of Ethnic Studies. Ethnic Studies is an interdisciplinary field that begins with the assumption that race and racism have been and will continue to be strong social and cultural forces in American society (Hu-Dehart, 1993). It builds on the pioneering work of Carter G Woodson (1933) and W.E.B. Du Bois (1903), Third World movements for decolonization (Fanon, 1963), Black independent schools and Afrocentric public schools, and tribal schools (Sleeter, 2011). Ethnic Studies—which was first identified as "Third World Studies" and changed at the moment of its institutionalization—emerged from a swiftly flowing confluence of revolutionary work and theorizing in the late 1960s. The Third World Liberation Front (TWLF) coalition formed at San Francisco State University and University of California, Berkeley was a momentous transnational project that aspired to undo over 400 years of world history and was inspired by anticolonial, anti-racist strivings aimed at addressing what W.E.B. Du Bois memorably termed "the problem of the twentieth century" (Okihiro, 2011). Prior to the 1960s, the large corpus of scholarship by Black intellectuals (and other scholars of color) was rarely taught at colleges and universities (Rojas, 2007). The TWLF demanded inclusion, access, democracy, representation, and new academic units buttressing multicultural and anti-racist curricula in both postsecondary and K-12 contexts (Umemoto, 1989).

Furthermore, Ethnic Studies centers race and racism as the primary terrain of academic inquiry and interrogates the construction and deconstruction of racial projects. Omi and Winant's (1994) seminal work on racial formation provides a critical framework in deconstructing social institutions as "racial projects," where racial categories are at once made real, but are also contested and reconfigured. Schools and curricula themselves have become "racial projects" where racial inequity has become naturalized. Ethnic Studies scholars and K-12 teachers also attempt to counter that inequity by tapping into the untold and untapped knowledge production of communities of color that is often absent from mainstream curricula at the secondary and postsecondary levels. Ethnic Studies, as a field, is very broad and critical in that it seeks to deconstruct the forces that contribute to the normalizing of racialized inequity and in that it also seeks to affirm and include multiple voices, perspectives, and artifacts within the corpus of sanctioned knowledge. Recent studies of Ethnic Studies high-school courses have demonstrated robust academic and media literacy skills (Morrell, Dueñas, Garcia, & López, 2013), the formation of critical literacy skills and an ethical responsibility to self and community (de los Ríos, 2013), and students as reconstructors of history (Jocson, 2008). From exposure to Ethnic Studies curricula, students are better able to develop a language of critique and possibility; and students of color are far more likely to have access to their histories and a fuller humanity in the educational arena.

The coupling of critical pedagogy and Ethnic Studies serves as a response and intervention to a racialized education crisis. Through combining the student-as-agent approach of critical pedagogy and race conscious inquiry that grounds Ethnic Studies, we feel it possible to create powerful curricula that simultaneously develop academic literacies, self-efficacy, and collective action for racial justice. The necessity of this approach is made even clearer by the continued growth of "post-racial" ideologies that have naturalized racial inequity in schools (King, 1991; Philip, 2011).

America's "Race-Neutral" Curricula

The concept of "race-neutrality" permeates US curricula, schooling, and education policy (Wells, 2014). Schools as racial projects operate under the assumption that the process of becoming educated is a race-neutral or color-blind experience. On the contrary, not only formal school curricula but also informal, hidden, and null curricula work to maintain economic, political, societal, and cultural order (Apple, 1982; Bernstein, 1975). Since the beginning of schooling, curricula have served as a tool for acculturation and a depository of white supremacist ideals and values. As Tyack (1974) recounts, it has been the epistemologies, values, and beliefs of White Anglo Saxon Protestants (WASPs) that have been historically (and currently) deemed of most worth in public schools.

> Schoolmen… held a common set of WASP values, professed a common core (that is, pan-Protestant) Christianity, were ethnocentric, and tended to glorify the sturdy virtues of a departed tradition. They took their values for granted as self-evidently true—not subject to legitimate debate. (Tyack, 1974, p. 109)

As "the key institution in the practical process of social differentiation and selection and the heart of the ideological process through which inequality is made to seem legitimate" (Shapiro & Purpel, 1993, p. 62 as cited in Goodwin, 2010, p. 3110), schools and school curricula have been key in maintaining hegemony. Furthermore, Sleeter (2002) argues that curricula and standards alike advance a dominant ideology by disregarding the scholarship of historically oppressed groups and attempting to build students' allegiances to the existing social order.

Recent cases across the country convey the ways in which white supremacy is standardized through "race-neutral" curricula. The struggle over Texas history standards is a prime example (Au, 2013; Vasquez Heilig, Brown, & Brown, 2012). A bloc of conservative evangelical Christians on the state Board of Education eliminated the Seneca Falls Convention and women's suffrage activist Carrie Chapman Catt from the standards, while also removing Harriet Tubman off the list of good citizens. Texas also swapped out Martin Luther King Jr. Day, minimized the incarceration of Japanese Americans during WWII, reduced the discussion of slavery, and removed references to United Farm Worker labor leader, Dolores Huerta (Foner, 2010; McKinley 2010).

Furthermore, the ideological battle in Tucson, Arizona over representation, historical memory, and epistemology was seen through the dismantling of the once academically successful Raza/Mexican American Studies Program in the Tucson Unified School District (Cabrera, Meza, Romero, & Rodriguez, 2013). This program was based on socioculturally and historically contingent curriculum and pedagogy (Romero, Arce, & Cammarota, 2009) and drew from counter-hegemonic frameworks like Mesoamerican epistemologies (Rodríguez, 2012). The Mexican American Studies Program has been empirically shown to increase the achievement of its students using typical indicators (Cabrera, Milem, & Marx, 2012; Cappellucci et al., 2011) and yet was deemed "un-American," "divisive," promoting "sedition," and encouraging students to "overthrow the government" (Sleeter, 2011).

Howard (2010) has argued that color-blind perspectives in curriculum development and schooling perpetuate racial inequality and "reproduce racial and cultural hegemony in school practices" (p. 53). Thus curriculum—as a tool for acculturation and a conduit for whitestream epistemologies and values (Urrieta, 2009)—has

historically promoted the de-Indigenization, axiological subjugation, miseducation, and the assimilation of students of color to the dominant Western culture.
In effect, educational practices that appropriate "color-blind" ideologies are not
color-blind at all—these strategies of erasure are simultaneous practices of whiteness. Reconfiguring learning spaces from color-blindness to race-consciousness is
significant in Ethnic Studies approaches.

Ethnic Studies in American High Schools

As we contemplate a more widespread use of a critical pedagogy of Ethnic Studies
in America's high schools, it is important to understand the rich tradition of Ethnic
Studies teaching in these settings that already exists. Erroneously, many believe
that Ethnic Studies have only been taught in universities and colleges. However,
the tradition of high-school Ethnic Studies is as long and rich as the postsecondary
context that we know and hear much more about.

As early as 1968, students at Berkeley High School in Northern California were
demanding an African American Studies department (Ogbar, 2004; Rojas, 2007),
which has now been a part of that school's curriculum for more than 45 years.
In addition, the Chicana/o Blowouts in East Los Angeles, also of 1968, became
the largest student mobilization in US history (Acuña, 1996); students attending
Garfield, Lincoln, Belmont, Roosevelt, and Wilson high schools protested against
the schools' substandard material conditions and quality of education. One of the
key points of protest for the students at Garfield, Roosevelt, Wilson, and Lincoln
high schools was the lack of curriculum dealing with Chicana/o history, language,
and culture (García & Castro, 2011; Ochoa, 2008).

It is out of that rich tradition of pedagogy and praxis in California schools that
dates back nearly 50 years that we offer three case studies of recent work employing what we have come to call critical pedagogies of race with high-school students. The first of these cases explores students' critical close readings of federal
legislations affecting their lives and futures and their organizing of social justice
community posadas to raise awareness and create local solutions. The second case,
from Roosevelt High School, shows how López looked to community resources
to design a Community Cultural Treasures Project that united teachers, nonprofit
arts organizations, and literacy directors to create an assignment that addressed the
life, culture, local history, and voice of students. The final case study describes
a 12-year project where high-school students used youth participatory action
research (YPAR) to unpack issues of social and racial injustice in their neighborhoods, schools, and communities. The case exemplifies the tremendous passion
and purpose youth bring to racial justice work and it also shows the potential to
leverage this intense engagement to increase academic achievement and college
access.

Pomona High School

Despite research conveying that Latina/o families are the least likely to participate in political activism (Bloemraad, Voss, & Lee, 2011; Martínez, 2005), up
to 5 million (mostly Latina/o) immigrants and their allies took part in a historic
national mass mobilization in spring of 2006 (Zepeda-Millán, 2014). An unprecedented wave of immigrant activism captured the nation's attention with a series of
mass demonstrations to protest *The Border Protection, Antiterrorism, and Illegal
Immigration Control Act of 2005* (H.R. 4437), which sought to change the penalty
for being undocumented from a civil violation to a federal felony. The bill also
targeted anyone who assisted "people without papers" by punishing them with
monetary fines and incarceration (Zepeda-Millán & Wallace, 2013). de los Ríos, a
teacher at Pomona High School (PHS) at the time, observed that many of her students and their families, im/migrants themselves, developed an oppositional consciousness (Morris & Braine, 2001) around this nativist legislation as deportations
and the separation of families were at an all-time high in their communities. From
these experiences emanated a series of *charlas* (community discussions) and later
a vision for a high-school curriculum that would center topics like im/migration,
investigate conceptual themes from women and Ethnic Studies, labor history, and
English literature, and allow students to explore the lived experiences of Chicana/
o-Latina/o young people and other people of color and connect them to larger
historical trajectories. Pomona High School's Chicana/o-Latina/o Studies courses
and program became the product of this vision and the first college-preparatory
Ethnic Studies courses offered in the Pomona Unified School District (de los Ríos
& Ochoa, 2012).

True to Ethnic Studies' disciplinary commitment to grassroots communities
(Okihiro & Tsou, 2006), PHS's Chicana/o-Latina/o Studies courses offer multiple opportunities for high-school students to engage in grassroots community
organizing projects. One of these cultivates civic engagement and critical literacies alongside *jornaleros* (day laborers) and staff of the Pomona Day Labor
Center, also known as the Pomona Economic Opportunity Center (PEOC). The
PEOC not only provides a safe place for workers and their potential employers
to meet up and negotiate a day's work, it also organizes day laborers so that they
are active leaders in their own communities who take on issues important to day
laborers and the greater immigrant community. As the founding teacher of the
Chicana/o-Latina/o Studies course, de los Ríos hoped that her students would
not only develop both critical and academic literacies through this partnership,
but also gain knowledge and skill sets that would help them better address their
material conditions (Freire, 1970) within a pervasive anti-migrant hegemony
(Gonzáles, 2013). At the commencement of the collaboration, the skillful organizing demonstrated by the *jornaleros*, the Director Susan Foster, Pitzer College
Professor José Calderón, and others provided and continues to provide our high-
school students with fruitful learning experiences and fecund soil for critical
thinking.

In the winter of 2008, students enrolled in the PHS Chicana/o-Latina/o Studies courses began organizing social justice posadas with *jornaleros* from the PEOC (de los Ríos, 2013). Since then, hundreds of young people, parents, and community members participate in a candlelight procession every year in resistance to the increasing anti-immigrant sentiments and call for a path to citizenship for the 12 million undocumented immigrants in the United States. Rooted within a framework of service-learning, Chicana/o-Latina/o Studies students partner up with Pomona Day Laborers—many of whom are immigrants from México and Central America—to organize a community procession that seeks to promote awareness around current state and federal policies affecting immigrants, especially undocumented students. This project is a modern adaptation of the popular religious ritual celebrated throughout the US Southwest and México. A *posada,* meaning inn or shelter in Spanish, is traditionally celebrated in the season of Advent with the biblical reenactment of Joseph and Mary traveling home-to-home seeking shelter and refuge during the week before Christmas. While this project is not a religious posada, it still draws from the community's funds of knowledge and honors long-standing spiritual rituals and culturally relevant practices. Rather than centering the biblical narrative of the Holy Family's experience with rejection when seeking acceptance, the posada concentrates on the current social climate of undocumented students and immigrant families seeking amnesty, justice, and opportunity. Instead of singing the traditional religious songs, historical social justice songs like "De Colores" are bilingually sung, and poetry and chants that advocate for human rights are read and chanted. Prior to the posada, high-school students engage in a rigorous unit that explores some of the important concepts and theories necessary to understand immigration.

First, students read excerpts of Francisco Jimenez' book *The Circuit* and Helena Maria Viramontes' book *Under the Feet of Jesus. The Circuit* is an auto-biographical novel based on the author's journey as a young boy migrating from Mexico to the US and living in migrant labor camps in California. Similarly, Viramontes' book tells the story of a young girl and her migrant family's arduous struggle with working the fields in the summer months. These novels provide an important context for migrant labor and California agricultural history. Additionally, for 2 weeks, students study the history of immigration as a global phenomenon, agricultural labor, and wage discrimination and hear first-hand *testimonios* from *jornaleros* in the Los Angeles and San Bernardino areas. Later, high school students compare wages and labor conditions from the Delano Grape Strike in 1965 to various twenty-first century agricultural strikes and conduct close readings of both federal and state legislations affecting immigrant families.

Moreover, students have developed academic position papers, written letters to local council members, and spoken publicly at various forums in the community advocating for both the California and Federal DREAM Act and comprehensive immigration reform. Utilizing a non-hierarchical and asset-based approach to unite Pomona day laborers and Pomona High School students, this collaboration continues to be unique in that it brings together two marginalized communities that are usually kept apart—the grassroots labor community and the urban public K-12 sector. It entails the co-creation of a liberatory space—a Social Justice Community Posada—that engages families, teachers, and administrators in critical discussion, collective action, and literacies of humanity and justice.

The organizing of the actual posada occurs primarily after school with the *jornaleros*; students work in committees with day laborers for 4 weeks. Together they form a procession route in downtown Pomona, contact businesses and local and national newspapers, create songs of justice and peace, research bilingual poems that stand in solidarity with immigrants, and ultimately build community with their neighbors, including the local business where they would eventually visit and sing. Students have also created iMovies, Prezis, and photo essays documenting their journeys with this assignment. These digital artifacts are often used for the following year's posadas as teaching tools and have also been presented at national conferences to not only convey students' passion for social justice, their twenty-first century literacies, and the critical thinking skills that derive from this project but also serve as examples of young people who are powerfully and civically engaged and active in fighting for the self-determination and dignity of their communities. Lastly, the institutionalization of the partnership between Pomona High School and the PEOC has given students a stronger sense of membership within the school campus community where students have articulated feeling significantly "safer" as members of immigrant and transnational communities both inside and outside of school (de los Ríos, 2013).

Roosevelt High School

Serving culturally rich Chicano/a-Latino/a communities such as the east side of Los Angeles offers educators opportunities to design Ethnic Studies units that address students' history, culture, and humanity. As a result of the nation's reliance on high stakes testing and standardized curricula, teachers are restricted from freely building student community literacy and implementing culturally empowering pedagogies. However, by taking interdisciplinary approaches, partnering with local community organizations, and building alliances across cultural communities, educators can supersede irrational and dehumanizing hegemonic forces (Darder, 2002). In the spring of 2013, López, a history teacher at Roosevelt High School, engaged his 10th grade World History students in a community grounded Ethnic Studies project.

López participated in the designing of the Community Cultural Treasures Project that brought together teachers and nonprofit community arts and literacy directors to create a project that addressed the life, culture, local history, and voice of students. Partnering with long-standing and respected community arts leaders was fundamental for the success of this project, because they brought a wealth of knowledge and connections to leaders who have historically transformed and continue to transform the neighborhood into a culturally rich hub. Students learned to identify community-based cultural assets and generate empowering community knowledge through a critical textual product (Morrell, 2008) that offered an alternative and liberating counter-narrative to the dominant discourse. Students published a book of biographies, poems, narratives, and interviews that challenged racist notions of their neighborhood and shared their work to community members at a local theater arts space.

To generate the content for the book, students were guided in setting up interviews with *community cultural treasures*, individuals who have made positive contributions to the culture and people of East Los Angeles. Students conducted in-depth interviews with people from their neighborhood who promote the preservation of Boyle Height's culture and ethnic wealth. Seeing positive images of community members who are transforming and expanding the cultural landscape is critical for the development of empowered youth. Projects such as these allow for students to read about people who have made powerful contributions throughout history, and more importantly collaborate with them in the writing of their own community history. Students who have a passion for art chose to interview Willie Herron and Wayne Healy, two of the first public artists who began painting cultural murals in East Los Angeles in the 1970s. Other students sat down with local musical artists from the bands Quetzal and La Santa Cecilia to explore how their music addresses and celebrates the Latino community. Students also met directors of community spaces, such as Casa 0101, a theater arts center that puts on productions on community themes, and *Espacio 1839*, a local bookstore, radio station, and cultural art space where community culture advocates and young people converge to create and share diverse forms of empowering arts and approaches to change and community building. There were over 70 different community-based cultural assets that students identified, engaged with, and wrote about. Many were local food vendors and resilient people who reflect the cultural diversity and ethnic wealth of Boyle Heights in East Los Angeles.

Students told stories of Boyle Height's musicians, muralists, activists, cultural landmarks, educators, cultural workers, and family in their book product, *La Vida Diferente* (A different life). Through the process of having students meet and listen to stories of their community's culture, they were exposed to existing cultural capital and learned to perceive their community as a space that culturally empowers its members, rather than seeing their neighborhood through a deficit lens. Ethnic Studies amplifies the voices of students and communities that have historically been spoken for. The student writings were products that dispelled racist stereotypes of Chicana/o-Latina/o communities generated in the dominant media.

In the classroom, students were learning how to write in multiple genres and building their literacy skills by moving through the writing and editing process. Tutors from a local nonprofit organization volunteered in both López's class and his partnering English class to offer students support in their written pieces. Students had a lot of support through this project, which was central to its success, and fundamental in what Ethnic Studies teachers must do—gather support and resources from local communities. It is critical for educators to seek out local organizations and develop projects that connect students to the community and the community to the classroom. One of the many positive outcomes that came out of this project was that students became aware of and connected to the many resources, spaces, and people in East Los Angeles that they can tap into for support, guidance, and inspiration. For example, a student Paula became aware of a community cycling club for women of color, and can now turn to the group of empowered women while expanding her support network of people that can help her navigate through society as a female of color. Another student Giselle interviewed public artist Raul González, who has painted many murals around Boyle Heights, many with youth, on themes that promote community culture, history, and empowerment. Giselle became much more interested in murals and later helped paint a mural at her school.

When the book was published, a book-release celebration was organized at a local theater space. Family, teachers, and people who were interviewed for the book were invited to hear students read their pieces. This culminating event was transformational for youth, who had in their hands the fruits of their hard work; they experienced shifting identities as writers, historians, scholars, and authors of community culture. The space facilitated an intersection of community leaders of the past and cultural advocates of the present, which included the youth who authored the book. López believes that authentic critical Ethnic Studies curricula and projects must create opportunities for students to participate in the reading of the world, rather than it being imposed by teachers and academics (Freire, 1998).

Unlike alienating curriculum, this project had the support of community members and cultural workers. Through this nurturing and caring approach in building student skills and scholarship students further revealed their community cultural wealth, while contributing to the struggle for racial justice (Yosso, 2005). This project aims at highlighting to educators who are working to create humanizing curriculum, the crucial importance to not develop projects in isolation but rather work in solidarity (Freire, 1998) with the community they serve, including students. Working in community develops stronger relationships within the school and the neighborhood. As a result of this project, López developed new relationships with community cultural workers who are interested in working on future projects to support student learning and empowerment. The youth-authored book is currently used by teachers at Roosevelt High School in their Ethnic Studies and English courses.

The project also aimed at developing in students a love for their community. Connecting students with cultural workers of East Los Angeles who have a deep love for their community and commitment to social justice helps students see what community love looks like. Ethnic Studies curriculum must create avenues for students to see manifestations of love, which humanizes the learning environment and supports student learning and self (Morrell et al., 2013). Teachers must also possess a love for the community they serve if they wish to impart in students this value. Duncan-Andrade and Morrell (2008) call on educators to practice revolutionary love, which is the manifestation of love in the classroom that is strong enough to bring about radical change, which requires endless dedication, passion, commitment, and belief in the potential of every student. The cultural workers and community cultural treasures that students interviewed possess this radical love for their community and people. Teachers who possess this commitment and love will be much more successful in developing the value of community love through their pedagogical practices in students.

Critical Ethnic Studies pedagogy and curriculum development that is grounded in community and culture and includes student critical textual production and product distribution contribute to student critical consciousness, community literacy, cultural empowerment, and humanization. As public schools continue to move toward non-White pluralities, curricula need to address the cultural needs of students. Ethnic Studies offers a humanizing and empowering approach to education, challenging the historical role of schools that has racially oppressed and systemically alienated students of color.

Ethnic Studies pedagogy has numerous benefits for students such as an increase in academic confidence in writing, identity development, and critical literacies. At Wilson High School in Los Angeles, teachers who taught through an Ethnic Studies lens had students improve their writing abilities and self-confidence and develop a positive caring student–teacher relationship (Morrell et al., 2013). One Wilson High teacher indicates that her assignments allowed her to "better understand her students and create a classroom environment that is welcoming to all" (p. 58). Another teacher asserts that students learned to write reflective poems and produced a deep analysis of their world, while drawing parallels to Chicano writers from the Chicana/o movement. Students benefit from being exposed, for the first time, to concepts of oppression and learn to examine their own personal histories (pp. 111–112). Los Angeles educators who taught lessons on identity in their Ethnic Studies courses and units made meaningful connections to students, while constantly affirming their potential during the school year, resulting in successful academic outcomes (p. 156). At Roosevelt High School, students learned to document public places within their community using media devices and create community youth counter-narratives. In the Ethnic Studies course, students were successful in producing videos that addressed existing community problems and youth cultural expressions (p. 92).

The Council of Youth Research (CYR)

On a hot August day, Morrell was in the Tom Bradley Room, the 26th floor of Los Angeles City Hall, setting up students' PowerPoint presentations and digital video documentaries. Audience members and members of the media were starting to file in as the high school students prepared with their groups for their presentations. Over the course of the next 3 hours they would speak to the deputy mayor of Los Angeles and the staff of his Office of Education about the conditions of youth in Los Angeles schools. The students had consulted literature from social theory and the sociology of education that offered various reasons that youth drop out or are pushed out of Los Angeles public schools. Students were divided into five research teams, each tasked with studying a particular neighborhood and school where the

4 year completion rates hover between 25 and 40 % (meaning somewhere between 60 and 75 % of incoming ninth graders do not finish high school with a diploma 4 years later). They presented various forms of data they collected and analyzed including interviews, surveys, photographs, participant observation, digital video, and descriptive statistics. The 25 minute presentations provided only a snapshot of the larger body of work, which also included a formal academic research report that the students coauthored in small groups. All of this work was completed in the scope of a 6-week summer course that brought together high-school students attending underperforming schools across Central, South, and East Los Angeles. After the culmination of the presentations, the students heard from the deputy mayor, his staff, and ultimately the Mayor of Los Angeles, Antonio Villaraigosa. They were also interviewed by various members of the print and film media and featured on the front page of the *Los Angeles Times*. The students' reports, PowerPoint slides, and digital video documentaries were sent to the mayor's office for use in work with Los Angeles schools and they were also uploaded onto the websites of the Institute for Democracy, Education, and Access (IDEA) at UCLA, the university sponsor of the program. Several students were involved in a week-long written debate, also carried by the *Los Angeles Times*, with a former school board member about the best ways to move forward in reforming schools to serve the needs of underperforming schools better.

The City Hall presentations served as a capstone for an annual course that brought high-school students of color[1] to the university each summer course to study Youth Participatory Action Research for Educational Justice. For 12 years (1999–2011) Morrell and his colleagues offered a 5-week college-level course for high-school students that taught them about the process of conducting research in their schools and communities to promote social, racial, and educational justice. In preparation for conducting research in schools and communities, the students read a great deal from social theory, the social sciences, Ethnic Studies, and educational research. Students also composed in various genres including field notes, journals, interview transcripts, research reports, and personal essays that were referred to as critical memoirs.

During the academic year, the Council of Youth Research (CYR) students collaborated with UCLA and the mayor's office of education to collect and analyze information about life in Los Angeles schools. The work, conducted largely in the context of English and Social Studies classrooms, was distributed to students, teachers, parents, and more globally to policymakers, elected officials, and community organizations around the city. Students also began to share their work more broadly. For instance, students traveled to the California State Capitol to dialog with legislators around issues of educational injustice. Students involved with

---

[1] Schools selected for the Council of Youth Research were essentially 100 % non-White. Over the 12 years of the project 99 % of the students identified as members of non-White ethnic groups, the largest being Latino (over 60 %) and African American (35 %). The CYR demographics closely correlate to those of the schools where the project took place.

the Council also traveled to Seattle, Denver, New Orleans, and San Francisco to speak at the annual meetings of the American Educational Research Association (AERA), a professional organization of over 15,000 members. At one of these annual meetings, the students were granted a Presidential Session, focused solely on the promise of Youth Research.

Council students have also been involved in social media, creating Twitter feeds, Facebook pages, blogs, and YouTube channels where they share their PowerPoint presentations, research reports, and video documentaries. Local and national print and television media outlets regularly featured students and their work.

The goals of the project were to promote academic literacy development, civic engagement, and critical racial consciousness for the young people involved, while also providing a knowledge base that could help to transform the curricular and pedagogical practices in English and Social Studies classrooms by pushing educators to think about how to merge a critical pedagogy of race within the demands of these academic disciplines.

When looking for evidence of impact, one can point to the transformation in the students themselves. Whether through student written critical memoirs, comments made in presentations, focus group interviews, or informal personal reflections, students identified that the CYR provided a unique space for student voice inside an education system where they were often muted. Additionally, much of the ethos for research questions, actual research design, and the carrying out of studies came from students themselves. Finally, the students had ownership over much of the process of production and distribution of research, which ultimately led to the creation of digital video documentaries (a student idea) as a complement, or even a supplement on occasions, to the traditional research report.

Morrell, Dueñas, Garcia, and López (2013) have reported elsewhere about the academic progress of the students; there was clear evidence of higher student graduation and college access within the CYR student populations when compared to historical trends in the schools where the project took place. In Morrell's dissertation study (Morrell, 2004) of the original cohort of students, more than 95 % graduated high school and matriculated into college in a school where the graduation rate for students of color hovered around 50 %. In follow-up studies, we identified increased mathematical reasoning (Rogers, Morrell, & Enyedy, 2007), the development of college-level writing (Morrell, 2008), nearly 100 % high-school graduation rates (Mirra & Morrell, 2011), and powerful examples of critical media production (Morrell et al., 2013).

There are two additional spaces where there appears to be evidence of change. One is at the school sites themselves. In one high school, Council students created a social action club that grew to possess tremendous influence throughout the school. Led by students, this organization dedicated itself to bringing youth together to address problems in the school and the community. In their first year, club members conducted research on the police department's ticketing of tardy students, held press conferences and lunchtime rallies, and helped to plan a major conference that focused on research and organizing for social justice.

Other campuses throughout the city with Council students followed suit in creating their own social justice clubs. Students modeled a problem-posing pedagogy when establishing their clubs, as they wanted to honor youth voice and they also wanted young people to have the opportunity to share their concerns with each other, away from the influence of adults. Several members of these student-led groups became active in working with the administrations to improve campus climate. Students also used their research skills to create "bottom up" measures of successful schools and they shared their survey instruments and interview protocols with others via our project website and other social media outlets.

In another example, CYR members invited the principal and several department chairs to their research presentations at City Hall. From this initial involvement, the principal became an enthusiastic supporter of the project, coming to visit the students as they worked after school, coming into the teacher's classroom for presentations, and offering himself to be interviewed by student research teams from around the city. The school was in the process of transitioning into small learning communities, each having its own theme and identity. One of these communities, formed around concern for social justice, came to be called Agents of Change (AOC). It is important to correlate the timing of these events, the connection between the principal and the Council, and the naming of the small learning community's first leader, a teacher who had been involved in several summer seminars with the CYR.

The students attending this school also established relationships with their local State Senator who attended their presentations, the president of the school board who participated in interviews with them, and the Superintendent of the city schools. During the following academic year, the principal was promoted to local Deputy Superintendent and was replaced by one of the assistant principals, also a strong supporter of the CYR. During her first few weeks on the job changes in school security threatened the safety of students. In a routine conversation with the Superintendent, the Council students shared their concerns. Within days, the District Superintendent had spoken with the local Deputy Superintendent, who then connected with the principal about how to address the problem of inadequate security on campus. While there are many other ways that this issue could have been handled, there is no mistaking the influence and credibility that the students in the Youth Council garnered in the school and the local community.

Implications for Pedagogy

Redefining Rigorous Instruction

Too often in conversations about educational reform, "rigorous" instruction is juxtaposed against instruction that is relevant and meaningful to students. The underlying assumption is that work that students enjoy (or are able to do) must not be rigorous. If we aspire to make practices such as the ones outlined in this article more prevalent in classrooms across the country, we have to challenge these misconceptions. In each of the case studies teachers worked to create curricula that developed the academic competencies of reading, writing, critical analysis, public speaking, media literacy, and critical language awareness, to name a few.

Those who are committed to a critical pedagogy of race in secondary schools must also be committed to developing academic skills that students can use to better navigate their professional, social, and civic futures. However, we argue that this can be done through a curriculum that focuses on social awareness, reclaiming lost and stolen histories, and the struggle for equity and racial justice. Even further, we argue that curricula that expose students to multiple historical viewpoints, that position youth as agents of change, and that appeal to young people's sense of fairness and equality will increase engagement and interest, which will lead to increased academic achievement. One of the key reasons that young people are often not interested in school is not because they do not care about education; rather they do not see education as connected to their lives. A critical pedagogy of race is rigorous and relevant in that it is centered within the everyday and historical experiences of young people and it pushes them to connect intellectual rigor with the pursuit of a fuller humanity. As Paulo Freire says, "to study is one's revolutionary duty!"

Ethnic Studies Across the Curriculum

Although the mandated tests and teacher evaluation systems designed to measure student achievement threaten to push the Common Core State Standards in the wrong direction, this reform, with its focus on deeper learning, critical citizenship, and cross-curricular literacy actually has far more "progressive" potential than is currently being realized (Wells, 2014). Ethnic Studies curricula have been successfully implemented in disciplines currently regulated by the Common Core State Standards such as history and English. López has collaborated with English teachers on a 10th grade inquiry-based unit, Voices of Change, where students in both World History and English explored the essential question, "What needs to change to generate more justice and equity in Boyle Heights?" Another example includes López partnering with an 11th grade English teacher to develop an interdisciplinary unit on the Chicana/o Student Movement. Students read *The Revolt of the Cockroach People* by Oscar Zeta Acosta in their American Literature class while examining in their US History class news articles of the 1968 walkouts, and interviewing former leaders in their quest to answer, "How can we resist educational and social inequalities and achieve social justice?" These units dealt with CCSS.ELA-LITERACY.RH.11-12.3 and CCSS.ELA-LITERACY.RH11-12.3, two English Language Arts standards that emphasize students' evaluation of various explanations and viewpoints of historical events, their determination of which viewpoints best accord with textual evidence, and their acknowledgment of where the texts leave matters uncertain. Each of these units also focus on close and critical reading and evidence-based argumentative writing, which are hallmarks of the new Common Core State Standards and essential skills for college, career, and civic readiness.

Similarly, de los Ríos has drawn from CCSS.ELA-LITERACY.RH.11-12.7 to evaluate multiple sources of information presented in diverse media, including the musical genre Mexican Corridos, to explore issues of feminism and immigration in her Spanish for Native Speakers courses in order to promote cross-curricular literacy. She too has collaborated with other Spanish teachers to facilitate and teach Ethnic Studies units entirely in Spanish. There are numerous opportunities to collaborate with teachers across departments and within their disciplines. Creating a culture of collaboration around Ethnic Studies in which teachers are creating powerful units that address race, racialization, and youth culture while applying critical pedagogy is fundamental for the sustainability of Ethnic Studies courses and programs. Within school spaces, it is important to bring together knowledgeable teachers in the field of Ethnic Studies with less familiarized teachers who desire to learn more about transforming their curriculum frameworks and pedagogical approaches.

There remains a need for trainings, conferences, and institutes that help educators access tools to develop Ethnic Studies curricula. An excellent example—which no longer exists—was Tucson Unified School District's (TUSD) Institute for Transformative Education, which brought together thousands of K-12 educators to engage in the praxis of Ethnic Studies pedagogies. Today, a number of teachers from Tucson, Arizona—many of whom are former teachers in the now dismantled TUSD Raza/Mexican American Studies Program—recently developed a 3-day summer institute that intellectually engages and scaffolds the implementation of Ethnic Studies methodologies throughout K-12 contexts. The Xican@ Institute for Teaching and Organizing (XITO) is a unique blend of theory, practice, and community responsive organizing and serves as an extraordinary model of the type of institutes that are needed to build national capacity on Ethnic Studies pedagogy and practices.

Implications for Policy and Praxis

Nationally, high school students' access to Ethnic Studies courses remains limited. That could change with Assemblyman Luis Alejo's (D-Watsonville) recent introduction of AB 101, a bill requiring California to form a task force that would study how to best implement a standardized Ethnic Studies program for high school students throughout the state. Such a program would address important gaps in students' knowledge and, coming from one of the most diverse states in the nation, serve as a powerful model for the rest of the country. More specifically, Tintiangco-Cubales and colleagues (2014) address the need for teacher credentialing programs to instruct future educators in the teaching of Ethnic Studies, and recommend that the state of California include Ethnic Studies coursework in the subject matter preparation of teachers. The aforementioned article also makes connections to the origins of Ethnic Studies as being responsive to grassroots communities. A community responsive pedagogy, as conveyed in the case studies mentioned in this article, is a hallmark of Ethnic Studies methodologies.

Teacher unions in cities like Los Angeles, Chicago, and New York are calling for schools to teach anti-racist curriculum, and for teachers to engage in local community struggles and organizations. In Los Angeles there has been an active campaign known as *Schools LA Students Deserve* that is working with educators and United Teachers of Los Angeles (UTLA) leadership to implement a list of changes in the school district, and one of these suggestions urged more Ethnic Studies course offerings for students. These efforts led to the recent historical resolution of mandating a college-preparatory Ethnic Studies course as a high-school requirement in the Los Angeles Unified School District (LAUSD). Following the examples of LAUSD and, most recently, San Francisco Unified School District's recent resolution with Ethnic Studies, we suggest that K-12 school districts offer Ethnic Studies courses beyond the frequent "social science elective," and strongly urge that that Ethnic Studies be implemented as a high school graduation requirement in all American high schools. Elected officials and school leaders must come together to garner support for state policy to make Ethnic Studies a nationwide high school graduation requirement.

We are at a critical crossroad in American history—a breaking point at which efforts to ignore critical pedagogies of race will further clash with the racial and cultural complexity of our day-to-day lives. We recommend that policymakers address race-conscious policies, practices, and material conditions that perpetuate segregation and inequality, while simultaneously tapping into the changing racial attitudes of Americans by supporting racially diverse schools and race-conscious curricula and pedagogical practices.

Brown at 60: Rethinking American Education

While the American educational landscape has changed a great deal over the past 60 years, race remains a salient issue. Though conversations in the late 1940s and early 1950s centered upon the benefits of integrating African American students into a largely White schooling system, in 2014 we face an entirely different demographic and socioeconomic reality. We no longer have a school system that is predominantly White and we no longer have the comfort (if we ever did) of living in happy isolation removed from the diverse global society. As politicians and pundits discuss the "demographic imperative" or the need for global literacies, there is a growing admission that American schools and the world at large are tremendously heterogeneous spaces. There is also some tacit admission that at present, we do an inadequate job of preparing all students for this domestic and global reality.

Rethinking American education on the 60th anniversary of the *Brown* decision must entail questioning the education that all of our students receive, particularly as it relates to race, ethnicity, and intercultural understanding. While the quality and focus of mainstream education were largely unquestioned during the *Brown* deliberations, we no longer have that luxury. We must be willing to face the tough reality that the content of our curricula inadequately reflects the diversity of the nation. Further, our inability to deal with race effectively has consequences for all of our students. We firmly believe that increasing all students' access to a critical Ethnic Studies curriculum not only helps to realize the ideals of *Brown*; it also helps to prepare our students academically, socially, and culturally for the world today.

References

Acuña, R. (1996). *Anything but Mexican: Chicanos in contemporary Los Angeles*. New York: Verso.

Apple, M. (1982). *Education and power*. Boston: Routledge & Kegan Paul.

Au, W. (2013). Coring social studies within corporate reform: The Common Core standards, social justice and the politics of knowledge in US schools, *Critical Education 4*(5).

Bartolomé, L. I. (1994). Beyond the methods fetish: Toward a humanizing pedagogy. *Harvard Educational Review, 64*(2), 173–194.

Bernstein, B. (1975). *Class, codes, and control*. London: Routledge.

Bloemraad, I., Voss K., Lee, T. (2011). The protests of 2006: What were they, how do we understand them, where do we go? In K. Voss & I. Bloemraad's (Eds.) *Rallying for immigrant rights*. Berkeley, (pp. 3–43) CA: University of California Press.

Cabrera, N. L., Milem, J. F., & Marx, R. W. (2012). *An empirical analysis of the effects of Mexican American Studies participation on student achievement within Tucson Unified School District*. Report to Special Master Dr. Willis D. Hawley on the Tucson Unified School District Desegregation Case, Tucson, AZ. Retrieved from http://works.bepress.com/nolan_l_cabrera/17/.

Cabrera, N. L., Meza, E. L., Romero, A. J., & Rodriguez, R. (2013). "If there is no struggle, there is no progress": Transformative youth resistance and the School of Ethnic Studies. *The Urban Review*. doi:10.1007/s11256-012-0220-7.

Cappellucci, D. F., Williams, C., Hernandez, J. J., Nelson, L. P., Casteel, T., Gilzean, G.…. (2011). Curriculum audit of the Mexican American studies department Tucson Unified School District Tucson, Arizona. Cambium Learning, Inc.; National Academic Educational Partners, F. L. Miami Lakes. Retrieved from http://www.tucsonweekly.com/images/blogimages/2011/06/16/1308282079-az_masd_audit_final_1_.pdf.

Council of Great City Schools. (2012). Characteristics of the Great City Schools, 2009–2010. Retrieved August 31, 2014.

Darder, A. (2002). *Reinventing Paulo Freire: A pedagogy of love*. Westview Press.

Du Bois, W. E. B. (1903). *The souls of black folk*. Chicago, IL: A.C. McClurg & Co.

Duncan-Andrade, J., & Morrell, E. (2008). *The art of critical pedagogy: Possibilities for moving theory to practice in urban schools*. New York: Peter Lang.

Fanon, F. (1963). *The Wretched of the Earth*. New York, NY: Grove Press.

Feistritzer, C. E. (2011). *Profile of teachers in the US 2011*. National Center for Education Information.

Foner, E. (2010). Twisting history in Texas. *The Nation, 290*, 4–6.

Freire, P. (1970). *Pedagogy of the oppressed*. New York: Continuum.

Freire, P. (1998). *The Paulo Freire reader*. New York: Continuum.

Freire, P., & Macedo, D. (1987). *Literacy: Reading the word and the world*. Westport, CT: Bergin & Garvey.

García, M. T., & Castro, S. (2011). *Blowout!: Sal Castro & the Chicano struggle for educational justice*. University of North Carolina Press.

Gonzales, A. (2013). *Reform without justice: The Homeland Security state and Latino migrant politics*. Oxford: Oxford University Press.

Goodwin, A. L. (2010). Curriculum as colonizer: (Asian) American education in the current context. *Teachers College Record, 112*(12), 3102–3138.

Grant, C., & Sleeter, C. (1990). *After the school bell rings (2nd ed.)*. Philadelphia, PA: Falmer.

Howard, T. (2010). *Why race and culture matter in schools: Closing the achievement gap in American Schools*. New York: Teachers College Press.

Hu-Dehart, E. (1993). The history, development, and future of Ethnic Studies. *Pi Delta Kappan, 75*(1), 50–54.

Jocson, K. M. (2008). Kuwento as multicultural pedagogy in high school Ethnic Studies. *Pedagogies: An International Journal, 3*(4), 241–253.

King, J. (1991). Dysconscious racism: Ideology, identity, and the miseducation of teachers. *Journal of Negro Education, 60*(2), 133–146.

Kucera, J., & Orfield, G. (2014). *New York State's extreme segregation: Inequality, inaction, and a damaged future*. A research report published by the UCLA Civil Rights Project.

McLaren, P. (1994). *Life in schools: An introduction to critical pedagogy and the foundations of education*. New York: Longman.

Martínez, L. (2005). Yes we can: Latino participation in unconventional politics. *Social Forces, 84*(1), 135–155.

McKinley Jr., J. C. (2010, March 12). Texas conservatives win curriculum change, *The New York Times*. Retrieved from http://www.nytimes.com/2010/03/13/education/13texas.html.

Mirra, N., & Morrell, E. (2011). Teachers as civic agents: Toward a Critical Democratic Theory of Urban Teacher Development. *Journal of Teacher Education, 62*(4), 408–420.

Morrell, E. (2004). *Becoming critical researchers: Literacy and empowerment for urban youth*. New York: Peter Lang.

Morrell, E. (2008). *Critical literacy and urban youth: Pedagogies of access, dissent, and liberation*. New York: Routledge.

Morrell, E., Dueñas, R., Garcia, V., & López, J. (2013). *Critical media pedagogy: Teaching for achievement in city schools*. New York: Teachers College Press.

Morris, A., & Braine, N. (2001). Social movements and oppositional consciousness. In J. Mansbridge & A. Morris (Eds.), *Oppositional consciousness: The subjective roots of social protest* (pp. 20–37). Chicago, IL: University of Chicago Press.

National Center for Education Statistics. (2014). Racial/ethnic enrollment in public schools (April 2014). Retrieved August 31, 2014.

National Collaborative on Diversity in the Teaching Force. (2004). *Assessment of diversity in America's teaching force: A call to action*. Washington D.C.

Ochoa, G. L. (2008). Pump up the blowouts: Reflections on the 40th anniversary of the Chicana/o school blowouts. *Rethinking Schools, 22*(4), 50–53.

Ogbar, J. O. G. (2004). *Black power: Radical politics and African American identity*. Baltimore: The John Hopkins University Press.

Okihiro, G. Y. (2011). Preface. *Journal of Asian American Studies (JAAL), 14*(2), 167–169.

Okihiro, G. Y., & Tsou, E. (2006). On social formation. *Works and Days 47/48, 24*(1, 2), 69–88.

Omi, M., & Winant, H. (1994). *Racial formation in the United States: From 1960s to 1990s*. New York: Routledge.

Philip, T. (2011). An "ideology in pieces" approach to studying change in teachers' sensemaking about race, racism, and racial justice. *Cognition and instruction, 29*(3), 297–329.

de los Ríos, C. V. (2013). A curriculum of the borderlands: High school Chicana/o-Latina/o studies as sitios y lengua. *The Urban Review, 45*(1), 58–73.

de los Ríos, C. V., & Ochoa, G. L. (2012). The people united, shall never be divided: Reflections on collaboration, community, and change. *Journal of Latinos and Education, 11*(4), 271–279.

Rodríguez, R. C. (2012). Tucson's maiz-based curriculum: MAS-TUSD profundo. *Nakum Journal, (2)*1, 72–98.

Rojas, F. (2007). *From Black power to Black studies: How a radical social movement became an academic discipline.* Baltimore, MD: John Hopkins University Press.

Rogers, J., Morrell, E., & Enyedy, N. (2007). Contexts for becoming critical researchers: Designing for identities and creating new learning opportunities. *American Behavioral Scientist, 51*(3), 419–443.

Romero, A., Arce, S., & Cammarota, J. (2009). A Barrio pedagogy: Identity, intellectualism, activism, and academic achievement through the evolution of critically compassionate intellectualism. *Race Ethnicity and Education, 12*(2), 217–233.

Rumberger, R. (2011). *Dropping out: Why students drop out of high school and what can be done about it.* Cambridge: Harvard University Press.

Shapiro, H. S., & Purpel, D. E. (Eds.). (1993). *Critical school issues in American education.* New York, NY: Longman.

Sleeter, C. E. (2002). State curriculum standards and the shaping of student consciousness. *Social Justice, 29*(4), 8–25.

Sleeter, C. E. (2011). *The academic and social value of Ethnic Studies: A research review.* Washington D. C: National Education Association.

Tintiangco-Cubales, A., Kohli, R., Sacramento, J., Henning, Agarwal-Rangnath, R., & Sleeter, C. (2014). Toward an Ethnic Studies pedagogy: Implications for K-12 schools from the research. *The Urban Review.*

Tyack, D. B. (1974). *The one best system.* Cambridge, MA: Harvard University Press.

Umemoto, K. (1989). "On strike!" San Francisco State College Strike, 1968–1969: The role of Asian American students. *Amerasia Journal, 15*(1), 3–41.

Urrieta, L. (2009). *Working from within: Chicana and Chicano activist educators in whitestream schools.* Tucson: University of Arizona Press.

US Department of Education. (2010). *The blueprint for educational reform.* Washington DC: Department of Education.

Vasquéz Heilig, J., Brown, K., & Brown, A. (2012). The Illusion of Inclusion: A Critical Race Theory Textual Analysis of Race and Standards. *Harvard Educational Review, 82*(3), 403–424.

Wells, A. S. (2014). *Seeing past the "colorblind" myth of education policy: Addressing racial and ethnic inequality and supporting culturally diverse schools.* Boulder, CO: National Education Policy Center.

Woodson, C. G. (1990/1933). The Mis-education of the Negro. Trenton, NJ: Africa World Press.

Yosso, T. J. (2005). Whose culture has capital? A critical race theory discussion of community cultural wealth. *Race Ethnicity and Education, 8*(1), 69–91.

Zepeda-Millán, C., & Wallace, S. (2013). Racialization in times of contention: How social movements influence Latino racial identity. *Politics, Groups, and Identities, 1*(4), 510–527.

Zepeda-Millán, C. (2014). Weapons of the (Not So) Weak: Immigrant mass mobilization in the US South. *Critical Sociology, 40*(5), 1–19.

Incoherent Demands: Outcomes-Focused, Race to the Top-Aligned Policies and Their Impact on Urban Teaching and Learning

Jill C. Pierce

From Inputs to Outcomes

Education reforms in recent decades have increasingly focused on student and teacher outcomes. These reforms mark a movement away from earlier federal policies that concentrated on inputs: on students' equitable access to educational resources, on compensatory programs, and on social welfare supports (Darling-Hammond, 2010). Educational policies in the Race to the Top (RttT) funding era emphasize teachers' performances and students' test scores (US Department of Education (DOE), 2009) and thus locate themselves ideologically far from the *Brown vs. Board of Education* decision and the early iterations of Title I legislation. While high expectations for outcomes are not inherently misguided, the No Child Left Behind (NCLB) era that began in 2002 demonstrated that an exclusive focus on test scores subjects urban[1] schools to extreme pressure and degrades the quality of education offered to low-income students of color (Berliner, 2007; Kim & Sunderman, 2005; Nichols & Berliner, 2007). To gain insight into whether the outcomes demanded of teachers and students were similarly reductive in the first years of RttT-aligned policies, I interviewed urban, New York City (NYC) teachers about how new and longstanding

---

[1]In this chapter, I sometimes refer to low-income students of color as an urban population, and also refer to their teachers as urban educators, following the logic of Noguera (2003). I discuss decisions and policies concerning students of color (the *Brown* decisions and resultant desegregation policies) and low-income students (Title I legislation), and although these groups of students overlap significantly, they are undeniably distinct (Rothstein, 2013). My use of the term "urban" as a shorthand obscures some of these differences.

J.C. Pierce (✉)
New York University, Metro Center, 726 Broadway, New York, NY 10003, USA
e-mail: jcp451@nyu.edu

© Springer International Publishing Switzerland 2016
P.A. Noguera et al. (eds.), *Race, Equity, and Education*,
DOI 10.1007/978-3-319-23772-5_10

policies impacted their planning and instruction in 2013 and 2014. I wanted to understand how teachers of low-income students of color reacted to and navigated a complex mix of reforms from city, state, and federal levels. I found that urban teachers described tensions among several types of policies—tensions they often framed as threatening the quality of teaching and learning in their classrooms.

Input-Focused Education Reforms

The *Brown vs. Board of Education* decision (1954) signified an acknowledgement that unequal access to resources constrained the educational opportunities of students of color. *Brown* and *Brown II* focused on equality of resources, and the Title I legislation of 1965 embraced a similar emphasis by providing funding to target inequities facing low-income students. There was an acknowledgement that external constraints functioned as more than just "excuses" in the educational lives of urban children (see Meier, 2002; Rothstein, 2013), particularly during President Johnson's War on Poverty. Legislation in this period reflected "a strong concern about social welfare" (Jennings, 2001, p. 5), and educational policies enhanced services not only for low-income students of color but also for bilingual students and students with disabilities (Jennings, 2001; Rebell & Wolff, 2008). Beginning in the late 1960s, black students saw test-score gains that correlated with the enactment of desegregation policies and the initiation of Title I and other anti-poverty programs (Grissmer & Flanagan, 1999; Orfield & DeBray, 1999). The benefits associated with these policies, moreover, were not limited to increases in test scores but extended to other areas of academic and social progress (Rothstein, 2013; Wells & Crain, 1994, 1997; see Ayscue & Orfield, this volume). The gains seen by black students in particular indicate that

> there may have been a major change in the quality of blacks' school experience beginning in the late 1960s. This change in school experiences could reflect social and legal changes aimed at equalizing educational opportunity, additional educational resources that were especially helpful for black students, and the implementation of civil rights legislation creating new job opportunities for academically successful blacks (Grissmer & Flanagan, 1999, p. 48).

As might have been expected, addressing opportunity gaps beyond the classroom correlated with an increased likelihood that low-income students of color would experience academic gains (see Noguera, 2003).

To be clear, the mandates of *Brown* and *Brown II* were unevenly enforced and Title I funds unevenly distributed. Desegregation efforts typically met with great opposition, Title I funding was frequently misappropriated, and the compensatory program itself "posed no threat to segregated institutions" (Kantor & Lowe, 2013, p. 30). Thus low-income students of color experienced limited and inconsistent benefits from an era of imperfect commitment to civil rights, income equality, and meaningful educational opportunities (Rebell & Wolff, 2008). However, gains were made, and policymakers could have examined problems with implementation and committed to increased support for desegregation and compensatory funding programs (Orfield, 1999).

Outcomes-Focused Accountability Measures

Instead, rather than double down on dismantling segregation and increasing resources to address opportunity gaps for low-income students, educational and social policies and legal decisions in the mid-to-late 1970s and 1980s turned in other directions. Courts moved away from enforcing desegregation, and President Reagan reduced Title I expenditures and other anti-poverty spending (Jennings, 2001; Kantor & Lowe, 2013; Orfield & Eaton, 1996). The 1983 A Nation at Risk report (National Commission on Excellence in Education, 1983) placed responsibility for academic underachievement on the shoulders of ill-prepared teachers, blaming them

> for a myriad of societal ills: the erosion of U.S. economic competitiveness and productivity, the decline in student academic achievement, teenage pregnancy, juvenile delinquency and crime, the coarsening of our everyday discourse and culture, a decline in morals, gender and racial discrimination, and so on (Ingersoll, 2007, pp. 20–21).

A Nation at Risk facilitated a nationwide emphasis on educational outcomes and accountability for students, teachers, and schools perceived to be failing in their roles (Ravitch, 2013). As Mehta says,

> the paradigm established by A Nation at Risk defined the terms of the debate: schooling is critical for economic development; schools overall are underperforming and require across-the-board solutions; failures of student performance lie with schools and not broader social factors; and the success of solutions will be measured by test scores…The idea of standards and accountability was appealing because it was consistent with the definition of the problem—it promised across-the-board improvement, it focused on outputs over inputs, it focused on schools, and it could be measured by test scores (Mehta, 2013, p. 157).

Emphasizing accountability rather than educational inputs, decades of policymakers have downplayed and dismissed the social contexts of schooling and the detrimental effects of poverty and racial isolation, as well as the institutional factors within schools that complicate teachers' ability to raise all students' achievement (Carter & Welner, 2013; Darling-Hammond, 2010; Lipman, 1998, 2004; Noguera, 2003; Payne, 2008; Rebell & Wolff, 2008).

A Nation at Risk laid the groundwork for the accountability measures emphasized in the NCLB Act (a reauthorization of the Elementary and Secondary Education Act—of which Title I is a part—signed in 2001). NCLB mandated disaggregation of test scores by racial and other subgroups, and in many ways it represented a welcome focus on the disproportionately low academic performance of students of color (Carter & Welner, 2013; Fruchter, 2007; Noguera & Wing, 2006; Rebell & Wolff, 2008). In fact, Kantor and Lowe argue that some black and Latino organizations "believed that accountability offered a more robust sense of opportunity than Title I, which had been framed in a language of cultural deprivation that blamed poor children for their own educational failures" (2013, p. 37). For many, NCLB's discursive focus on high expectations was promising.

Yet "high expectations become a punitive false promise if combined with low resources, low opportunities, and low supports" (Carter & Welner, 2013, p. 10), and in reality, NCLB perpetuated rather than resolved disparities (Carter & Welner, 2013;

Fruchter, 2007; Kantor & Lowe, 2013; Noguera, 2008). The act "wound up reinforcing class- and race-based differences in access to educational resources rather than
increasing the resources available to those who lacked them" (Kantor & Lowe, 2013,
p. 37). NCLB discounted questions of school, teacher, and student capacity, failed
to hold policymakers accountable for providing educational inputs, and enacted the
most punitive measures on the most struggling schools (Carter & Welner, 2013;
Fruchter, 2007; Kantor & Lowe, 2013; Noguera, 2008; Rebell & Wolff, 2008). The
act left many urban students

> caught in a downward cycle, facing poverty-related obstacles outside school as well as a
> system that generates a constant churning of teachers, principals, and schools. Even if it
> is called 'accountability,' this turmoil should not be mistaken for progress; in fact, it often
> results in just the opposite (Carter & Welner, 2013, p. 4).

When accountability measures subject schools to high-stakes testing and sanctions, one counterproductive result is an exodus of highly qualified teachers
from struggling schools (Lipman, 2004). Another is a narrowing of curricula to
tested subjects (frequently English and math), to the exclusion of subjects such
as art and music (Berliner, 2007; Meier, 2002; Tienken & Zhao, 2013). Within
tested subjects, moreover, teachers often resort to rote, skill-and-drill methods,
teaching to tests and denying enriching pedagogy to the students most in need
of high-quality educational experiences (Berliner, 2007; Darder & Torres, 2004;
Darling-Hammond, 2010; Lipman, 2004; Meier, 2002; Payne, 2008; Tienken &
Zhao, 2013; see Lipsky, 2010).

NCLB set requirements for proficiency levels that were never realistic in the
absence of increased capacity (Fruchter, 2007; Ryan, 2004), and most states
received waivers from these requirements ahead of their 2014 deadlines (Wong &
Reilly, 2014). Yet reforms since NCLB have not necessarily capitalized on the lessons learned from earlier high-stakes accountability systems. With a host of new
reforms aligned to the RttT funding program in schools, it is a propitious time to
ask how new and longstanding policies are interacting to play out in urban contexts, how they are impacting teaching and learning, and whether they are subject-
ing teachers and students to educational threats similar to those experienced in the
first decade of NCLB.

Reform Coherence and RttT-Aligned Policies

It is also a key time to examine the coherence of RttT-aligned reforms, which constitute a complex mix of policies (several of which I describe below). RttT offered
states a total of 4.35 billion dollars, and to secure their eligibility for funding,
many states adopted new standards, assessments, and teacher evaluation systems
(see US DOE, 2009). In New York State, which received RttT funding, these new
reforms intersected with pre-existing policies such as state tests: it often happens
in educational reform that policies

accumulate one on top of another, adding to rather than simply replacing what went before…Practitioners have faced a surge of new laws, regulations, and reform ideas coming on top of a system of curriculum and instruction that was already many layers deep in partially assimilated innovations. Often the messages sent by policy elites in any one year's laws or regulations have conflicted with what went before or came after, creating inconsistency and confusion (Tyack & Cuban, 1995, pp. 63–64).

Policy coherence is fundamental to student and teacher success, particularly in struggling schools (Payne, 2008). Streamlined policies "can result in more consistent (and thus stronger) signals to both teachers and students about what is important for teachers to teach and for students to learn" and can "allow for more focused and more efficient instruction" (Goertz, Floden, & O'Day, 1996, p. 2). Yet reforms in recent decades have frequently proved incoherent, particularly when high-stakes tests have coexisted alongside distinct approaches to assessing student learning (Berliner, 2007). Darling-Hammond observed that even before NCLB, teachers' instructional impact was "undermined by curriculum guides, teacher evaluation systems, and testing programs reflecting contradictory images and standards for teaching" (2001, p. 219; see also Cohen, 1995; Datnow, 2005; Fuhrman, 1993; Newmann, Smith, Allensworth, & Bryk, 2001; Payne, 2008). In the era of RttT and beyond, we should be assured that schools are guided by a set of compatible policies that offer a coherent vision of teaching and learning. Absent a much-needed focus on inputs for urban students (Fruchter, 2007), teachers should at least feel that new and longstanding educational reforms cohere sensibly to help them facilitate high-quality learning experiences for their students.

The mix of new and longstanding policies governing high school teachers' work in 2013 and 2014 was complex, and I focus on the impact of a handful of policies in this study.[2] New York State responded to the receipt of RttT funding by adopting a standards framework called the Common Core Learning Standards (hereafter, Common Core) (NY State Education Department (SED), 2014a). Students' scores on Common Core-aligned local assessments factored into many teachers' evaluation scores, which also included student data from existing assessments such as the New York State Regents exams (longstanding determinants of high school students' eligibility for graduation) (NYC DOE, 2014c). During this study, forty percent of New York City teachers' evaluation scores were based on students' performance on these state and local assessments, and the remaining sixty percent derived from measures including administrators' observations of classroom instruction. Observations were structured around New York's version of Charlotte Danielson's Framework for Teaching (NYC DOE, 2013c, 2014b). This complex mix of teacher evaluation criteria and student standards and assessments was accompanied by citywide instructional expectations, new requirements for teacher tenure, and other new and longstanding policies (NYC DOE, 2013a, 2015).

---

[2]I focus on policies that teachers discussed most frequently with me in interviews about their planning and instruction.

In this study I aimed to find out how urban teachers reacted to many of the reforms at play in their schools in 2013 and 2014. I asked high school teachers working with low-income students of color in New York City how teaching and learning in their classrooms were impacted by new and longstanding educational policies. Below, I briefly describe the methods I used to carry out this inquiry.

Interviewing Teachers

In interviews with teachers, I concentrated on teachers' planning and instruction: how and why did teachers privilege particular activities, skills, units, and practices over others? How did new and longstanding policies influence their curricular and instructional choices? How were teachers navigating multiple exigencies, and did those exigencies seem sensible to them?

I spoke with six high school teachers[3] about their curriculum planning processes, their instruction, and their understanding of the policies they faced beginning with the onset of the 2013–2014 school year. The teachers I interviewed worked at public, NYC high schools that predominantly served low-income Black and Latino students. I conducted two rounds of semi-structured interviews with each teacher (one English, one art, one math, one science, and two social studies teachers), for a total of more than an hour of conversation with each interviewee.[4] Each teacher had somewhere between 2 and 15 years of experience, and all but one had taught for more than 3 years: I sought out interview subjects with multiple years of experience who had planned and taught under a different (ostensibly looser) set of instructional demands citywide. I included in my sample four teachers who taught courses culminating in Regents exams, in order to consider the exigencies that state testing places on teachers. I coded the data both topically and thematically (Reissman, 2008; Rubin & Rubin, 2012; Saldaña, 2013), first by hand and then using ATLAS.ti, a qualitative data analysis program. As I coded and analyzed the interview data, I looked for patterns that emerged in how teachers discussed their planning and instruction and the mix of policies they faced.

Local Assessments: "Trying to Bridge the Gap"

In 2013, many high school teachers faced the dilemma of preparing students for both new (local) and longstanding (state) assessments. The skills prioritized on each form of exam struck teachers as distinct. As they struggled to design

---

[3]I have changed the names and identifying details of each interviewee.

[4]Many interviewees also gave me copies of curricular artifacts including year-long planning calendars, lesson plans, daily assignments, and in-class tests.

streamlined, coherent curricula, teachers felt pulled in multiple instructional directions at once—an overarching challenge they faced in the initial years of RttT-aligned reforms.

Students' scores on the new local assessments began to factor into teachers' evaluation scores in the fall of 2013 (NYC DOE, 2013b). These local assessments were not administered in every subject area, and some teachers' evaluation scores were tied only to state assessments. Yet several of the teachers I interviewed worked with local assessments as well as Regents exams. In 2013 and 2014, Regents exams did not reflect many of the skills demanded by the Common Core, whereas local assessments were Common Core-aligned.

Local social studies assessments tested students' ability to write using both claims and counterclaims, a skill emphasized in the Common Core Writing Standards for Literacy in Social Studies and Science (NY SED, 2014a) but not in social studies Regents exams. Social studies teacher Ms. Langdon lamented, "Now I have to teach point and counterpoint, and I know that they do it in English, but for social studies it's a little different. So now it's just more stuff that we have to fit in, and it kills a lot more time, which we don't have." Teachers of Regents-based courses spoke frequently of the limited time they had to prepare students for success on high-stakes assessments. Getting students acclimated to new rounds of local testing cut into that time significantly. Mr. Rayne (social studies) echoed Ms. Langdon's frustration when describing his first year of exposure to local assessments:

> I know for my class, I'm going to have to teach them one thing for the local assessments that will come in April and then I'm going to have to teach them a completely different thing on the Regents, and it confuses the kids. They walk into the Regents and they're going, "Do I need counterclaim, or not need counterclaim? I don't remember."

Preparing students to master a discrete skill on one test when they would not need it on the following (state) exams struck teachers as time-consuming and confusing—a conflict reminiscent of the contradictory messages that Darling-Hammond argues can complicate teachers' jobs and undermine effective, streamlined instruction (2001; see also Ball, Maguire, & Braun, 2012). New York City demands "coherent" curricula from its teachers (NYC DOE, 2014a; see also NYC DOE, 2013a), yet those who faced pressure to help students pass existing, non-Common Core-aligned state assessments identified incoherence in the need to simultaneously guide students to success on distinct local assessments. Goertz, Floden, and O'Day (1996) argue that "if curricular goals and assessments are aligned, teachers do not have to divide their time between teaching a curriculum that stresses certain knowledge and skills on the one hand and preparing students for standardized tests which assess different skills and knowledge on the other" (p. 2). In the case of the teachers I interviewed, mismatched assessments pulled teaching and learning in multiple, seemingly contradictory directions throughout the year.

Some teachers felt enough frustration with the incompatibility they saw among assessments that they opted out of the "locals" process in their second year of evaluations that incorporated Measures of Student Learning (MOSL) (NYC DOE, 2014c).[5] Mr. Rayne considered himself lucky to have served on his school's MOSL committee and to have been able to recommend that in 2014–2015, his evaluations be tied only to students' Regents scores. Describing his year with local assessments, he explained, "it was just an added stress for the kids. To put them through something they're not going to be tested on [on the Regents]."[6] Teachers including Mr. Rayne refrained from framing their critiques of the new local assessments as an objection to the Common Core's foci (which I discuss below). In fact, many teachers I interviewed expressed impatience for a time when state assessments would be aligned to the new standards—a time when teachers might be able to stop emphasizing more skills than they had time to teach. To English and math teachers, the timeline for when Regents exams would be Common Core-aligned seemed mostly clear (see NY SED, 2014b). Science and social studies teachers, however, expressed confusion across interviews about the impact the Common Core would have on their state assessments. "It would be nice to see now what a prospective Regents test would look like in terms of the expectations," sighed Mr. Lambert (science). Mr. Rayne expressed that teachers in his department hoped for this to happen "eventually" but were unclear about the timeline and specifics of the eventual change: "I'm hoping, I'm hoping…that they're going to move the Regents to be more like the local. Eventually. So then it will be the same. But for right now we're trying to bridge the gap between the two."

"Bridging the gap" between Regents and more recent, RttT-aligned reforms proved difficult for many teachers. The state exams represented thick layers of exigencies, and local assessments and instructional and observational guidelines often rested uncomfortably alongside these high-stakes exams. So frequently did I hear teachers reference demands associated with the Regents exams during interviews—interviews that I expected would revolve more centrally around new standards, assessments, and evaluations—that I devote the next section to teachers' discussions of these exams.

---

[5]A number of changes were made to the teacher evaluation process between the first and second years of implementation (see NYC DOE, 2014c).

[6]Teachers identified a number of other problems with local assessments: art teacher Ms. Nelson noted that because there were no local assessments in her subject area, her MOSL scores were tied to students' performance on local English assessments, and thus not to results of her own teaching. Students often questioned the purpose of the local assessments, and when students failed to "take them seriously" during the fall round of administration, teachers sometimes did not object. Tasked with demonstrating student growth between the fall and spring assessments, many teachers viewed the growth as a kind of performance they could elicit simply by introducing and incorporating the exam in their classes differently in the spring than they had done in the fall. Thus teachers positioned student growth on local assessments as a contrived performance—a kind of game to be played (Ball, 2000; see also Anderson, 2009).

The Regents: Testing "How Well Kids Take Tests"

Regents exams determined teachers' curricular choices, impacted how they structured student learning, and, for the first time in 2013, factored into teacher evaluation criteria in NYC. These assessments exerted extreme pressure on urban high school teachers and students alike, and many teachers felt that Regents exams fundamentally diluted the quality of education they could offer their students.

In order to graduate from high school, general education students in New York State must pass five Regents exams: two in social studies and one each in English, science, and math (NY SED, 2010). Given their high-stakes nature, these exams are often the most powerful driver of high school curricula. Mr. Carter (English) told me that at his school, "we did a self-evaluation and saw that we are having a lot of students who are accumulating credits, passing classes, but not passing Regents. So we realized that we need to have a stronger focus on high-stakes assessments to prepare them for those tests." At Mr. Carter's school, this focus included adding new weeks of testing in the form of midterms and finals: four weeks in all. These testing periods were in addition to time newly devoted to preparing students for the local assessments and administering those tests. In many classrooms, teacher-designed midterms and finals heavily prioritized the skills tested on Regents exams, which seemed to reign supreme in driving instruction.

Mr. Rayne explained that in structuring each week of social studies instruction, he designed his classes around the Regents exam format of document-based questions (DBQs), thematic essays, and multiple-choice questions. Students' past performance on each of these question formats fundamentally shaped his curriculum:

> The biggest thing is we want to focus on thematic essays and the DBQ writing…So when I planned every unit, I put in three to four class days of writing. So every unit ends with some type of essay, whether it's thematic or DBQ. And then I plan everything around that. So, as far as objectives go, I only use past Regents questions, I don't make up any questions on my own. So the kids are used to them.

I frequently heard that teachers and their administrators were focusing attention on getting students "used to" testing—helping students' minds and bodies accommodate to the format of test questions and the task of sitting for hours-long assessments (see Ball et al., 2012). After a year of amplified testing at Mr. Rayne's school, he found that his students indeed "knew what to expect…it's not nearly as hard to get them to sit as it was last year." I had the sense that for many teachers, the culture of schooling was becoming "increasingly saturated with practices, language, and values shaped by increasing performance on standardized tests" (Lipman, 2004, p. 77), and that many teachers were embracing the need for additional rounds of testing as common sense. (In part, this may have been because for the first time in 2013, students' Regents scores factored into teachers' evaluation scores.)

Yet the very teachers who spoke of students accommodating to testing often offered strong critiques of the skills emphasized on Regents exams. They felt that the assessments prized the "regurgitation of facts," "rote memorization," and other low-level skills. When I asked how he felt about being in what he identified as a test-focused teaching environment, Mr. Ulmer asked:

> Do I really think that the Regents exam is telling anybody how much my kids know? No, I don't think that at all. I think that they test how well kids take tests… how well kids can do simple calculations. Is that important for life? Not really. Math is—you know, people always say math is so connected to real life, and I believe that. And if you can do simple calculations, that's great. Are you ever going to need to do that in the supermarket? No, you have a calculator to do that. There's just no usefulness in only knowing calculations and skills.

Mr. Ulmer concluded that we now have an education system in which students are over-tested with exams that fail to provide teachers with useful knowledge (see Darder & Torres, 2004)—a sentiment echoed by the other teachers of Regents-based classes. Although they cast Regents exams as unhelpful, teachers in 2013 and 2014 were more beholden than ever to these assessments, which now impacted their own evaluations in addition to students' possibilities of graduating.

Regents exams forcefully shaped teachers' time and design of curricular materials. They also strongly influenced how teachers facilitated student learning in their classrooms. Given Regents exams' focus on "fact recall" (Mr. Rayne and Mr. Lambert), teachers felt pressure to cover a great deal of material in a short amount of time. Many of them voiced the impression that the best way to do this was to concentrate on teacher-directed dictation and individual student work (see Berliner, 2007). The exigencies of high-stakes testing led them to believe that they had limited time to facilitate other forms of instruction. However, adding to teachers' sense of facing incoherent demands was their understanding that they needed to consistently display to administrators a commitment to student-to-student discussions and small-group work.

Student-to-Student Discussions: "Having Students Really Teach Each Other"

"Student-to-student discussion" and "collaborative learning" were key components emphasized in the Citywide Instructional Expectations of 2013-2014 (NYC DOE, 2013a). Teachers felt that during observations, administrators were frequently looking for students to be engaged in collaborative work. Danielson's Framework for Teaching, which guides observations, refers to small-group work in several of its eight components used for evaluative purposes in New York (NYC DOE, 2013c, 2014b). Collaboration is also a skill emphasized throughout the Common Core (NY SED, 2014a).

Each teacher I interviewed mentioned the necessity of demonstrating that his or her classes consistently incorporated "peer-to-peer interaction," "group work," or "student-to-student discussion." Mr. Carter said that in his English class, he tried to focus on having students really teach each other. Student interaction is one of the areas that our school's lacking in...according to our observation, our first round of observations. That was the area that we scored the lowest on as a staff. So we're focusing on student-to-student interaction.

Art teacher Ms. Nelson said that "group work is something [administrators] want to see," and she noted that in her discipline students naturally understood that their peers' aesthetic judgments and reflections were just as valuable as her own. Many teachers seemed to have an understanding of "good teaching" as involving collaborative student work. Although Mr. Rayne disliked group work as demanded at his school (in formulaic ways, as he described it), his ideal instructional design would involve a significant number of group-based activities. He considered his student teaching situation to have been just such an ideal:

What we did a lot of that I absolutely loved was simulations and acting out plays... it was great....That's definitely something I loved to do—we did Galileo's trial, we did Columbus' trial, we acted out the Crusades, where different groups were different religious groups, and we did the war and kids came up with a war plan...If there was no Regents at the end, I would definitely be doing more of those types of things. Because I think the kids get more out of that, personally.

Mr. Ulmer agreed that students "got more out of" collaborative activities, as opposed to individual work. Yet he and the other teachers of Regents-based courses (Mr. Carter, Ms. Langdon, and Mr. Lambert) submitted that group work was often too time-consuming in the face of students' impending exams.

Teachers also expressed fundamental misgivings about collaboration as an appropriate instructional method through which to prepare students for success on high-stakes assessments. Both Mr. Carter and Mr. Rayne mentioned that when it comes time for students to sit and take tests, they must do so individually. "Real-life, real-time testing means sitting on your own and silently working with material," explained Mr. Carter. In Mr. Rayne's view,

on tests, they work on their own, so they need the skill by themselves...[They] can't write a paragraph together. They have to do it themselves. At some point, you're going to have to sit there and write an essay by yourself.

Several teachers expressed the belief that individual work was best suited to prepare students for fact recall and essay writing on exams. Yet, as Ms. Langdon said, "if I did that in an observation? Forget it. You know, no peer-to-peer [interaction]." Teachers thus felt tension between what observations required of them and what they felt preparation for high-stakes tests demanded of students.

Scholars argue that collaboration is vital to twenty-first century education: to preparing students for success in a diverse, global workforce (Berliner, 2007; Darling-Hammond, 2010). Newmann, Marks, and Gamoran (1995) urge that when students engage in "substantive conversation" with those around them, they build "an improved and shared understanding of ideas or topics" (p. 2). Collaboratively-built understanding (see also Slavin, 1983), combined with other practices that Newmann et al. identify as central to "authentic pedagogy," has been associated with increased achievement for individual students on standardized tests (1995).

Yet while teachers at progressive schools serving affluent students may accept this premise (Lipman, 2004; see Ravitch, 2013), most teachers I interviewed could imagine no such link. They appeared to draw an impenetrable mental line between test preparation and group work for reasons related to time and to the forms of practice (skill and drill; solitary essay writing) associated with preparing students for individual success on tests. This was true even among teachers who believed that in ideal (non-test-based) scenarios, collaboration led to greater student learning.

In her observation of one Chicago school, Lipman (2004) noted that third grade teacher Ms. Washington abandoned cooperative work for one-third of the school year to prepare for high stakes assessments: "During that time, the students put away their novels, basal readers, and math manipulatives, and [Ms. Washington] rearranged clusters of desks in rows and forbade students to work together because that would be cheating on the ITBS and ISAT [exams]" (pp. 78–79). Many teachers I interviewed indicated a similar impulse to abandon collaborative work in the face of high-stakes assessments. Yet while they experienced pressure to raise students' test scores, they faced a simultaneous demand to display (to administrators during observations) that their lessons involved student-to-student interaction and discussion. While these exigencies may not be inherently contradictory, to many teachers they felt incoherent and difficult to navigate.

Moving Away from Inquiry: "Losing the Good Parts of Teaching"

Many teachers spoke to me about other tensions they experienced between what they thought to be "good teaching" and the pedagogical practices they thought tests necessitated. A central tension revolved around the use of inquiry in the classroom. As defined by Harvey and Daniels (2009), inquiry involves students' creation of questions about a topic and their subsequent search for patterns that provide insight into the topic. The language of inquiry can be seen in Danielson's Framework (NYC DOE, 2013c) and its emphasis on ensuring that students are taking an active rather than passive role in learning, are working to "initiate higher-order questions" (p. 33), and are "discovering patterns" (p. 34). The framework guides administrators to search for "evidence of some student initiation of inquiry and student contributions to the exploration of important content" (p. 36). Many teachers I interviewed also worked for schools currently or formerly funded by a support network that emphasized inquiry as a vital instructional strategy.

Teachers saw a tension between inquiry (what they sometimes called "exploration" or "discovery" learning) and direct instruction, which they felt was demanded by test preparation. Mr. Ulmer mentioned this tension to me several times. Before 2013, he engaged in math workshops, summer institutes, coaching sessions, and collaborative scoring meetings in which he came to see inquiry as the "right" way to teach. In describing his first year as a teacher, he said:

> All this stuff that the [school's support network] was teaching me—all the inquiry stuff, I was so excited about that. I was perfecting that, the kids really were able to write what they were thinking and were sharing things with each other. Really good, really good engagement in the class usually, and I felt like they were really learning.

Mr. Ulmer continued by noting that recently he felt he was "losing the good parts of teaching. I'm losing that investigation thing...I'm going with what I need to do rather than what I think is right or what I want to do." What he "needed" to do was lead his students to achieve a certain percent passing rate on a particularly difficult Regents exam in order to be considered eligible for tenure (this was the goal his administrators expressed to him). As I found in speaking with other untenured teachers, Mr. Ulmer expressed less concern with his own job security and new tenure requirements than with the idea that students would not learn authentically if his sole focus was raising scores on a high-stakes assessment.

Wrestling with his beliefs in the face of this assessment caused Mr. Ulmer to have a difficult school year beginning in 2013, and to doubt his own understandings about pedagogy:

> I struggled a lot, just because of this Regents thing. At the end, [my instruction] looked a lot different. Because even though I still tried to incorporate investigation—still tried to get interesting things in there—it was mainly focused on: "Can you complete this worksheet? Because these are the questions you're going to see on the test." And it wasn't good for me, it drained me a little bit. I wasn't feeling...I was really having a hard time last year.

Mr. Ulmer expressed hope that it might be possible to engage in inquiry and simultaneously prepare students for the Regents exam. Yet elsewhere he framed these goals as incompatible, citing the fact that there was simply too much content to cover before the test to devote time to exploratory learning. Mr. Rayne agreed: "I can't do the discovery lesson where they discover the material every day because I have so much material. I think sometimes you just have to give it to them. And say, kids, you have to remember this, and unfortunately that's the way it is." He expressed the belief, as did Mr. Ulmer, that such an approach "is not the most ideal way to teach." Yet Mr. Rayne and Mr. Ulmer indicated that logistically, a "coverage"-oriented method of instruction (Harvey & Daniels, 2009; Lipman, 2004) is necessitated by high-stakes tests.

Newmann, King, and Carmichael (2007) write that

> according to conventional wisdom, basic skills and key information in subject areas are best taught through traditional drill and practice, and if not explicitly taught and memorized, students, especially those from disadvantaged backgrounds, are unlikely to succeed on tests of basic skills, or on standardized tests of subject matter content. These assumptions make teachers reluctant to demand construction of knowledge and in-depth understanding through elaborated communication, because it takes time away from explicitly covering all the material that might be required on a test (p. 26).

Newmann et al. found these assumptions untrue: students challenged to engage in higher-order thinking and knowledge construction actually performed better on tests than students facing lesser demands from teachers. Yet in my study, I found that teachers often echoed—though not without ambivalence—the conventional wisdom described by these authors: that urban students could not succeed on tests without direct, drill-based instruction. As Mr. Carter said, "I felt like the initial focus was on inquiry-based learning and group work, and we need to still incorporate that. But we need to support individual success on tests. On high-stakes tests." It appeared that shifting instructional priorities for teachers and an increased focus on test preparation left teachers in tension about the kind of instruction they should prioritize for students. Teachers' confusion reminded me of Ball's questions about teaching in an era of performativity, when teachers must demonstrate their calculable worth through scores and figures:

> Within all this…purposes are made contradictory, motivations become blurred and self worth is uncertain. We are unsure of what aspects of work are valued and how to prioritize efforts. We become uncertain about the reasons for actions. Are we doing this because it is important, because we believe in it, because it is worthwhile? Or is it being done ultimately because it will be measured or compared? (Ball, 2003, p. 220).

The measurements teachers faced in 2013 and 2014 were more exigent than ever due to evaluations they faced, and teachers responded to increased test pressures by questioning their priorities in the classroom. How were teachers supposed to satisfy the demands of both "fact-recall"-oriented tests and observations? During observations, students needed to demonstrate that they were actively constructing knowledge and teachers needed to facilitate "higher-order thinking" and rigorous instruction (NYC DOE, 2013c, 2014a). Both test and observation outcomes determined teachers' evaluation scores, and the seemingly different visions of teaching and learning prioritized in each left teachers to navigate what they often felt were irreconcilable contradictions.

Shared Definitions: "What Really Is *Rigorous*?"

While RttT-aligned reforms such as observational guidelines aimed to cultivate "a common language and vision of instructional effectiveness that teachers and evaluators can share" (NYC DOE, 2013b, p. 8), gaps in understanding clearly persisted in the first years of these reforms. These gaps subjected teachers to a further sense of incoherence as they struggled with definitions of rigor and of other terms used in evaluation-related documents.

Ms. Langdon noted a lack of clarity about terms that arose during her administrators' visits—an issue she tied to the Citywide Instructional Expectations of 2013-204 (NYC DOE, 2013a). This document emphasizes that students should experience "rigorous instruction," and references to rigor also appeared in Danielson's *Framework*, New York City's School Quality Review Rubric, and the Common Core (NYC DOE, 2013c, 2014a; NY SED, 2014a). After a round of informal observations in which her principal brought network representatives to several classrooms, Ms. Langdon received feedback about a lack of rigor in her own class. Yet she noted that she and her administration did not have a shared understanding of that term. "Where do you find that definition of what really is *rigorous*?" she wondered:

> Because if [the students] can't do it, you can't tell me it's not rigorous enough. I think this is rigorous enough that they struggle with it and don't finish. But then someone comes in and looks at it and says this isn't rigorous.

This question of what constitutes rigor is vital in the context of teaching low-income students of color. Many urban students enter high school unaccustomed to "demanding" curricula, having confronted low educational expectations in their prior schooling (Payne, 1984, pp. 111–115). Differences in opinion about rigor could lead to productive discussions about how to provide students with needed supports to engage in challenging academic work. However, to date, it did not sound as though Ms. Langdon and her colleagues were developing shared under-standings of appropriately rigorous work for their students.

New York provides a number of resources that showcase exemplars of stu-dent work, curriculum, and instruction (Engage NY, 2014). Yet many teachers expressed the sense that these materials assume too high a level of student prepa-ration. Teachers also noted that videos demonstrating highly effective teaching in particular components of Danielson's Framework failed to paint a holistic portrait of masterful instruction. While teachers agreed that the framework described much of what they understood to comprise good teaching, some gaps in understanding persisted. Mr. Lambert, who had been teaching for more than a decade, joked that "you can hover over 'Highly Effective' territory forever, but you will never land." He credited this disconnect to administration-led meetings about Danielson's Framework that took place in professional development sessions, where he said model practice was never demonstrated:

> I definitely can appreciate the fact that it's difficult to have "Highly Effective" in every single category, but the fact that they have not been able to demonstrate it? How do you have this category that nobody meets?…We kept seeing what's ineffective, what's ineffec-tive, what's ineffective—how about we see what's highly effective and compare ourselves to that?

Here, Mr. Lambert suggested that teachers on the ground lacked shared under-standings of policy terms with the people above them in the reform chain (see Darling-Hammond, 2001; Scott, 1998; Spillane, Reiser & Reimer 2002). Both Mr. Lambert and Ms. Nelson described Danielson's Framework as "subjective," and Ms. Nelson believed that there were no clear criteria for judging whether one had achieved proficiency in a given Danielson dimension. "There might be places you thought you did well," she said, "and then administrators or you look at the framework, and the language makes you think you didn't do well." This disconnect is not inherently negative, for it may push school communities to collaboratively define effective, engaging instruction. Yet as of 2014, many teachers remained par-tially confused about the terms, measurements, and demands (see Scott, 1998) of a framework that policymakers insist "establishes a common language and increases dialogue about effective instruction" (NYC DOE, 2014b, p. 3). This confusion suggested a further sense of policy incoherence—one that emerged from ambiguity surrounding purportedly straightforward policies.

Common Core: "Maybe I'm not Doing Everything I'm Supposed to Do?"

In discussing the Common Core, teachers also expressed confusion—although they noted their strong support for the standards' foci as well.

Many teachers said that the standards underscored skills they already prioritized in their classrooms. They initially implied that the Common Core factored into their planning only retroactively, once their units and lessons were already designed. Mr. Carter (English) explained this process: he chose his content first and then the projects, assessments, and texts he would use to teach and reinforce this content. "Then," he noted, "I think, well, do these meet the standards, and which standards do they meet?" Several teachers agreed that they produced curriculum maps and unit plans without first referencing the Common Core.

If the standards are implemented only when teachers drop selected mandates into already-planned curricula, there is a good chance that some standards are overlooked and that the Common Core framework is not being used as intended: to influence the creation of curricula that address specific sets of competencies. This may lead to further instances of incoherence in which standards intended to shape students' skills statewide are haphazardly incorporated from one classroom or school to the next. I wondered about this in examining teachers' yearlong curriculum maps, from which select grade-level standards were often missing. In none of the curricular artifacts teachers brought with them to interviews did I find reference to the Common Core Language Standards, which are designed to scaffold students' mastery of written conventions (NY SED, 2014a). At first glance, I questioned whether the Common Core had much formative impact on teachers' planning, and I wondered what inconsistencies might result if teachers referenced the standards after the fact of planning. Ms. Langdon, too, wondered aloud: "I don't know. Maybe I'm not doing everything I'm supposed to do with it?" As Porter, Fusarelli, and Fusarelli (2015) found in their case study of the new standards' enactment, "an incomplete understanding on the part of teachers of the Common Core" can hinder implementation (p. 124).

Yet as I continued speaking to teachers, they made it clear that the Common Core did influence their design of curriculum in overarching ways. Mr. Lambert noted that in science, the Common Core drove him to concentrate on how students expressed their understanding of scientific concepts. "I think it's good," he said, "because you have to be able to articulate in science—it's not just about application." Mr. Ulmer and Mr. Carter noted that they tried to emphasize Common Core-aligned reading, writing, problem-solving, and higher-order thinking skills in their classrooms. While teachers' processes of implementing the standards may have left some individual skills and understandings unaddressed, teachers appeared supportive of the framework's instructional emphases. Teachers framed most frustrations about the new standards as ones brought about by the related tests and their implementation, not by the standards themselves.

This distinction between the Common Core and their corresponding tests complicates some of the portrayals of the standards in popular media. Sharp critiques of the standards' design do not mesh with the impressions of many high school teachers, who indicate that many of the standards support in-depth learning. These teachers' support for the Common Core, together with their critiques of high-stakes assessments, resonate with Noguera's argument that while the Common Core are not a silver bullet, they could *ideally* function "...to eliminate the unevenness that presently characterize[s] educational standards among the states... [and] to engage students to reason, problem solve, write and process information in ways that challenge their higher order thinking skills" (Hess & Noguera, 2013). Unfortunately, Noguera observes, the new standards materialize in their most high-stakes, visible form as tests for which students (and their teachers) are not provided adequate preparation or support.

Still, the Common Core may be pushing some teachers to consider a focus on higher-order thinking in their classrooms, a focus that seems to be supported by the Danielson Framework, the Citywide Instructional Expectations, and NYC's School Quality Review rubric (NYC DOE, 2013a, c, 2014a). Teachers did point to gaps in understanding and enacting some of these policies, confusing as the mandates were in the absence of time for substantive dialogue about them. Yet overall, the greatest incoherence teachers identified was between high stakes tests and the educational vision presented in many of the RttT-aligned reforms of 2013 and 2014—reforms that prized critical thinking and collaborative work over rote memorization.

Incompatible Outcomes

In the first years of RttT-aligned policies, some urban high school teachers were left confused about the skills and instructional strategies they should prioritize. State exams involved such high stakes that some teachers focused the majority of their instructional efforts on teaching to these tests. Yet they also faced new rounds of local assessments that measured distinct skills and new expectations for their teaching that encouraged the facilitation of collaboration, inquiry, and higher-order thinking (rather than the rote memorization they felt standardized tests necessitated). As Berliner (2007) argues, in their current form "high stakes tests and the curriculum goals for the twenty-first century are incompatible" (p. 138). Confusingly, both seemed to be emphasized in new and longstanding policies that NYC teachers experienced in 2013 and 2014.

When I asked about the new amalgam of standardizations that teachers faced, I expected to hear stronger critiques of the new evaluation system and new standards. What I heard instead were resounding denouncements of testing, even by those who accommodated to the rituals and pedagogy they thought were best-suited to the demands of high-stakes exams. The teachers I interviewed worried about the degraded state of student learning that was accompanying testing in 2013 and 2014, suggesting that the lessons of NCLB were not being heeded in the RttT era. There is reason to fear that new and longstanding reforms will continue to result in "the opposite of the rhetoric…[as] more and more children are 'left behind'"—as before, curricula may narrow "as (mostly) working-class and minority youth are condemned to a regime of test-prep and little more" (Garrison, 2009, pp. 103–104; see also Berliner, 2007; Darder & Torres, 2004; Lipman, 2004). As teachers of Regents-based courses described their instruction to me, it appeared to contain many elements of such a regime. Despite what we know to be the dangers of test-based accountability measures, we find ourselves in the midst of reforms that exert extreme pressure on teachers and students through high-stakes testing. This appears true even in the face of some new policies that demand "higher-order," more challenging learning experiences for students. As local and state assessments come to resemble one another more closely, teachers may feel some relief from the need to teach seemingly incongruous skills. But the general pressure to tailor curriculum and instruction to standardized, high-stakes tests is unlikely to disappear, given state mandates and federal funding programs.

In a time when education reform is focused on outcomes rather than inputs, teachers of low-income students of color seem to be facing incoherent messages about what students need to learn…Is it higher-order thinking skills, inquiry, and collaboration, which many teachers sense are fundamental to high-quality learning experiences? Or is it the narrow skills assessed on high-stakes tests: accountability measures that tend to penalize rather than support low-income students of color and their teachers? In the absence of providing greater support to address the needs of urban students outside the classroom, policymakers should be providing schools with a coherent vision of teaching and learning, or with the support to develop their own such visions locally. Without doing this, and without decreasing the stakes associated with standardized testing, we run the risk of continuing to deny low-income students of color high-quality educational experiences in urban schools.

References

Anderson, G. (2009). *Advocacy leadership: Toward a post-reform agenda in education*. New York, NY: Routledge.

Ball, S. J. (2000). Performativities and fabrications in the education economy: Towards the performative society? *Australian Educational Researcher, 27*(2), 1–24.

Ball, S. J. (2003). The teacher's soul and the terrors of performativity. *Journal of Education Policy, 18*(2), 215–228.

Ball, S. J., Maguire, M., & Braun, A. (with Hoskins, K. & Perryman, J.) (2012). *How schools do policy: Policy enactments in secondary schools*. New York, NY: Routledge.

Berliner, D. (2007). The incompatibility of high-stakes testing and the development of skills for the twenty-first century. In R. Marzano (Ed.), *On excellence in teaching* (pp. 113–143). Bloomington, IN: Solution Tree Press.

Brown v. Board of Education of Topeka, 347 U.S. 483 (1954).

Carter, P., & Welner, K. G. (2013). *Closing the opportunity gap: What America must to do give every child an even chance.* New York, NY: Oxford University Press.

Cohen, D. K. (1995). What is the system in systemic reform? *Educational Researcher, 24*(9), 11–17, 31.

Darder, A., & Torres, R. D. (2004). Manufacturing destinies: The racialized discourse of high-stakes testing. In A. Darder & R. Torres (Eds.), *After race: racism after multiculturalism* (pp. 78–96). New York, NY: New York University Press.

Darling-Hammond, L. (2001). *The right to learn: A blueprint for creating schools that work.* San Francisco, CA: Jossey-Bass.

Darling-Hammond, L. (2010). *The flat world and education: How America's commitment to equity will determine our future.* New York, NY: Teachers College Press.

Datnow, A. (2005). The sustainability of comprehensive school reform models in changing district and state contexts. *Educational Administration Quarterly, 41,* 121–153.

Engage NY (2014). https://www.engageny.org/.

Fruchter, N. (2007). *Urban schools, public will: Making education work for all our children.* New York, NY: Teachers College Press.

Fuhrman, S. H. (1993). *Designing coherent education policy: Improving the system.* San Francisco, CA: Jossey-Bass Publishers. Retrieved from http://files.eric.ed.gov/fulltext/ED359626.pdf.

Garrison, M. J. (2009). *A measure of failure: The political origins of standardized testing.* Albany, NY: State University of New York Press.

Goertz, M. E., Floden, R. E., & O'Day, J. (1996). The bumpy road to education reform (RB-20-June 1996). Philadelphia, PA: Consortium for Policy Research in Education. Retrieved from http://www.aocmedi.literacy.org/sites/default/files/policybrief/861_rb20.pdf.

Grissmer, D., & Flanagan, A. (1999). Making Title I more effective: Lessons from recent research. In G. Orfield & E. H. DeBray (Eds.), *Hard work for good schools: Facts not fads in Title I reform* (pp. 46–54). Cambridge, MA: The Civil Rights Project, Harvard University.

Harvey, S., & Daniels, H. (2009). *Comprehension and collaboration: Inquiry circles in action.* Portsmouth, NH: Heinemann.

Hess, F., & Noguera, P. (2013, October 8). How can we fix the very broken American education system? American Enterprise Institute. Retrieved from http://www.aei.org/article/education/how-can-we-fix-the-very-broken-american-education-system/.

Ingersoll, R. (2007). Short on power, long on responsibility. *Educational Leadership, 65*(1), 20–25.

Jennings, J. F. (2001). Title I: Its legislative history and its promise. In G. D. Borman, S. C. Stringfield, & R. E. Slavin (Eds.), *Title I: Compensatory education at the crossroads* (pp. 1–24). Mahwah, NJ: Lawrence Erlbaum Associates.

Kantor, H., & Lowe, R. (2013). Educationalizing the welfare state and privatizing education: The evolution of social policy since the New Deal. In P. L. Carter & K. G. Welner (Eds.), *Closing the opportunity gap: What America must to do give every child an even chance* (pp. 25–39). New York, NY: Oxford University Press.

Kim, J. S., & Sunderman, G. L. (2005). Measuring academic proficiency under the No Child Left Behind Act: Implications for educational equity. *Educational Researcher, 34*(8), 3–13.

Lipman, P. (1998). *Race, class and power in school restructuring.* Albany, NY: State University of New York Press.

Lipman, P. (2004). *High stakes education: Inequality, globalization, and urban school reform.* New York: RoutledgeFalmer.

Lipsky, M. (2010). *Street-level bureaucracy: Dilemmas of the individual in public service.* New York, NY: Russell Sage Foundation.

Mehta, J. (2013). *The allure of order: High hopes, dashed expectations, and the troubled quest to remake American schooling*. New York, NY: Oxford University Press.

Meier, D. (2002). *In schools we trust: Creating communities of learning in an era of testing and standardization*. Boston, MA: Beacon Press.

NYC DOE. (2013a). 2013–2014 Citywide instructional expectations. Retrieved from http://schools.nyc.gov/NR/rdonlyres/C8CFE95F-9488-458B-AEBF-1A21AD914F64/0/201314Citywide InstructionalExpectationsMay62013.pdf.

NYC DOE. (2013b). *Advance guide for educators*. Retrieved from http://schools.nyc.gov/NR/rdonlyres/814596C9-702B-4AAE-989E-A576B34D17CF/0/AdvanceGuideforEducators 101813.pdf.

NYC DOE. (2013c). Danielson 2013 rubric: Adapted to New York Department of Education Framework for Teaching Components. Retrieved from http://schools.nyc.gov/NR/rdonlyres/8A4A25F0-BCEE-4484-9311-B5BB7A51D7F1/0/TeacherEffectivenessProgram1314Rubric 201308142.pdf.

NYC DOE. (2014a). 2014–2015 Quality Review Rubric. Retrieved from http://schools.nyc.gov/NR/rdonlyres/8C11A001-7E78-469D-996F-B0C3703CEA81/0/201314QualityReview Rubric.pdf.

NYC DOE. (2014b): Advance guide for educators: 2014–2015. Retrieved from http://www.uft.org/files/attachments/advance-guide-2014-15.pdf.

NYC DOE. (2014c). Phase 1: Measures of student learning selection (MOSL) selections. http://www.uft.org/files/attachments/mosl-selection-guide-2014-15.pdf.

NYC DOE. (2015). Tenure for newer teachers. Retrieved from http://www.uft.org/new-teachers/tenure.

NY SED. (2010). Part 100 Regulations: 100.5 Diploma Requirements. Retrieved from http://www.p12.nysed.gov/part100/pages/1005.html.

NY SED. (2014a). *New York State P-12 Common Core Learning Standards for English language arts & literacy*. Retrieved from https://www.engageny.org/resource/new-york-state-p-12-common-core-learning-standards-for-english-language-arts-and-literacy.

NY SED. (2014b). Transition to Common Core Regents examinations in English language arts and mathematics, original issue date: March 2013; Fifth Update: December 2014 Retrieved from http://www.p12.nysed.gov/assessment/commoncore/transitionccregents1113rev.pdf.

National Commission on Excellence in Education. (1983). *A nation at risk: The imperative for educational reform*. Retrieved from http://datacenter.spps.org/uploads/sotw_a_nation_at_risk_1983.pdf.

Newmann, F. M., King, M. B., & Carmichael, D. L. (2007). Authentic instruction and assessment: Common standards for rigor and relevance in teaching academic subjects. Report prepared for the Iowa Department of Education. Retrieved from http://centerforaiw.com/sites/centerforaiw.com/files/Authentic-Instruction-Assessment-BlueBook.pdf.

Newmann, F. M., Marks, H. M., & Gamoran, A. (1995). Authentic pedagogy: Standards that boost student performance. *Issues in Restructuring Schools, 8*, 1–4. Retrieved from http://wcer.wisc.edu/archive/cors/Issues_in_Restructuring_Schools/Issues_No_8_Spring_1995.pdf.

Newmann, F. M., Smith, B., Allensworth, E., & Bryk, A. S. (2001). Improving Chicago's schools: School instructional program coherence: Benefits and challenges. Chicago, IL: Consortium on Chicago School Research. Retrieved from https://ccsr.uchicago.edu/sites/default/files/publications/p0d02.pdf.

Nichols, S. L., & Berliner, D. C. (2007). *Collateral damage: How high-stakes testing corrupts America's schools*. Cambridge, MA: Harvard Education Press.

Noguera, P. A. (2003). *City schools and the American dream: Reclaiming the promise of public education*. New York, NY: Teachers College Press.

Noguera, P. A. (2008). *The trouble with black boys…and other reflections on race, equity, and the future of public education*. San Fransisco, CA: Jossey-Bass.

Noguera, P. A., & Wing, J. Y. (Eds.). (2006). *Unfinished business: Closing the racial achievement gap in our schools*. San Francisco, CA: Jossey-Bass.

Orfield, G. (1999). Strengthening Title I: Designing a policy based on evidence. In G. Orfield & E. H. DeBray (Eds.), *Hard work for good schools: Facts not fads in Title I reform* (pp. 1–20). Cambridge, MA: The Civil Rights Project, Harvard University.

Orfield, G., & DeBray, E. H. (Eds.). (1999). *Hard work for good schools: Facts not fads in Title I reform*. Cambridge, MA: The Civil Rights Project, Harvard University.

Orfield, G., & Eaton, S. E. (1996). *Dismantling desegregation: The quiet reversal of* Brown v. Board of Education. New York, NY: The New Press.

Payne, C. M. (1984). *Getting what we ask for: The ambiguity of success and failure in urban education*. Westport, CT: Greenwood Press.

Payne, C. M. (2008). *So much reform, so little change: The persistence of failure in urban schools*. Cambridge, MA: Harvard Education Press.

Porter, R. E., Fusarelli, L. D., & Fusarelli, B. C. (2015). Implementing the Common Core: How educators interpret curriculum reform. *Educational Policy, 29*(1), 111–139.

Ravitch, D. (2013). *Reign of error: The hoax of the privatization movement and the danger to America's public schools*. New York, NY: Knopf.

Rebell, M. A., & Wolff, J. A. (2008). *Moving every child ahead: From NCLB hype to meaningful educational opportunity*. New York, NY: Teachers College Press.

Reissman, C. K. (2008). *Narrative methods for the human sciences*. Thousand Oaks, CA: Sage.

Rothstein, R. (2013). Why children from lower socioeconomic classes, on average, have lower academic achievement than middle class children. In P. L. Carter & K. G. Welner (Eds.), *Closing the opportunity gap: What America must to do give every child an even chance* (pp. 61–74). New York, NY: Oxford University Press.

Rubin, H. J., & Rubin, I. S. (2012). *Qualitative interviewing: The art of hearing data*. Thousand Oaks, CA: Sage.

Ryan, J. E. (2004). The perverse incentives of the No Child Left Behind Act. *NYU Law Review, 79*(3), 932–989.

Saldaña, J. (2013). *The coding manual for qualitative researchers* (2nd ed.). Thousand Oaks, CA: Sage.

Scott, J. (1998). *Seeing like a state: How certain schemes to improve the human condition have failed*. New Haven, CT: Yale University Press.

Slavin, R. E. (1983). When does cooperative learning increase student achievement? *Psychological Bulletin, 94*(3), 429–445.

Spillane, J., Reiser, B., & Reimer, T. (2002). Policy implementation and cognition: Reframing and refocusing implementation research. *Review of Educational Research, 72*(3), 387–431.

Tienken, C. H., & Zhao, Y. (2013). How common standards and standardized testing widen the achievement gap. In P. L. Carter & K. G. Welner (Eds.), *Closing the opportunity gap: What America must to do give every child an even chance* (pp. 111–122). New York, NY: Oxford University Press.

Tyack, D., & Cuban, L. (1995). *Tinkering toward utopia: A century of public school reform*. Cambridge, MA: Harvard University Press.

US DOE (2009). Race to the top program: Executive summary. Washington, DC. Retrieved from https://www2.ed.gov/programs/racetothetop/executive-summary.pdf.

Wells, A. S., & Crain, R. L. (1994). Perpetuation theory and the long-term effects of school desegregation. *Review of Educational Research, 64*(4), 531–555.

Wells, A. S., & Crain, R. L. (1997). *Stepping over the color line: African-American students in white suburban schools*. New Haven, CT: Yale University Press.

Wong, K. K., & Reilly, M. (2014, August). *Education waivers as reform leverage in the Obama administration: State implementation of ESEA flexibility waiver request*. Paper presented at the annual meeting of the American Political Science Association, Washington, DC.

Mexican American Educational Stagnation: The Role of Generational Status, Parental Narratives, and Educator Messages

Casandra D. Salgado

Introduction

Scholars debate whether years of education for Mexican American youth improve or stagnate across generations (Alba, Abdel-Hady, Islam & Marotz, 2011; Duncan & Trejo, 2011; Telles & Ortiz, 2008). Parent-to-child comparisons show educational advancement between immigrant parents and their second-generation children (7–8 years vs. 12–13 years), and educational advancement between second-generation parents and their third-generation children (10–11 years vs. 12–13 years) (Telles & Ortiz, 2008).[1] Despite parent-to-child educational advancement, second- and third-generation children attain on average 12–13 years of education, suggesting limited educational progress or stagnation for Mexican Americans.[2] Educational stagnation among Mexican Americans is surprising since the third generation has parents who are more educated than those of the second

---

[1] The second generation refers to the U.S.-born children of immigrants and the third generation refers to the U.S.-born grandchildren of immigrants.

[2] While most quantitave data does not permit disaggregation by generational status beyond the third generation, Telles and Ortiz (2008) find that Mexican Americans' limited educational progress continues into the fourth generation. I use the term educational stagnation to refer to Mexican Americans' limited educational progress.

A version of this chapter was originally published as an article with the following citation: Salgado, C. D. (2015). Racial lessons: Parental narratives and secondary schooling experiences among second- and third-generation Mexican Americans. *Race and Social Problems, 7*(1), 60–72.

C.D. Salgado (✉)
Department of Sociology, University of California, Los Angeles (UCLA),
264 Haines Hall, 375 Portola Plaza, Los Angeles, CA 90095-1551, USA
e-mail: casandrasalgado@ucla.edu

© Springer International Publishing Switzerland 2016
P.A. Noguera et al. (eds.), *Race, Equity, and Education*,
DOI 10.1007/978-3-319-23772-5_11

generation. Yet the improvement in schooling we expect to find between second- and third-generation children is largely absent. Additionally, educational stagnation suggests that the educational incorporation of Mexican American youth differs from that of other racial and ethnic groups. In fact, Mexican American high school dropout rates are more than twice as high as those of Asians and Whites, and the discrepancy continues in college graduation rates (Burciaga, Pérez Huber & Solórzano, 2010; Covarrubias, 2011). The lower educational attainment of Mexican Americans indicates that their educational experiences qualitatively differ from those of Asians and Whites.

To explain educational stagnation among Mexican Americans, the prevailing hypothesis attributes second-generation educational advancement (compared to that of the immigrant generation) to the optimism instilled by their Mexican-born parents (Kao & Tienda, 1995, 1998), and third-generation educational stagnation (compared to that of their second-generation counterparts) to the disillusioned prospects for upward mobility instilled by their U.S.-born parents (Gibson & Ogbu, 1991). Yet, others emphasize that Mexican American youth regardless of generational status are vulnerable to negative school conditions that lead to their low educational attainment (Telles & Ortiz, 2008; Valenzuela, 1999). While existing hypotheses on educational stagnation remain inconclusive, the second and third generations complete similar years of education. Whether educational stagnation is attributable to generational differences in academic motivation between the second and third generation, or negative school conditions that lead to their low educational attainment regardless of generational status, remains in question.

The sociological literature on Mexican American educational attainment focuses on how parental narratives impact the educational experiences of the second generation and misses how parental narratives affect the third generation. The undertheorization of third-generation parental narratives skews existing knowledge of how parental narratives influence Mexican American schooling. Nevertheless, an exclusive emphasis on parental narratives glazes over the school inequalities that affect Mexican Americans. Scholars are thus left with an inadequate analysis of how parental narratives *and* school conditions shape Mexican American educational trajectories. Since research focuses on the second-generation schooling advantage relative to the immigrant generation, the present study shifts the reference group to the third generation to examine how parental nativity *and* the school context influence Mexican American educational incorporation.

The present study also evaluates how student racial composition in high school influences Mexican American schooling conditions. In *Brown v. Board of Education* (1954), the Supreme Court outlawed racial segregation of schools by ruling that such segregation was inherently unequal. Sixty years after *Brown*, the role of student racial composition in schools remains critical to education research. While Latino students have become the most highly segregated minority group in California (Orfield & Ee, 2014), the effects of segregation and integration on Latino schooling conditions is unclear. Specifically, both segregated and integrated schools may reproduce racial stereotypes of Mexican Americans that lead to their low educational attainment (Goldsmith, 2004; Ochoa, 2013; Pizarro, 2005). An analysis of racialized treatment toward Mexican Americans in segregated and integrated schools is key to further specifying how the schooling context affects their educational incorporation.

In this paper, I investigate how generational status, that is, second and third generation, shapes the parental narratives and high school experiences of Mexican American young adults. First, I discuss how the content of narratives of Mexican-born and U.S.-born parents differ for second- and third-generation Mexican Americans, respectively. Second, I discuss the educational barriers of Mexican Americans in diverse and majority-Latino high schools and how those barriers may guide them toward the community college system. I show the potential importance of racialized school practices on Mexican Americans' educational experiences and trajectories.

Parental Narratives: Immigrant Optimism, Blocked Opportunities, and Racial Socialization

The literature on academic achievement among children of immigrants attributes their educational success (as compared to that of the immigrant generation) to the optimism instilled by their immigrant parents (Kao & Tienda, 1995). Immigrants represent a positively selected and highly motivated group, and therefore they may emphasize the importance of academic achievement to their children (Qian & Blair, 1999). Immigrant optimism largely derives from the dual frame of reference among immigrant parents. Dual frame of reference refers to immigrants who often interpret conditions in the new host country in direct reference to their own experiences in their country of origin (Suárez-Orozco, 1989). For immigrant parents, the desire to see their children attain high levels of education may also reflect their greater faith in American schools, especially when they are more recently arrived in the United States (Glick & White, 2004).

For second-generation youth, scholars also emphasize the "immigrant bargain" or the expectation that the second generation will redeem their parents' sacrifice in coming to the United States by succeeding in school and work (Kasinitz, Mollenkopf, Waters, & Holdaway, 2009; Louie, 2012; Smith, 2006). While similar bargains occur in nonimmigrant families, the life-defining sacrifices of migration on the part of immigrant parents convert the bargain into an urgent tale of success or failure (Louie, 2012; Smith, 2006). Accordingly, second-generation youth understand that school and work success validates parental sacrifice while failure incurs a burden of shame (Smith, 2006). Immigrant optimism and the immigrant bargain may also help the second generation confront negative school conditions. By extension, U.S.-born children of Mexican American parents benefit less from the immigrant narrative due to their United States frame of reference and, therefore, are more vulnerable to the negative effects of schooling.

Scholars posit that third-generation educational stagnation (as compared to that of their second-generation counterparts) is attributable to the messages of blocked opportunities instilled by their U.S.-born parents (Gibson & Ogbu, 1991; Kao & Tienda, 1998). Native-born parents may be disillusioned with their prospects of upward mobility, and may bring their own past relationships with schools into play when rearing their children (Luttrell, 1997). For Mexican American parents, perceptions of negative treatment by their children's educators may reinforce past experiences of alienation in schools (Romo, 1984). As a result, Mexican American parents may transfer leveled educational aspirations to their children. While the marginalization of Mexican American parents appears to be central to how they rear their children, we know less about how discrimination shapes the content of parental narratives and academic motivation for third-generation children.

Racial socialization research may elucidate the messages that Mexican Americans receive from their U.S.-born parents. Racial socialization refers to the verbal and nonverbal processes of promoting children's awareness of discrimination and preparing them to cope with it (Hughes et al., 2006). While Latino youth report more racial socialization than White youth (Huynh & Fuligni, 2008), they report less racial socialization than Black youth (Hughes, 2003). This suggests that Mexican-origin parents may believe that discrimination is an unavoidable reality for their children and may talk to their children about possible discrimination experiences (Huynh & Fuligni, 2008). While parental messages of blocked opportunities may negatively impact third-generation schooling, racial socialization may facilitate the academic success of third-generation youth. Specifically, racial socialization can contain messages that enhance youths' positive views of their ethnic group and self-esteem, which is positively associated with youths' academic orientations and outcomes (Chavous et al., 2003). Thus, I examine the content of immigrant optimism and racial socialization for members of the second and third generation.

Schooling: Oppositional Identity, Racialization, and School Racial Composition

The literature on educational outcomes of Mexican-origin youth theorizes that oppositional identities among U.S.-born youth relative to immigrant youth may contribute to their educational stagnation (Gibson & Ogbu, 1991). Matute-Bianchi (1986), for example, finds that nonimmigrant Chicano or *cholo* students reject academic-oriented behaviors to maintain the integrity of their respective identities. Conversely, the dual frame of reference among immigrant youth facilitates their academic success. While U.S.-born, Mexican-origin students are depicted as lacking the same drive as immigrant students, it is apparent that educators' stereotypes worked against Mexican-origin youth regardless of nativity (Matute-Bianchi, 1986). Therefore, the focus on oppositional identities misses how oppressive school structures adversely affect the schooling of immigrant and nonimmigrant youth and instead blames youths' individual attributes.

When the schooling context is analyzed more centrally, the role of deficient school practices in the marginalization of U.S.-born, Mexican-origin students becomes evident (Ochoa, 2013; Pizarro, 2005; Stanton-Salazar, 2001; Valencia, 2002). Valenzuela (1999), for example, attributes educational stagnation among Mexican Americans to subtractive schooling, a process by which schools subtract educational resources from youth through a pattern of mutual alienation and distrust between students and teachers. Deficient student–teacher relationships are a product of a larger schooling context that impedes learning. Furthermore, Conchas (2006) shows that caring student–teacher relationships are unavailable to Mexican Americans, as they are isolated in remedial programs. The absence of guidance from educators in remedial programs leads to Mexican American insecurities regarding their intellectual abilities and lackluster motivation to plan for college. Beyond youths' individual attributes, these studies document that deficient school practices may be present for Mexican Americans regardless of generational status. Therefore, an examination of the schooling context is critical to exploring further reasons for the leveling of educational progress among Mexican Americans.

Scholars also contend that racial discrimination and stereotyping are central to Mexican American schooling (Ochoa, 2013; Telles & Ortiz, 2008; Valencia, 2002). Racialization refers to the ways in which ideas about race sort individuals into the American racial hierarchy (Telles & Ortiz, 2008). Therefore, ideas about the worth of Mexican Americans, especially compared to those about Asians and Whites, lead to their educational disadvantage. Similarly, research demonstrates that educators' perceptions of Latinos as inferior leads to discrimination in the form of holding them to lower academic standards and tracking them into less challenging courses (Lucas & Gamoran, 2002; McKown & Weinstein, 2008; Tenenbaum & Ruck, 2007). Educators are also reluctant to invest in the education of Latinos (as compared to that of Asians and Whites) in the form of resources ranging from classroom assistance to college guidance (Marx, 2006; Oakes, 2005; Pizarro, 2005). These findings substantiate the larger racialization process in schools that limits Mexican American educational progress.

However, existing evidence on the racialized treatment of Mexican Americans in diverse and majority-Latino schools shows mixed results. In diverse schools, research documents that racial stereotypes foster low expectations of Latinos and track them into less rigorous courses (Conchas, 2006; Ochoa, 2013). Yet, diverse schools may increase Latino students' access to challenging curricula and thereby increase their college attendance (Goldsmith, 2009; Orfield & Ee, 2014). In majority-Latino schools, research details how Eurocentric curricula alienate Mexican-origin students, which leads to their low educational attainment (Valenzuela, 1999). However, majority-Latino schools may increase Latino college expectations and self-worth, which also increases their college attendance (Frost, 2007; Goldsmith, 2004). Since schools may reproduce existing racial hierarchies, how student racial composition shapes Mexican American schooling remains in question. The qualitative data reported here permit an evaluation of how racialized treatment in diverse and majority-Latino schools affects Mexican American schooling.

Few qualitative studies have examined how generational status—more specifically, the second and third generations—shapes the parental narratives and educational experiences of Mexican Americans. In this paper, I examine how the contents of parental and educator messages[3] socialize and affect the high school experiences of Mexican American young adults. Additionally, I investigate how racialized treatment (stereotyping and discrimination) toward Mexican Americans may operate in diverse and majority-Latino high schools.

Data and Methods

This article draws from 41 interviews with U.S.-born Mexican American young adults in Los Angeles County, CA. I located my research in Los Angeles County since it has one of the largest Mexican-origin populations within California (Brown & Lopez, 2013). I recruited respondents from two community colleges with majority-Latino student populations. Participants selected were second- and third-generation Mexican Americans of working-class families.

Generational Status

I define the second generation as children of immigrants, whose parents migrated to the United States as adults (at least 16 years of age) and did not attend school in the United States. I interviewed 18 of the second generation. I define the third generation as those who have U.S.-born parents, and have at least three grandparents who were born in Mexico. Among the third generation, most had two U.S.-born parents (14 respondents) or had parents that came to the United States as newborns or before the age of eight (6 respondents). I also include those who had a U.S.-born mother and Mexican-born father (3 respondents) with the third generation since parental messages and class backgrounds were similar to those of students who had two U.S.-born parents. I interviewed 23 of the third generation.

Other Selection Criteria

I interviewed 20 women and 21 men. For the second generation, I interviewed 10 men and 8 women. For the third generation, I interviewed 12 women and 11 men.

---

[3]Educator messages refer to the messages that students receive from teachers, counselors, and administrators about their academic ability, worth, and potential.

I interviewed respondents between 17 and 25 years of age. Most participants are between 18 and 20-years old, are recent high school graduates, and are able to recollect their high school experiences with ease.

I controlled for class background by focusing on working-class Mexican Americans. I selected respondents whose parents have a high school degree or less. While most immigrant parents were self-employed or employed in factory and construction jobs, most U.S.-born parents were employed in clerical, mechanical, and transportation jobs. Using this selection criterion, I investigate the effect of factors like parental narratives, rather than the effect of parents' educational resources, on their children's educational experiences.

Community College Students

Mexican American community college students are an ideal population for this study for two main reasons: (1) most Mexican Americans begin and end their postsecondary careers at community college whether they graduate or not and (2) Mexican Americans in community college are diverse in their academic achievements and experiences (Burciaga et al., 2010). For U.S.-born, Mexican Americans in the United States, 17 % have less than a high school degree, 36 % earn a high school degree, 31 % attend some college, and 16 % earn a bachelor's degree or higher (Current Population Survey, 2012). While somewhat selective compared to the many Mexican Americans who do not pursue college, community college students are an ideal population since most Mexican Americans have a high school degree or attend some college.

As community college students, participants are more successful than their Mexican-born or U.S.-born parents who have a high school degree or less. Despite parent-to-child educational progress, second- and third-generation children attain on average 12–13 years of education (Alba et al., 2011; Telles & Ortiz, 2008). Therefore, community college students are an ideal population through which to examine educational stagnation since most Mexican Americans end their postsecondary careers at community college. As high school graduates, participants are also more successful than those who did not complete high school. This suggests that high school graduates would have fewer negative and racialized school experiences than those who did not complete high school. As a result, this study provides a conservative test of racialization.

Research Sites

I selected Mexican American students at two community colleges in East Los Angeles County. Both community colleges are Hispanic-Serving Institutions, postsecondary institutions that serve 25 % or more of Latino full-time student enrollment. I chose these college campuses for two main reasons: (1) majority-Latino neighborhoods surround both colleges and shape the composition of student enrollment and (2) they are similar in Latino student enrollment (at least 40 %) and Latino transfer rates compared to other Los Angeles County community colleges (Los Angeles Community College District, 2012).

I recruited respondents through one-on-one recruitment, classroom announcements and campus flyers. Most respondents were recruited through classroom announcements and few through one-on-one recruitment or campus flyers. Recruitment content asked if students wanted to participate in a study on the educational messages they received from family members and educators, and their educational experiences and trajectories. Of the 152 students contacted, 41 met the selection criteria and were interviewed in library or conference rooms at their campus.

High Schools

All respondents attended public school at the primary and secondary levels. Respondents are from the San Gabriel Valley and cities throughout East Los Angeles County, CA. Most respondents graduated with a high school diploma with the exception of one who earned a GED (General Education Development) diploma. In high school, most respondents did not take honors or advanced placement classes and had average grade point averages (2.0–3.0 GPA). Given these background characteristics, most participants are average students and few are high achievers.

Most respondents attended majority-Latino high schools with at least 40 % or more Latinos. While most high schools were majority-Latino, they varied in whether they included a sizeable minority of non-Latino students, namely Asians or Whites. Diverse schools include 10–55 % Asian and White students and Latino schools include 90–98 % Latino students. Since diverse student composition may be narrowly defined, the study provides a conservative test on the effects of a diverse student-body on Mexican American schooling.

Data Analysis

Each interview lasted between 45 and 90 minutes, was conducted between August 2011 and October 2012, and was recorded and transcribed verbatim. Interviews consisted of three sections: (1) academic course trajectory and extracurricular participation, (2) high school-to-college transition, and (3) parental and educator messages about college. I inductively analyzed the interviews to identify broad themes that were subsequently organized by the primary explanations for how generational status shapes Mexican American schooling: (1) parental motivation, (2) negative treatment by teachers, and (3) academic tracking by counselors.

Findings

Parental Narratives

The interviews made clear the expectation that Mexican Americans will redeem their parents' sacrifices through their educational success. In particular, participants drew upon multiple parental messages as educational motivation (see Table 1). On the one hand, parental messages on substandard working and financial conditions often included parental explanations for not attending college. On the other hand, parental messages about the need to challenge negative Mexican stereotypes often included parental accounts of negative labor market experiences. Nonetheless, parental messages regarding higher education clustered into two major themes: (1) substandard working and financial conditions and (2) the need to challenge negative Mexican stereotypes. While an equal proportion of second- and third-generation respondents stressed their parents' unfavorable economic conditions as educational motivation (six out of ten), a substantial proportion of the third generation also emphasized the need to challenge negative Mexican stereotypes (four out of ten). While the content of parental messages for the second and third generations differed, the effect of parental messages was the same—members of the second and third generations were equally motivated to pursue higher education.

Table 1 Frequency distribution of parental narratives by generational status ($N = 41$)

	Generational status	
	Second ($N = 18$)	Third ($N = 23$)
Parental narratives		
Substandard work and financial conditions	11	14
	(0.6)	(0.6)
College opportunities not available in Mexico	8	0
	(0.4)	(0)
Financial family obligations thwarted college aspirations	0	9
	(0)	(0.4)
Challenge negative Mexican stereotypes	0	10
	(0)	(0.4)
Negative labor market experiences	0	7
	(0)	(0.3)

Note Numbers in parentheses are proportions. The sample size (N) represents the number of participants. Frequencies do not equal the total number of participants in each generational status category, as participants reported more than one theme for parental narratives

Second- and Third-Generation Motivation: Substandard Working and Financial Conditions

An equal proportion of the second and third generations emphasized their parents' substandard working and financial conditions as postsecondary motivation (six out of ten). Furthermore, parental messages on substandard economic conditions often included parental explanations for not pursuing college. While the second generation conveyed that college was not a viable option for their parents in Mexico, the third generation explained that their parents' financial familial obligations thwarted their college aspirations (four out of ten for both).

Many second-generation participants reported parental messages regarding the arduous working conditions of their immigrant parents as postsecondary motivation (six out of ten), and less so their parents' hardships in Mexico or their own potential hardships in Mexico if their parents had not migrated to the United States. Julian, an 18-year-old, reported for example that his immigrant father's current job prompted him to pursue higher education.

> My father wants us to get an education because he never had the opportunity to get an education. [My father says,] "You better go to college or you will be working a dead-end job and getting the same wage as me and that's not enough."

While Julian was aware that his parents migrated from Mexico to the United States in search of better work opportunities and that college was not an available option for his parents in Mexico, his father's working conditions were what prompted him to further his education. Julian further explained that he did not "want to work every day for little pay" like his parents. Therefore, his father's warnings about low-wage work provided the basis of his postsecondary motivation to obtain a higher paying job. Similarly, most second-generation respondents reported that their parents' arduous, low-wage jobs with inconsistent pay reinforced their decision to pursue higher education. Accordingly, they used their immigrant parents' working conditions in the United States as points of reference to excel in school and to exceed their parents' class status.

Similarly, most third-generation respondents referenced their U.S.-born parents' low-wage work and financial hardships as postsecondary motivation (six out of ten). Daniel, a 20-year-old, reported how his U.S.-born father's advice regarding a college degree to obtain better pay and financial stability encouraged him to attend a 4-year college.

> My dad says, "I know that if I would have gone to [a 4-year] college and received this stupid piece of paper [diploma] we would never have any of these financial problems." My dad has this friend named Ian and he got a degree in political science. They got hired at the same time and have the same job, but Ian always made more money because of the piece of paper. My dad says, "That's why I make less than he does in the same position."

Daniel's father emphasized that obtaining a bachelor's degree in any field of study would provide better work and financial opportunities. The advice of Daniel's U.S.-born father was reinforced by the housing troubles that Daniel's

family was experiencing. He reported, "I don't want to end up like my parents...
I don't want to feel like I don't know where I'm going to live next month." As a
result, Daniel was motivated to receive a college diploma to evade the financial
obstacles of his family. Many third-generation respondents also reported that they
were encouraged to attend college to avoid the same financial obstacles as their
U.S.-born parents.

Additionally, Daniel reported that his father could not attend college because he
had to financially support his parents and siblings. Daniel said, "My dad tried to
go to college, but he realized that his mother really needed him to work and help
provide for the family." Many third-generation respondents explained that their
parents could not continue on to college from high school due to financial familial obligations associated with their low-income status. Given these experiences,
the third generation was encouraged to take advantage of the college opportunities
afforded to them. Conversely, the second generation did not report parental messages of limited postsecondary opportunities due to financial familial obligations
and instead, emphasized that postsecondary opportunities were not available to
their parents in Mexico (see Table 1).

Together, the content of parental messages regarding substandard working
and financial conditions show subtle differences by respondent's generation (see
Table 1). While the second generation stressed that college was not an option due
to the absence of college opportunities for their parents in Mexico, the third generation stressed that college was not an option due to their parents' financial familial
obligations (four out of ten for both). Nonetheless, both second- and third-generation participants were expected to redeem their parents' sacrifices through their
educational success.

Third-Generation Motivation: Challenging Negative Mexican Stereotypes

An equal proportion of second- and third-generation participants reported messages of substandard working and financial conditions as educational motivation
(six out of ten), yet the third generation further emphasized the need to challenge
negative Mexican stereotypes (four out of ten). Parental messages about the need
to challenge negative Mexican stereotypes often included parental accounts of
negative labor market experiences (three out of ten). Notably, parental accounts of
negative labor market experiences reinforced third-generation motivation to challenge Mexican stereotypes such as perceptions of being ignorant, unable to speak
proper English, low-income, lazy, or like gang members. In contrast, the second
generation did not report the need to challenge negative Mexican stereotypes or
describe their Mexican-born parents' negative labor market experiences as educational motivation (zero out of ten for both).

Briana, a 21-year-old, reported that her U.S.-born mother encouraged her to pursue college so that she could have a job where she was treated fairly. Briana explained that the negative treatment her mother previously experienced from White coworkers at a salon was the central source of her mother's messages regarding educational motivation.

> My mother told me to do something that I liked… she feels useless because she didn't go to school or anything… My mom worked as a salon receptionist with White girls. Those White girls treated her like she was stupid and she knows perfect English, and they [still] treated her as if she was dumb. "Have Irma do this, have Irma wash the towels or sweep the floor." My mom can't stand to be talked down to like she's ignorant… [She] told me that I should prove everyone wrong who thinks I can't [pursue my goals].

Briana explained that her mother knew "perfect English" to emphasize that her mother's White coworkers treated her negatively simply because of her Mexican background and regardless of her nativity. Furthermore, the discrimination her mother experienced made her feel useless and incompetent. As a result, Briana's mother encouraged her to pursue higher education to avoid workplace discrimination in less-prestigious occupations, and to challenge the negative stereotypes that non-Mexicans have of Mexican-origin people. Many third-generation participants also conveyed that parental messages of "proving wrong" the ideas that Mexican Americans are less capable than others coupled with evading similar negative labor market experiences as their parents were central to their educational motivation. For the second generation, parental messages on negative labor market experiences or the need to challenge negative Mexican stereotypes were not as evident (see Table 1).

Third-generation respondents also pointed to their parents' blocked job opportunities as educational motivation. Jeffrey, a 20-year-old, discussed how his U.S.-born father was denied a position in the United States Air Force due to racial discrimination. When asked how his U.S.-born father's stories influenced his own educational goals, Jeffrey responded:

> It keeps me going. I don't know how to explain it… When my dad was 19, he tried to go to the Air Force. My dad scored the highest on the [placement] test compared to Whites. The drill sergeant was surprised that he was Frank Diaz. They placed him in refrigeration even though he tested into air traffic controller. He felt like it was racism, so he got out of the Air Force… He tried to speak up about it, but no one listened to him… Sometimes he looks it up on the computer and he says, "Man, they're making $40,000 a year! Imagine if I would be making that much? We could've had a different life."

Jeffrey's father was employed in two part-time jobs, as a youth counselor and a truck driver. Jeffrey explained that his father continued to feel defeated and upset by the unfair treatment he received by the Air Force officer. Rather than be discouraged by this narrative, Jeffrey reported, "It makes me want to better myself, educate myself." Accordingly, Jeffrey recognized that Mexican Americans are perceived as less deserving of prestigious occupations in the labor market. To respond to and to challenge those negative perceptions, Jeffrey emphasized that he wanted to further his education. Similarly, other third-generation respondents underscored that they wanted to pursue higher education to overcome their parents' employment barriers as well as to challenge negative stereotypes regarding the low educational status of Mexican Americans. Conversely, among the second generation, parental accounts of discrimination in the labor market as the basis of post-secondary motivation was not as apparent (see Table 1).

In short, the content of parental messages for the second and third generations differed (see Table 1). While an equal proportion of second- and third-generation respondents stressed their parents' unfavorable economic conditions in the United States as educational motivation (six out of ten), third-generation respondents also stressed the need to challenge negative Mexican stereotypes as motivation (four out of ten). Nonetheless, the effect of parental messages for the second and third generations was the same—they were equally motivated to pursue college. Despite encouraging parental messages, members of the second and third generations had limited knowledge of the high school-to-college transition as first-generation college students. Therefore, educator messages regarding participants' college options may have played a critical role in guiding their educational trajectories.

High School Experiences

While respondents reported encouraging messages to pursue higher education from their parents, regardless of parents' nativity, they reported negative treatment by their educators in high school. The second and third generations perceived the same negative treatment, which was reported in two significant ways: (1) low expectations and marginalization by teachers, and (2) low expectations and academic tracking by counselors (see Table 2). While most respondents (35 of 41) perceived low expectations by educators, the presence or absence of non-Latino students shaped how respondents explained the negative treatment by educators. Specifically, students who attended diverse schools reported that they were treated differently from non-Latino students, namely Asians and Whites. Conversely, students who attended Latino schools did not have non-Latino students with whom to compare their negative treatment, yet they reported that educators simply held low expectations of Mexican Americans.

Low Expectations and Marginalization by Teachers

Respondents acutely recalled the low expectations and marginalization they perceived from teachers in the classroom. Those who attended diverse schools perceived more instances of low expectations by teachers than those who attended Latino schools (seven out of ten and three out of ten, respectively). Respondents who attended diverse schools described needing to prove their academic intelligence to teachers due to teachers' low expectations of Mexican Americans compared to Asians and Whites. Jesse, a 20-year-old, reported feeling underestimated

Table 2 Frequency distribution of educator messages by school racial composition ($N = 41$)

	School racial composition	
	Diverse ($N = 25$)	Latino ($N = 16$)
Educator messages		
Low expectations and marginalization by teachers		
Preference for Asian and White students	17	0
	(0.7)	(0)
Low academic achievement standards	0	5
	(0)	(0.3)
Low expectations and academic tracking by counselors		
Questioned intellectual ability	9	0
	(0.4)	(0.0)
Lackluster 4-year college guidance	10	7
	(0.4)	(0.4)
Did not report low expectations	2	4
	(0.1)	(0.3)

Note Numbers in parentheses are proportions. The sample size (*N*) represents the number of participants. Frequencies do not equal the number of participants in each school racial composition category, as participants reported more than one theme for educator messages

when he excelled on course exams because he did not fit the studious, middle-class-White-student profile.

> I went to a school with a lot of White kids, who had money and got good grades. I didn't fit that image at all… When they would see my test scores, they would scratch their head… I was accused of cheating multiple times. It was very frustrating because I wasn't cheating and I knew I wasn't. It got so far that I had meetings with the principals and I had to take tests by myself. I felt like I was very underestimated. They made me retake tests to prove that I did it myself.

Jesse explained that he had to retake more than one exam because his White teachers and principals thought he cheated on his exams.[4] He emphasized that he "did not fit the White-student mold that typically received the A grades" he had earned because of his dark phenotype, Mexican ancestry, and working-class background. Jesse's account suggests that White teachers favored White students, which made him feel marginalized. Consequently, Jesse felt frustrated and powerless because teachers could not believe that he was both intelligent and Mexican-origin. Similarly, many respondents reported experiences of having to convince educators that they could compete with the top Asian and White students in their classes due to perceived biases that Mexican Americans are academically inferior compared to Asian and Whites.

---

[4]I report educators' race/ethnicity to specify how respondents percieved educators' negative treatment.

Respondents who attended diverse schools also reported low expectations by educators when they perceived that the intellectual cultivation of Asian students was favored in the classroom. Ramona, a 19-year-old, explained that teachers always looked to the Asian students for the answers to the questions posed in class, which made her feel marginalized.

> Teachers would pick the [Asian students] more. You would raise your hand and the teachers would always pick on the Chous or Chans and not the Rodriguezes or Guerreros... It was like, why even go to class if they're not even going to pay attention to me? I was like I'm here too, why don't you pick on me? I know the answer. I need help, help me! It was always them [the Asian students] that got [the] attention.

Ramona felt frustrated that her teachers, who were mostly White, were more invested in the schooling of Asian students than Latino students. She also questioned whether teachers valued her intellectual efforts and whether she should attend class because she felt invisible relative to her Asian classmates. Ramona's example demonstrates how Mexican American students can disconnect and disinvest from their classes due to the less favorable treatment they perceive from teachers. Similarly, many respondents who attended diverse schools perceived that teachers had higher expectations for Asian or White students and lower expectations for Latino students. The preferential treatment of non-Latino students by teachers conveys the message that educating Asian and White students is more favorable than educating Mexican American students, which can negatively influence Mexican American academic engagement and performance.

Respondents who attended Latino schools reported fewer instances of low expectations by educators than those who attended diverse schools (three out of ten and seven out of ten, respectively). This may be because those who attended Latino schools could not compare their experiences to those of other non-Latino students. Nonetheless, respondents understood the low academic standards directed at them by teachers in Latino schools. For example, Jeffrey, a 20-year-old, explained that teachers set low academic standards from day one in class.

> Everyone at my school didn't pay attention. The teachers didn't say anything. I had teachers that would say, "If you want a C, sit in the front and if you want a D, sit in the back of the class." I [also] thought it was normal for students to talk in class until I came here [to community college.]

Jeffrey's account exemplifies the ways in which teachers may assume Mexican Americans to neither be academically engaged nor excel in class and consequently, instill low academic standards. Furthermore, Jeffrey's example specifies how teachers' low expectations convey the message that Mexican Americans are unworthy of quality academic instruction. Together, low expectations and low-quality academic instruction impeded Jeffrey's academic development. While respondents who attended Latino schools reported fewer instances of low expectations and marginalization by teachers than those who attended diverse schools (see Table 2), Jeffrey's example demonstrates how low expectations may operate in Latino schools.

Additionally, Jeffrey attributed the low expectations of his teachers and low-quality school curriculum to his "below average" performance on the SAT, the main standardized test used in admissions to most 4-year colleges. When asked if low expectations by educators affected whether he attended a 2- or 4-year college, Jeffrey said, "Yea, I took the SAT my junior year. I scored really low on everything. I was embarrassed. I tried to study for whatever I could. The questions that I read, I thought it was a different language." Jeffrey perceived that the subpar academic instruction he received in school hindered his 4-year college prospects. Many respondents who attended Latino schools also perceived and explained that low expectations by teachers resulted in substandard curricula that did not prepare them for the 4-year college admissions process. While respondents who attended diverse schools more often perceived low expectations by teachers relative to their Asian and White counterparts (seven out of ten), respondents who attended Latino schools simply reported low academic standards by teachers (three out of ten).

Low Expectations and Academic Tracking by Counselors

Respondents who attended diverse schools reported more instances of low expectations by counselors regarding their intellectual ability than those who attended Latino schools (four out of ten and zero out of ten, respectively). This may be because those who attended diverse schools could compare their negative treatment to that of non-Latino students. Namely, respondents who attended diverse schools perceived that counselors questioned their academic ability when they wanted to enroll in rigorous courses such as Advanced Placement and honors. Eighteen-year-old Carmen, for example, reported that her Latina counselor expected her to receive mediocre grades and tracked her into non-college-preparatory courses because of her Mexican ancestry.

> My counselor never let me go beyond average. I bring home a C and my mother would say that a C is bad and the counselor would say that a C is good. My mom would say [to my counselor], "No. I don't want her to get a C. I want her to get help. What does she need?" And the counselor would say, "No, no, that's fine, there are kids out there that are worse." My mom would say, "I don't care. I want my daughter to do better." My counselor knew that I was better than a D and an F, but a C was okay.

Carmen also perceived that her counselor facilitated certain opportunities for Asian students and not Latino students. While her counselor offered Advanced Placement courses to her Asian friends in school, Carmen was never offered those same courses. Furthermore, Carmen's account exemplifies the competing messages that students can receive from their parents and educators. While her mother advocated for Carmen to obtain extra assistance in school, her counselor affirmed that performing at an average academic level was acceptable. Because of her counselor's advice, Carmen only enrolled in courses that satisfied high school graduation requirements. Therefore, the average expectations of her counselor may have thwarted Carmen from satisfying 4-year college admissions requirements.

Similarly, many respondents who attended diverse schools perceived that their counselors' low expectations for Latino students filtered them into non-college preparatory courses. In contrast, among those who attended Latino schools, low expectations by counselors in the form of questioning students' intellectual ability when they wanted to enroll in more rigorous courses was not as evident (see Table 2).

An equal proportion of respondents who attended diverse and Latino schools reported that they did not apply to 4-year colleges because their counselors provided lackluster college guidance or modest motivation to pursue higher education (four out of ten for both). Janelle, a 19-year-old who attended a diverse school, explained that she did not satisfy admissions requirements for the California State University or University of California campuses since her Asian American counselor simply advised her to attend community college.

> I knew that I didn't have the chance to go to a 4-year because I didn't have the Spanish and Math requirements. I figured that I should start here [at community college] and then transfer somewhere later. [Did your counselor ever recommend that you go to summer school or how to make-up those classes?] No, she said that I was on the right track for community college. She never really pushed me to go to a 4-year college. She just said, "You'll do fine in community college."

Janelle also reported that her counselor encouraged her to take Regional Occupational Program classes, which are nonacademic classes for low-tracked students, over A–G courses that fulfilled California requirements for 4-year college admissions. Although Janelle's school offered extensive A–G courses, she was placed in courses for low-tracked students. Additionally, Janelle perceived that her counselor only offered positive reinforcement about attending community college because she was not deserving of 4-year colleges. Respondents who attended diverse and Latino schools reported similar messages that their counselors did not push them to attend 4-year colleges due to their low expectations. While counselors may have been acting in line with their roles in directing average-performing students of working-class families to community colleges, respondents perceived their modest messages about college as negative treatment.

Participants also reported that their counselors did not advise them about college or the differences between 2 and 4-year colleges, which indicated lackluster college guidance (see Table 2). Twenty-year-old Roy stated, "The only thing counselors cared about is making sure that you graduate. They were like, 'you need this class to graduate and that's it.'" Twenty-year-old Sonia explained, "They never really said anything. They never really said to go to community college or 4-year college as long as you continue your education." Throughout high school, Roy and Sonia, who attended different Latino schools, met with their counselors at least once a year, but were never advised about college. Similar to Janelle who stressed that her counselor never "pushed" her to attend 4-year colleges, Roy and Sonia were never explicitly encouraged to attend 4-year colleges. These accounts further exemplify how respondents perceived that their counselors diverted them from attending 4-year colleges. Other participants who attended diverse and Latino schools similarly perceived that their counselors' modest motivation of students to continue their education after high school did not prompt them to attend 4-year colleges.

In all, the messages that Mexican Americans received in high school regarding their intellectual abilities show that they perceived low expectations by educators as barriers in their pursuit of higher education. While most respondents (35 of 41) reported negative treatment by educators, the absence or presence of non-Latino students shaped how they perceived negative treatment. Namely, Mexican Americans who attended diverse schools were more likely to report low expectations by teachers and counselors since they could compare their negative treatment to that of non-Latino students (see Table 2). In contrast, Mexican Americans who attended Latino schools did not have non-Latino students with whom to compare their perceived negative treatment and therefore were more likely to report instances of low expectations by counselors. Additionally, the comparison of educator messages at diverse and Latino schools indicates that Mexican Americans are held to the same low academic standards. Consequently, the low expectations that Mexican Americans faced in high school, whether diverse or Latino in student composition, may have limited their postsecondary options and diverted them to the community college system.

Discussion

This study examined how generational status shapes the parental narratives and high school experiences of Mexican Americans. My findings show that second- and third-generation respondents received encouraging parental messages to pursue higher education. Furthermore, most participants (regardless of generational status) perceived low expectations by educators in high school, whether they attended a diverse or Latino school. Therefore, I argue that educator messages are equally or more important than parental narratives in shaping Mexican American educational incorporation. My findings support a longer line of research calling attention to the importance of educators and their significant influence over students' educational trajectories (Conchas, 2006; Ochoa, 2013; Stanton-Salazar, 2001; Telles & Ortiz, 2008; Valenzuela, 1999).

Scholars posit that the leveling of educational progress for Mexican Americans is attributable to generational differences in parental narratives. While the second generation is advantaged by their parents' immigration narrative (Kao & Tienda, 1995; Smith, 2006), the third generation is disadvantaged by their parents' blocked opportunities narrative (Gibson & Ogbu, 1991). In contrast, I show that while the content of parental narratives differed by generational status, the effect of parental narratives for members of the second and third generation was similar—they were equally motivated to pursue higher education. Both second- and third-generation participants stressed their parents' unfavorable economic conditions in the United States as educational motivation, yet the third generation also emphasized the need to challenge negative Mexican stereotypes. Since the effect of parental narratives for members of the second and third generation was similar, I argue that parental narratives alone inadequately account for educational stagnation among Mexican Americans.

Scant research has qualitatively compared the content and effect of parental narratives for the second and third generation. Racial socialization research suggests that Latino parents may educate their children about membership in a lower-status group within the American racial hierarchy as a means to facilitate their educational attainment (Hughes, 2003; Huynh & Fuligni, 2008). My findings contribute to research on Mexican-origin racial socialization. I find that both second- and third-generation participants stressed their parents' unfavorable economic conditions in the United States as educational motivation, yet the third generation also stressed the need to challenge negative Mexican stereotypes. Since parental narratives on racial stereotypes were not as evident for the second generation, I show that racial socialization was more prevalent among the third generation than the second generation. For third-generation participants, racial socialization underscored succeeding in school to evade the same negative labor market experiences of their U.S.-born parents and to challenge negative Mexican stereotypes. Consequently, members of the third generation emphasized pursuing college to overcome negative stereotypes regarding the low educational status of Mexican Americans.

For parental narratives, my findings also indicate that perspectives on racial membership in the United States may shift across generations, which affects racial socialization. As some Mexican American parents may perceive that they will never be accepted as "Whites," especially relative to Mexican immigrant parents, they may come to see their status as racialized minorities and find it important to educate their children about racial inequality. Among Mexican American parents, racial socialization conveys that achieving upward mobility is possible by succeeding in school, despite the racial inequalities that their third-generation children may experience.

Scholars debate the extent to which generational differences matter in how Mexican Americans respond to negative school conditions. Some propose that the second generation may more effectively mobilize ethnicity to escape the potential disadvantages in schools (Gibson & Ogbu, 1991; Matute-Bianchi, 1986). However, others find that Mexican Americans, regardless of generational status, are negatively affected by racialized school practices (Telles & Ortiz, 2008; Valenzuela, 1999). My findings support research which shows that the racialized treatment of Mexican Americans in school leads to their low educational attainment. Notably, I find no generational differences in how Mexican Americans perceived and responded to their racialized treatment in high school. Furthermore, my findings substantiate the significance of educators' low expectations as evidence of racialized treatment toward Mexican Americans. Namely, educator messages regarding respondents' academic ability and worth negatively affected their academic engagement or whether they enrolled in college preparatory courses. Respondents also relied on school information to successfully transition to 4-year colleges, yet they perceived that schools failed to provide those college resources.

Therefore, I argue that racialized educator messages may be a key factor in explaining educational stagnation among Mexican Americans.

Studies comparing the racialized treatment of Mexican Americans in diverse and Latino schools remain scant. In diverse schools, scholars document how Mexican Americans are held to lower expectations compared to Asians and Whites (Conchas, 2006; Ochoa, 2013). In Latino schools, research demonstrates that cultural-deficit assumptions on the part of educators impede the academic achievement of Mexican American youth (Valenzuela, 1999). Unlike previous studies, my findings speak to the Mexican American experience at both diverse and Latino schools. Notably, I find that Mexican Americans confronted racialized treatment and were exposed to low expectations at both diverse and Latino schools. Mexican Americans in diverse schools were more likely to perceive *lower expectations* by educators, as they compared their negative treatment to that of Asian and White students. In contrast, Mexican Americans in Latino schools did not have non-Latino students with whom to compare their negative treatment and therefore were more likely to simply perceive *low expectations* by educators. Additionally, students from diverse schools perceived more negative treatment than those from Latino schools.

Sixty years after *Brown* (1954), the role of student racial composition in Latino school conditions remains in question, in terms of whether segregated or integrated schools have positive or negative effects on Latino students' schooling (Goldsmith, 2004, 2009; Orfield & Ee, 2014). Nonetheless, the message—unequal school conditions for minority youth relative to White youth—behind the *Brown* decision remains relevant for Mexican Americans. My findings demonstrate that Mexican Americans confronted low expectations whether they attended diverse or Latino institutions. Since the content of educator messages was similar at diverse and Latino schools, my findings suggest that dominant racial stereotypes, depicting Mexican Americans as less capable than Asians and Whites, are reproduced within schools. Therefore, racial stereotyping in the form of educators' low expectations may widen unequal school opportunities for Mexican Americans and Latinos at large, especially relative to their Asian and White counterparts (Goldsmith, 2004, 2009; Ochoa, 2013).

Limitations and Future Research

A remaining critical question is whether the content and effect of parental and educator messages among Mexican American community college students differ from those directed at students who did not graduate from high school, graduated from high school but did not attend college, or attended a 4-year college. Since community college students in the present study are somewhat selective compared to the many Mexican Americans who do not pursue higher education, it is imperative to examine the degree to which the content of parental and educator messages affects the educational experiences of Mexican Americans with different educational trajectories. This is key in specifying whether (1) parental or educator messages have more or less influence on the educational trajectories of Mexican Americans and (2) whether the racialized content and effect of educator messages substantiate a larger process of racialization for Mexican Americans in high school.

It is equally important that future research on educational stagnation among Mexican Americans compares how various demographic characteristics (e.g., gender, class, and phenotype) shape the content and effect of parental and educator messages. A comparative methodological approach will further inform how within-group differences among U.S.-born, Mexican-origin youth shape their educational attainment. Furthermore, interviews asked participants to address the significant influences from their family and school contexts that shaped their high school and college trajectories in retrospect. Subsequent research should examine the content and effect of parental and educator messages as Mexican Americans transition from high school to college. Additionally, since the interview sample was limited to the East Los Angeles Metropolitan Area, quantitative research should further explore the basis of educational stagnation by examining the frequency and types of educational messages among a larger sample of Mexican Americans.

Lastly, my findings indicate that schools with a diverse teaching staff, rather than student body, may reduce the reproduction of racial stereotypes in schools and thus better serve Mexican American/Latino students. Future research should compare how the racial composition of educators and students in high school influences the educational environment and trajectories of Latino youth. This is critical in specifying the school practices by which racial stereotypes are reproduced or challenged in the school system.

Conclusion

I have shown that generational differences in parental narratives inadequately account for educational stagnation among Mexican Americans. Furthermore, my findings substantiate the importance of racialized educator messages in high school that negatively affect Mexican Americans' educational experiences and trajectories. Therefore, I argue that educator messages are equally as or more important than parental narratives in shaping Mexican American educational incorporation. Given these findings, the present study has contributions for both assimilation and school segregation research. Since low expectations by educators exacerbated educational stagnation, assimilation research should be more attentive to how the schooling context shapes the educational incorporation of various racial and ethnic groups. Moreover, low expectations by educators signal the reproduction of the racial hierarchy in schools. School segregation research should further consider how racial discrimination and stereotyping operate in segregated and integrated schools, which in turn, may widen unequal school opportunities.

Acknowledgments   The author wishes to thank Armida Ornelas, Vilma Ortiz, Ariana J. Valle, Laura E. Enriquez, Karina Chavarria, Irene I. Vega, the Race and Immigration Research Group at UCLA, and the editors and anonymous reviewers for their valuable comments.

References

Alba, R., Abdel-Hady, D., Islam, T., & Marotz, K. (2011). Downward assimilation and Mexican Americans: An examination of intergenerational advance and stagnation in educational attainment. In M. Waters & R. Alba (Eds.), *The next generation: Immigrant youth in a comparative perspective* (pp. 95–109). New York: New York University Press.

Brown, A., & Lopez, M. H. (2013). *Mapping the Latino population, by state, county and city.* Washington, DC: Pew Research Center. Retrieved from Pew Hispanic Research Center website: http://www.pewresearch.org/hispanic.

Brown v. Board of Education of Topeka, 347 U.S. 483 (1954).

Burciaga, R., Pérez Huber, L., & Solórzano, D. (2010). Going back to the headwaters: Examining Latina/o educational attainment and achievement through a framework of hope. In E. Murillo, S. Villenas, R. Galván, J. Muñoz, C. Martínez, & M. Machado-Casas (Eds.), *Handbook of Latinos and education: Theory, research, and practice* (pp. 422–437). New York: Routledge.

Chavous, T. M., Bernat, D. H., Schmeelk Cone, K., Caldwell, C. H., Kohn Wood, L., & Zimmerman, M. A. (2003). Racial identity and academic attainment among African American adolescents. *Child Development, 74*(4), 1076–1090.

Conchas, G. Q. (2006). *The color of success: Race and high-achieving urban youth.* New York: Teachers College Press.

Covarrubias, Alejandro. (2011). Quantitative intersectionality: A critical race analysis of the Chicana/Chicano Educational Pipeline. *Journal of Latinos and Education, 10*(2), 86–105.

Current Population Survey. 2012. *Annual Social and Economic Supplement.* [Machine-readable datafile]. Washington, DC: United States Bureau of the Census.

Duncan, B., & Trejo, S. J. (2011). Intermarriage and the intergenerational transmission of ethnic identity and human capital for Mexican Americans. *Journal of Labor Economics, 29*(2), 195–227.

Frost, B. F. (2007). Texas students' college expectations: Does high school racial composition matter? *Sociology of Education, 80*(1), 43–65.

Gibson, M. A., & Ogbu, J. U. (1991). *Minority status and schooling: A comparative study of immigrant and involuntary minorities.* New York: Garland Publishing.

Glick, J. E., & White, M. J. (2004). Post-secondary school participation of immigrant and native youth: The role of familial resources and educational expectations. *Social Science Research, 33*(2), 272–299.

Goldsmith, P. R. (2004). Schools' racial mix, students' optimism, and the Black-White and Latino-White achievement gaps. *Sociology of Education, 77*(2), 121–147.

Goldsmith, P. R. (2009). Schools or neighborhoods or both? Race and ethnic segregation and educational attainment. *Social Forces, 87*(4), 1913–1941.

Hughes, D. (2003). Correlates of African American and Latino parents' messages to children about ethnicity and race: A comparative study of racial socialization. *American Journal of Community Psychology, 31*(1–2), 15–33.

Hughes, D., Rodriguez, J., Smith, E., Johnson, D., Stevenson, H. C., & Spicer, P. (2006). Parents' ethnic-racial socialization practices: a review of research and directions for future study. *Developmental Psychology, 42*(5), 747–767.

Huynh, V. W., & Fuligni, A. J. (2008). Ethnic socialization and the academic adjustment of adolescents from Mexican, Chinese, and European backgrounds. *Developmental Psychology, 44*(4), 1202–1208.

Kao, G., & Tienda, M. (1995). Optimism and achievement: The educational performance of immigrant youth. *Social Science Quarterly, 76*(1), 1–19.

Kao, G., & Tienda, M. (1998). Educational aspirations of minority youth. *American Journal of Education, 106*(3), 349–384.

Kasinitz, P., Mollenkopf, J. H., Waters, M. C., & Holdaway, J. (2009). *Inheriting the city: The children of immigrants come of age.* New York: Russell Sage Foundation.

Los Angeles Community College District. (2012). *Student enrollment by ethnicity Fall 1972-Fall 2012.* Los Angeles Community College District: Research and Statistics. Retrieved from http://research.laccd.edu/student-characteristics/enrollment-by-ethnicity.htm.

Louie, V. (2012). *Keeping the immigrant bargain: The costs and rewards of success in America.* New York: Russell Sage Foundation.

Lucas, S., & Gamoran, A. (2002). Tracking and the achievement gap. In J. Chubb & T. Loveless (Eds.), *Bridging the Achievement Gap* (pp. 171–198). Washington, DC: Brookings Institution Press.

Luttrell, W. (1997). *Schoolsmart and motherwise: Working-class women's identity and schooling.* New York: Routledge.

Marx, S. (2006). *Revealing the invisible: Confronting passive racism in teacher education.* New York: Routledge.

Matute-Bianchi, M. E. (1986). Ethnic identities and patterns of school success and failure among Mexican-descent and Japanese-American students in a California high school: An ethnographic analysis. *American Journal of Education, 95*(1), 233–255.

McKown, C., & Weinstein, R. S. (2008). Teacher expectations, classroom context, and the achievement gap. *Journal of School Psychology, 46*, 235–261.

Oakes, J. (2005). *Keeping track: How Schools Structure Inequality.* New Haven, CT: Yale University Press.

Ochoa, G. L. (2013). *Academic Profiling: Latinos, Asian Americans, and the achievement gap.* Minneapolis, MN: University of Minnesota Press.

Orfield, G., & Ee, J. (2014). *Segregating California's future: Inequality and its alternative 60 years after Brown v. Board of Education.* UCLA: The Civil Rights Project.

Pizarro, M. (2005). *Chicanas and Chicanos in school: Racial profiling, identity battles, and empowerment.* Austin, TX: University of Texas Press.

Qian, Z., & Blair, S. L. (1999). Racial/ethnic differences in educational aspirations of high school seniors. *Sociological Perspectives, 42*(4), 605–625.

Romo, H. (1984). The Mexican-origin populations differing perceptions of their childrens' schooling. *Social Science Quarterly, 65*(2), 635–650.

Smith, R. C. (2006). *Mexican New York: Transnational lives of new immigrants.* Berkeley, CA: University of California Press.

Stanton-Salazar, R. D. (2001). *Manufacturing hope and despair: The school and kin support networks of U.S.-Mexican youth.* New York: Teachers College Press.

Suárez-Orozco, M. M. (1989). *Central American refugees and US high schools: A psychosocial study of motivation and achievement.* Stanford, CA: Stanford University Press.

Telles, E. E., & Ortiz, V. (2008). *Generations of exclusion: Mexican-Americans, assimilation, and race.* New York: Russell Sage Foundation.

Tenenbaum, H. R., & Ruck, M. D. (2007). Are teachers' expectations different for racial minority than for European American students? A meta-analysis. *Journal of Educational Psychology, 99*(2), 253–273.

Valencia, R. R. (Ed.). (2002). *Chicano school failure and success: Past, present, and future.* New York: Routledge.

Valenzuela, A. (1999). *Subtractive schooling: US-Mexican youth and the politics of caring.* Albany, NY: SUNY Press.

"There's Nothing for Us Here": Black Families Navigating the School/Prison Nexus 60 Years After *Brown*

Lawrence T. Winn and Maisha T. Winn

In her groundbreaking historiography of African American families who partici-pated in the historic "Great Migration"—or the purposeful exodus of Black people from their homes in southern cities and towns to northern and western cities such as Chicago, Detroit, Milwaukee, Newark, New York, Philadelphia, Los Angeles, and Oakland—Wilkerson posits

> The people did not cross turnstiles of customs at Ellis Island. *They were already citizens* [our emphasis]. But where they came from, they were not treated as such (Wilkerson, 2010, p. 10).

Like immigrant families from outside the United States, millions of African Americans in the early part of the twentieth century began moving from the south to the north (Drake & Cayton, 1993). The U.S. Census Bureau noted that between 1910 and 1940, the Great Migration resulted in nearly 2 million Blacks leaving the south in search of opportunities. During the Great Migration, Blacks strategi-cally and purposefully sought more security and a new way of living for them-selves and their children. After the First World War and continuing throughout the 1970s, these families clung to dreams of owning property and more robust employment opportunities in a new land. Today, a new—yet smaller—migration

---

A version of this chapter was originally published as an article with the following citation: Winn, L. T., & Winn, M. T. (2015). Expectations and realities: Education, the discipline gap, and the experiences of Black families migrating to small cities. *Race and Social Problems, 7*(1), 73–83.

L.T. Winn (✉) · M.T. Winn
University of Wisconsin, Madison, WI, USA
e-mail: lawrence.winn@wisc.edu

M.T. Winn
e-mail: mtwinn@wisc.edu

© Springer International Publishing Switzerland 2016
P.A. Noguera et al. (eds.), *Race, Equity, and Education*,
DOI 10.1007/978-3-319-23772-5_12

245

is taking place for similar reasons. Big cities, like Chicago, Illinois that African American families once coveted as greener pastures during the Great Migration are now losing African American families—or fragments of families—to smaller cities like Madison, Wisconsin in search of safer neighborhoods, better jobs, and access to quality education for their children. These families are finding that this new environment does not always yield what they hoped, and this is especially true in the area of education. In the mid-1990s, Madison was considered "The New Promised Land" for many African Americans who migrated from Chicago (Mills, 1995); however, recent U.S. Census Bureau data demonstrates that people are leaving Madison and returning to Chicago for reasons that have not been well documented (Milewski, 2014).

As we reflect on the 60th anniversary of the historic *Brown versus Board of Education* ruling and consider the progress made in eliminating racial barriers, our ideas are informed by our phenomenological case study exploring the trajectories of working class and working poor African American families and youth participants in two community organizations who are part of the new migration from cities like Milwaukee and Chicago to Madison, Wisconsin, which boasts better public schools, more green spaces, less crime, and progressive politics. The purpose of this study is to understand how working class and working poor African American parents and youth from Chicago who moved to Madison, Wisconsin experience racial disparities—with particular attention to school discipline policies—in their new environment. Our objective is to understand the points of convergence as well as the tension between participants' expectations of their new city and the realities they experienced with specific focus on education and school discipline policies. These families relocated to Madison hoping to access a better education system, obtain quality employment, and live in safer communities. Using participant observation and qualitative interviews with members in a coalition of working class African American mothers and grandmothers, Making Our Mark (MOM), and a youth-centered collective of teenage males, The BOND,[1] we seek to understand the dreams and hopes participants carried from larger cities and the realities they experienced in their new environment. Our study is guided by the following questions:

- What are the experiences of African American working class families who migrate from large urban cities to small cities?
- In what ways do their experiences converge with and differ from their initial expectations?
- How do these new migrants navigate racial disparities in schools with particular attention to discipline policies?

We chose to focus on Madison, Wisconsin because we believe that much of the focus in education research can be "urbancentric"—that is, there is a great amount of attention on racial disparities in large cities, especially when considering school

---

[1]"MOM" and the "BOND" are pseudonyms.

reform (Calloway, 2014). However, racial disparities in nonurban communities can be equally as staggering as those found in large cities (Wisconsin Council on Children and Families, 2013). Such disparities can be found in education, criminal justice, healthcare, and the workforce. Yet, some African American families continue to receive messages that some smaller and seemingly quieter cities may yield more opportunities for their families. Like the men and women in Wilkerson's study, participants in this study also left neighborhoods and schools that were intensely policed and fraught with violence. However, they encountered symbolic violence in their new environment and in schools. And like families who partook in the Great Migration, the families in our study were presumably "already citizens" even though the treatment they received from whence they came and where they settled often told them otherwise. Citizenship was tenuous even in their new environment.

African American families in our study may not have endured the brunt of southern Jim Crow laws, but their lives have become entangled in what Alexander (2010) refers to as the "New Jim Crow." According to Alexander, mass incarceration in the United States has created a caste system in which African American males, in particular, are unable to participate as democratic citizens due to loss of rights from felony convictions resulting in probation, incarceration, and isolation. The culture of mass incarceration has seeped into public schools and into the lives of families in this study—families whose members are often viewed as potential public enemies (Kim, Losen, & Hewitt, 2010; Laura, 2014; Losen & Skiba, 2010; Meiners, 2007; Meiners & Winn, 2011; Nocella, Parmar & Stovall, 2014; Rios, 2011; Skiba, Michael, Nardo, & Peterson, 2002). This has been especially true for Black and Latino boys whose struggles in American public schools are well documented in education research (Fergus, Noguera, & Martin, 2014; Howard, 2013; Kunjufu, 1985; Noguera, 2009). Zero-tolerance policies, or policies "that may be accelerating student contact with law enforcement," have led to disproportionate numbers of African American, Latino, and Indigenous youth being pushed out of schools and communities (Skiba, 2014, p. 27). Participants in our study believed that they were removing their children and grandchildren from miseducation in the Chicago area public schools and neighborhood violence into a place where they might be viewed through a new lens of possibility. However, participants in our study are finding themselves enmeshed in the maze of zero-tolerance policies in a self-professed liberal and progressive city that is unsure how to be gracious to its new neighbors.

Ultimately, we argue that while progress has been made in eliminating racial barriers and expanding racial equality through education since the historic *Brown vs. Board of Education* ruling, much of the progress has been undermined by the systematic policing of Black and Latino families in schools and communities.

As equity-oriented scholars, we wish to move away from "damage centered" research that often omits stories of resilience and the success of working class and working poor communities (Tuck, 2009). Using a cultural-historical activity theory framework (CHAT), we seek to *historicize* (Gutierrez, 2008) and *humanize* (Paris & Winn, 2013) the lives of our participants by acknowledging and privileging the history of migration for African Americans as well as the ways in which

African Americans have continuously struggled to be viewed as citizens in the context of the United States. CHAT invites theory to be practiced by "situating theory in the present, sociopolitical, and cultural-historical contexts" (Stetsenko, 2014). CHAT, along with a "humanizing" approach to qualitative inquiry (Paris, 2011; Paris & Winn, 2013), guides our phenomenological case study methodology to seek out the agentive acts of African American working class and working poor communities including their desire to seek out coalitions that help them navigate racial disparities that impact their lives in schools and in out-of-school contexts.

Methods

Sites

We chose two neighborhood organizations in Madison, Wisconsin, in a working class and working poor community that is primarily African American. These organizations meet in community rooms in members' apartment complexes. Participants in both organizations are African Americans who have relocated or migrated from large cities—primarily Chicago—to Madison. The first working group, MOM, is a coalition of mothers and grandmothers who gather to discuss issues around housing and more recently healthcare; however, their conversations started to focus on the education of their children and grandchildren as well as their experiences navigating tensions for these young people and learning how to advocate on their behalf. The BOND is a collective of African American boys ages 14–18 who meet to discuss a range of topics from politics, history, and popular culture. In addition to meeting in the apartment complex community room, they have "field trips" throughout the city. Our interest in understanding how African Americans experience migration from large urban cities to small cities, along with recent policy reports on racial disparities in the state of Wisconsin—and Madison in particular—prompted our scholarly inquiry. Wisconsin ranked last (50th) in the United States for the well-being of African American children on indicators ranging from educational access to home life, in comparison to being ranked #10 for white children (Annie E. Casey Foundation, 2014). During the 2010–2011 academic year, only 50 % of Black high school students in Dane County—which houses Madison—graduated on time; 21 % of Black students were suspended from school compared to 2.3 % of the county's White students; and Black juveniles (ages 10–17) were arrested at a rate of 6 times that of White juveniles.

Participants

For the purpose of this study, we sought community nominations for parent perspectives. Lawrence T. Winn had access to community organizers because of his

Table 1 The BOND Participants

Name	Age	Grade level	City of origin
William	14	Middle School	Chicago
Kevin	14	Middle School	Chicago
Paul	14	High School	Chicago
Cedric	15	High School	Chicago
Chris	16	High School	Chicago
Eddie	16	High School	Chicago
Dave	16	High School	Chicago
Pryor	18	High School	Chicago
Chappelle	18	High School	Chicago

research on racial disparities in Dane County that resulted in a published report. Ms. Love, Ms. Ruby, and Ms. Yvette, who define themselves as mothers/grandmothers, were consistently nominated as "pillars" in the community. Lawrence T. Winn became a participant observer in the BOND in February 2013 and for the purpose of this study, selected the two participants, Pryor and Chappelle, who at age 18 had the most years of experience in Madison public schools. Table 1 shows the complete list of the BOND participants, their ages, grade levels, and city of origin. All of the MOM participants' children and grandchildren had been suspended at least once and all of the BOND participants had been suspended multiple times.

Data Collection

Lawrence T. Winn was a participant observer in the BOND and collected field notes at the weekly meetings from February 2013–February 2014. Maisha T. Winn attended the BOND meetings quarterly and also collected field notes. Because Lawrence T. Winn had more of a rapport with the youth in the BOND, he conducted qualitative interviews that were semi-structured with an open-ended protocol that invited narrative responses. All interviews were approximately 60 minutes in length and took place at community institutions or the community rooms in housing units. Maisha T. Winn attended MOM meetings and the both authors cofacilitated interviews with MOM participants. Documentary sources such as the Madison Metropolitan School District (MMSD) Code of Student Conduct (2014) as well as the District's Behavior Education Plan (approved in March 2014 with plans for implementation in September 2014) were collected and analyzed.

Data Analysis

All interviews were transcribed and analyzed for "significant statements" (Creswell, 2007; Moustakas, 1994). We used horizonalization to organize significant statements into themes. This process allowed us to generate a textual description of how participants experienced their lives in Madison with a specific focus on their transactions with schools and school discipline policies and practices. Additionally, we conducted a discourse analysis of the MMSD's outgoing Code of Student Conduct and incoming new Behavior Education Plan. More specifically, we used Gee's (2011) building task questions such as "How is this piece of language being used to make things significant or not and in what ways?" (significance); "What sort of relationship or relationships is this piece of language seeking to enact with others (present or not)?" (relationships); and "What perspective of social goods is the piece of language communicating (i.e., what is being communicated as to what is taken to be 'normal,' 'right,' 'good,' 'correct,' 'proper,' 'appropriate,' 'valuable,' 'the way things are,' 'the way things ought to be…') (politics)" (Gee, 2011, pp. 17–19).

School Discipline Policies in Madison

Here, we take time to explicate current policies around school discipline in MMSD and juxtapose them with new policies that seek to dismantle the relationship between schools and punishment. We offer this analysis because participants in our study experienced the frustration over how school discipline policies and practices have been mapped onto their voices and bodies. This is an effort to provide the context for how the lives of participants in our study often collided with schools.

On Monday, March 31, 2014, the MMSD Board approved the new superintendent's Behavior Education Plan (hereafter referred to as the BEP). The BEP will replace the "Classroom Code of Conduct and Student Conduct and Discipline Plan" (hereafter referred to as "The Code"). Prompted by data like the aforementioned reports on racial disparities in Dane County, the new Superintendent Jennifer Cheatham and her team sought to respond to zero-tolerance policies that disproportionately impacted African American children[2]. In The Code, 18 out of the 30 pages were devoted to "Behavior violations" organized from Level I to Level IV. Level I violations included "Behaviors that negatively affect the orderly operation of the learning environment," while Level IV focused on "Behaviors that significantly endanger the health or safety of others, damage property or cause serious disruption." For example, "throwing objects…or otherwise releasing any non-authorized object (including a snowball)" is considered a Level IV violation. Youth Court is also available in some of the schools to address offenses that take place beyond the school campus.

In an effort to respond to racial disparities in MMSD's schools, the District instituted Positive Behavioral Interventions and Support (PBIS) before data collection for this study. Restorative justice practices, which are alternative responses

---

[2]The Code preceded Cheatham's appointment.

to harm in which those who were harmed and those who caused harm are brought together to engage in consensus building in how to respond in a way that keeps both parties engaged, present, and active, were also introduced and implemented as part of a grant that the district awarded the local YWCA that counts "eliminating racism" in addition to "empowering women" as part of its mission. Through the grant, the YWCA trained students and staff persons in restorative practices and peacemaking/keeping circles to resolve conflicts between students and students and teachers. These circles could be used for offenses that did not involve weapons or drugs in lieu of suspensions and other forms of isolation.

While the language and certainly the structure of The Code lacked the discourse of restoration, it did hint at MMSD's efforts to begin including restorative practices as evidenced by the section entitled "Instruction. Intervention. Consequence. Restoration." Restorative practices were the last step in "consequences" and, therefore, not always used as a way to disrupt in school and out-of-school suspensions as much as they were used to re-engage youth who previously experienced removal and isolation. Restoration was nestled among "community service, making amends, actions to repair harm, mediation, circle/conference, youth court, fix it plan or restitution," but quite possibly lost its potential by being one of the last steps. In the BEP, there is a strategic and purposeful movement to use a restorative discourse or a discourse that acknowledges racial disparities in discipline and punishment in schools and communities, and voices a desire for a scenario whereby all students have an opportunity to be civic actors (Winn, 2013). Ideally, a restorative discourse would be supported by pedagogical practices. A restorative discourse requires a purposeful effort to keep all children in classrooms and school communities as opposed to seeing suspensions as an initial response to harm. This is particularly important because much of the language in zero-tolerance, which was certainly evident in The Code, is up for interpretation. Studies show that when a violation reads that a student's actions may "cause or seriously disrupt" learning, Black and Latino students' actions are more likely to be viewed as disruptive (Gregory, Skiba, & Noguera, 2010; Kim et al., 2010; Losen & Skiba, 2010; Meiners & Winn, 2011; Nocella, Parmar, & Stovall, 2014). Participants in our study, from whom you will hear in the next section—and the mothers/grandmothers in particular—always found the rationale for their children/grandchildren's suspensions to be ambiguous.

In the BEP, MMSD posits that this document is a "shift in philosophy and practice with respect to behavior and discipline..." that seeks to "focus on building student and staff skills and competencies." Later, the BEP asserts it was "designed to reflect a district commitment to student equity" citing "disturbing data" in national reports about who gets disciplined, for what, how much, and what is at stake for children who disproportionately experience punishment (MMSD, 2014). The BEP highlights three key factors in the data the school district consulted: (1) African American students with "particular disabilities" were more likely to experience discipline; (2) Students who experience suspensions often repeat grades; and (3) Suspensions and expulsions are often precursors to entering the juvenile justice system. Language in The BEP is proactive with statements like

"All students have the right to..."; "All parents/guardians have the right to..."; "All teachers/staff have the right to...", while intervention and discipline live side by side with restorative circles offered during "intensive intervention" or "short term removal responses," signaling the district's desire to make restorative practices one of the first responses as opposed to the last. These shifts are timely, yet it remains to be seen if the change in language will inspire a change in disposition, classroom culture, and overall school culture (Winn, 2014a, b). In the next sections, we explore data from parents and youth about their experiences with school discipline under "The Code."

"All Our Kids Are Getting Suspended": MOMS Navigating Schools

Ms. Love, Ms. Ruby, and Ms. Yvette organized working class and working poor African American mothers in their community informed by a model Ms. Love learned about at the U.S. Social Forum in Detroit in 2010. The organization, Making our Mark (MOM), first started discussing issues like problems with landlords and mold in apartments; however, during their gatherings the participants, according to Ms. Love, realized that "All our kids are getting suspended. Getting tickets. Getting diagnosed. I never heard of 'bipolar' until I moved to Madison." During our interview with Ms. Love she described why she left Chicago: "I came [to Madison from Chicago] to bond with my grandchildren." Her initial reaction to Madison was "It was like a little suburb," and she found it "cleaner, quieter, and smaller" than life in Chicago. Like Ms. Love, Ms. Ruby was also recognized in the African American working class neighborhood they moved to as a person one could count on because of her ability to access resources and resolve problems. She moved to Madison seeking a more peaceful life after trying Evanston, Illinois first. Both of these mothers/grandmothers followed adult children to Madison and became their grandchildren's advocates while their adult children worked long hours. Initially, Ms. Ruby was excited that her grandchildren would attend schools in Madison where the reputation for public education was very strong. According to Ms. Ruby,

> [African Americans] are told that the school's system is great: 'It is such a great school system.' It is better than some of the schools in Chicago or in Milwaukee—true enough, I am sure—but it is not that great that I can shout over it.

Ms. Yvette distinguished herself by describing her move from Chicago to Madison as, "I didn't come here wanting." Ms. Yvette had a home she inherited from her grandfather on the South side of Chicago; however, over time she witnessed the neighborhood deteriorating. In the late 1980s, Ms. Yvette's mother moved to Madison from Chicago and she brought her children to visit their grandmother. Ms. Yvette recalled her children's enthusiasm about Madison:

I seen how [my kids] was able to play and it was nice. And it was on Moses Street.[3] My kids said, 'Mom, we should move here. We should move here.' I didn't move here until 1999. Me and the kids and my sister and her kids…we stayed.

While Ms. Yvette was reluctant to leave her home in Chicago, she thought Madison was "a nice place to live because the apartments were more modern than the apartments in the city." Ms. Yvette also thought Madison was esthetically more beautiful: "I seen how green the grass was here and it was like a whole total, different environment, and I decided to make that change."

One of the first issues Ms. Love and Ms. Ruby encountered was that their children and grandchildren were categorized as struggling learners in the context of their new school district. For example, Ms. Love posited that her daughter was "advanced" in Chicago schools prior to arriving in Madison and "never in trouble." However, when Ms. Love's daughter entered Madison public schools in the fifth grade she kept getting sent to the "time-out" room. "That's not a good place… that's not a place for my daughter," Ms. Love asserted as she revisited her conversation with the elementary school principal. Ms. Love made the point that how she experienced her daughter at home and what the school told her about her daughter's behavior were "two different stories." Her daughter maintained that she was being held to a different standard than "other" children. Ms. Love explained to the principal: "My daughter sees how you treat other children…you checked her off without telling me about it." Ms. Ruby faced similar issues in her grandchildren's schools in Madison. She argued that suddenly the teachers and administrators were seemingly unaware as to how to build relationships with African American students:

Ms. Ruby: Now one of my grandsons had problems with his middle school; as a matter of fact a couple of my granddaughters had the same problems with the same principal… It is like she does not know how to deal with us African Americans. It seems like she will give another person a break but not our kids. She will not give them a break because they should know better. And I do not understand that. If [Black children] should know better then why should [white children] not know better?

Unlike Ms. Love, Ms. Ruby asserted that the principal was possibly "racist." Ms. Love never mentioned the words "racism" or "racist" at any point during her interview. She simply conveyed that she worked harder at trying to understand the school district's practices so she could support her daughter. For example, Ms. Love could see that the school was determined to get her to seek out a psychologist for her daughter because they thought she had Attention Deficit Hyperactivity Disorder or ADHD:

Ms. Love: I said okay. We goin' to do what you asked us to do…the principal said that when my daughter was in the fifth grade they saw AD or A-something.

Interviewer: ADHD?

Ms. Love: We tried them pills and they didn't work. All they did was make her sleepy. We went to the doctor and there wasn't anything wrong with her.

---

[3]Moses Street is a pseudonym for a street largely associated with working class and working poor African American and Latino families.

Between the fifth and eighth grades, Ms. Love's daughter was suspended twice for nonviolent- and nondrug-related incidents, and after the second suspension Ms. Love was informed that her daughter would be expelled. Ms. Love hypothesized that the school had to rescind their decision to expel her daughter because their decision was not supported by any of the school district's policies. She also expressed that she thought the school was surprised that she took the time to call the district office. The second key issue that MOM participants faced was the schools telling them their children and grandchildren had ADHD. While Ms. Yvette maintained that her children did well in the schools and had "caring" teachers, she believed that "things changed" once her grandchildren entered the system:

Ms. Yvette: When my kids started the teachers were caring but now I have grandkids. One of my grandson[s] goes to one of the middle schools and it's totally different. Like, for example, they wanted to expel him because of his behavior problem and they said only in one class he had problems. When my grandkids have problems at school it's not just a parent meeting. It's a parent and grandma meeting. I come. I get involved. The school calls me and I go. I went and had a meeting and I said, 'Out of all the classes he has, why is it that this class he has a problem with?' I asked my grandson, 'What is it? You don't like the teacher?' 'No, grandma,' he said, 'That's not it. You can't think in that class and the teacher don't stop people from bothering you and the teacher tells you to deal with it…so I try to deal with it and then I get in trouble.' I told the principal, 'Is there any way you can give me a list of his classes and how many students are in those classes?' Come to find out…that class had over 25 students and the teacher was new so I think that's a lot of the reasons why it's different from the days when I moved here, and the kids can't function.

Ms. Yvette challenged the school by reaching out to the school district office. According to Ms. Yvette, once she reached out the school district office the principal could "suddenly hear her" and invited her to talk about her grandson again. Together they worked out a plan of action that did not unfairly put the onus on her grandson who was being recommended for special education classes. Ms. Yvette made it a point to address what she viewed as an eagerness on behalf of the school system to recommend Ritalin. "And [an]other thing…here in Madison, they want to put the kids on Ritalin," Ms. Yvette posited. "You know, if kids are not sitting down or if kids not minding you then they have a problem. You know? ADHD. But they don't know a lot of kids can't function with a lot of noise." Racial disparities in special education are well documented (Harry & Klingner, 2006); additionally, there is data supporting the assertion that most children who experience suspensions, expulsions, and other forms of isolation are in special education (U.S. Department of Education, 2014). Ms. Ruby encountered similar dispositions at her grandchildren's schools and theorized that the schools believed all African American children had ADHD:

Ms. Ruby: When [my grandson] was in middle school, [the school] had a crazy way of dealing with things. You *know* [African American children] all have ADHD—so they think. I don't think either of my grand kids have ADHD but that was what the school has diagnosed them as [having]. They would just let [my grandson] walk out [of] class if he felt overwhelmed or felt like he needed to take a walk he could just walk out of class and take a walk. No! You don't give him any other privileges than any other child. He is not special…and he is not learning. I don't know if you are afraid of him or think he going to go off or what it is you know but treat him just like you treat everybody else.

The only time Ms. Love referenced racism or disparities was in her retelling of an incident that involved a white male student who hit her daughter with a football. When her daughter retaliated, the school said she "damaged" him and it was a "Level IV offense" under the Code of Student Conduct. Ms. Love's tactical goal, now that her daughter is 15 and in a high school, is to be present at the school ("I'm up at the school. I'm on my point") and make unannounced visits. After fighting to get one of her grandsons in a "much better school" in the district, Ms. Ruby found herself in the same scenario as in his previous school. She was told that her grandson had ADHD and needed a formal diagnosis from a doctor. Again, her grandson was being disinvited from the classroom and encouraged to walk around to "get some air he needs" when what he really needed, according to Ms. Ruby, was to be in class learning like his peers. Ms. Ruby was gravely concerned that the schools promoted the practice of isolation and removal. In her two grandsons' cases, teachers gave them the option to "take a walk," which was equally as disruptive to their learning as an imposed dismissal by a teacher. Ms. Ruby started receiving more calls from the schools and her grandchildren were being suspended multiple times largely due to their "attitude":

> Ms. Ruby: [The suspensions are] always because of attitude or something he said or done… always. And to me it never makes sense whatever it is. The majority of time it never makes sense. And then when you go to them to ask them about it they can't give you a reason that makes sense. They will show you something in [The Code] and will say, 'The discipline code says that.' But it also says dot dot but you forgot to read the whole sentence. Okay? I can read and I will read. They don't know how to talk to some of the parents I don't think. They try to treat them inferior. I know that I am not inferior to any of them…They did not expect me to go to the school or they did not expect for me call them back. And then when I really got to know them and they found what capacity I was working in—Oh, that was really a shock. Oh, what I am I suppose to be doing? Because I am the grandmother I should be sitting at home fiddling my thumbs I guess.

Ms. Ruby was aware that the school could have possibly stereotyped her in various ways; first, the school personnel seemed to be surprised that she was working in a leadership capacity as opposed to being a stay home grandmother "fiddling" her thumbs. Next, she felt the school personnel underestimated how far she would go to understand school policy. Referencing the outgoing Code of Student Conduct, Ms. Ruby found that teachers often referred parents—especially parents of African American children—to this document when their children were being punished for particular behaviors and that the mere referral to The Code would end the conversation. For Ms. Ruby, referencing school policies only started the conversation because not only did she read the policy, but also she interrogated the text and reminded teachers and administrators of their responsibilities. One of the prevailing issues with school discipline policies under the zero-tolerance regime is the arbitrariness of what is considered "disruptive" or *who* is considered disruptive.

Many parents and guardians as well as the students themselves walk away from disciplinary hearings or punishments with the same feeling that Ms. Ruby encountered. Ms. Ruby took on her grandchildren's education with great passion because she knew how hard and how much their parents were working and the sheer amount of phone time and meetings at the schools would result in missed wages. These mothers/grandmothers contrasted in that Ms. Love focused on how to navigate the system, while Ms. Ruby had ideas about how the schools could be strengthened.

When asked what suggestions she had for addressing the miscommunication between the schools and families, Ms. Ruby began to talk about the need for more African American teachers. According to Ms. Ruby, if the district had more African American teachers, there would be an opportunity for parents, guardians, and students to have allies at the school:

> Ms. Ruby: I think there needs to be more African American teachers. Because hopefully they will [better] understand where a child is coming from than the teachers that they have now. [Some teachers] don't think what the problem might be and [they] just judge and don't know what [they] are judging or why…I just think [teachers] should understand the kids more…how to talk [to them]…how to treat them. They don't even have African American history. How can you not have African American history? I don't understand that. How are they suppose know where they came from?

In many ways, Ms. Ruby alluded to the thought that perhaps if there were more African American teachers she could rule out institutional racism and the targeting of African American children in schools for disciplinary and exclusionary practices. While Ms. Ruby critiqued the white teachers for treating African American children like "delicate flowers" who would wither if one pushed too much, she imagined African American teachers as being more sympathetic and investigative, as learning what may have been impacting students outside of school as well as in school, and as supporting students in moving forward. In what seemed like a brief moment of surrender, Ms. Ruby summarized the experience as "this is what they do here." Ms. Ruby credited this new environment for her grandchildren's learning ("They do learn"); speaking ("They talk better"); and calm disposition ("Their attitude is different"). Ultimately, Ms. Ruby believed that some of the schools were better than many in large districts; however, she was not completely convinced. Ms. Yvette believed that both the community and the schools were equally responsible for the problems and the solutions:

> Ms. Yvette: Not only do the school system fail but some of our parents fail their kids. As far as the school system, they need to break down the classroom size and bring more social services in the schools, have more one-on-ones, just don't label no one. Have psychotherapy. You know what I'm saying? When you take care of a child try to take care of every aspect to grab this child. You know what I'm saying? So until we have that…A child just don't be born with problems! So until we grasp that, until we have teachers that care, until we have time to say, 'I noticed you had an attitude this morning. Do you want to talk about it?' How can you see a child coming into your class 6 or 7 months and you don't see a difference? Until we start or until they put teachers in that care—and you should be able to identify what's going on with your students—if they doing good in this class why are they not doing good in the other class? Grown ups need to intervene. And

a lot of white teachers don't have time. They think that's the kids' dialect. No! You tell them, 'Watch your mouth up in here.' And get control of your classroom. These kids are out of control.

Similar to the other mothers, Ms. Yvette wanted teachers to be consistent with their expectations from both Black and white students. Ms. Yvette believed that the teachers should clarify these expectations while exhibiting an ethic of care. While working class and working poor parents are often characterized as not caring about what happens in schools or invisible when it comes to parent participation, the mothers/grandmothers in MOM offer a different view of parent involvement and engagement. In the next section, we turn to the perspectives of Black youth who migrated with their families from Chicago to Madison, from the big city to the small city.

"There's Nothing Here for Us": Youth Navigating Schools

BOND members Pryor and Chappelle both moved to Madison from Chicago and spoke candidly about their lives in Madison. Both boys were the only two BOND members who were bussed from their neighborhood to attend a high school in an affluent community that was a popular location for university faculty's children to attend. Pryor agreed with most of his peers in The BOND and mothers in MOM that Madison was "safer" than Chicago:

Pryor: It is safer here but the police stay on you. The west side of Madison used to be a lot worse but I could still go outside and play. Not in Chicago. But in Chicago you get more love because there are more black teachers. Black teachers can relate to us. It seems like more opportunities out here but not really because they make it hard. You need an ID for everything. Blacks from Madison also act funny. Act like they don't want us to be here.

The notion of safety for Pryor focused on explicit dangers such as gun violence and gang rivalry. However, embedded in his assessment was the notion that there were other significant changes such as lack of opportunities and the absence of Black teachers who could "relate" to Black students. Acknowledging Madison's opportunities, Pryor asserted that identification was needed, signaling a particular kind of system that had to be navigated with social capital and preplanning. Youth could not merely walk into a center and expect to engage in activities. Pryor also experienced isolation from Blacks born and raised in Madison and believed that they did not want Blacks from Chicago in their city.

Chappelle had a slightly different perspective than Pryor; he argued that Madison was essentially the same as Chicago:

Chappelle: Nothing is different from Chicago. Same thing. Since Madison is smaller, it is easier to get into trouble. You get into trouble over the littlest thing. Chicago is way bigger. Chicago had more rec centers that stayed open later and open to all. You could hang out there and avoid trouble and messing around. Here you have to pay fees and get memberships like at the YMCA.

Both Pryor and Chappelle underscored the perks of big cities—more anonymity and more activities for youth around the clock. Again, the notion of membership was invoked in Chappelle's interview. He argued that there were fewer options for himself and his peers, which often resulted in them "get[ting] into trouble for the littlest thing." Chappelle echoed Pryor's acknowledgement of Chicago teachers:

> Chappelle: The schools in Chicago were better cause the teachers cared about us and treat us like kids. There were more black teachers…They taught us life skills. Black teachers in Chicago cared about us. They stayed on you and helped you along the way. They tell you when you are behind before it is too late and you can't pass.

Contrary to the negative press Chicago Public School (CPS) teachers endured, the BOND members recalled their teachers and experiences in CPS with fondness and—we would argue—longing. The need to inform a student "when you are behind before it is too late and you can't pass" seemed obvious, but it was not Chappelle's experience in his new city:

> Chappelle: White teachers don't care. They let you get behind. They don't teach anything engaging or interesting. They want you to act like them.
>
> Interviewer: What do you mean?
>
> Chappelle: They want you to act white! Not me because I do me.
>
> Interviewer: What about the black teachers in Madison?
>
> Chappelle: There were no black teachers at Beacon High School[4]. Not even black janitors.

Reflective of America's teaching force, Madison's teaching force is largely white and female. In her seminal study of successful teachers of African American students, Ladson-Billings (1994) posits that teachers do not have to share students' cultural and ethnic heritage to provide academically rigorous learning opportunities for students; however, they should practice culturally relevant pedagogical practices (Ladson-Billings, 1995). Most recently, Paris (2012) argues for culturally sustaining pedagogies to support the democratic engagement of multiethnic and multilingual youth in schools. Chappelle's observation that his teachers in Chicago taught "life skills" mirrors historiographies of segregated schools in the south that served African American children. Siddle-Walker (1996) argues that African American teachers in segregated schools set high expectations for their students and it was these expectations that drove academic success in spite of being in substandard facilities. Conversely, Chappelle saw his white teachers' interests in him as being conditional because their primary concern, according to Chappelle, is that Black students act "like them" or "act white." Chappelle's declaration "I do me" was an affirmation of his self-worth as well as a challenge to the notion that he had to change the core of his identity in order to receive the education that he was entitled to in American public schools.

We observed that the interview protocol asked about "experiences living in Madison," and both Pryor and Chappelle started discussing schooling and

---

[4]All school names are pseudonyms.

education. When asked to discuss "problems Black youth face in Madison," Pryor invoked school again. According to Pryor, the primary issues for himself and his peers were "nothing to do" and "police." He continued his concern that Blacks who were established in Madison were ashamed of the Black youth from urban cities:

> Pryor: A staff member at Beacon High School said, 'You little black kids don't learn-we don't want y'all here.' We don't act like them and I'm not trying to fit in like them. [Blacks who move here join] gangs because there ain't nothing to do. We need something outside of the box beside basketball. Teach me how to build something. I like building, I want to learn construction work.

Pryor implied that Black youth were often confined to a monolithic vision of hoop dreams and if they had any place in the school it was on the basketball team; however, he had other desires. Sadly, joining gangs had become a pastime for some youth as it gave them "something to do." During one of the BOND sessions, members were asked if they had experienced suspensions. All of the boys' hands went up that evening and then they asked a barrage of questions: "Do you mean recently?" "You mean beginning in elementary school?" "This school year only?" Their questions blindsided the adult facilitators in the room because the nature of the follow-up questions indicated that not only had every boy around that table experienced suspension, but also they had been suspended multiple times. It was often difficult for them to explain why they were suspended because their actions were not straightforward offenses like drugs or weapons but instead involved speaking out of turn or being "disruptive" in class. Pryor was forthcoming about being suspended:

> Pryor: I moved here in 6th grade. I was suspended from eighth grade about 24 times. I was suppose to go to the private school for high school but the teacher suspended me for nothing so I could not attend. There were no black teachers at Beacon. I was not learning nothing interesting or new. I learn more from the streets. The white kids were cool but they don't know.

Chappelle argued that the monolithic depiction of Black youth as disruptive was visible in school and off campus:

> Chappelle: [People in Madison] always think we are up to something no good. Most of the time they might be right but still they can't stay on us for no reason. Also, there is nothing to do unless you get into trouble. Kids ride the bus for fun and get into trouble. Also discrimination. Whites don't want us here. Like, my first day in Madison a white man said you are from Chicago uh? The way he said it and for him to say it was not cool. They don't want us here in Madison.

Like Pryor, Chappelle also felt as if Black youth were expected to change their personality and behavior in order for them to be considered citizens. Chappelle posited that Black youth from Madison had been taught "their" ways, or White ways, which helped them fit in more and, from his vantage point, secured their citizenship:

Chappelle: If you don't act like them you can't succeed in school.

Interviewer: Who are them?

Chappelle: White people. Black kids raised here are taught their ways. So they alright.

Chappelle did eventually get the Black teacher he hoped for in "night school"; since he was not on track for graduation, he had to enroll in an alternative program:

Chappelle: I am taking night classes. Now I have a Black teacher. Why now? Why night school I get a Black teacher?

Interviewer: What is he/she like?

Chappelle: I like her because she is teaching me interesting things like street law. That makes it interesting. It's real life.

While the struggle for the youth looks different from the struggle for the parents, grandparents, and guardians, Pryor and Chappelle provide evidence that it can be complicated—at best—for migrant youth to negotiate their learning experiences. These youth feel the push and pull of being in a place that does not have the same kind of life-threatening dangers, yet they do not feel safe in the very place that is supposed to treat them with equity and an ethic of care that should not be reserved for particular kinds of youth. Safety in this context is debatable, as is who gets counted as worthy of being protected.

Community Youth Organizations: Creating Opportunities for Suspended Youth

When schools "push out" youth—either by suspension policies or teaching curriculum that is not "engaging or interesting"—community-based youth organizations often provide safe places for youth to be productive (Baldridge, Hill, & Davis, 2011). The BOND is an example of one of these community-based youth organizations that help Black youth who migrated to Madison and encountered challenges in the schools navigate their new city. The BOND is one of the few places where the youth can voice their opinions, participate in workshops, collaborate on projects, and learn their civil and legal rights. On any given session, fifteen to twenty youth along with several adult mentors discuss topics such as "Money or Power?" "Black Youth and the Police," "Being Wealthy and Being Rich," "The word Nigger and Nigga," "Why aren't there any Black teachers?" "Education and Careers," and "Allen Iverson or Derrick Rose?" Although many of the youth access much of their information through social media and the Internet because schools "don't teach anything engaging or interesting" (Chappelle) and "don't have any black teachers who can relate" (Pryor), the majority of the youth sense a disconnection from the rest of "mainstream" society. As suggested by

Pryor that "it seems like more opportunities out here but not really because they make it hard…you need an ID for everything," BOND members are aware of the limitations to resources and opportunities. Many of the opportunities (internships, mentoring professionals, cultural activities, etc.) afforded to youth in neighboring communities—often white and middle class—are not made available or easily accessible to Black youth such as the members of The BOND. This lack of opportunities leads to a racial gap in social capital for black youth—in particular, those who live in isolated communities and are suspended from school.

In February 2014, The BOND conducted a survey to learn more about its youths' educational and career aspirations. The survey categories included community, relationships, education and careers, leadership, and cultural activities. Seventeen youth filled out the survey. The findings show that there is an opportunity and exposure gap for Black youth. For example, when asked whether "I have personally met and learned about the work of the following: doctor, lawyer, or scientist," survey respondents revealed that 4 out of 17 participants have met and learned about the work of a doctor; 3 out of 17 participants have met and learned about the work of a lawyer; and 0 out of 17 participants have met and learned about the work of a scientist. Chappelle said that the only reason he met a lawyer was because he "had to go downtown to juvey [juvenile justice center]." Many of the youth said that they never met a black lawyer, doctor, or scientist. When asked the question of whether they attended or visited an educational or cultural space outside of their community in the past year, survey respondents revealed that 0 out of 17 youth attended a live performance; 2 out of 17 youth visited a museum; 6 out of 17 youth visited the library; 2 out of 17 youth visited an art gallery exhibit; and 4 out of 17 youth toured a university. What is striking about this data is that only 4 of the 17 youth visited a university when the University of Wisconsin, Madison is less than 5 miles and 10 minutes from the location of the BOND meetings and where many of the youth reside.

The BOND has used this data to increase opportunities for its youth and to expose the youth to cultural activities, educational programs, and professionals outside of their community. With a grant from the City of Madison's Emerging Opportunities Program, lawyers, professors, and scientists have led workshops, and the youth have attended live performances, visited the public library, and toured the University of Wisconsin, Madison several times. During one recent trip to the UW, Madison, Chappelle and Pryor attended a seminar featuring one of the leading scholars in urban education. Faculty, graduate students, and local teachers participated in the discussion. Throughout the seminar, the featured scholar asked Pryor and Chappelle for their opinions about teacher instruction, suspension policies, and classroom learning environments. After the seminar, Pryor said "If I had a teacher like him, I would love school." Chappelle responded "Man, that was fun." This was Chappelle and Pryor's fourth time on campus in the past six months. The BOND is teaching its youth strategies to navigate spaces of "whiteness" and to "decode the system" (Stanton-Salazar, 1997) in a liberal and progressive city and introducing them to spaces where social capital is exchanged.

Discussion

So what do these stories from working class African American families who migrated from one large city to a small city tell us about their hopes, dreams, experiences, and discoveries? And how can we use these stories to think about revisiting school discipline policies and practices that continue to isolate particular youth? What can we learn from these lived experiences that can help us achieve the equality for all students that was intended in the *Brown v. Board of Education* historic ruling? In these stories are themes of desire—not a static notion of desire but one that is fluid and liberating. As Tuck (2010) offers, desire can be "smart" and "agentive." From the mothers'/grandmothers' perspectives, this new migration for working class African American families was a strategic effort to access high-quality education for their children and grandchildren and high quality of life. Ms. Love, Ms. Ruby, and Ms. Yvette imagined their roles as supporting their adult children in their parenting efforts. However, as Ms. Love, Ms. Ruby, and Ms. Yvette became increasingly involved with the schools and experienced racial disparities in discipline policies and practices, they were motivated to find ways to reclaim the rights of Black children in school contexts. As they collected their own data, they became more critical of the policies and their new city that was originally characterized as having the best of everything and definitely being "better than" Chicago. Ms. Love, Ms. Ruby, and Ms. Yvette asserted their citizenship and their rights as parents, grandparents, and community organizers. Ms. Love, Ms. Ruby, and Ms. Yvette dismantle stereotypes about African American parents—and single parenting in particular—and their reported stories demonstrate involvement in the schools and a keen interest in the academic experiences of their children and grandchildren. However, there is a mismatch in values and expectations that is vast and not easily bridged. One of the recurring tensions was that mothers/grandmothers did not want their children/grandchildren taking walks, getting fresh air, or missing classroom instruction. They viewed this as a form of isolation and implicit bias against their students.

Pryor and Chappelle detailed this mismatch in their narratives of their lives in schools and beyond. As consummate outsiders they felt their options and opportunities were limited. They could either be like their White teachers, and Black students who received a stamp of approval from White teachers, or live in a monolithic box of what it meant to be Black as well as what it meant to be an outsider from the big city. We wish to underscore that Pryor and Chappelle did not view education or being educated as synonymous with whiteness; they are Black youth who wanted to be themselves *and* be viewed as worthy citizens in their schools and communities. They did, however, feel that in order to receive the education they needed to be successful, they would have to take on personalities, dispositions, and practices that they believed to be "white." To be sure, when both Pryor and Chappelle were asked, "What strategies, skills or resources are necessary to ensure that you or other African American youth have opportunities after high school?" Chappelle responded, "Be friendly. Fit in with the whites. You can't be you. [But] I will always be me. I am not going to fit in." Pryor had a similar response: "Be white. White is right. Be a good faker. They won't accept you for who you are." While these reflections can be characterized as being resistant to school and education, we posit that these youth are identifying tensions that are evident in the well-documented experiences of minoritized youth in American public schools.

These youth and their families are negotiating past and present realities in their new environment. By moving from a big city to a small city environment, participants engaging in this new migration held the belief they would find better homes, schools, and quieter lives. While participants in our study did feel safer from the threat of physical violence, they had not imagined the struggle that would ensue in the education system that presented a symbolic violence in the form of suspensions, expulsions, and other forms of isolation. In a progressive move, MMSD is responding to local and national racial disparities in school discipline policies and practices in their implementation of the aforementioned Behavior Education Plan (BEP). The BEP requires teachers to keep students in the classroom for incidents that in the past were addressed with referrals and sending students out. In the BEP, restorative practices will be implemented early and often, including restorative conversations that will make an effort to reach youth prior to tensions rising or acts of harm being committed. In American public schools, most of the students causing harm have actually been harmed by the infrastructure of schooling. It is possible that through restorative conversations—that is conversations that are focused on "why" particular choices were made, the context for the choices made, and next steps for accountability—youth, their families, teachers, and administrators will actually take time to listen to each other.

West Oakland, California, and Alameda County have documented their use of restorative justice in schools and the ways in which they use this practice to resist zero-tolerance policies that have negatively impacted minoritized youth (Kidde & Alfred 2011; Sumner, Silverman, & Frampton 2010). A key factor in these two cases that can inform the work in Madison is the way schools in West Oakland and Alameda County utilize families in the process of supporting youth in being accountable for their actions and fostering a desire to be a part of the classroom and school communities. A case study in Cole Middle School in West Oakland found that suspension declined by 87 % with the implementation of restorative justice practices. This case study, which included participant observation, open-ended interviews, a questionnaire, and data from the Oakland Unified School District, found that "school-based restorative justice" should be "grounded in the norms, values, and culture of the students, school, and community" (Sumner et al. 2010, p. 3). Parents and guardians in this study indicated that they were made aware of concerns with their children early in the process, thus giving families an opportunity to create a community response that supported students. In Alameda County, a collective of stakeholders including their School Health Services (SHS) and a nonprofit organization, Restorative Justice for Oakland Youth (RJOY), partnered in creating a guide for educators working with youth in classrooms and outside of classrooms including "intervention circles"; "peer juries"; and "restorative conferencing"

(Kidde & Alfred, 2011, p. 13). In both studies, families are a key component of working with students to develop solutions and create a system of accountability.

Teacher education and teacher educators are essential to disrupting the short-comings of policies after *Brown v. Board of Education.* Confronting racism and racial bias in responding to student behaviors is complicated work that has to be embedded in the training of future teachers. With so many policy changes in schools, teachers often feel as if one more task is being added to their full plates. In order to achieve equity for all students, teachers need support to do this work. Elsewhere, Winn argues for a "Restorative English Education" and ulti-mately a "Restorative Teacher Education" (Winn, 2013). In a Restorative Teacher Education, pre-service teachers learn how to use their curricular powers to keep their students present, engaged, and willing participants in classroom communi-ties. A Restorative Teacher Education invites teachers across content areas to inte-grate restorative practices into their content area by selecting readings, required experiences, activities, and other culturally *sustaining* (Paris, 2012) practices that use students' "funds of identity" (Esteban-Guitart & Moll, 2014) to foster a rig-orous academic setting. In sum, teachers would leave their preparation programs with restorative dispositions or a mindset that sending students out for incidents that do not involve violence or drugs is not an option. Addressing this work in teacher preparation programs is a long-term solution that can take some of the pressure off school systems to find time for teachers to be trained.

References

Alexander, M. (2010). *The new jim crow: Mass incarceration in the age of colorblindness.* New York: The New Press.

Annie E. Casey Foundation. (2014). *Race for results: Building a path to opportunity for all chil-dren.* Baltimore. Retrieved from http://www.aecf.org.

Baldridge, B. J., Hill, M. L., & Davis, J. E. (2011). New possibilities: (Re)engaging black male youth within community-based educational spaces. *Race Ethnicity and Education, 14*(1), 121–136.

Calloway, C. G. (2014). *Race, rural education and relationship to "the urban": A selective lit-erature review of rural education.* An unpublished manuscript for Education Policy 911, University of Wisconsin-Madison.

Creswell, J. W. (2007). *Qualitative inquiry and research design: Choosing among five approaches.* Thousand Oaks: Sage.

Drake, S., & Cayton, H. R. (1993). *Black metropolis: A study of negro life in a northern city.* Chicago: University of Chicago Press.

Esteban-Guitart, M., & Moll, L. C. (2014). Lived experience, funds of identity and education. *Culture and Psychology, 20*(1), 70–81.

Fergus, E., Noguera, P., & Martin, M. (2014). *Schooling for resilience: Improving the life trajec-tory of Black and Latino Boys.* Cambridge: Harvard Education Press.

Gee, J. P. (2011). *An introduction to discourse analysis: Theory and method* (3rd ed.). New York and London: Routledge.

Gregory, A., Skiba, R., & Noguera, P. A. (2010). The achievement gap and the discipline gap: Two sides of the same coin? *Educational Researcher, 39*(1), 59–68.

Gutierrez, K. (2008). Developing a sociocritical literacy in the third space. *Reading Research Quarterly, 43*(2), 148–164.

Harry, B., & Klingner, J. K. (2006). *Why are so many minority students in special education?*. New York: Teachers College Press.

Howard, T. (2013). *Black Male(d): Peril and promise in the education of African American males*. New York: Teachers College Press.

Kidde, J., & Alfred, R. (2011). Restorative justice: A working guide for our schools. Alameda County. Alameda County School Health Services Coalition. Retrieved November 9, 2014 from http://healthyschoolsandcommunities.org/Docs/Restorative-Justice-Paper.pdf.

Kim, C., Losen, D., & Hewitt, D. (2010). *The school-to-prison pipeline: Structuring legal reform*. New York: New York University Press.

Kunjufu, J. (1985). *Countering the conspiracy to destroy black boys* (Vol. 1). African American Images.

Ladson-Billings, G. (1995). Toward a theory of culturally relevant pedagogy. *American Educational Research Journal, 32*(3), 465–491.

Ladson-Billings, G. (1994). *The Dreamkeepers: Successful teachers of African American children*. San Francisco: Jossey-Bass.

Laura, C. (2014). *Being bad: My brother and the school-to-prison pipeline*. New York: Teachers College Press.

Losen, D. J., & Skiba, R. J. (2010). Suspended Education: Urban middle schools in crisis. The Civil Rights Project/Proyecto Derechos Civiles. Retrieved June 24, 2014 from http://escholarship.org/uc/item/8fh0s5dv.

Madison Metropolitan School District (2014). *Behavior Education plan for middle and high school students*. Retrieved June 24, 2014 from https://legalsvcweb.madison.k12.wi.us/files/legalsvc/secondary%20code%20-%20web.pdf.

Meiners, E. R., & Winn, M. T. (2011). *Education and Incarceration*. New York and London: Routledge.

Meiners, E. R. (2007). *Right to be hostile: Schools, prisons, and the making of public enemies*. New York and London: Routledge.

Milewski, T. D. (February 8, 2014). Census numbers who that many people go from Madison to Chicago than vice-versa. *The cap times*. Retrieved October 12, 2014 from http://host.madison.com/news/local/writers/todd-milewski/census-numbers-show-that-more-people-go-from-madison-to/article_52707394-8f7a-11e3-aa58-0019bb2963f4.html.

Mills, S. (March 28, 1995). Madison—The New Promised Land. *Chicago tribune*. Retrieved from http://articles.chicagotribune.com/1995-03-28/news/9503280167_1_mayor-paul-soglin-generous-welfare-benefits-wisconsin.

Moustakas, C. (1994). *Phenomenological research methods*. Thousand Oaks: Sage.

Nocella, A. J., Parmar, P., & Stovall, D. (Eds.). (2014). *From education to incarceration: Dismantling the school-to-prison pipeline*. New York: Peter Lang.

Noguera, P. A. (2009). *The trouble with Black boys...and other reflections on race, equity, and the future of public education*. San Francisco: Jossey-Bass.

Paris, D. (2011). 'A friend who understand fully': notes on humanizing research in a multiethnic youth community. *International Journal of Qualitative Studies in Education, 24*(2), 137–149.

Paris, D. (2012). Culturally sustaining pedagogy: A needed change in stance, terminology, and practice. *Educational Researcher, 41*(3), 93–97.

Paris, D., & Winn, M. T. (2013). *Humanizing research: Decolonizing qualitative inquiry with youth and communities*. Thousand Oaks: Sage Press.

Rios, V. (2011). *Punished: Policing the lives of Black and Latino boys*. New York and London: New York University Press.

Stanton-Salazar, R. D. (1997). A social capital framework of understanding the socialization of racial minority children and youths. *Harvard Educational Review, 87*, 1–40.

Siddle Walker, V. (1996). *Their highest potential: An African American school community in the segregated south*. Chapel Hill: University of North Carolina Press.

Skiba, R. J. (2014). The failure of zero tolerance. *Reclaiming children and youth, 22*(4), 27–33.

Skiba, R. J., Michael, R. S., Nardo, A. C., & Peterson, R. (2002). The color of discipline: Sources of racial and gender disproportionality in school punishment. *Urban Review, 34*, 317–342.

Stetsenko, A. (2014). *From participation to transformation: Implications of a transformative activist stance for human development.* A paper presented at the 4th Congress of the International Society for Cultural and Activity Research (ISCAR), Sydney, Australia.

Sumner, M. D., Silverman, C. J., & Frampton, M. L. (2010). School-based restorative justice as an alternative to zero-tolerance policies: Lessons from West Oakland. In Thelton E (Ed.), *Henderson center for social justice*. Berkeley, University of California, Berkeley School of Law (Boalt Hall). Retrieved November 8, 2014 from http://www.law.berkeley.edu/files/11-2010_School-based_Restorative_Justice_As_an_Alternative_to_Zero-Tolerance_Policies.pdf.

Tuck, E. (2010). Breaking up with Deleuze: Desire and valuing the irreconcilable. *International Journal of Qualitative Studies in Education, 23*(5), 635–650.

Tuck, E. (2009). Suspending damage: A letter to communities. *Harvard Educational Review, 79*(3), 409–427.

U.S. Department of Education Office for Civil Rights. (2014). *Civil rights data collection: data snapshot school discipline*. Retrieved June 24, 2014 from http://www2.ed.gov/about/offices/list/ocr/docs/crdc-discipline-snapshot.pdf.

Wilkerson, I. (2010). *The warmth of other suns: The epic story of America's Great Migration*. New York: Random House Books.

Winn, M. T. (2013). Toward a restorative english education. *Research in the Teaching of English, 48*(1), 126–135.

Winn, M. T. (2014a). *Toward a restorative english education pedagogy in the third space.* A paper presented at the International Congress on Activity Research (ISCAR). Sydney, Australia

Winn, M. T. (2014b). *Building lifetime circles: English education in the age of mass incarceration.* A paper presented at the European Forum for Restorative Justice. Belfast, Ireland

Wisconsin Council on Children and Families. (2013). *Race to equity: A baseline report on racial disparities in Dane County*. Retrieved from http://racetoequity.net/dev/wp-content/uploads/WCCF-R2E-Report.pdf.

The Diversity of School and Community Contexts and Implications for Special Education Classifications

Roey Ahram

Brown v. Board of Education of Topeka brought to the national stage the long debated question about whether schools that were segregated by race could facilitate equal educational outcomes. In the course of studying the impact of segregation and desegregation there have been numerous studies examining how the relationship between the socioeconomic and/or racial demographics of a school or community are related to student outcomes. Generally, these studies have found that all groups of students who attend more diverse schools are more likely to experience improved short-term and long-term academic outcomes— e.g., improved test scores and grades across the curriculum, as well as improved graduation rates—as well as a host of other positive life outcomes (Mickelson & Nkomo, 2012). Additionally, racial segregation has a measurable negative impact on student achievement (Borman & Dowling, 2010). This chapter seeks to broaden the existing conversations about the diversity of schools, tying them with existing and new research on the extent to which socioeconomic and racial demographics—i.e., community contexts—are related to special education disproportionality. In so doing, it adds to the collective understanding of how socioeconomic and/or racial demographics may influence equitable student outcomes.

Disproportionality is a broadly ascribed term denoting the over- and underrepresentation of culturally and linguistically diverse students (typically Black, Latino, and Native American) assigned to particular educational classifications or classroom placement types, or receiving particular educational services (National Education Association of the United States & National Association of School Psychologists, 2007). With respect to educational classification, students may experience disproportionality with respect to their group's representation within

R. Ahram (✉)
New York University, Metro Center, 726 Broadway, New York, NY 10003, USA
e-mail: ra977@nyu.edu

© Springer International Publishing Switzerland 2016
P.A. Noguera et al. (eds.), *Race, Equity, and Education*,
DOI 10.1007/978-3-319-23772-5_13

the overall population of students with disabilities, or within the population of students classified by particular disability categories—most notably, judgmental categories of disability, which are identified subjectively and are generally assigned after students enroll in school (Donovan & Cross, 2002). These judgmental disability categories include emotional disturbance (ED), learning disability (LD or SLD), mental retardation or intellectual disabilities (MR or ID), other health impairments (OHI), and speech/language impairments (SLI). This particular study focuses its attention on the overrepresentation of Black students classified as students with disabilities.

In a 2014 report, the U.S. Department of Education estimated that Black students are more than 1.4 times more likely to be classified as disabled compared to non-Black students (U.S. Department of Education, Office of Special Education and Rehabilitative Services, Office of Special Education Programs, 2014). This, however, is not a new phenomenon. The overrepresentation of particular groups of students in special education has been part of the education literature for more than four decades. Beginning in 1968, Lloyd Dunn's formative study "Special Education for the Mildly Retarded: Is Much of it Justifiable?" showed that Black students and students from low socioeconomic backgrounds were overrepresented in special classes for children deemed to have mild mental retardation (Dunn, 1968). Since then, Dunn's research has been corroborated and expanded upon by a multitude of studies involving a variety of research strategies and data sources, including national school datasets (compiled by the U.S. Department of Education's Office of Civil Rights) (e.g., Donovan & Cross, 2002; Finn, 1982; Heller, Holtzman, & Messick, 1982). The scope and sum of research on disproportionality is indicative of the persistent and pervasive nature of this phenomenon.

Disproportionality continues to warrant scrutiny given the negative social and educational outcomes that may result from it and the deeply rooted educational disparities that appear to perpetuate it. Special education disproportionality is problematic both in terms of educational outcomes and equity perspectives. From an educational outcomes standpoint, research has shown that (1) special education services vary widely in their effectiveness at raising students' academic achievement (Donovan & Cross, 2002; Fierros & Conroy, 2002; Gottlieb & Alter, 1994; Harry & Klingner, 2006); (2) special education classifications are often associated with enduring and negative stigmatization (Donovan & Cross, 2002; Gartner & Lipsky, 1999; Wagner, Newman, Cameto, Levine, & Marder, 2007); and (3) special education placements are effectively permanent classifications (Fierros & Conroy, 2002; Harry & Klingner, 2006). With respect to the effectiveness of special education services, research on special education programs show, in some (but not all) instances, special education classifications result in little more than ability segregation, with minimal benefits for students who are excluded from general education. Students receiving special education services achieve only marginal (if any) gains in academic proficiency in their placements (Gottlieb & Alter, 1994) and experience limited access to a rigorous and full curriculum, reducing the likelihood of their eligibility for admissions to a post-secondary institution (Fierros & Conroy, 2002; Harry & Klingner, 2006), and resulting in diminished employment opportunities over the course of their lifetimes (Donovan & Cross, 2002; Harry & Klingner, 2006). From a social-emotional perspective, students receiving special education services typically have limited interaction with academically mainstreamed peers and face social stigmatization associated with being labeled intellectually, physically, or emotionally disabled (Donovan & Cross, 2002; Gartner & Lipsky, 1999). Moreover, students classified as disabled are more likely to report feelings of loneliness and to express concerns of being disliked by non-classified students (Wagner et al., 2007). Programmatic ineffectiveness and social stigmatization are compounded by the fixedness of special education labels (Harry & Klingner, 2006). For students of color, these effects are even greater given that they are more likely to be placed in restrictive classroom environments that effectively isolate them from their peers in general education classrooms (Fierros & Conroy, 2002). Losen (2002) characterizes the harmful effects of racial imbalances in special education as placing students of color in triple jeopardy—first in the increased likelihood of being misclassified as disabled, then in the greater likelihood of being placed in more restrictive settings, and finally in the higher odds of receiving poor quality services within those settings.

While the outcomes of special education placements are, in and of themselves, disconcerting, the presence of special education disproportionality may also be indicative of larger societal disparities linked to broader inequities. Meier, Stewart, and England (1989) argue that disproportionality is a form of segregation that may be associated with discrimination and academic bias in the educational experiences and processes that precede special education placements. Harry and Klingner (2006) suggest that disproportionality is, amongst other things, the result of institutional academic bias ingrained in school districts and teachers, and a constructed and misapplied notion of students' deficit. As such, the persistent and widespread evidence of disproportionality underscores concerns about the relationship between race, perspectives of student ability, and educational equity.

Several large-scale quantitative studies have analyzed state- and district-level datasets to examine the relationship between community contexts and disproportionality—i.e., the relationship between various socioeconomic indicators (e.g., median home price, proportion of students qualifying for free or reduced lunch) and racial demographic indicators (e.g., proportion of students of color) with different measures of disproportionality (e.g., Coutinho, Oswald, & Best, 2002; Oswald, Coutinho, Best, & Singh, 1999; Oswald, Coutinho, Best, & Nguyen, 2001; Skiba, Poloni-Staudinger, Simmons, Feggins-Azziz, & Chung, 2005). In several papers, Oswald and Coutinho have examined the relationship between various special education classifications and community context variables such as educational, demographic, and economic factors at the school district level (see Coutinho et al., 2002; Oswald et al., 1999; Oswald et al., 2001). Their research, along with a study by Skiba et al. (2005), has studied the relationship between special education classifications and community context variables, finding consistent and, sometimes, conflicting relationships. Generally, these studies show that the level of poverty in a school district and the demographic composition of the school district are both related to the rate at which Black students are classified in particular disability categories, however, the direction and significance of those relationships varies by study (Table 1).

Analyzing state-level data, Zhang and Katsiyannis (2002) reported inverse correlations between state poverty and disability classifications in states with higher concentrations of poverty. In those states, fewer Hispanic students were classified as learning disabled and fewer American Indian and Alaskan, Asian and Pacific Islander, African American, and White students were classified with an emotional disturbance than in states with less concentrated poverty. Looking broadly at state-level data, Zhang and Katsiyannis (2002) looked at the relationship between

Table 1 District-level community context studies

Study	District-level community context	Direction of relationship	Special education disproportionality
Oswald et al. (1999)	Poverty	+	Black/African American MMR
	Poverty	−	Black/African American SED
Oswald et al. (2001)	Poverty	−	Black/African American[a] MR
	Poverty	−	American Indian[a] MR
	Poverty	+	White MR
	Non-White Students	−	Black/African American MR
Coutinho et al. (2002)	Poverty	+	Black/African American LD
	Poverty	+	Hispanic LD
	Poverty	+	Asian[a] LD
	Poverty	−	White LD
	Poverty	−	American Indian and Alaskan LD
	Non-White Students	−	Black/African American LD
	Non-White Students	−	Hispanic LD
	Non-White Students	−	Asian[a] LD
	Non-White Students	−	White LD
	Non-White Students	+	American Indian and Alaskan LD
Skiba et al. (2005)	Poverty	+	Black/African American MMR
	Poverty	−	Black/African American LD
	Poverty	−	Black/African American SL

[a]Male

state poverty levels and the percentage of students in each racial group (American Indian, Asian/Pacific Islander, Hispanic, African American, and White) classified according to several disability categories (all disabilities, emotional disturbance, learning disabilities, and mental retardation). They found that among 20 group pairings of race and disability, only six correlations were significant, all of which represented inverse correlations between state poverty. Specifically, the lower the state poverty level, the higher the rate of Hispanic students classified as disabled or learning disabled, and the higher the rate of American Indian and Alaskan, Asian and Pacific Islander, African American, and White students classified with an emotional disturbance (Table 2).

District-level analyses use correlations and regressions to examine the relationship between various measures of community context and disproportionate outcomes. In their attempts to better frame theories of special education disproportionality, these analyses elucidate possible relationships between socioeconomic and/or racial demographics and special education classifications for a student belonging to different racial and ethnic groups.

Oswald et al. (1999) examined the relationship between community and school context variables and disproportionate outcomes of African American students classified as having mild mental retardation (MMR) or having serious emotional disturbance (SED). Their analysis drew from 1992 U.S. Department of Education, Office of Civil Rights (OCR) and the National Center for Educational Statistics (NCES) Common Core of Data (CCD), and identified significant associations between two socioeconomic factors and disproportionality. First, higher levels of poverty within a community are related to a higher disproportionate representation of African American students classified as MMR. In school districts with high poverty rates, their analysis showed no difference in the rate at which African American students were classified as MMR compared to the rate for non-African American students, while in school districts with low poverty rates, African American students were more likely to be classified as MMR compared to non-African American students. The researchers also found that higher levels of poverty within a community corresponded with lower levels of disproportionate representation of African American students classified as SED. That is, in school districts with low poverty rates, there was little to no difference in the rates at which African American students were classified as SED compared to

Table 2 State-level community context studies

Study	State-level community context	Direction of relationship	Special education outcome
Zhang & Katsiyannis (2002)	Poverty	−	Hispanic SWD
	Poverty	−	Hispanic LD
	Poverty	−	American Indian and Alaskan ED
	Poverty	−	Asian and Pacific Islander ED
	Poverty	−	Black/African American ED
	Poverty	−	White ED

non-African American students, while in school districts with high poverty rates, African American students were more likely to be classified as SED compared to non-African American students.

Studies by Oswald et al. (2001) and Coutinho et al. (2002) examined disproportionality in mental retardation (MR) and learning disability (LD) classifications based on an updated OCR dataset. Oswald et al.'s (2001) analysis found that the relative likelihood of African American students being classified as MR decreased as poverty increased.[1] Moreover, for African American students, the rate of MR classification dropped as community poverty increased, whereas for White students, the classification rate increased, narrowing the difference between rates of classification for Black and White students.[2] These findings suggest that higher levels of poverty within a community are linked to lower rates of disproportionate representation by African American students classified as MR.

Coutinho et al.'s (2002) analysis found that the relative likelihood of African American students being classified as learning disabled (LD) increased as poverty increased. The increases were due to increases in the classification rates of African American students as LD and reductions in the classification rate of White students as LD, widening the gap between classification rates of Black and White students. This demonstrates that higher community levels of poverty are related to a higher disproportionate representation of African American students classified as LD. Comparatively, higher community levels of poverty are related to lower disproportionate representation of African American students classified as MR.

Skiba et al. (2005) conducted a district-level analysis of a single state, specifically focused on classification of African American students in five special education categories—mild mental retardation (MMR), moderate mental retardation (MoMR), emotional disturbance (ED), learning disability (LD), and speech and language (SL). Their analysis showed that disproportionality decreased for SL and LD classifications when poverty increased, and increased for MMR classification as poverty increased. Based on these findings, Skiba et al. (2005) concluded that poverty served as a poor predictor of disproportionality.[3] Together, Oswald et al. (1999), Oswald et al. (2001), Coutinho et al. (2002), and Skiba et al. (2005) demonstrate the possibility that the socioeconomic context of a community is related

---

[1]Odds ratios comparing the classification rates of Black students to White students were used as measures of relative likelihoods.

[2]This is counter to Oswald et al.'s (1999) findings.

[3]Their model also examined school-level variables, showing that suspension–expulsion rates are correlated to disproportionality in ED classifications, dropout rates are negatively correlated to disproportionality in MoMR classifications and positively correlated to disproportionality in SL classifications, achievement levels are positively correlated to disproportionality in MMR classifications and negatively correlated to disproportionality in SL classifications, and student–teacher ratios were positively correlated with disproportionality in MMR classifications. Moreover, the study's logistic regression demonstrates that race (the proportion of African American students) was a better predictor of disproportionality than poverty and that school suspensions and expulsions proved to be the most significant predictor of disproportionality.

to disproportionality in that poverty does appear to be related to disproportionality. However, since poverty seems to influence different groups of students' chances of being classified as disabled differently, is not a consistent predictor of disproportionality.

With respect to school district racial demographics, the likelihood of an African American student being classified as a student with MR and LD appears to drop as the percentage of non-White students in a school district increases. Oswald et al.'s (2001) analysis revealed that the odds ratio of African American students being classified as MR decreased as the percentage of non-White students in school districts increased. Similarly, Coutinho et al.'s (2002) analysis found that the relative likelihood of African American students being classified as LD decreases as the percentage of non-White students enrolled in a district increased. According to both sets of analyses, the rate of being classified as a student with a learning disability dropped for African American, Hispanic, and White students as the percentage of non-White students in a school district increased.[4] Across the three studies, findings showed that identification rates of Black and Hispanic males as learning disabled and Black males and females as mentally retarded and/or emotionally disturbed decreased as the percentage of non-White students in a district increased (Coutinho et al., 2002; Oswald et al., 1999; Oswald et al., 2001). These statements support the generalization that disproportionality tends not to occur in schools with high concentrations of students of color (Ladner & Hammons, 2001).

While these studies have produce mixed (and sometimes contradictory) findings with respect to the size and direction of the relationship between socioeconomic and racial demographic factors and disproportionality, taken as a whole, they appear to substantiate a plausible relationship between community context and the rates at which different groups of students are classified with disabilities, across disability categories.[5] Compared to the concentration of poverty, the concentration of non-White students in a school seems to be a more reliable predictor of disproportionality.

Analysis of Data from a Single State

Using ordinary least square (OLS) regression, analyses in this chapter look at both the relative risk that Black students have of being classified as disabled compared to non-Black students as well as the risk Black students have of being classified

---

[4]MacMillan and Reschly (1998) raised concerns about Oswald et al.'s (1999), Oswald et al.'s (2001), and Coutinho et al.'s (2002) use of data from the Office of Civil Rights, arguing that it oversamples from large urban districts, thus limiting the ability to generalize the findings to a national level.

[5]The contradictory nature of these findings may put into question the validity of the hypothesis of differential susceptibility.

as disabled independent of the risk experienced by any other students. The analysis tests the influence of race, poverty, district personnel, and district achievement variables on special education disproportionality. This study is a secondary analysis of district-level special education, enrollment, and achievement data from a state education association (SEA), combined with data from the NCES Common Core, and data from the U.S. Census's Small Area Income and Poverty Estimates (SAIPE).

As in earlier studies (e.g., Coutinho et al., 2002; Oswald et al., 1999; Oswald et al., 2001; Skiba et al., 2005), special education classification data, student racial demographic data, community socioeconomic data, and student academic achievement data were analyzed. Student enrollment and special education classification data, disaggregated by race and ethnicity, were gathered from the 2010–2011 school year from 680 school districts in a large northeastern state. These data were provided by the SEA and merged with data from the NCES Common Core, which included information on student–teacher ratios for each district. Data from the SAIPE were also included to provide an estimation of the number of children in the district between the ages of 5 and 17 and an estimation of the number of children in the district between the ages of 5 and 17 living below poverty. 3rd grade English Language Arts (ELA) and math achievement data from the state education agencies online report system were included as average measures of students' achievement in the district. After merging the data from across these sources, 676 school districts were available for analysis.

In order to hedge against the influence of small school districts representing low populations of students with disabilities and low populations of Black students with disabilities, data from only 263 schools of the original 680 were analyzed.[6] While the 263 school districts constitute only slightly more than a third of the original dataset, these 263 school districts represent a large majority of the total number of enrolled students and an even greater majority of those students with disabilities who were included in the original dataset.[7]

This modified dataset was used for an analysis of disproportionate special education classifications of Black students across all disability categories.

The descriptive variables used in this analysis included the total enrollment size (Enroll), proportion of the school district student population who are Black or African American, proportion of the school district's community school age

---

[6]The following district enrollment criteria were used to construct the final dataset: (a) at least 75 students with disabilities enrolled; (b) a minimum of 30 Black students (disabled and nondisabled) enrolled; (c) at least 75 non-Black students (disabled and nondisabled) enrolled; and (d) at least 10 Black students with disabilities.

[7]Based on the 649 school districts in the original dataset for which there is enrollment data, these 263 school districts serve 71.6 % of the total number of students enrolled in the entire dataset. Moreover, based on the 652 school districts in the original dataset for which there is special education enrollment data, these 262 school districts served 73.8 % of the total number of students with disabilities enrolled in the entire dataset.

Table 3 Description of key descriptive variables

Variable	Description
Enrollment	Total district enrollment from the state education agency, internal data 2010–2011 school year
Percent Black	Percent of Black and African American students enrolled in district
Percent poverty	Percent of children ages 5 through 17 living in families below the poverty line in district
Student–teacher ratio	Ratio of the total district enrollment to the number of teachers in a school district
3rd Grade ELA	The mean scaled score on the state 3rd grade English Language Arts exam

children who live below the poverty line, student-to-teacher ratio, and academic performance—i.e., mean student performance on 3rd grade English Language Arts (ELA) exam (Table 3).[8]

This study focuses on the relative risk that Black students have of being classified as disabled compared to all other students (i.e., the relative risk ratio[9]) as well as the risk Black students have of being classified as disabled, otherwise known as the risk index.[10,11]

Relative Risk. A relative risk is broadly defined as the ratio of the probability (or likelihood) of an event occurring for one group compared to the probability of the event occurring for a comparison group (Durlak, 2009). For this study the relative risk of Black students being classified with a disability is the ratio between the quotient of the number of Black students classified with a disability divided by the total number of Black students enrolled, and the quotient of the number of non-Black students classified with a disability, divided by the total number of non-Black students enrolled in the district.[12] A relative risk of one indicates that Black students have the same chance as all other students of being classified with a

---

[8]Originally, the academic performance of students from several grade levels was considered for this analysis, but they proved to be highly correlated with each other.

[9]This is a point of departure from Skiba et al. (2005), which used Z-scores.

[10]Reporting relative risk ratios alone can pose a problem in that relative risk values are not comparable to each other. A relative risk of 2.0 in one case is not the same as relative risk of 2.0 in another due to proportions. For example, in school district A, 10 % of Black students are classified as disabled, while 5 % of non-Black students are classified as disabled. At the same time, in school district B, 30 % of Black students are classified as disabled, while 15 % on non-Black students are classified as disabled. In both school district A and B, Black students are twice as likely to be classified as disabled compared to all other students, but Black students in school district B are three times more likely to be classified as disabled compared to Black students in school district A. For this reason, this study also will use the risk index of Black student being classified as disabled.

[11]The risk that non-Black students have of being classified as disabled will be used as an independent variable in this model.

[12]$RR_{Black} = \frac{SWD_{Black}/(SWD_{Black}+GEN_{Black})}{SWD_{Other}/(SWD_{Other}+GEN_{Other})}$.

disability. A relative risk of greater than one indicates increased chance for Black students being classified as disabled—i.e., overrepresentation—and a relative risk of less than one indicates a decreased chance—i.e., underrepresentation.

Lipsey and Wilson (2000) and Hosp and Reschly (2003) explain that relative risk ratios are difficult to interpret since they are centered on one, with a minimum value of zero and an undefined maximum value. They therefore suggest using a transformation of the natural log of relative risk in inferential analysis. Using the natural log transformation of the relative risk, zero becomes the point at which Black students have the same risk as all other students of being classified as disabled. A relative risk of zero indicates that Black students have the same chance as all other students of being classified with a disability. A relative risk of greater than one indicates an increased chance for Black students being classified as disabled—i.e., overrepresentation—and a relative risk of less than one indicates a decreased chance—i.e., underrepresentation. This transformation improves the usability of relative risk ratios in the calculation of inferential statistics (Lipsey & Wilson, 2000).[13]

Risk Index. The risk index is the probability (or likelihood) that a particular group will experience a particular outcome, independent of the risk of any other group. With respect to special education, the risk index is also known as the classification rate. This study is interested in the risk index of Black students being classified as disabled. For this paper the risk index of Black students being classified with a disability is the quotient of the number of Black students classified with a disability divided by the total number of Black students enrolled.[14] The greater the risk index, the greater the likelihood that Black students have of being classified as disabled, independent of the classification rate of other students.

Analysis and Results

Two regression analyses were used to examine the relationship between community contexts and disproportionality outcomes. Regression analysis is a technique for assessing the relationship between a single dependent variable and multiple independent variables (Tabachnick & Fidell, 2007). Each analysis seeks to answer the primary research question: *What is the relationship between school districts' community context (i.e., socioeconomics and racial demographic characteristics) and disproportionality outcomes?* The first analysis examines the relative risk that Black students have of being classified as disabled. In this analysis, relative risk

---

[13]As such, in the descriptive statistics, both the relative risk of Black students being classified with a disability as well as the natural log transformed relative risk. When reporting inferential statistics, only the natural log transformed relative risk is reported (though for the sake of clarity in the writing, the natural log transformed relative risk will be referred to as the relative risk).

[14]$RI_{Black} = SWD_{Black}/(SWD_{Black} + GEN_{Black})$.

ratios are used as response variables and those that follow are used as predictor variables (i.e., descriptor): the concentration of Black and African American students enrolled in the district, the concentration of children living below the poverty line, total district enrollment, student-to-teacher ratio, and the mean scaled score on the state 3rd grade ELA exam. The second analysis builds upon the first, examining the risk index (the classification rate of Black students) relative to community context variables. In this analysis, the risk index of Black students is used as the response variable with the following included as predictor variables: the risk index of non-Black students being classified as disabled, the concentration of Black and African American students enrolled in the district, the concentration of children living below the poverty line, total district enrollment, student-to-teacher ratio, and the mean scaled score on the state adopted 3rd grade ELA exam.

These analyses used Pearson product-moment correlations to help specify the initial model, followed by standard (or simultaneous) multiple regressions in which all of the descriptive variables were entered in each model simultaneously. Additionally, partial and semipartial correlations were calculated for each of the descriptive variables. The partial and semipartial correlations were used to separate the effects of the descriptive variables on the outcome variable in order to assess the unique contribution of the descriptive variable on the outcome variable.

The dataset included a wide range of school districts of various sizes, with the smallest district enrolling 733 students and the largest encompassing 35,555 students, with an average school district size of 4,464.56 students. Though on average, school districts enrolled a low percentage of Black students (11.47 %), some districts in the sample were predominately composed of Black and African American students. The average percent of children in poverty across the school districts in the dataset is 12.32 %. The average student-to-teacher ratio in the dataset was 12.7 to 1. The average mean ELA score was 665.8 (Tables 4 and 5).

The average (mean) school district has a classification rate for Black students of 0.20 and a classification rate of non-Black students of 0.13. This means in

Table 4 Descriptive statistics of socioeconomic and demographic variables

Variable	Mean	SD	Min	25th %tile	Median	75th %tile	Max
Enrollment	4464.56	4113.69	733.00	2053.00	3493.00	5266.00	35555.00
Percent Black	11.47	13.89	0.83	2.90	5.79	13.85	79.51
Percent poverty	12.32	7.96	2.41	6.01	10.05	17.28	38.70

SD Standard Deviation; *Min* Minimum value; *25th %tile* 25th percentile; *75th %tile* 75th percentile; *Max* Maximum value

Table 5 Descriptive statistics of staff and student academic variables

Variable	Mean	SD	Min	25th %tile	Median	75th %tile	Max
Student–teacher ratio	12.72	1.40	9.60	11.70	12.70	13.70	16.60
3rd Grade ELA	665.83	6.17	646.00	662.00	666.00	670.00	683.00

SD Standard Deviation; *Min* Minimum value; *25th %tile* 25th percentile; *75th %tile* 75th percentile; *Max* Maximum value

Table 6 Descriptive statistics of special education variables

Variable	Mean	SD	Min	25th %tile	Median	75th %tile	Max
Risk index (Black)	0.20	0.07	0.05	0.16	0.20	0.23	0.62
Risk index (non-Black)	0.13	0.03	0.07	0.11	0.13	0.15	0.43
Relative risk (Black)	1.58	0.51	0.67	1.21	1.46	1.82	3.62
Relative risk (Black)[a]	0.41	0.31	-0.40	0.91	0.38	0.60	1.29

SD Standard Deviation; *Min* Minimum value; *25th %tile* 25th percentile; *75th %tile* 75th percentile; *Max* Maximum value
[a]Natural Log Transformed

Table 7 Bivariate Pearson correlations between key variables

	Percent Black	Percent poverty	Enrollment	Student–teacher ratio	3rd Grade ELA	Risk index (non-Black)
Percent poverty	0.448*					
Enrollment	0.322*	0.190*				
Student–teacher ratio	0.023	−0.097	0.313*			
3rd Grade ELA	−0.544*	−0.750*	−0.228*	−0.038		
Risk index (non-Black)	0.077	0.274*	0.109	−0.087	−0.223*	
Relative risk (Black)	−0.314*	−0.282*	−0.164	−0.045	0.285*	−0.333*
Relative risk (Black)[a]	−0.329*	−0.272*	−0.143	−0.029	0.271*	−0.327*
Risk index (Black)	−0.265*	−0.088	−0.102	−0.105	0.117	0.394*

*$p < 0.05$
[a]Natural Log Transformed

the average school, among Black students, 20 % are classified as disabled, while among non-Black students, 13 % are classified as disabled. The average school district in the dataset had a relative risk ratio of 1.58. This means that in the average school district Black students are 1.58 times more likely to be classified with a disability compared to all other students (Table 6).

Table 7 presents the Pearson product-moment correlations among demographic, socioeconomic, school, achievement, and disproportionality measures. Several of the descriptive variables were significantly correlated with the relative risk of Black students being classified as disabled.[15] The concentration of poverty in a

---

[15]The interrelationship between the descriptive variables helps define the regression model. The proportion of Black students and the concentration of poverty in a school district were moderately correlated. Skiba et al. (2005) do, however, note that poverty and race may operate differently with respect to disproportionality. Therefore, both variables were included in the regression model. There was a moderate positive correlation between the proportion of Black students in a school district and the overall district enrollment, and a strong negative correlation between the proportion of Black students in a school district and the average ELA achievement.

school district was weakly correlated with the overall district enrollment. Additionally, the relationship between the proportion of students in poverty and the average ELA achievement in a district was strongly negatively correlated. There was a weak negative correlation between the concentration of poverty in a school district and the risk index of non-Black students. District size (enrollment) was moderately correlated with the student-to-teacher ratio, and weakly negatively correlated with the average ELA achievement in a district. Also, there was a weak negative correlation between the average ELA achievement in a district and the risk index of non-Black students. The high correlations between the descriptive variables, particularly the average ELA achievement and poverty, signifies that multicollinearity poses a concern when developing a regression model.

Using Cohen's convention for correlation coefficients (Cohen, 1988), there was a moderate negative correlation between the proportion of Black students in a school district and the relative risk of Black students being classified as disabled. Similarly, there was a weak negative correlation between the proportion of students in poverty and the relative risk of Black students being classified as disabled. There was also a weak negative correlation between the overall enrollment of a district and the relative risk of Black students being classified as disabled. Academic achievement data was correlated with the relative risk of Black students being classified as disabled. There was a weak positive correlation between the average ELA achievement in a district and the relative risk of Black students being classified as disabled.[16] There was a weak negative correlation between the proportion of Black students in a school district and the risk index of Black students being classified as disabled. There was a moderate positive correlation between the risk index of non-Black students being classified as disabled and the risk index of Black students being classified as disabled.

In both analyses, a standard multiple regression was performed. In the first analysis, the standard multiple regression was performed between the relative risk of Black students being classified as disabled and the percent of Black and African American students enrolled in district, the percent of children ages 5 through 17 living in families below the poverty line in district (concentration of poverty), the total district enrollment, and the ratio of the total district enrollment to the number of teachers in a school district (student-to-teacher ratio).

In the second analysis, the standard multiple regression was performed between the risk index of Black students being classified as disabled and the risk index of non-Black students being classified as disabled, the percent of Black and African American students enrolled in district, the percent of children ages 5 through 17 living in families below the poverty line in district (concentration of poverty), the total district enrollment, and the ratio of the total district enrollment to the number of teachers in a school district (student-to-teacher ratio).

---

[16]There is a moderate negative correlation between the risk index of non-Black students and the relative risk of Black students being classified as disabled, $r = 0.3333$, $n = 263$, $p < 0.0001$. This correlation is tautological to the definition of relative risk—as the risk of non-Black students decreases, the relative risk of Black students increases.

Table 8 Standard multiple regression of school and community variables on the (Natural Log of the) relative risk of Black students classified as disabled

	Coef. (b)	Robust Std. Err	Beta (β)	Partial Corr.^{2}	Semipartial Corr.^{2}
Percent Black[a]	-0.105***	0.021	-0.348	0.094***	0.086***
Percent poverty[a]	-0.037	0.034	-0.075	0.005	0.004
Enrollment[a]	-0.041	0.030	-0.089	0.007	0.006
Student–teacher ratio	0.001	0.016	0.005	0.000	0.000
Constant	0.358	0.232			

$R^2 = 0.168$; Adjusted $R^2 = 0.155$
***$p < 0.01$, **$p < 0.05$, *$p < 0.1$
[a]Natural Log Transformed

Given the high correlation between the proportion of students in poverty and the average ELA achievement in a district, achievement was removed from both models (Tabachnick & Fidell, 2007).

Relative Risk Analysis[17]

Table 8 displays the unstandardized coefficients (b) and intercept, robust standard errors, standardized coefficients (β), partial correlations, semipartial correlations, R^2, and adjusted R^2. The overall model was statistically significant, $F(4, 257) = 12.95$, $p < 0.001$, with R^2 at 0.168. The adjusted R^2 value of 0.155 indicated that slightly more than 15 % of the variability in (the natural log of) disproportionality was predicted by the (natural log of the) percent of Black and African American students enrolled in district, the (natural log of the) percent of children ages 5 through 17 living in families below the poverty line in district (concentration of poverty), the (natural log of the) total district enrollment, and the ratio of the total district enrollment to the number of teachers in a school district (student-to-teacher ratio). Of those descriptive variables, only the (natural log of the) percent of Black and African American students enrolled in district significantly predicted disproportionality, $b = -0.105$, $p < 0.001$. The size and direction of the relationship suggests that the lower the percentage of Black students enrolled in

[17]Based on the number of univariate outliers and the skew of the descriptive variable, the decision was made to transform the several descriptive variables to reduce the number of outliers and improve the normality and homoscedasticity of the residuals. Natural log transformations were used on the percent of Black and African American students enrolled in district, the percent of children ages 5 through 17 living in families below the poverty line in district (concentration of poverty), and the total district enrollment variables. One case with missing data was removed from the data, but none of the outliers were removed, $N = 262$. This did not have any significant impact on the correlations between the variables.

a school district, the higher the likelihood that Black students would be classified with a disability at a disproportionate rate compared to all other students.

Partial and semipartial correlations were calculated to identify each variable's unique variance in the models. The semipartial correlations show that the (natural log of the) percent of Black students in a school district explains 8.62 % ($p > 0.001$) of variance in the (natural log of the) relative risk of Black students being classified with a disability.

Risk Index Analysis[18]

Table 9 displays the unstandardized coefficients (b) and intercept, robust standard errors, standardized coefficients (β), partial correlations, semipartial correlations, R^2, and adjusted R^2. The overall model was statistically significant, $F(5, 256) = 14.65$, $p < 0.001$, with R^2 at 0.273. The adjusted R^2 value of 0.267 indicates that slightly more than a quarter of the variability in (the natural log of) the risk index of Black students being classified as disabled was predicted by the (natural log of the) risk index of non-Black students being classified as disabled, the (natural log of the) percent of Black and African American students enrolled in district, the (natural log of the) percent of children ages 5 through 17 living in families below the poverty line in district (concentration of poverty), the (natural log of the) total district enrollment, and the ratio of the total district enrollment to the number of teachers in a school district (student-to-teacher ratio). Of those independent variables, both the (natural log of the) risk index of non-Black students being classified as disabled and the (natural log of the) percent of Black and African American students enrolled in district significantly predicted disproportionality, $b = -0.498$, $p < 0.001$ and $b = -0.120$, $p < 0.001$ respectively. The size and direction of the relationship suggests that the higher the risk that non-Black students had of being classified as disabled and lower the percentage of Black students enrolled in a school district, the higher the likelihood that Black students would be classified with a disability at a disproportionate rate compared to all other students.

---

[18]Similar to risk ratio analysis, based on the number of univariate outliers and the skew of the descriptive variables, the decision was made to transform the several descriptive variables to reduce the number of outliers and improve the normality and homoscedasticity of the residuals. Natural log transformations were used on the risk index of Black students being classified as disabled, the risk index of non-Black students being classified as disabled, the percent of Black and African American students enrolled in district, the percent of children ages 5 through 17 living in families below the poverty line in district (concentration of poverty), and the total district enrollment variables. In one case, missing data was removed, but none of the outliers were removed ($N = 262$). This did not have any significant impact on the correlations between the variables.

Table 9 Standard multiple regression of school and community variables on the (Natural Log of the) risk index of Black students classified as disabled

	Coef. (b)	Robust Std. Err	Beta (β)	Partial Corr.^{2}	Semipartial Corr.^{2}
Risk index (non-Black)[a]	0.498***	0.101	0.351	0.133	0.112
Percent Black[a]	−0.120***	0.020	−0.397	0.132	0.111
Percent poverty[a]	0.019	0.034	0.039	0.001	0.001
Enrollment[a]	−0.024	0.030	−0.053	0.003	0.002
Student–teacher ratio	−0.008	0.015	−0.034	0.001	0.001
Constant	−0.608	0.263			

$R^2 = 0.273$; Adjusted $R^2 = 0.267$
*** $p < 0.01$, ** $p < 0.05$, * $p < 0.1$
[a]Natural Log Transformed

Partial and semipartial correlations were calculated to identify each variable's unique variance in the models. The semipartial correlations showed that the (natural log of the) percent of Black students in a school district explains 11.1 % ($p > 0.001$) of variance in the (natural log of the) risk index of Black students being classified with a disability.

Combined, the regression models show that the proportion of Black students in a school district was inversely related to the relative risk that Black students had of being classified as disabled, and the risk that Black students had of being classified as disabled, independent of the risk of all other students. For every 1 % decrease in the proportion of Black students in a school district, the relative risk of Black students being classified as disabled increased 0.11 %, and the risk of Black students being classified as disabled (i.e., the classification rate of Black students) increased 0.12 %.[19] At the same time, as shown in the correlation matrix, the risk index of non-Black students was not correlated with the percentage of Black students enrolled in a school district. Thus, as clearly shown in Table 10, Figs. 1 and 2, as the proportion of Black students decreased, the classification rate of Black students increased while the classification rate of non-Black students remained the same. This suggests that as the percentage of Black students in a school decreased the *increase* in disproportionality was related to the increased risk that Black students had of being classified as disabled (and the unchanged risk that all other students had of being classified as disabled).[20] Moreover, these findings suggest that

---

[19]This not a percentage point increase, but rather a percent change of the proportions. For example, a change from 75 % Black student enrollment to 65 % may represent a 10-percentage point change in the Black student enrollment, but it also represents a 15 % change in the Black student enrollment. The 1 % point change in the text refers to this second method of looking a percentage change and not the first.

[20]It should be noted that the risk index of Black students classified as disabled is not correlated with concentration of poverty in a school district, while there is a moderate positive correlation between the risk index of non-Black students and the concentration of poverty.

Table 10 Key special education outcomes by quintile of percent of Black students enrolled in a school district

Quintile of percent of Black	Average percent Black (%)	Average relative risk (Black)	Average risk index (non-Black) (%)	Average risk index (Black) (%)	Average risk index (Overall) (%)
1st Quintile	1.86	1.84	13.10	23.58	13.29
2nd Quintile	3.30	1.75	13.51	22.77	13.82
3rd Quintile	5.82	1.58	13.24	20.27	13.65
4th Quintile	11.62	1.44	12.79	18.17	13.41
5th Quintile	34.23	1.28	13.86	17.47	15.03

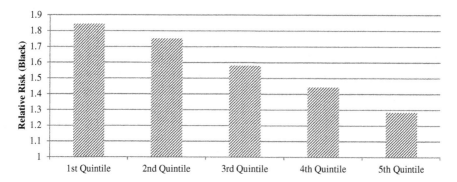

Fig. 1 Average relative risk of Black students being classified as disabled by quintile of percent of Black students enrolled in a school district

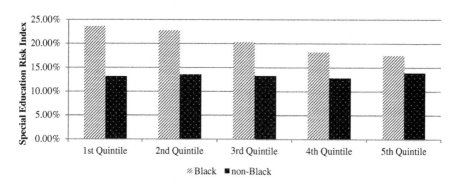

Fig. 2 Average special education risk index of Black and non-Black students and by quintile of percent of Black students enrolled in a school district

the percentage of Black students in a school district shared a unique relationship with the classification rate of Black students that it did not share with the classification of non-Black students.

Conclusion and Discussion

The analysis of district-level data shows that the percentage of Black students in a school district predicts a small amount of the variance in disproportionality. This analysis is in line with the findings of Coutinho et al. (2002), Oswald et al. (1999), and Oswald et al. (2001), who reported that the identification rate of Black and Hispanic males as learning disabled and Black males and females as mentally retarded and emotionally disturbed drops as the percentage of non-White students in a district increases. This analysis also corroborates Ladner and Hammons' (2001) assertion that disproportionality tends not to occur in schools with high concentrations of students of color.[21] The data also shows, however, that while school demographics mediate disproportionate outcomes, disproportionality is pervasive across school districts regardless of the community context. This suggests that special education disproportionality is not simply a product of community context. Nevertheless, the manner in which community context influenced disproportionality suggests that the community context, in particular the relationship between the proportion of Black students in a school district and those Black students' special education outcomes, is worthy of further investigation.

Building on existing studies, it is possible to construct a theoretical framework as to why context matters with respect to disproportionality and examine the implications of the findings. As will be explicated in more detail below, this framework holds that conceptions of race and ability overlap in such a way as to increase the likelihood that Black students (and other minority students) are at increased risk of being (mis-) classified as disabled. Moreover, these conceptions of race and ability are constructed not just at the individual-level, but are related to community context. Moreover, this framework has broader implications with respect to educational equity that inform how we as a society should view segregation and integration.

The Special Education Equity Paradox and Disproportionality

Special education and special education disproportionality represent two competing educational equity issues. When the Education for All Handicapped Children Act (EHA) and the Individuals with Disabilities Education Act (IDEA) were enacted, they were done so as a means of creating more inclusive schools. Prior to this legislation, most states gave school districts discretion with respect to whether or not they would enroll students with disabilities, and if so, what type of educational

---

[21]They found that districts with the lower concentrations of students of color reported higher special education classification rates, suggesting that additional research is needed to understand referral and classification processes in schools where fewer non-White students are enrolled.

services and support school districts were required to provide. The enactment of the laws increased access to education for students with disabilities, but also has led to a formalization of what Ferri and Connor (2005) describe as a "cognitive merging of race and ability" (p. 99) that has led to disproportionality.[22]

It could be argued that those students who are ultimately classified as disabled are in need of additional services—the questions are: are they in need of a special education classification to get those services, and do they have a disability? Students who are referred to the special education classification process tend to be struggling learners, however, they are not necessarily disabled (Harry & Klingner, 2006; Harry, Klingner, Cramer, Sturges, & Moore, 2007; Mehan, Hertweck, & Meihls, 1986). Nevertheless, Harry and Klingner (2006) point out that in considering special education classifications for struggling learners, schools seldom consider the classroom environment or students' past educational experiences and instead locate students' struggles as intrinsic deficits. Alternatively, when teachers see the role of instruction in students' learning difficulties and feel as if they have the capacity to address those difficulties through improved instruction, they are less likely to refer struggling learners to the special education referral process (Gravois & Rosenfield, 2002, 2006; Harry & Klingner, 2006; Knotek, 2003; Mehan et al., 1986).

With respect to racialized concepts of ability, O'Connor & Fernandez (2006) claim that labels of ability and disability are norm-referenced against White middle-class norms and argue that application of these norms within schools marginalizes culturally and linguistically diverse students. Moreover, they and other scholars point out that students' abilities and/or disabilities should not be perceived as artifacts that are uncovered or developed within the students, but rather as qualities constructed within the context of schools, based on not just student behaviors, but also how these behaviors are interpreted against the cultural norms

---

[22]Thus, educational practitioners might argue that by receiving a special education classification students are afforded additional resources and services that they might not otherwise get. Moreover, it could be argued that special education services provide additional support to struggling students and the overrepresentation of Black students in special education is indicative of response to need—providing struggling Black students with the supports they need to be successful in schools. Researchers enjoying this perspective have argued that Black students are in fact underrepresented in special education—indicating that despite being disproportionately overrepresented in special education, their educational needs (as defined both by their academic performance and their socioeconomic status) is such that Black students require additional special education services (Hibel, Farkas, & Morgan, 2010, Morgan et al., 2015). In a sense, this line of research argues that Black students (as well as Native American students, Hispanic Students, and language minority students) should be more disproportionately classified as disabled because they have a greater educational need. If this is the case, significant attention should be placed on the quality of those special education services being offered—as noted above research suggests special education services may not be an effective means of supporting student (Donovan & Cross, 2002; Fierros & Conroy, 2002; Gottlieb & Alter, 1994; Harry & Klingner, 2006), and carry with it the negative externalities of stigmatization (Donovan & Cross, 2002; Gartner & Lipsky, 1999; Wagner et al. 2007) and permanence (Fierros & Conroy, 2002; Harry & Klingner, 2006).

of society, schools, and individual teachers (Mehan, 1980; Mehan et al., 1986). This dynamic may lend itself to specific bias given that research on the social norms of culturally and linguistically diverse students reveals that these students exhibit culturally based interactional forms that often differ from the norms valued in schools (Gay, 2010; Hale, 2001; Tyler, Boykin, Miller, & Hurley, 2006).

Many scholars have described how differences in cultural norms produce discontinuities and contribute to misinterpretations of the abilities of culturally diverse students (Ferguson, 2003; Gay, 2010; King, 1991; Ladson-Billings, 1999; Nieto, 2004). This cultural disconnect may lead to inappropriate or incomplete judgments about student ability, in part because schools fail to recognize and leverage the funds of knowledge their students bring to the classroom (e.g., Delpit, 2006; Irvine, 1990; Moll, Amanti, Neff, & Gonzalez, 1992; Valenzuela, 1999). Moreover, mismatched cultural lenses and ways of being influence the extent to which schools perceive culturally and linguistically diverse students as academically ready for school (Heath, 1983). Ultimately, the incongruence between students' own cultural attributes and the cultural habits valued in their schools can promote negative perceptions of the ability of students of color that result in referrals into the special education classification process (Delpit, 2006; Ford, Harris III, Tyson, & Trotman, 2001; Harry, Klingner, Sturges, & Moore, 2002).

The special education classification process seeks out deficits in order to provide students with support. At the same time, the labels of ability and disability are imbued with concepts of race. As such, it could be argued that the special education classification is perfectly designed to produce disproportionality. Harry and Klingner (2006) lament that "special education's lofty intentions have been subverted by the fixation on identifying the 'something else [an intrinsic deficit or missing piece]' and locating the correct box with the correct deficit label" (p. 183). But there often is no "something else" or intrinsic deficit—rather there are biased conceptions of ability within the normative process of special education classification that effectively (though not necessarily intentionally) separate out culturally and linguistically diverse students, applying to them a special education label.

Context Matters

Perceptions of race and ability are key elements in why context matters. Traditionally, research on educational equity has pointed to inequitable distributions of educational resources that place Black students at a disadvantage. The amount of resources available to students in a school is an important determinant of their academic achievement (Greenwald, Hedges, & Laine, 1996). Unfortunately, students of color are overrepresented in poorly resourced, poorly performing schools (Darling-Hammond, 2013; Frankenberg & Orfield, 2012; Lee, 2004; Orfield & Lee, 2007; Rothstein, 2004). Even when controlling for the effects of school quality difference, achievement of classmate differences, and the distribution of student ability in a school, the concentration of Black students has

an adverse effect on the achievement of Black students—particularly high achieving Black students (Borman et al., 2004; Card & Rothstein, 2007; Hanushek,
Kain, & Rivkin, 2002). Ladner and Hammons' (2001) analysis of disproportionate outcomes, however, found that there was no relationship between special education classification and district resources. Moreover, minority students in urban
districts had lower special education classification rates. Similarly, this study
shows that there is no relationship between the special education classification
of non-Black students and the concentration of poverty (a proxy for community
resources). This indicates that racial demographics play a significant role in the
classification of culturally and linguistically diverse students—possibly more than
resources.

This is perhaps because labels of ability and disability are constructed outcomes that are less resource driven and more a reflection of the social, political,
and economic structures of our national, state, and local communities. For a large
number of special education classifications, particularly those in the judgmental categories, the line between abled and disabled (and even between classifications) varies among schools and school districts (Donovan & Cross, 2002; Harry
& Klingner, 2006). The findings from this study, along with those of other studies,
suggest that it is reasonable to posit that as contexts change, so too do concepts of
ability and disability. Based on these studies, it is unclear as to what exactly varies
between schools that might influence these concepts of ability and disability; however, research has offered insights into several ways that communities contribute to
schooling outcomes, including disproportionality.

Research on school effectiveness demonstrates that context variables such as
socioeconomic conditions and racial demographics can influence the implementation of school policies and practices, making it essential to examine them in
studies that look at school outcomes (Reynolds, Teddlie, Creemers, Scheerens, &
Townsend, 2000). This is because schools as institutions function within complex
social and political ecologies that inform the ways policies, practices, and processes unfold. Existing literature points to different ways in which district demographics can inform policies and procedures related to curriculum, instruction,
and special education (Anyon, 1980, 1981; Eitle, 2002; Harry & Klingner, 2006;
Meier et al., 1989), as well as how concepts of race are understood within school
contexts (Lewis, 2003), which may help explain why context matters with respect
to disproportionality, and why the risk of Black students being classified as disabled increases as the concentration of Black students in a school decreases.

Anyon (1980, 1981) identifies a correspondence between the social class of a
school's population and the type of curriculum and pedagogy of the school, and in
doing so argues that schools both reflect and reproduce the "tensions and conflicts of
the larger society" (1981, p. 38). This is true not just with respect to curriculum and
pedagogy, but also with respect to how special education classifications are employed.
Moreover, just as schooling as a whole can mirror broader issues within society, individual school districts can also be reflective of more local community contexts.

Based on their ethnographic research, Harry and Klingner (2006) found
that wealthier communities exerted more pressure on school districts to redirect

struggling students toward pathways leading to special education classification. These patterns may develop in response to external pressure on district leaders to produce favorable achievement results; Figlio and Getzler (2002) found that greater emphasis on high-stakes testing, such as state performance exams, increased the likelihood that low-performing students and students from low socioeconomic backgrounds would be placed in special education.

Meier et al. (1989) and Eitle (2002), in their respective analyses of local racial demographics, socioeconomics, and political–economic structures, posit that community demographics shape the political environment within schools in ways that influence Black students' access to educational opportunity. In school districts where Black community members represent a minority of the district or hold little political and economic influence relative to White community members, Black students are more likely to be relegated or segregated into special education classes. Moreover, Lewis's (2003) ethnographic research in schools demonstrates that community and school racial demographics can influence how concepts of race are constructed and operate within and around schools. Her work shows that the racial demographics of a school can influence how race labels (and subsequently, their symbolic meanings) are ascribed to students, and she explores the impact of this ascription, suggesting that more adverse concepts of race are developed and put forth in predominantly White communities. Mehan et al. (1986) provide a framework for understanding how the political environment of schools and conceptions of race come together in ways that produce disability labels. Their work posits that student ability and disability are culturally constructed within the context of schools (pp. 85–86). When a stakeholder such as a teacher refers students to special education, he or she is operating within the constitutive rules (policies and practices) of schools in defining ability and disability based on his or her general perceptions of his or her students within the specific school context (Anderson-Levitt, 1984; Mehan, 1980; Mehan et al., 1986).[23]

Collectively, research by Meier et al. (1989), Eitle (2002), and Lewis (2003) suggests that community context may influence perceptions of Black students' abilities and special education disproportionality by shaping the relationships among ability, disability, and race. Moreover, educational stakeholders—be they teachers, administrators, school boards, or parents—cannot escape the influence of their community context. They are embedded in their local school district contexts such that these contexts "shape their racial ideologies, beliefs about intelligence, ability to act in a discriminatory way, and opportunity to activate cultural and social resources" (Eitle, 2002, p. 599). These all come together to produce disability labels. Thus, as the demography of a school shifts so too do the constitutive rules regarding what constitutes student ability and disability.

While school and community resources are by and large related to student outcomes, and individual actors such as teachers, psychologists, and school

---

[23]As explained by the revisited hypothesis of differential susceptibility, these constitutive rules may be influenced by factors outside of schools (Anyon, 1980, 1981; Eitle, 2002; Harry & Klingner, 2006; Meier et al., 1989).

administrators play an important role the classification process and thus dispro-portionality, the research suggests that the phenomenon of disproportionality is also reflective of our collective community values and biases. Overall, the research suggests that the biases that drive disproportionality emanate from the community level through a complex political and social process—one that requires greater examination and consideration.

Another View of Segregation

The Justices in the *Brown v. Board of Education* (1954) decision found that:

> Separate educational facilities are inherently unequal. Therefore, we hold that the plain-tiffs and others similarly situated for whom the actions have been brought are, by reason of the segregation complained of, deprived of the equal protection of the laws guaranteed by the Fourteenth Amendment.

Since their ruling, there has been a large number of studies empirically con-firming the inequality of segregation—looking at the negative impact of school segregation on Black students—and the positive effects of desegregation that have confirmed this finding (e.g., Card & Rothstein, 2007; Frankenberg & Orfield, 2012; Lutz, 2011; Mickelson, 2015; Orfield, 2013; Orfield, Frankenberg, Ee, & Kuscera, 2014; Reber, 2005). These studies generally show that students in more diverse educational settings have better academic outcomes. The relationship sug-gested in this study (and others like it) adds to this literature in showing that Black students in hyper-segregated school districts serving predominantly non-Black stu-dents are put at a disadvantage, having an increased relative risk of being classi-fied as disabled, compared to Black students in less segregated school districts. Combined with the existing literature on segregation and desegregation, this study suggests that Black students' educational outcomes are negatively impacted by being in predominantly segregated educational environments, be those environ-ments predominantly Black or predominantly White.

References

Anderson-Levitt, K. M. (1984). Teacher interpretation of student behavior: Cognitive and social processes. *The Elementary School Journal, 84*(3), 315–337.

Anyon, J. (1980). Social class and the hidden curriculum of work. *Journal of Education, 162*(1), 67–72.

Anyon, J. (1981). Social class and school knowledge. *Curriculum Inquiry, 11*(1), 3–42.

Borman, G., & Dowling, M. (2010). Schools and inequality: A multilevel analysis of coleman's equality of educational opportunity data. *Teachers College Record, 112*(5), 1201–1246.

Borman, K. M., Eitle, T. M., Michael, D., Eitle, D. J., Lee, R., Johnson, L., & Shircliffe, B. (2004). Accountability in a postdesegregation era: The continuing significance of racial seg-regation in Florida's schools. *American Educational Research Journal, 41*(3), 605–631.

Brown v. Board of Education, 347 483 (US 1954).

Card, D., & Rothstein, J. (2007). Racial segregation and the black–white test score gap. *Journal of Public Economics, 91*(11), 2158–2184.

Cohen, J. (1988). *Statistical power analysis for the behavioral sciences* (2nd ed.). Hillsdale, NJ: Laurence Earlbaum Associates.

Coutinho, M. J., Oswald, D. P., & Best, A. M. (2002). The influence of sociodemographics and gender on the disproportionate identification of minority students as having learning disabilities. *Remedial and Special Education, 23*(1), 49–59.

Darling-Hammond, L. (2013). Inequality and school resources: What will it take to close the opportunity gap. In P. L. Carter & K. G. Welner (Eds.), *Closing the opportunity gap: What America must do to give every child an even chance* (pp. 77–97). New York, NY: Oxford University Press.

Delpit, L. (2006). *Other people's children: Cultural conflict in the classroom*. New York, NY: The New Press.

Donovan, M. S., & Cross, C. T. (2002). *Minority students in special and gifted education*. Washington, DC: National Academies Press.

Dunn, L. M. (1968). Special education for the mildly retarded: Is much of it justifiable? *Exceptional Children, 35*, 5–22.

Durlak, J. A. (2009). How to select, calculate, and interpret effect sizes. *Journal of Pediatric Psychology, 34*(9), 917–928. doi:10.1093/jpepsy/jsp004.

Eitle, T. M. (2002). Special education or racial segregation: Understanding variation in the representation of Black students in educable mentally handicapped programs. *Sociological Quarterly, 43*(4), 575–605. doi:10.1111/j.1533-8525.2002.tb00067.x.

Ferguson, R. F. (2003). Teachers' perceptions and expectations and the black-white test score gap. *Urban Education, 38*(4), 460–507.

Ferri, B., & Connor, D. (2005). Tools of exclusion: Race, disability, and (re) segregated education. *The Teachers College Record, 107*(3), 453–474.

Fierros, E. G., & Conroy, J. W. (2002). Double jeopardy: An exploration of restrictiveness and race in special education. In D. J. Losen & G. Orfield (Eds.), *Racial inequity in special education* (pp. 39–70).

Figlio, D. N., & Getzler, L. S. (2002). Accountability, ability and disability: gaming the system (No. w9307). National Bureau of Economic Research.

Finn, J. D. (1982). Patterns in special education placement as revealed by the OCR surveys. In K. A. Heller, W. H. Holtzman, & S. Messick (Eds.), *Placing children in special education: A strategy for equity* (pp. 322–381). Washington, D.C.: National Academy Press.

Ford, D. Y., Harris, J. J, III, Tyson, C. A., & Trotman, M. F. (2001). Beyond deficit thinking: Providing access for gifted African american students. *Roeper Review, 24*(2), 52–58.

Frankenberg, E., & Orfield, G. (2012). *The resegregation of suburban schools: A hidden crisis in American education*. Cambridge, MA: Harvard Education Press.

Gartner, A., & Lipsky, D. K. (1999). Disability, human rights and education: The United States. In F. Armstrong & L. Barton (Eds.), *Disability, human rights, and education: Cross cultural perspectives* (pp. 100–118).

Gay, G. (2010). *Culturally responsive teaching: Theory, research, and practice*. New York: Teachers College Press.

Gottlieb, J., & Alter, M. (1994). *Evaluation study of the overrepresentation of children of color referred to special education*.

Gravois, T. A., & Rosenfield, S. (2002). A multi-dimensional framework for evaluation of instructional consultation teams. *Journal of Applied School Psychology, 19*(1), 5–29.

Gravois, T. A., & Rosenfield, S. A. (2006). Impact of instructional consultation teams on the disproportionate referral and placement of minority students in special education. *Remedial and Special Education, 27*(1), 42–52.

Greenwald, R., Hedges, L. V., & Laine, R. D. (1996). The effect of school resources on student achievement. *Review of Educational Research, 66*(3), 361–396.

Hale, J. E. (2001). *Learning while black: Creating educational excellence for african american children*. Baltimore, MD: JHU Press.

Hanushek, E. A., Kain, J. F., & Rivkin, S. G. (2002). *New evidence about Brown v. Board of Education: The complex effects of school racial composition on achievement* (No. w8741). Cambridge, MA: National Bureau of Economic Research.

Harry, B., Klingner, J., Sturges, K. M., & Moore, R. F. (2002). Of rocks and soft places: Using qualitative methods to investigate disproportionality. In D. J. Losen & G. Orfield (Eds.), *Racial inequity in special education* (pp. 71–92). Cambridge, MA: Harvard Education Press.

Harry, B., & Klingner, J. K. (2006). *Why are so many minority students in special education?: Understanding race and disability in schools*. New York, NY: Teachers College Press.

Harry, B., Klingner, J. K., Cramer, E. P., Sturges, K. M., & Moore, R. F. (2007). *Case studies of minority student placement in special education*. New York, NY: Teachers College Press.

Heath, S. B. (1983). *Ways with words: Language, life and work in communities and classrooms*. New York, NY: Cambridge University Press.

Heller, K., Holtzman, W., & Messick, S. (1982). Placing children in special education: A strategy for equity. Panel on selection and placement of students in programs for the mentally retarded, Committee on Child Development Research and Public Policy, Commission on Behavioral and Social Sciences and Education, National Research Council.

Hibel, J., Farkas, G., & Morgan, P. L. (2010). Who is placed into special education?. *Sociology of Education, 83*(4), 312–332.

Hosp, J. L., & Reschly, D. J. (2003). Referral rates for intervention or assessment: A meta-analysis of racial differences. *The Journal of Special Education, 37*(2), 67–80.

Irvine, J. J. (1990). *Black students and school failure. Policies, practices, and prescriptions*. Westport, CT: Greenwood Press, Inc.

King, J. E. (1991). Dysconscious racism: Ideology, identity, and the miseducation of teachers. *The Journal of Negro Education, 60*(2), 133–146.

Knotek, S. (2003). Bias in problem solving and the social process of student study teams: A qualitative investigation. *The Journal of Special Education, 37*(1), 2–14.

Ladner, M., & Hammons, C. (2001). Special but unequal: Race and special education. In C. E. Finn, A. Rotherham J. & C. R. Hokanson (Eds.), *Rethinking special education for a new century* (pp. 85–110). Washington, DC: Thomas B. Fordham Foundation: Progressive Policy Institute.

Ladson-Billings, G. (1999). Preparing teachers for diverse student populations: A critical race theory perspective. *Review of Research in Education, 24*, 211–247.

Lee, C. (2004). *Racial segregation and educational outcomes in metropolitan Boston*. Cambridge, MA: The Civil Rights Project.

Lewis, A. (2003). *Race in the schoolyard: Negotiating the color line in classrooms and communities*. Piscataway, NJ: Rutgers University Press.

Lipsey, M. W., & Wilson, D. B. (2000). *Practical meta-analysis*. Thousand Oaks, CA: Sage.

Losen, D. J., & Orfield, G. (2002). *Racial inequity in special education*. Cambridge, MA: Civil Rights Project, Harvard University.

Lutz, B. (2011). The end of court-ordered desegregation. *American Economic Journal: Economic Policy, 3*(2), 130–168.

MacMillan, D. L., & Reschly, D. J. (1998). Overrepresentation of minority students: the case for greater specificity of the variables examined. *The Journal of Special Education, 32*, 15–24.

Mehan, H. (1980). The competent student. *Anthropology & Education Quarterly, 11*(3), 131–152.

Mehan, H., Hertweck, A., & Meihls, J. L. (1986). *Handicapping the handicapped: Decision making in students' educational careers*. Stanford: Stanford University Press.

Meier, K. J., Stewart Jr, J., & England, R. E. (1989). *Race, class, and education: The politics of second generation discrimination*. Madison: University of Wisconsin Press.

Mickelson, R. A. (2015). The cumulative disadvantages of first-and second-generation segregation for middle school achievement. *American Educational Research Journal*, 0002831215587933.

Mickelson, R. A., & Nkomo, M. (2012). Integrated schooling, life course outcomes, and social cohesion in multiethnic democratic societies. *Review of Research in Education, 36*(1), 197–238.

Moll, L. C., Amanti, C., Neff, D., & Gonzalez, N. (1992). Funds of knowledge for teaching: Using a qualitative approach to connect homes and classrooms. *Theory into Practice, 31*(2), 132–141.

Morgan, P. L., Farkas, G., Hillemeier, M. M., Mattison, R., Maczuga, S., Li, H., & Cook, M. (2015). Minorities are disproportionately underrepresented in special education longitudinal evidence across five disability conditions. *Educational Researcher, 44*(5), 278–292.

National Education Association of the United States, & National Association of School Psychologists. (2007). *Truth in labeling: Disproportionality in special education.* National Education Association.

Nieto, S. (2004). *Affirming diversity: The sociopolitical context of multicultural education* (4th ed.). Boston: Pearson/Allyn and Bacon.

O'Connor, C., & Fernandez, S. D. (2006). Race, class, and disproportionality: Reevaluating the relationship between poverty and special education placement. *Educational Researcher, 35*(6), 6–11.

Orfield, G. (2013). Housing segregation produces unequal schools: Causes and solutions. In P. L. Carter & K. G. Welner (Eds.), *Closing the opportunity gap: What america must do to give every child an even chance* (pp. 40–60). New York, NY: Oxford University Press.

Orfield, G., Frankenberg, E., Ee, J., & Kuscera, J. (2014). *Brown at 60: great progress, a long retreat and an uncertain future.* Los Angeles, CA: Civil Rights Project/Proyecto Derechos Civiles.

Orfield, G., & Lee, C. (2007). Historic reversals, accelerating resegregation, and the need for new integration strategies. *Civil Rights Project/Proyecto Derechos Civiles.*

Oswald, D. P., Coutinho, M. J., Best, A. M., & Nguyen, N. (2001). Impact of sociodemographic characteristics on the identification rates of minority students as having mental retardation. *Journal Information, 39*(5).

Oswald, D. P., Coutinho, M. J., Best, A. M., & Singh, N. N. (1999). Ethnic representation in special education the influence of school-related economic and demographic variables. *The Journal of Special Education, 32*(4), 194–206.

Reber, S. J. (2005). Court-ordered desegregation successes and failures integrating American schools since Brown versus Board of Education. *Journal of Human Resources, 40*(3), 559–590.

Reynolds, D., Teddlie, C., Creemers, B., Scheerens, J., & Townsend, T. (2000). An introduction to school effectiveness research. In D. Reynolds & C. Teddlie (Eds.), *The international handbook of school effectiveness research* (pp. 3–25). New York: Falmer Press.

Rothstein, R. (2004). *Class and schools: Using social, economic, and educational reform to close the achievement gap.* Washington, DC: Economic Policy Institute.

Skiba, R. J., Poloni-Staudinger, L., Simmons, A. B., Feggins-Azziz, L. R., & Chung, C. (2005). Unproven links can poverty explain ethnic disproportionality in special education? *The Journal of Special Education, 39*(3), 130–144.

Tabachnick, B. G., & Fidell, L. S. (2007). *Using multivariate statistics* (5th ed.). New York: Pearson Education Inc.

Tyler, K. M., Boykin, A. W., Miller, O., & Hurley, E. (2006). Cultural values in the home and school experiences of low-income African-American students. *Social Psychology of Education, 9*(4), 363–380.

U.S. Department of Education, Office of Special Education and Rehabilitative Services, Office of Special Education Programs. (2014). *36th annual report to congress on the implementation of the individuals with disabilities education act, 2014.* Washington, DC: Author.

Valenzuela, A. (1999). *Subtractive schooling: US-Mexican youth and the politics of caring.* Albany, NY: SUNY Press.

Wagner, M., Newman, L., Cameto, R., Levine, P., & Marder, C. (2007). Perceptions and expectations of youth with disabilities. A special topic report of findings from the national longitudinal transition study-2 (NLTS2). NCSER 2007-3006. *National Center for Special Education Research.*

Zhang, D., & Katsiyannis, A. (2002). Minority representation in special education a persistent challenge. *Remedial and Special Education, 23*(3), 180–187.

Index

© Springer International Publishing Switzerland 2016   293
P.A. Noguera et al. (eds.), *Race, Equity, and Education*,
DOI 10.1007/978-3-319-23772-5

CPSIA information can be obtained
at www.ICGtesting.com
Printed in the USA
LVOW02*1619091215

466140LV00001B/24/P